Shakespeare's
World of Images

DONALD A. STAUFFER

Shakespeare's World of Images

THE DEVELOPMENT
OF HIS MORAL IDEAS

"La fin couronne les oeuvres."
—*Henry VI*, Part 2, V, ii, 28

"Piu por dulzura que por fuerza."
—*Pericles*, II, ii, 27

"Number there in love was slain."
—*The Phoenix and Turtle*

INDIANA UNIVERSITY PRESS

Bloomington   *London*

QUOTATIONS IN THE TEXT ARE ALL TAKEN FROM THE ONE-VOLUME
Complete Works of Shakespeare,
EDITED BY AND COPYRIGHT BY GEORGE LYMAN KITTREDGE

COPYRIGHT, 1949, BY W. W. NORTON & COMPANY, INC.
FIRST MIDLAND BOOK EDITION 1966
LIBRARY OF CONGRESS CATALOG CARD NUMBER: 66-12754
MANUFACTURED IN THE UNITED STATES OF AMERICA

Contents

Preface

WHENEVER in this book a character from Shakespeare is mentioned, the name of that character should be taken as convenient shorthand for all the words and acts ascribed to it in the play. If the reader or the writer assumes that the character is a real person instead of a fiction in art, Shakespeare the illusionist is at his work again.

Shakespeare's
World of Images

CHAPTER ONE

The Country Mouse

HE COULD hardly have known that he was going to be famous. Even when he had the achievements to base it on, he took no thought of the morrow, in contrast to his younger friend Ben Jonson. Many of his works his fellow-actors and friends collected and published for the first time years after he was dead. How much greater reason for modesty and humility there was when he first hit London!

Shakespeare took his time. He was still tinkering, still experimenting, when Christopher Marlowe, who was just as young-old as Shakespeare, had spent all his certainty, brilliance, and passion, and was dead. Shakespeare was still looking around for himself. There were other forms of writing besides tragedies and history plays. There were comedies and those current fashions of erotic narrative poems and sonnets. He tried them all.

By 1592, when he was twenty-eight years old, we know definitely that he had been writing or revising plays long enough to throw a scare into older playwrights. But his competitors were established and had had the incalculable benefits of university educations. What of this ignorant newcomer, this upstart, this copier of his predecessors and betters? The less his contemporaries knew about him, the better for him.

Although it must have taken a period of hard work in London to bring him to the indignant notice of Robert Greene in 1592, precisely where he had been during any of the preceding seven years nobody knows. Before that he had grown up in a country town. The butcher's son next door was his lifelong friend. Shakespeare's father had been losing out in his affairs, attached to the descending rim of the wheel of fortune. Partly this was John Shakespeare's fault, because he could not bring himself to forget entirely the old Catholic faith which was now neither fashionable nor politic. His son William instinctively shared this loyalty to an established past, but it did not make the family life in Stratford easier. Furthermore, by the time he reached twenty-one the young man had become, in somewhat accidental and impetuous fashion, the husband of a wife considerably his senior and the father of three children. Dubiously schooled and brought up, with family chains rather than family connections, this rustic dared to assault London with its white tower built, they said, by Julius Caesar above the Thames.

At least in the publisher Richard Field there was one other man from Stratford in the great capital. This was the city to which Drake was just returning after girdling the globe, to be knighted by the Queen on the deck of the *Golden Hind* down the river at Deptford. And when the young man came to London, this was the seat of that nation which had destroyed, or was destroying, or was about to destroy, the power of Spain that floated in the Armada. He might well be humble.

He set to work like an industrious apprentice. Among the first plays which his fellows accredit to him were *Titus Andronicus* and the three chronicles concerning Henry VI. The first works of an artist, like the early years of one's life or the first days in school, remain in his mind because of their freshness and novelty and sense of discovery, and have an importance to him far beyond their absolute values. The newcomer to London can hardly be said to have put his own ideas into these early plays, for he had not as yet the confidence and experience that could stamp old matters with "Shakespeare" as a seal. Rather, he educated himself by turning over this assigned material with energy and ambition. He grounded his thoughts; he directed them almost by accident to themes and ideas which were to ripen in his later individual meditations.

TITUS ANDRONICUS

The maker of *Titus Andronicus*—so the play tells us—was a writer who could turn out smooth blank verse; who had read around enthusiastically in the Latin storytellers Ovid, Vergil, and the tragic Seneca; who was somewhat naïvely proud that he knew the Latin poets in the original; and who was so much at home with birds and animals and country scenes that he almost makes his bloody Roman city into a rustic village. Moreover, though this particular matter hardly distinguishes him from most of his rivals, he writes for stage effect alone, knows or cares nothing about tragedy, and cannot create—or does not bother to create—credible characters. The plot is so wild and extravagant that even the late Shakespeare could hardly have motivated its butchers convincingly.

The play is a storehouse of themes and episodes and attitudes and images and situations which Shakespeare was later to develop. It is much easier to assume that Shakespeare wrote it than to explain how so many of his later preoccupations got into a play written by someone else. The specific parallels are so numerous that they had better be consigned to a footnote or they will drown the argument.[1] Not one of these ideas or situations is well handled in *Titus Andronicus*. They are the raw materials, as yet half-shaped, which were later to become part of his thought. They are important because they bit into his mind when he was new at the game, when to turn out these ludicrous five acts of gore and chopped limbs may have cost him more labor than to write *Twelfth Night* or *Lear*. He is so eager and so ambitious. His audience must be impressed. Almost like a dog retrieving oddments to drop at his master's feet, he presents his classical gleanings, a procession of figures that were later to become important words in the language of his imagination—"bright-burning Troy," King Priam, Hecuba, "lovesick Dido" and her "wandering prince," the "great Alcides," Actaeon, Dian, Philomel, Hyperion, Pyramus. What studied nonchalance in referring to Tully's *Orator!* The University Wits will be matched, and Seneca and Ovid quoted without gloss in their own Latin. And what delight to contrive a scene which can quote Horace's "Integer vitae" as an integral part of the plot! At some time in those lost seven years, this young man had set himself deliberately to school. Though the early plays smugly parade this learning, Ovid remained beloved to the last, and the haunting stories of Dido's scanted passion, of Troy's fall, and of the career of the Eternal City were to become woven into the texture of his dreams.

Yet to his gruesome subject the young man brought more than his assiduous assimilation of books: he brought the one type of experience that he had so far made his own—his delight in nature. From the story of rape, mutilation, murder, and revenge laid in imperial Rome, let us construct two poems, of nature in clouded weather and in sunshine, by the simple process of lifting what lines we please:

The tempest song

Forc'd in the ruthless, vast, and gloomy woods . . .
The woods are ruthless, dreadful, deaf, and dull . . .
The trees, though summer, yet forlorn and lean,
O'ercome with moss and baleful mistletoe . . .
As flowers with frost or grass beat down with storms . . .
Here never shines the sun; here nothing breeds,
Unless the nightly owl or fatal raven . . .
One hour's storm will drown the fragrant meads . . .
With miry slime left on them by a flood . . .
Set fire on barns and haystacks in the night . . .
Here stands the spring whom you have stain'd with mud . . .
For all the water in the ocean
Can never turn the swan's black legs to white,

Although she lave them hourly in the flood . . .
O earth, I will befriend thee more with rain . . .
Than youthful April shall with all his show'rs.
In summer's drought I'll drop upon thee still,
In winter with warm tears I'll melt the snow,
And keep eternal springtime on thy face . . .
For now I stand as one upon a rock,
Environ'd with a wilderness of sea,
Who marks the waxing tide grow wave by wave . . .
By uproar sever'd, as a flight of fowl
Scatt'red by winds and high tempestuous gusts.

The song of spring and summer

As when the golden sun salutes the morn
And, having gilt the ocean with his beams,
Gallops the zodiac in his glistering coach
And overlooks the highest-peering hills . . .
The hunt is up, the morn is bright and grey,
The fields are fragrant, and the woods are green.
Uncouple here, and let us make a bay . . .
And climb the highest promontory top . . .
To hunt the panther and the hart with me,
With horn and hound we'll give your Grace bonjour . . .
Like stinging bees in hottest summer's day,
Led by their master to the flow'red fields . . .
This goodly summer with your winter mix'd . . .
Where, like a sweet melodious bird, it sung
Sweet varied notes, enchanting every ear!
The birds chaunt melody on every bush;
The snake lies rolled in the cheerful sun;
The green leaves quiver with the cooling wind
And make a checker'd shadow on the ground . . .
And whilst the babbling echo mocks the hounds,
Replying shrilly to the well-tun'd horns,
As if a double hunt were heard at once,
Let us sit down and mark their yellowing noise . . .
We may, each wreathed in the other's arms
(Our pastimes done), possess a golden slumber,
Whiles hounds and horns and sweet melodious birds

Be unto us as is a nurse's song
Of lullaby to bring her babe asleep.

Since these Jabberwocky "poems" are no more than artificial collocations, their only "meaning" is that Shakespeare from the start was nature's child. Like Wordsworth, he knew her lessons of terror and joy, and introduced them, somewhat incongruously, into his earliest works. Not since the Elizabethans have writers in English been able to summon up an out-of-doors at once so joyous and spacious, such a world of natural life and such a natural world of life. It is a nature by turns more ruthless, or more melodiously cheerful, than actuality. But its intensity comes from observation. Even Shakespeare's hunts, though they are idealized, are less conventional than Spenser's Garden of Adonis or Marlowe's passionate shepherd. This nature-poetry has been presented here at such length because the impulse from the vernal wood first taught Shakespeare of man. His moral evil and good were to spring from the earth which he knew so well. And the fragrant fields, the seasons, the storms, the sweet birds singing, which afforded him his first successful expression, were to remain in the last dramatic romances his final consolation.

These passages have been assembled here because they show also how an artist cannot keep himself out of his work. What are they doing in this bloody play? Read them in full to unwary listeners, and how many would guess they came from *Titus Andronicus?* This response to nature and delight in her power and beauty were Shakespeare's irrelevant contributions to the story. Apart from this, Shakespeare did not force his own beliefs and preoccupations upon the play, because as an artist he had as yet so few to express. Instead, he picked up nuclear ideas from this accidental composing in the accepted form of the tragedy of blood.

He wrote from ambition rather than from conviction. Deliberately he set himself to outdo *Gorboduc, The Spanish Tragedy, Tamburlaine.* He will out-Herod Herod, surpassing the medieval stage in direct naïveté. Everything will be superlatively hideous.

If Lavinia is raped and her tongue torn out, it must be "worse than Philomel," so that she must have her hands lopped off, too. Titus declares that he will be revenged "worse than Progne," and therefore the baked Thyestean pastry which Titus serves up "like a Cook" will be ground out of the bones of two grown sons rather than a mere single boy. If the protagonist is to butcher his wretched daughter on the stage, he has "a thousand times more cause" than his classical prototype Virginius.

One of the most disarming glimpses which we have of this young world-shaking dramatist is an original stage direction in the first act:

> Sound drums and trumpets; and then enter two of Titus' sons, and then two men bearing a coffin covered with black; then two other sons; then Titus Andronicus; and then Tamora, the Queen of Goths, and her two sons, Chiron and Demetrius, with Aaron the Moor and others, *as many as can be.*

If this is to be a tragedy, let us have murders and horrors "as many as can be." Let nothing and no one be spared. At the end of the play, "the poor remainder of Andronici," two of the few characters yet unmassacred, promise, if the Romans judge they have done aught amiss, that they will

> on the ragged stones beat forth our brains
And make a mutual closure of our house.
Speak, Romans, speak!

It is surprising that Shakespeare did not permit them to carry on to such an excellent and consistent conclusion.

The humorless and the idolaters suspect Shakespeare's authorship because of the revolting subjects. On the contrary, the frank simplicity of the *treatment* makes it more than ever the work of the gentle Shakespeare. It has the radical innocence of a child, which Shakespeare was so long in losing. There is much of Jack the Giant Killer in it, and in spite of its loud protestations—perhaps because they are so loud—no one can take it seriously as a presentation of moral evil. It should make splendid theatrical entertainment today if produced in the spirit of a revival of *Ten Nights in a Barroom* or *Uncle Tom's Cabin*. The audience might even place bets, as in reading horror stories and detective fiction, about who would die next or what the total number of the slain would be. Shakespeare used his inventiveness to think up some funny shockers,[2] and some excellent examples of bathos, where one must admit Shakespeare again outdoes all rivals:

> A very fatal place it seems to me. (II, iii, 202)
> Will 't please your Highness feed? (V, iii, 54)
> Why, there they are both, baked in that pie. (V, iii, 60)

Max Beerbohm wasted his time in writing *Savonarola Brown:* Shakespeare had already written it.

There is far more knowledge of evil in *Twelfth Night*. Considered, then, solely in the light of Shakespeare's moral development, this is a ludicrously charming play, for it shows him still in paradise, telling sad stories of the death of kings. It is a horrendous "Pyramus and Thisne" with Shakespeare as his own Bottom strenuously trying to please. And though he underlines its barbarities with repeated undramatic summaries—

> For I must talk of murthers, rapes, and massacres,
> Acts of black night, abominable deeds,
> Complots of mischief, treason, villanies
> Ruthful to hear, yet piteously perform'd

—it remains, like Bottom's, "A very good piece of work, I assure you, and a merry," "a part to tear a cat in, to make all split."

Titus Andronicus is based on book-knowledge, not on experience; and its motivations are all out of the storytellers. The play is full of "honour" and "justice"—mere words. Yet Shakespeare learned from writing it. For one thing, he learned not to attempt straight tragedy; he avoided further trials until *Romeo and Juliet*, which still fell short of tragedy, though in a different way. He learned to construct scenes and speeches with formal balance and repetition, to clarify a situation or drive home a point. He began to meditate on the grandeur that was Rome, and he became almost convincing when he considered how "to order well the state," or denounced her lawless sons that "ruffle in the commonwealth of Rome." Among the characters in the play, critics have taken only Aaron seriously. But Aaron is drawn with relative certainty principally because of his ancestors in preceding playwrights, right back to the medieval Vice. Aaron, also, is something the young writer has read about in books, rather than a person, or even a type, observed in experience. *Titus Andronicus,* therefore, an ambitious, learned, competent trial in an accepted form, is principally interesting for our purposes because it shows that one may write passably by echoing others and before one has anything of one's own to say. In Shakespeare's case, his moral convictions grew out of his own experience, and except for his delight in the fresh English countryside, his experience, in a form matured enough for the purposes of art, was yet to come.

HENRY VI, PARTS 1, 2, AND 3

Like *Titus Andronicus,* the three plays dealing with the life of Henry VI which Shakespeare wrote or remade served as parade grounds and practice fields where an amateur playwright could turn himself into a professional. Comparisons with the original sources show that Shakespeare already had the knack of occasionally inventing or copying dramatically effective scenes,[3] and that he could take a jumbled situation and through simplification, repetition, and balance clarify its significance for the least attentive.[4]

Up through *King John* among the history plays, through *Love's Labour's Lost* among the comedies, Shakespeare worked hard to perfect methods of formalized crystal-clear stage presentation. Only later did he realize that his art did not reflect life in the tight complication of *The Comedy of Errors,* or the artificiality of the scene in *Henry VI,* Part 3 (III, ii) in which 24 successive speeches fill one line of blank verse apiece, or the Chinese boxes and rigid minuets of *Love's Labour's Lost.* Not until he had run through such early formalized attempts did he experiment with more convincing ways of holding the mirror up to nature. He rubbed out the obvious traces of his art, expressing his ideas more indirectly, developing a supple informality, using variation instead of repetition or dynamic asymmetrical oppositions instead of mechanical balance, and indicating his judgments through the appropriate behavior of differing characters rather than through pompous orations and moralizing summaries. But anyone who mistakes this cunning and conscious concealment of his art for carelessness or lack of moral opinions should study more closely his first efforts. In the early histories, he preaches directly at the drop of a gauntlet. His moral instinct is obvious in his moralizing. Paradoxically, what he has to say carries no conviction, for he repeats stiffly the platitudes of the chroniclers and the saws of the pulpit. None of his own light shines through. He is still a dark planet, absorbing, not radiating, ideas.

The old plays and Holinshed's history of England give him jumbles to work with. He sorts over the rubble but cannot organize it into large consistent structures. He is still so empty, or unsure of himself, or respectful of others, that he has no adequate theory of history. A chronicler may consider his job performed if he says accurately: "This happened." But an historical dramatist has failed unless he shows how events grow out of character. As yet Shakespeare has no clear ideas of character, or of how characters may impinge upon one another. He is impressed by names and titles. At best, he assigns his characters one trait, so that they move like figures in a morality play—"brave" Talbot, "proud" Cardinal. At worst, they are mere noble names, grouped on opposing sides with as much individuality as pawns in chess. They somersault into new positions, with utter disregard for inner consistency, merely in order to explain the tangled facts of an anarchic period. They taunt each other:

> Ambitious Warwick, let thy betters speak.
> Blunt-witted lord, ignoble in demeanour!
> Pernicious bloodsucker of sleeping men!

Or they point schoolboy morals:

> So bad a death argues a monstrous life.
> Thrice is he arm'd that hath his quarrel just.
>   (2, I, iii; III, ii and iii)

The moralizings, the tournaments of insults, the galvanized activities of these proud preaching puppets, run all on a level. The verse strains, but never takes flight. Not yet has the writer learned the difference between stage effects and drama, and his efforts to bear the weight of the world on his young shoulders gave Greene some grounds for thinking even the name of Shakespeare sounded ridiculously bombastic.

Across these savage chronicles Shakespeare at times writes his signature. The first part of *Henry VI* slanders Joan of Arc so foully that many critics prefer to assign it to another author.[5] Yet two of the scenes (II, iv and IV, ii) are generally accredited to the young man from Stratford, largely because they breathe the country air—that love of nature which Shakespeare first found ways to express adequately. In one scene the heroic Talbot, about to die against the French, rallies the English with arguments that Shakespeare was later to expand in Henry V's speech before Agincourt, and with inspiriting images of the hunt that always filled Shakespeare with joyous excitement:

> How are we park'd and bounded in a pale,
> A little herd of England's timorous deer,
> Maz'd with a yelping kennel of French curs!
> If we be English deer, be then in blood;
> Not rascal-like, to fall down with a pinch,
> But rather, moody-mad and desperate stags,
> Turn on the bloody hounds with heads of steel
> And make the cowards stand aloof at bay. (IV, ii, 45–52)

The deer are superior because they are English, and the English are superior because they appreciate their deer. If we did not have the legend that Shakespeare had been driven from Stratford because of deer-stealing, it would be necessary to invent it.

The other scene is the famous plucking of the red and white

roses in the Temple Garden by the followers of the houses of
York and Lancaster. The wars of a kingdom are reduced pic-
torially to a choice between two flowers! Indeed, one character
at the start of the scene goes out of his way to explain that although he knows as little about legal matters as a jackdaw, he is a
fair judge of hawks, dogs, sword-blades, horses, and merry girls.
So, at this time, was Shakespeare. He was also a judge of roses.
They were no mere conventional symbols for him; they were
absolutes, to which all the beauties and dangers of life could
be referred, and particularly the flushing and paling of the human countenance which Shakespeare never tired of contemplat-
ing. It is not too much to say that in the early 1590's Shakespeare
knew more about roses than about politics and noblemen.

The quarrel that split the fifteenth century is transformed
into flower pictures:

> From off this brier pluck a white rose with me.
> Pluck a red rose from off this thorn with me.
> I pluck this pale and maiden blossom here . . .
> Lest, bleeding, you do paint the white rose red . . .
> Shall dye your white rose in a bloody red . . .
> Meantime your cheeks do counterfeit our roses;
> For pale they look with fear . . .
> Blush for pure shame to counterfeit our roses . . .
> Now by this maiden blossom in my hand. . . .

Set in this most momentous plucking of flowers since the days of
Proserpine and gloomy Dis is Shakespeare's seal:

> Hath not thy rose a canker, Somerset?

For in the double image of the canker and the rose Shakespeare
found a symbol whose meaning he was never to exhaust.

The subject matter of these plays first led the young writer
to meditate on England's destiny. Given half a chance, it was
not hard for any Englishman in the 1590's to be patriotic, so
short a time after the defeat of the Spanish Armada. Shakespeare's
confidence and pride in England developed in clarity and certainty throughout the decade. The echoes of its thrilling notes

have never ceased to resound; and the most obvious historical instance of Shakespeare's moral influence is his shaping the hearts of his countrymen, when they think or have thought of England, toward courage and responsibility and loyalty. Most of this was to come later, but in the first part of *Henry VI*, Talbot is an epic figure, dauntless because he is an Englishman; and Joan of Arc and the French are blackened because they dare to oppose such bravery. Shakespeare proves his patriotic point by making a Frenchman quote the chronicler Froissart that in the past "England all Olivers and Rowlands bred." Yet this may be "verified" even "more truly" in the present fifteenth century:

> For none but Samsons and Goliases
> It sendeth forth to skirmish. (I, ii, 30, 33–4)

The great vision of an ordered island under a rightful ruler, which he was to develop in the famous passages in *Richard II* and *Henry V*, Shakespeare already glimpses:

> My sovereign, with the loving citizens,
> Like to his island girt in with the ocean
> Or modest Dian circled with her nymphs,
> Shall rest in London till we come to him.
> (3, IV, viii, 19–22)

The passage is surrounded with phrases that idealize: "true-hearted friends," "not mutinous," "Men well inclin'd to hear what thou command'st," "my Hector and my Troy's true hope," "Well-minded Clarence," "Sweet Oxford, and my loving Montague," "happy farewell!" "pity . . . mildness . . . mercy," "These graces challenge grace."

But in the mutinous fifteenth century, as Shakespeare well knew, these graces were more apt to challenge rebellion. Immediately after Henry VI has set up this New Jerusalem in his mind, this lovingly harmonious kingdom where "the lion fawns upon the lamb," his rival Edward breaks in with "Seize on the shamefac'd Henry, bear him hence." What the material of the Barons' Wars taught Shakespeare most bitterly was that England, which no foreign enemy could destroy, was capable of de-

stroying itself. "England is safe, if true within itself." Henry
VI's reign was to Shakespeare a long dwindling twilight of shame
and treachery and an increasing fatal fever. "What madness, what
infamy," the pious King exclaims,

> That for a toy, a thing of no regard,
> King Henry's peers and chief nobility
> Destroy'd themselves and lost the realm of France!
>
> (1, IV, i, 145–7)

Shakespeare as yet has no skill in analyzing the causes; but he
records with some certainty what seems to him a pattern: that in
an unstable realm, the good must go down before "factious emulation," brute selfishness, blind politics. Thus, quarreling factions
will have no time to reinforce the brave Talbot in his struggle to
preserve the realm against impossible odds; the goodness of
Humphrey of Gloucester will band together his murderous opponents long enough to bring about his death; young princes and
stripling heirs will casually be stabbed, mere light punctuation
marks in a doom-fraught sentence. At last, as a climax to the three
plays, the mild and Christian Henry will be slaughtered by the
greatest self-seeker of them all, Richard Duke of York. All factions, all levels are tainted with the disease of injustice and the
fever of power. In a scene as brutal and bitter as any Shakespeare
wrote before *Troilus and Cressida*, Lord Say is brought before
Jack Cade. Lord Say a few scenes before had been confident:

> The trust I have is in mine innocence,
> And therefore am I bold and resolute. (2, IV, iv, 59–60)

He is a palsied old man whose head shakes. It is thoroughly in
the spirit of the Henry VI plays for Cade to say: "I'll see if his
head stand steadier on a pole or no. Take him away and behead
him." Lord Say defends himself eloquently and nobly, and therefore, says Cade: "He shall die, an it be but for pleading so well
for his life."

Shakespeare's early reading and shaping of history, then, is less
a statement of moral convictions than an observation on past
politics: a government without center or support makes the lives

of its citizens unsafe. Remove sanctions—and the saintly Henry VI is almost alone in wishing for them—and the law of the beast becomes operative. Shakespeare could not have felt that he had discovered or created this rule of history: it was for anyone to read in the accounts of Holinshed and the other Elizabethan chroniclers. During the long uncertain reign of Henry VI, the world might be described as Yeats characterized the twentieth century:

> The best lack all conviction, while the worst
> Are full of passionate intensity.

We cannot understand Shakespeare's later political plays, and their preoccupation with stable government as the sole ground in which the individual moral life may grow naturally, unless we realize how deeply Shakespeare was immersed in gloomy history during his impressionable early years as a journeyman playmaker. His good characters are not convincing, while he writes more knowingly about his bad characters simply because he has acknowledged as obvious that in the fifteenth century, to the villain belong the spoils.

Shakespeare and his readers accept the quarreling plotters in the Henry VI plays almost as a convention—like the conventions of the murdered man and the seemingly innocent murderer in a modern detective story—and with just about the same amount of moral concern. Talbot dies in Part 1, Humphrey of Gloucester in Part 2, the king himself in Part 3, all honorable men. Nobody really cares. Good and bad, they die off one by one in the clash of interests. Action speeds up, so that in the last play in the Henry VI trilogy Fortune's wheel makes two and a half revolutions, rival rulers are alternately up and down, and the treacherous shifting from one side to another almost requires ledger-bookkeeping. But finally the mainstays of the King—Clifford and Warwick—have been killed in battle, the three brothers stab Prince Edward, Queen Margaret is taken prisoner, and in the fatal Tower of London, so fitting a temple for these plays, Richard Crookback has stabbed his king.

Ten little Indians sitting in a line.
One fell off, and then there were nine.

The little Indians have disappeared one after another—it is hardly more seriously moral than that—and now we know that the last little Indian will be Richard, because he is the bloodiest and most ruthless of them all. He is best able to take care of himself, and in these plays survival is each man's whole business. Moral scruples and pity are ineffectual and fatal.

RICHARD III

Shakespeare, then, logically as well as chronologically, proceeds to *Richard III*, the inevitable crown to the Henry VI plays, and the final touch in this sweeping historical canvas. If his later tetralogy (*Richard II, Henry IV*, Parts 1 and 2, and *Henry V*) grows to a triumphant united England in the character of Henry V, this tetralogy sweeps inexorably to its fearful anarchic close in the greatest anarch of them all—Richard III.

Richard is simply drawn. He is competent, but he is also evil because he is bounded by self-interest. The moral conception of proud force is no invention of Shakespeare's. Everyone knows that he finds it in Marlowe and that Marlowe finds it in Machiavelli as understood by the Elizabethans. It is as old as Cain, or Lucifer before him. Indeed, this book is not written because Shakespeare's moral ideas are new, but because they are so old, so central and applicable to human nature, and so firmly based on the maximum of experience, the minimum of theory.

This image of the almost completely evil man is the first important moral idea clear in Shakespeare's mind, though even here it is accepted intellectually rather than realized with the complete emotional understanding that created Edmund and Iago. Since Shakespeare is consistent throughout his life in his interpretation of pure moral evil, it is worth our while to let his Richard speak, even though his philosophy is not distinguishable from that of Marlowe's Jew of Malta or Milton's Satan. Shakespeare is well under thirty years of age when his Richard says:

I that have neither pity, love, nor fear . . .
I have no brother, I am like no brother;
And this word 'love,' which greybeards call divine,
Be resident in men like one another,
And not in me! I am myself alone. (3, V, vi, 68 ff.)

Here is the essence of evil for Shakespeare: that a man should be *himself alone*, cutting himself off from the community of men "like one another," denying the brotherhood which underlies the ordinary human emotions of pity, love, fear. Holding such a philosophy, Richard finds in self-interest his only possible delight; in the same soliloquy he turns against his blood-brother:

Clarence, thy turn is next, and then the rest,
Counting myself but bad till I be best.

Not in abasement, then, but in an almost purring self-approbation, Richard describes himself:

Why, I can smile, and murther whiles I smile . . .
I'll drown more sailors than the mermaid shall . . .
And set the murtherous Machiavel to school . . .
That I should snarl and bite and play the dog.

He is, as Queen Margaret describes him, a "devil's butcher," whose almsdeed is murder, and who never refuses petitioners for blood. In his own mind, Richard cannot be mistaken. His cheerful certainty grows out of his heartlessness. "He's sudden if a thing comes in his head," says his brother Edward. Involved solely in his own desires, what scruples could possibly intervene? "Sprawl'st thou?" he says above the body of the stabbed Prince Edward, and stabs him again; when he is prevented from killing Queen Margaret, he coolly demands: "Why should she live to fill the world with words?" He nurses no grievances, for he counts it natural that other men should act against him. Like Iago and Edmund, Shakespeare's other pure villains, he acts in gay excitement, for there is no moral war within himself.

Like them also, he has a superb intellect, and can amuse himself by rationalizing his attitudes. In his first long soliloquy he analyzes himself masterfully. Echoing Tamburlaine, he reveals his "soul's desire." It is the crown of England, which flatters him with impossibilities as he considers how many heirs stand between him and such sweet fruition. If the kingdom is unattainable, what is the world's next best pleasure? A lady's lap. But love has forsworn him in giving him his misshapen body, which he can describe without shrinking—"mine arm like a wither'd shrub," "an envious mountain on my back," "like to a chaos, or an unlick'd bear-whelp." No love, then; and he returns to his soul's desire and the obstacles that lie this side of achievement. Here there is unrest, yet it springs not from ethics but from his family genealogy:

> And I—like one lost in a thorny wood,
> That rents the thorns and is rent with the thorns,
> Seeking a way and straying from the way,
> Not knowing how to find the open air
> But toiling desperately to find it out—
> Torment myself to catch the English crown;
> And from that torment I will free myself
> Or hew my way out with a bloody axe. (3, III, ii, 174–81)

With this resolution, Richard again becomes gay, laughing at his own skill in dissembling, which will lead him to the crown. The torment in the thorny wood cannot last long, and is never a moral struggle. Let the poor dupes in the brotherhood of man agonize over their high principles! As for Richard, he could say of any man of aspiration and humane ideals what he said of Icarus:

> And yet, for all his wings, the fool was drown'd.

This sharply conceived sketch of Richard is wholly drawn from the third part of *King Henry VI*. It is no wonder that Shakespeare can proceed to develop such villainy with loving confidence in *Richard III*. Richard's delight in his own power to sway stupid, virtuous weaklings is intensified. He woos and wins the Lady Anne, wife of the dead Prince Edward whom Richard killed openly, while she is following as chief mourner the funeral coffin of Richard's other victim Henry VI. The "bottled spider" plays the part of the plain harmless man, soft, pitiful, and childish-foolish, with such brazen assurance that even his victims waver in their distrust. Only that fountain of venom, the old Queen Margaret, remains constant in her hatred, and she seems merely to refresh him with her curses.

Terror accelerates. As inevitably as in *Macbeth*, evil action generates further evil actions, until Richard can hardly be bothered to maintain the disguise of piety except for the pleasure of torturing simple gulls, now silent before his lies through fear, not ignorance. His brothers disappear in death, and the two young Princes are taken to the ominous Tower, after Richard has cautioned his sweet nephew against the world's deceit:

> No more can you distinguish of a man
> Than of his outward show . . .
> God keep you from them, and from such false friends!

Hastings is condemned by Richard before his lords on the incredible charge of conspiring with a witch to wither up the tyrant's arm. Yet no one dare object. Only in soliloquy can England's citizens defend free speech and analyze the inevitable effects of government by fear:

> Here's a good world the while! Who is so gross
> That cannot see this palpable device?
> Yet who so bold but says he sees it not?
> Bad is the world, and all will come to naught
> When such ill dealing must be seen in thought. (III, vi, 10–4)

Richard now speaks openly of murder, and loses at last his chief agent Buckingham. But even as the forces rise against this "most deadly boar" and the battle of Bosworth Field nears, Richard, his last wife dead, becomes "a jolly thriving wooer" and reaches his height of intellectual sadism at the end of a tremendous scene of poisonous seduction. His brother's widow speaks her last remonstrance: "Yet thou didst kill my children." And Richard replies:

But in your daughter's womb I bury them,
Where, in that nest of spicery, they will breed
Selves of themselves, to your recomforture.

Against such monstrous evil, justice at length rises as the pageant of his past victims cross the stage. Nemesis becomes Mnemosyne when the ghosts of the murdered speak to him dreaming in his tent: "Despair and die!"; and to Richmond, the future Henry VII and grandfather of Shakespeare's Queen: "Live and flourish!"

Yet at the end, after he has fronted the truth: "I shall despair. There is no creature loves me; And if I die, no soul shall pity me," he remains firm in his central belief: "Richard loves Richard: that is, I am I," and curses his conscience as a coward. He cannot see himself as his own judge, nor come as close as Doctor Faustus to repentance. To escape his fear and despair, he need only fly Bosworth Field, trading his kingdom for a horse. He is consistent to the end: "Our strong arms be our conscience, swords our law!" His heartlessness has been elevated almost into a fabulous dragon force inimical to England: "A thousand hearts are great within my bosom." In the end, he does not feel Faustus' terror or Macbeth's hideous inner death, but retreats proudly into Iago's silence and is killed in battle in a scene in which he does not speak at all. "The bloody dog is dead."

So Shakespeare leaves him, superbly great in courage, assurance, decision, even in humor; infinitely small in his blind selfishness. The world he constructed with such magnificent logic is destroyed, for its false premises affront the moral law.

Yet on the deepest level, the play does not carry full conviction. In past centuries it has been popular because it is a fascinating and melodramatic horror story. Shakespeare has imagined vital human speech and human traits clothing a moral abstraction of evil. The idea back of Richard was well known to the Elizabethans, traditional in Christian thought, already popularized by Marlowe and by Machiavelli. More important, it had been presented with subtle malevolence and maturity in Thomas More's life of Richard III which constituted Shakespeare's ultimate source. But the final impression is that the competence with which the young dramatist drew his first great serious figure rests upon an intellectual acceptance of human evil rather than upon full imaginative realization of such evil in all its possibilities. Shakespeare has fashioned Richard's essential nature on an hypothesis rather than on observation or experience. As a dramatic presentation of an evil man, because he is too completely evil, Richard is not quite good enough.

THE NARRATIVE POEMS AND THE EARLIEST COMEDIES

The figure of Richard Crookback may seem an odd starting point in considering Shakespeare's ideas on love as a moral force. Yet there we must begin, for genius is not bound to rule and order, and its convictions develop through the most unlikely imaginings—indirectly, or by negatives, or by haunted and dangerous roads that lead away from final haven. Love, conceived as an emotion that binds one human being to another, is the dominant energy that organizes Shakespeare's moral beliefs. For twenty years he wrote it into his great symphony, in which it sounds with pure confidence in two major movements alone—in the middle comedies and in *Antony and Cleopatra*. At the start, the theme of love is impure, mixed with a bewildering passion, presented falteringly, or stated as a theorem rather than realized as an experience. Shakespeare, in these earliest stages, best defines love by its opposites. His ideal love, like his ideal government, begins with negative realizations.

Consider the two amazing "love" scenes in *Richard III*. They are both unhistorical, both unnecessary to the plot. Since the same gloatingly horrible theme is developed in each scene, except that the second also persuades a Queen to be a female Pandarus, the first is enough to consider.[6] The subject is the bending, unnerving, swerving, shaking, breaking of a person's will. Richard glories in it, and Shakespeare does not scant it. To make the sadistic wooing even more glaring in insult, Shakespeare has Richard stop the funeral procession and speak to Lady Anne as mourner for her murdered father-in-law Henry VI. Only after Anne has spent herself in cursing and has consigned Richard to hell does he mention with superb effrontery a fitter place—"Your bedchamber." Perhaps there is no difference. Now he plays upon her selfishness and pride: all he has done was caused by her beauty, that did haunt him in his sleep. The snake is charming the bird. When he is sure of his control, this artist in depravity takes one more step toward delight: he lends her a sharp-pointed sword. He kneels.[7] He offers her his naked breast. While she holds the sword the master strikes her with the direct avowal that he killed King Henry. This is not enough. Well, then, he stabbed young Edward her husband.

> But 'twas thy heavenly face that set me on.
> *She falls the sword.* (I, ii, 182)

There must be one further step in her abasement. Taking the sword, he swears to kill himself if she so bids. Her will is sapped, and she has become his prey. Helpless, she acknowledges the victor.

Richard's subsequent soliloquy shows the springs of his conduct. He may say exultantly: "Was ever woman in this humour woo'd? Was ever woman in this humour won?" Love, to Richard as to Iago, is "a permission of the will." Since he is himself alone, he cannot bind himself to others, but may find sport in binding them to him. In the bending of their will against their will, he plumes up his own. He exults in Anne's perversion:

> What? I that kill'd her husband and his father
> To take her in her heart's extremest hate,
> With curses in her mouth, tears in her eyes,
> The bleeding witness of my hatred by!

And again:

> And will she yet abase her eyes on me,
> That cropp'd the golden prime of this sweet prince
> And made her widow to a woful bed?

Anne's degradation at his hands gives him for the moment a cheerful pride in his own misshapen self.

Moral beliefs develop out of the realization of evil as well as of good. The attraction existing between human beings Shakespeare first successfully presented on its evil side—when it is used as an instrument for worshipping the self. This is not love, but its opposite. If we wish to use the Shakespearean shorthand, we may call it lust.

> Love comforteth like sunshine after rain,
> But Lust's effect is tempest after sun.
> Love's gentle spring doth always fresh remain;
> Lust's winter comes ere summer half be done.
> Love surfeits not, Lust like a glutton dies;
> Love is all truth, Lust full of forged lies.

The preceding neat little stanza in praise of love comes from *Venus and Adonis*. It is clear and repetitious enough to be a commercial advertisement over the radio. The trouble is that neither Venus nor Adonis believes it. One is too hot and the other too cold. The pleasures of the poem come from Shakespeare's early knack at describing country sights and scenes, and from his acquired ability, under the sanction of Ovid and his rout, to bathe in lascivious blisses at luxurious leisure. An erotic poem is no fit place to look for moral beliefs, apart from the belief that is implied in a poet's granting himself the licence to be licentious. But it is worth a moment to contrast *Venus and Adonis* with Marlowe's *Hero and Leander*, which does contain a scene of complete sensual fulfilment. Shakespeare's conception is more tantalizing. *Venus and Adonis* offers fulfilment to neither party. Instead, it portrays an almost monstrous passion, in which we see

> Venus toute entière à sa proie attachée.

Shakespeare's Venus, under all the cloying imagery and sweet baits of the senses, remains the realized embodiment of "sweating lust," unappeasable, whose most poignant knowledge is of irreparable loss without having ever attained a moment of true possession. And Adonis—fastidious, petulant, callow, unapproachable, unawakened, self-absorbed—is killed before he experiences the attraction of one human being for another even on the level of lust. He is negative, the paradoxical object of un-quenched sensuality—desirable because undesiring. The echoless wastes of his snowy purity are not to be trodden by mortals or by gods. Cool kin to Hermaphroditus and Narcissus, he dies with the ice still in his arteries. Adonis belongs with Richard III, who de-fined himself to be no beast because he knew no touch of pity. In this poem only the beasts—the stallion, the boar, even poor Wat the hare—achieve any sort of emotional fulfilment.

The Rape of Lucrece Shakespeare promises as a "graver la-bour." The sensuous decoration of *Venus and Adonis* gives way a year later to a more somber rhetoric and sententious moraliz-ing in the style of the *Mirror for Magistrates.* Yet the poem mines the same vein, the same ungovernable and terrible instinct leading to destruction. Unsuspecting and helpless virtue is ruined in the person of Lucrece—a kind of wooden Desdemona. Tarquin's tigerish step leads him to the awful action in spite of his self-upbraidings, as if he, no less than Lucrece, were powerless before the compulsion of passion. The dynasty of the Roman kings is banished as a result of his moment of frenzy. Lucrece knows her-self to be so foully stained that she stays the suicidal knife only long enough to demand revenge. The poem does not traffic with the delights of sensuality, which is presented as an unmitigated calamity. In the world of Tarquin's inflamed thoughts, if virtue feeble were, "Heaven itself would ravish her."

In these two poems, then, the only formally acknowledged heirs of Shakespeare's invention, love is the generating theme. But it is love in one aspect only—love led awry, love undisci-plined, love insatiate, love unrequited, love the destroyer. Al-though his art is not adequate to his theme, Shakespeare's instinctive choice of subject hints at the base on which his later convictions were to rise: he sees clearly the power and the terror of an overmastering fever.

Yet Shakespeare never lived for long in one exclusive mood. Always he had the gift of making assumptions. In his *Comedy of*

Errors, love is a game, and its bewilderments, since they are to be mechanically contrived, are laughable. Because the heart need not be in it, Shakespeare can write quite a passable formal wooing in rhyme that foreshadows Romeo's courtship of Juliet, or can describe with relish the embroilment of the wrong Dromio with his billowy Luce-Nell-Dowsabel, or can dispense wise counsel regarding jealousy through the lips of the old Abbess Aemilia.

The Two Gentlemen of Verona may blame its unreality on the conventions of the Renaissance romance, just as *The Comedy of Errors* is better Plautus than Shakespeare. The typical Renaissance romance makes love into a game of tag, or, if one is ambitious, into a minuet or square-dance. Given two men and two women, the possibilities of entanglement may be mathematically calculated. Shakespeare conscientiously tried out in *The Comedy of Errors* and *The Two Gentlemen of Verona* the permutations and combinations that he handles most brilliantly and exhaustively in *A Midsummer Night's Dream.*[8] Love is a sweet unreason— sweet to the lover, unreasonable to all but him. Through watching its errors, therefore, all lookers-on may enjoy its comedy. Within the form of the conventional Italian-French-Spanish romance, this odd passion must lead its devotees through amusing situations and hairbreadth escapes at last to pleasure.

Writing under some such unexpressed assumptions, Shakespeare dramatized a run-of-the-mill story in *The Two Gentlemen of Verona.* Here he first touched the tone of his own characteristic comedy, transmuting the spirit of the romances into a love so true and certain that it can support the catastrophic swervings of the plot and the laughter and bawdry of low characters. Insofar as they have any personality at all, which is not much, Julia and Valentine and Silvia derive theirs from their own warm and unchanging love. One need hardly be reminded that the answer to the famous song, "Who is Silvia?" proclaims her to be holy, fair, wise, endowed with grace, admirable, kind, beautiful, pitying, and excelling all mortals. Julia is adept at describing "the inly touch of love," [9] and Valentine in two glowing speeches earns himself a place among love's doctors. He says of his lady:

> She is my essence, and I leave to be
> If I be not by her fair influence
> Foster'd, illumin'd, cherish'd, kept alive. (III, i, 182–4)

For he has found at last that "Love's a mighty lord."

Shakespeare's secret, learned early, is that such exalted sentiment must be kept sweet by seasoning. Valentine's praise is rendered more convincing because in the first scene he has been railing at Proteus for being "a votary to fond desire." And Julia, aware of her own coyness, knows that love may be wayward and foolish, "like a testy babe." We accept more willingly Julia's obedient wooing of Silvia for her own Proteus because it occurs in a play where the contemptible Thurio, crawfishing, says with dull common sense:

> I hold him but a fool that will endanger
> His body for a girl that loves him not.

The fine flowerings of the trio of lovers—Julia, Valentine, Silvia—grow in the atmosphere of this ordinary world, in which a tavern-keeper can fall asleep during a scene of betrayal, because it does not concern him, and in which one of the clowns can remind us that "Though the chameleon Love can feed on the air, I am one that am nourish'd by my victuals."

Such ideal love is real, the argument runs, because it exists in a believable world. Moreover, it is so strong that it can confidently suffer insult and reversal. Shakespeare gives it plenty of chances to prove its quality in opposition to Proteus, who notably furnishes the key to Shakespeare's moral ideas at this early time. Proteus is, in his own eyes, a triple traitor—to leave his Julia, to love fair Silvia, and to wrong his friend Valentine. Yet Shakespeare practically accuses him of "angel-like perfection." To his friend Valentine

> He is complete in feature and in mind
> With all good grace to grace a gentleman.

And to Julia he is of "divine perfection"; his looks are her soul's food.

Shakespeare does not develop the irony far. It is all love's fault. What can even an angel do against love, which is so powerful and so unreasonable? Proteus blames his actions on this errant god:

> And ev'n that pow'r which gave me first my oath
> Provokes me to this threefold perjury. (II, vi, 4–5)

He has had his moment of self-analysis:

> Is it mine eye, or Valentinus' praise,
> Her true perfection, or my false transgression,
> That makes me reasonless, to reason thus? (II, iv, 196–8)

But he sweeps such maunderings aside and accepts with alacrity a choice whose end he already knows:

> If I can check my erring love, I will;
> If not, to compass her I'll use my skill. (II, iv, 213–4)

The three lovers who have been lucky enough not to find desire a disease, help the changeable Proteus in his affliction. They, too, recognize sympathetically that it is not his fault. Love itself is a fool, and all lovers, all, are fond. " 'Tis pity love should be so contrary," says Julia. But though 'tis pity, 'tis true, and must be accepted as a fact of nature in which all lovers participate, the bad and the good. And therefore when Julia, fully aware of her lover's perfidy, exclaims: "Alas, poor fool! Why do I pity him?" the scholiasts might have a merry argument as to whether the poor fool is Proteus or Julia herself. "Were man but constant, he were perfect!" Since he is not constant in fact and act, he must be made so in the level of one's dreams. Even so early, then, Shakespeare was aware that compensation for the frailty of others may lie in the mind's unswerving loyalty to what it cherishes. If the world be false, all the more reason that one should to one's own world be true. Julia makes this clear when she reproaches her maid:

> Now, as thou lov'st *me*, do him not that wrong
> To bear a hard opinion of his truth!
> Only deserve my love by loving him. (II, vii, 80–2)

Love, then, can afford to be generous because in itself it is so unshakable. And this generosity cannot be carried too far. In one of those surprising scenes where Shakespeare suddenly abandons his characters in his enthusiasm for his thesis, Valentine proves that love is boundless as the sea. Proteus stands revealed in all his baseness before the three lovers. Now he declares himself repentant. And Valentine is so delighted at this quick conversion that he gives away the happiness of three perfect lovers for the benefit of the strayed fourth:

> And, that my love may appear plain and free,
> All that was mine in Silvia I give thee.

This is too much even for Julia, and she swoons. She has little to worry about. In such an atmosphere of generosity, the most changeable penitent would find small joy in returning to his fickleness, and the play ends with "One feast, one house, one mutual happiness."

The Two Gentlemen of Verona is hardly more than a light sketch, its lines hasty and undeveloped. Shakespeare's own inventions, additions to the original story, are the theme of friendship and the prodigality of love in the denouement. In this play, Shakespeare makes his first bold, characteristic, important moral assumption: that perhaps you can give away your cake and eat it too. Love—is it not conceivable?—can be so confident, so illimitable in its romantic devotion, so generous, that it can dissolve the mistaken world into its own smiling happiness.

CHAPTER TWO

The School of Love

SHAKESPEARE was not often a direct moralist. But in the
glad confident morning of his powers, from the time he
turned thirty until he had passed thirty-five, he was sure that love
made (or could make) the world go round most pleasantly, and
he could not keep his conviction out of his plays. He even found
delight in formulating it as a truth that must be taught to all
truants. Love is to be the great schoolmaster.

He had little use for platitudes as practical instruments for our
moral betterment. Often he makes fun of them, and when he
introduces them seriously, they come merely as culminations for
lessons already learned in action. Yet he had a profound respect
for experience as a schooling; many of his most melodramatically
contrived situations [1] are deliberately designed to carry a character painfully far—unnecessarily far, if good advice instead could
conceivably have set him straight—in order that that character
might write the living moral on his heart.

The final scene of *The Two Gentlemen of Verona*, for instance,
with almost unforgivable artificiality, enthusiastically insists upon
allowing Proteus to learn from the most horrible mistakes. Valentine watches purposefully from his retreat; Julia, disguised as a

page, remains unhappy in her asides; and Silvia, sweetly preaching, is about to be physically violated by Proteus, who is quite aware that he is betraying the spirit of love itself: "I'll love you 'gainst the nature of love—force ye." Not until Proteus has directly proclaimed "I'll force thee yield to my desire" does Valentine step out and upbraid him. He might have done it earlier, but how much less effective, then, would have been his chidings! That Valentine, and Shakespeare through him, is deliberately using the laboratory method of direct experiment in order to convey a moral lesson may be seen from Valentine's utterance as he withdraws into hiding: "Love, lend me patience to forbear awhile." It is evident also in Valentine's immediate forgiveness that follows hot on the heels of Proteus' shamed heart-sorrow:

> Then I am paid . . .
> Who by repentance is not satisfied
> Is nor of heaven nor earth.

Love, if it will but lend patience, may reform the erring through their own mistakes.

LOVE'S LABOUR'S LOST

Love's Labour's Lost might well be called "The School for Lovers." It stands just at the divide between Shakespeare's early essays and his first successes. There is something still coltish about it, something of the freshness of an amateur. Its formal tricks and metrical experiments seem disarmingly self-conscious and a trifle awkward even when they come off successfully. And perhaps Shakespeare is still most amusingly the country mouse in the joyous awe with which he watches (and portrays) the elegances of his courtly cousins. He, too, has been admitted to Arcadia.

Looking for profound significances in this happily ingenious literary exercise would be breaking a butterfly upon a wheel. Everyone knows, or should know, Berowne's fine formal speech in praise of Love. Shakespeare evidently took enough pains to write it in more than one version, since its original publication repeats its central ideas with variations. The ideas are simple enough: that love is learned in a lady's eyes; that it doubles any man's natural powers; that all poetry is inspired by love; and that love is the true learning through which men find themselves. This oration might be considered as no more than a panegyric composed to order in praise of "Saint Cupid." Its seriousness is proved, however, as is always the case in Shakespeare, by the drift and construction of the action as a whole. The four young ambitious men—the King of Navarre and his three lords—are acting unnaturally in cutting themselves off from their kind, or from their feminine complements, in the mistaken three-year search for bookish wisdom. Nature must assert itself. The women themselves, therefore—the Princess of France and her three ladies—will be their gentle lessoners. First must come their humbling through experience, in a complicated, formally con-trived scene during which each learns that his companion has fallen in love, and reproaches him for breaking his vow, only to be himself reproached in turn. Then, leagued to prosecute their love, the four young men learn that their ladies, too, have minds of their own. They undergo the discipline of mockery and taunt-ings; they are "all dry-beaten with pure scoff"; they are laughed at, bewildered, and again forsworn. They are still too proud of themselves, and Berowne admits the truth of the princess' descrip-tion of their laughable wooing: "When great things labouring perish in their birth." It looks as though their pretentious labors of love would indeed be lost.

Nature again breaks in, this time on the farcical level: two men, Don Adriano and Costard, are about to fight over a woman, Jaquenetta. The play is getting out of hand in a hurly-burly of uproarious brawls and flashing wit-combats on the theme of love—when with melodramatic suddenness a serious note is struck. A messenger announces the death of the princess' father. "The scene begins to cloud," and each of its aristocratic actors finds "a new-sad soul." Now is the time for those honest plain words that best pierce the ear of grief. The taffeta-phrases and spruce affectation have already been forsworn. "Those heavenly eyes" of love are felt to be the true selves of the lovers, more constant than the deformed humours, the ridiculous, unbefitting, wanton, skipping strains, the varying strange shapes and particoated presences of loose love. Yet though the young men through their spokesman Berowne have learned that their fickle lightness misbecomes love's constancy, they have not yet sealed their belief in action. The princess passes sentence on the king:

> go with speed
> To some forlorn and naked hermitage,
> Remote from all the pleasures of the world . . .
> If frosts and fasts, hard lodging and thin weeds
> Nip not the gaudy blossoms of your love,
> But that it bear this trial, and last love—
> Then, at the expiration of the year,
> Come challenge me. (V, ii, 803–5, 810–4)

Shakespeare has not done with his moralizing. The reader is often slightly uncomfortable, and perhaps the author was also, at the way in which, in these early plays, the young aristocrats bait their inferiors. The witty page Moth has been "put out of his part" by their fleering. Costard defends the discomfited hedge-priest—"a foolish mild man; an honest man, look you, and soon dash'd." Holofernes has reproved his unruly audience as a schoolmaster should: "This is not generous, not gentle, not humble." Even Don Adriano de Armado is jolted out of his high-flown speech into a sensible protest: "Sweet chucks, beat not the bones of the buried."

The young bloods do not act with charity. Love must learn, through a woman's eyes, to look at the world, to be generous, gentle, and humble. Rosaline therefore takes her ringleader Berowne in hand, to weed this wormwood, these mocks and wounding flouts, these idle scorns, from his brain:

> Visit the speechless sick and still converse
> With groaning wretches; and your task shall be,
> With all the fierce endeavour of your wit
> To enforce the pained impotent to smile.

And when the alarmed Berowne protests that it is impossible "to move wild laughter in the throat of death," Rosaline replies that the trial may rightly choke his gibing spirit.

> throw away that spirit,
> And I shall find you empty of that fault,
> Right joyful of your reformation.

With self-conscious smugness Shakespeare proclaims:

> Our wooing doth not end like an old play:
> Jack hath not Gill.

Shakespeare is more often a man of the Renaissance than of the Reformation. Therefore, lest this advice to his audience and city cousins should seem too stern, the play veers again toward farce to enforce the moral of humility, as we learn that Armado, too, has "vow'd to Jaquenetta to hold the plough for her sweet love three year," and ends with one of his loveliest songs, in which the country pictures of the spring and winter season vie for supremacy in beauty.

Even though the love of *Love's Labour's Lost* is well-bred, gay, capable of elevating the spirit, and in its essence self-neglecting and ideal, neither here nor elsewhere does Shakespeare forget that it grows from the earth. He laughs with Costard at the "most sweet jests," the "most vulgar wit,"

> When it comes so smoothly off, so obscenely, as it were, so fit!

Cupid's butt-shaft was once a thyrsus, and love remains an odd mixture today, as it was in the days "when King Pippen of France was a little boy" or "when Queen Guinover of Britain was a little wench." Shakespeare never forgets that "Love has pitched his mansion in The place of excrement."

THE TAMING OF THE SHREW

Shakespeare's two farces, *The Taming of the Shrew* and *The Merry Wives of Windsor*, teach further lessons in the school of love. If *The Two Gentlemen* enforces the commandment, Thou shalt not be fickle, then *The Shrew* continues with Thou shalt not be headstrong, and *The Merry Wives* ends with Thou shalt not be covetous. In a sense all these amorous injunctions are but variant voices from the oracle of love.

The Taming of the Shrew shows fast and direct writing. It is most poetically imaginative in the uproariously rough descriptions and actions that present Petruchio taming his Kate. Its justice is rude though wholesome. If Katherine is reduced to tears, her own earlier harshness has made her sister Bianca weep. She learns the effect of the inconsiderate wilfulness which she had herself so long practiced, by being subjected to that same unloving mood. She is starved, kept sleepless, thwarted, deprived of new clothes, and ruthlessly crossed—for roughness must grind down roughness. Petruchio, master of "the taming school," applies the eye-for-an-eye code in his own way: "He kills her in her own humour." The soaring falcon must learn to know "her keeper's call." Nor is this swashbuckling domestication by Petruchio at all allied to the brutal wooing of Richard Crookback, for its hearty affection aims merely at reducing to the pattern of society Kate's admirable though misdirected qualities of wit, warmth, and independence.

No less than Milton, Shakespeare accepts the natural subordination of woman to man in the state of marriage. Patience and obedience are the watchwords, and Petruchio swears that Kate "will prove a second Grissel." Katherine's sweet and wager-winning obedience in the last scene is calculated to please and astonish. Her speech on wifely obedience, though dear to harried husbands, is too long, too well-known, and too much a lecture to be set down here. Shakespeare is again obviously at his ethical preachments, even in the climax of a farce; and indeed the contrasts in this play and their final resolution well illustrate the qualities in a woman which Shakespeare dwells on with admiration: gentleness, grace, patience, obedience, kindness, the "soft low tongue and lowly courtesy," affability, modesty, mild behaviour, and temperance. Most of these womanly qualities fit in neatly with the ideal of wifely obedience which this play so openly celebrates. Since

Shakespeare's natural tendency was to work from the personal and the immediate to the general and the timeless, it is not beyond supposition that his ideas on order and duty in the state derive ultimately from his speculations on subordination and obedience in the family.

Such a belief in wifely duty—since it is Shakespeare's—is not stern and sour-faced. Mere mention of the two Portias, Hotspur's Kate, and Desdemona shows sufficiently that in Shakespeare's mind obedience neither turns independent spirits into slaves, nor trammels up the free gifts of mutual love. Shakespeare's most laughable invention in *The Taming of the Shrew* is his paradox that Petruchio's crude unkindnesses are impelled by irresistible love and consideration for his mate. The taming is a slapstick version of courtly love: Petruchio does not manhandle Kate, steers clear of physical violence, usually is overbearing and harsh only with others, and accuses her openly—how exasperating to the accused!—of all those virtues she has never shown. This most irritating of his disciplines is a conscious part of Petruchio's purpose; he piously announces his perverse strategy of calling her vices virtues, his roughness reverence:

Ay, and amid this hurly I intend
That all is done in reverend care of her; . . .
This is a way to kill a wife with kindness. (IV, i, 206–7, 211)

Kate winces under her awareness of the treatment:

And that which spites me more than all these wants—
He does it under name of perfect love. (IV, iii, 11–2)

Doubly galling and ironical, it is perfectly true.

Wise saws would not have tamed Kate. Far along in the action she can still flare up against Petruchio: "Your betters have endur'd me say my mind." Her father and sister have given up, and she needs no ten-foot pole to keep away suitors. But the school of experience remains the sure road to betterment; and Petruchio's outrageous victory, in which at her husband's request Kate calls the sun the moon and addresses the wrinkled old man as "Young budding virgin, fair and fresh and sweet," blazons the success of the taming school in the actions of its most brilliant graduate.

One point remains. Even on this flagrantly farcical level, Shakespeare plays with his preoccupation as to the nature of reality. Most of the conflicts here between appearance and reality, between shadow and substance, are generated from the outside. How can Christopher Sly be sure he is a drunken tinker when all those around him assure him that he is a lord? And is not the old father Vincentio almost justified in doubting his identity when everyone on the stage is crying away to prison with the dotard and impostor? In many fashions, this is a comedy of supposes, in which it follows, for example, in the logic of the imagination, that a supposed Lucentio must beget for himself a supposed father. But in a subtler mode of thinking, presented merely as an undeveloped suggestion, Petruchio's wilful suppositions as to the character of Katherine, though they are grounded at the start in no detectable reality, are the first mental acts that bring that character into being. "Love wrought these miracles" even on the purely humorous level. There is something deeper than humor, however, in Petruchio's calling Katherine affable, modest, and mild: in the outcome, thinking makes it so. Yet since the songs of Apollo are hushed after the words of Mercury, it is best to go no further than a hint: that in this tumultuous piece there may be more than horseplay.

THE MERRY WIVES OF WINDSOR

At first glance it would appear odd that among Shakespeare's comedies, his farces should contain the most obvious moral lessons. Perhaps the spirit of farce is so simple that artistically it needs an equally simple moral to match. *The Merry Wives of Windsor* [2] organizes its gallery of town and country portraits and genre paintings about a plot. And the plot takes as theme the chastisement of those two renegades of love, Sir John Falstaff and Master Frank Ford. Shakespeare could not be more blunt in his analysis. The figure whom he here calls Falstaff is a mere mountain of greed for money and victuals. He interprets others through his single passion, and finds in Mistress Ford's smiles "the leer of invitation" and in Mistress Page's good nature "the appetite of her eye." He will use their base desires as means to rifle their husbands' purses. "I will be cheaters to them both, and they shall be exchequers to me." Even his retainers, Pistol and Nym, see themselves as panders to base humours. Falstaff is triply a fool and knave in founding his plots on sensuality, in using lustful desires to further even more sordid and trivially base appetites, and in mistaking the character of the Windsor wives. Such badness, however it may be buttered with careless wit, must be trounced; and by the time Falstaff has undergone his third rough-and-tumble lesson, he is dejected deeper than any plummet.

If Falstaff is to be shown in love, if romantic love is equally impossible to the genuine Falstaff and to this weak imitation, and if this is to be a smacking farce, then horseplay must grow out of horn-play. Most theatres have found cuckoldry funny only when wives and lovers league against impotently raging and suspicious husbands. The health of Shakespeare's notions regarding married love (or more precisely, regarding the relations of sex to society) is marked by his almost invariable [3] refusal to portray illicit or extra-marital love with any degree of sympathy. Love is loyalty. The two wives of Windsor, therefore, immediately indignant at Falstaff's advances, set out to avenge their sullied honor, though it is stained only in Falstaff's mind. "Against such lewdsters and their lechery" no action is a betrayal. In the third and final chastisement of Falstaff, both wives and both husbands are in league to make a horned monster out of the fat knight who had tried to plant horns on the husbands' heads.

The husbands had not been privy to Falstaff's first two ignominies. In their own assured integrity the wives had felt it no less necessary to teach the jealous Ford how shameful his suspicions were. Other playwrights might point the moral of jealousy by punishing ungrounded suspicions through fulfilling them in reality. For example, the most famous line in one of Molière's short farces bitterly tells the cuckolded hero-husband that he has asked for it: "Tu l'as voulu, Georges Dandin!" Not so in Shakespeare. Jealousy is shamed by twice proving it to be groundless; then it is forgiven. Again, the impregnability of Shakespeare's natural and wholesome instincts has been made evident in this double moralizing—that neither the leering lover nor the green-eyed husband deserves sympathy.[4] Mistress Ford, therefore, after the first successful lesson to her two refractory pupils, exults to her friend: "I know not which pleases me better, that my husband is deceived, or Sir John." And the two wives set merrily ahead in their second plot to try Ford's jealousy further, and to purge Falstaff's "dissolute disease," which is such that a single dose will scarce prove effective. They must be certain that "The spirit of wantonness is sure scar'd out of him." Yet since the rites of marriage and the rights of love are both on their husbands' side, the jealous Ford is at last received back repentant, and a period is brought to the jest, the husbands' feelings restored, by making Falstaff into "public sport."

In the sub-plot also, the woman in love, because she is constant and knows her own heart, is the rightful judge and contriver, as she is in all of Shakespeare's happy comedies. Once more the theme of "Thou shalt not be covetous" is enforced. Mistress Page, dazzled by the supposed court connections of the well-moneyed French Doctor Caius, has chosen him for her daughter Anne; Master Page has settled on the awkward amateur athlete and tepid wooer Abraham Slender, also well-moneyed. But Anne sees through them both, and coolly judges her father's championing of Slender:

> O, what a world of vile ill-favour'd faults
> Looks handsome in three hundred pounds a year!

Her choice is the young gallant Fenton. The love between Anne Page and Master Fenton is the standard for judgment; the ideal is the temperate, socially acknowledged, well proportioned, unforced union of independent spirits. Fenton looks forward "in the lawful name of marrying To give our hearts united ceremony." He chides her parent for mistaken plans:

You would have married her most shamefully,
Where there was no proportion [5] held in love.
The truth is, she and I (long since contracted)
Are now so sure that nothing can dissolve us. (V, v, 234–7)

The problem of proportion is, indeed, the moral problem of all comedy. Shakespeare, in his great comedies, continually confronts what is for him a basic issue: the reconcilement, or domestication, of ideal, romantic, limitless love with social common sense. He believes in both. In *The Merry Wives of Windsor*, farce and occasional-piece though it is, Cupid is essentially a "child of conscience; he makes restitution." Even here the dramatist observes proportion, and although the only song in the play is over-sober in its attack on "sinful fantasy," "lust and luxury," the "bloody fire Kindled with unchaste desire," its last notes close with "candles and starlight and moonshine." Mistress Page forgives all villains at the end:

> Good husband, let us every one go home
> And laugh this sport o'er by a country fire,
> Sir John and all. (V, v, 255–7)

And it is she also who justifies the title, and in the process justifies the moral belief that laughter and virtue are not alien:

> We'll leave a proof by that which we will do,
> Wives may be merry, and yet honest too.
> We do not act that often jest and laugh;
> 'Tis old but true: Still swine eats all the draff. (IV, i, 106–9)

A MIDSUMMER NIGHT'S DREAM

The last two lines quoted furnish in motto form what might be considered as a Shakespearean conception of comedy that parallels Aristotle's theory of the function of tragedy. Tragedy may purge the mind of painful or excessive emotions of pity and fear; comedy in similar fashion may channel off excrescent, or uneasy, or painful emotions and desires by transforming them in the imagination and fulfilling them in art. In this way art itself serves as an instrument toward virtue: it will keep our natures, which may be swinish, from quietly and privately feeding on their own draff or garbage; it will open the pen of morbid introspection into the healthier, freer air of society; "dishonesty" will not be acted out in life, because it will find its deputy in the jests and laughter of the imagined worlds of art. The social world shall shine its sane unchanging rays into the idiosyncratic prisons of individual lives; the brooding that consumes itself shall be transformed into active images. Bacon's dictum, "But it is not good to stay too long in the theatre" may be reversed: It is not good to stay too long *outside* the theatre.

Of all of Shakespeare's comedies *A Midsummer Night's Dream* dives deepest into this imaginary world. The psychological theory that art is play finds ample evidence here, for the theme of love is multiplied and divided and diversified into myriad gambolings and dartings and involutions and returns and jokes. None of them seems serious. Here is the free play of the imagination on the forms of love. It is as if the artist had given his fancy permission to rove, unchecked by any rules except the demands of art. Love dances to many tunes and tempos. Here is the stately pavane of the courtly lovers Theseus and Hippolyta, subtle and dignified. Here is the formal minuet of the four young lovers, each changing partners until all possible variations have been run through. Here is the ballet of the fairy king and the fairy queen with their ethereal trains. Here is the burlesque *pas de deux* between Titania and the ass-headed weaver. And as a coda, here is the goat-dance, the satyr dance, of the very tragical mirth of Pyramus and Thisne.

Since it is no more than a dream of gentle marriages, no thought shall be severe, for "satire keen and critical" is "Not sorting with a nuptial ceremony." Yet also, since it is a dream, every metamorphosis of the strange god may be glanced at, and all his enemies mentioned without harm. Love is physical, mental, blind, rash, fickle, loyal, doting, modest, miserable, natural, true, faithful, a dove and a serpent, a madness, a mystery, a union in friendship from childhood, an enchantment, a curse and a blessing. Its enemies are hate, jealousy, delight in domineering, sport at watching others jangle—even chastity itself. "Thrice blessed," Theseus proclaims in his faint praise of single blessedness,

> Thrice blessed they that master so their blood
> To undergo such maiden pilgrimage. (I, i, 74-5)

And immediately he adds: "But earthlier happy is the rose distill'd." Love outweighs the claims of fortune and of birth, yet its praises are continually qualified by every whim of thought. "Reason and love keep little company together now-a-days." Love may be wayward and stubborn in its nature, so that when one lover says, "Do I not in plainest truth Tell you I do not nor I cannot love you?" another lover naturally replies, "And even for that do I love you the more."

This paradox of love's perversity is matched by the dilemma as to whether love is physical or mental. "Love looks not with the eyes, but with the mind," Helena says, but the lovers' mental images are of physical beauty; and as in *Love's Labour's Lost*, love is first learned in a mortal's *eyes*. Even when love is fully requited, this odd little god Cupid may be a torturer, as Hermia ironically knows:

> Before the time I did Lysander see,
> Seem'd Athens as a paradise to me.
> O, then, what graces in my love do dwell
> That he hath turn'd a heaven unto a hell! (I, i, 204-7)

But all of these paradoxical fancies are too light in spirit to weigh down the action with irony. Mendelssohn's shimmering surfaces admirably catch its mood in music. Only twice in the play does Shakespeare slow down the mad gallop of mirth and fantasy to linger for a moment in seriousness.

The first passage follows the most famous line in the play: "The course of true love never did run smooth." Then ensues a duet between the two lovers Hermia and Lysander embroidering the theme, which Hermia rounds out with her "good persuasion":

> If then true lovers have been ever cross'd,
> It stands as an edict in destiny.
> Then let us teach our trial patience,

> Because it is a customary cross,
> As due to love as thoughts and dreams and sighs,
> Wishes and tears, poor Fancy's followers. (I, i, 150–5)

For a moment the gentle lesson of patience through all trials hovers over the fantastic shiftings of the plot.

Again at the end of the play, the action settles to rest as desire and order are reconciled. Demetrius finds "all the faith, the virtue of my heart" in Helena, and after sickness, feels that he has, "as in health, come to my natural taste." Hippolyta softly chides Theseus' skepticism regarding these antique fables and these fairy toys, and suggests that there is a mystery and purpose in them that his philosophy dreams not of:

> But all the story of the night told over,
> And all their minds transfigur'd so together,
> More witnesseth than fancy's images
> And grows to something of great constancy;
> But howsoever, strange and admirable.

And Theseus himself, in the spacious thought of the close, opens love into wider panoramas of mortal brotherhood. It becomes the gift, man to man, of good intentions. Every act of good will is an offering of love, to be received in the spirit in which it is tendered.

> And what poor duty cannot do,
> Noble respect takes it in might, not merit . . .
> Love, therefore, and tongue-tied simplicity
> In least speak most, to my capacity.

The gossamer of this play, therefore, is more than cobweb. It ends with the rhyming nuptials of solemnity and jollity. Imagination has broken all limits—the imagination of the lunatic, the lover, and the poet. Poet and lover, at least, are in sympathy; and as for the madman, let him too be pardoned. Perhaps the greatest lunatic in this moon-drenched marriage-play is the Moon herself; yet the cold and fruitless moon, wandering companionless, may contribute her own peculiar beauty; and her "imperial votaress, fancy free," may be paid one of the supreme tributes of poetry.

The dream, then, recedes.

> These things seem small and undistinguishable,
> Like far-off mountains turned into clouds.

Yet it does not fade into the light of common day, but opens into a larger dream. We are never out of the theatre, and imagination can shape, must needs shape, the plot. "I have had a dream, past the wit of man to say what dream it was." Perhaps Bottom is right to add that "Man is but an ass if he go about to expound this dream." But glancingly, delicately, the dramatist gives us a swift glimpse and an assurance: "The best in this kind are but shadows; and the worst are no worse, if imagination amend them."

ROMEO AND JULIET

Among the enemies that beset the course of true love, Shakespeare in *A Midsummer Night's Dream* realizes momentarily, with a poignancy that almost destroys the dream itself, that the most dangerous enemy is Time. Seeking some source of belief that will not alter, Shakespeare has settled upon love, which he often equates with faith or loyalty. Yet how can its truth be sealed unalterably, if the moving finger of Time has the power to mar, to alter, or to destroy? Shakespeare had already given to the wronged Lucrece a long diatribe against "Misshapen Time," whose artistic irrelevance only emphasized Shakespeare's preoccupation. "Injurious, shifting Time," the "ceaseless lackey to Eternity," has as its servant "Opportunity"—that is, chance, or accident—which sets life-as-it-is in place of life-as-it-ought-to-be.[6] The quality of Time that Shakespeare feels most piercingly is its power, helped by its servants Opportunity and Oblivion, to blot and spoil and change whatever is noble and dignified. If brevity is the soul of wit, it is also the foe of worth. The ideal good can be changed only for the worse by Time, if Time has power at all. This cosmic pathos Shakespeare most frequently presents in wide symbols of the world's decay:

> To ruinate proud buildings with thy hours . . .
> And waste huge stones with little waterdrops.
>
> (*The Rape of Lucrece*, 944, 959)

In Lysander's lines in *A Midsummer Night's Dream*, Time the quick murderer is etched in stiletto strokes as the destroyer of true love:

> War, death, or sickness did lay siege to it,
> Making it momentany as a sound,
> Swift as a shadow, short as any dream,
> Brief as the lightning in the collied night,
> That, in a spleen, unfolds both heaven and earth,
> And ere a man hath power to say 'Behold!'
> The jaws of darkness do devour it up:
> So quick bright things come to confusion. (I, i, 142–9)

Such a tragic thunderclap startles the moonlit landscapes and fantastic laughter of the midsummer night. To convey his vivid intuition of the place and duration of love in the dark world of time, Shakespeare finds the lightning-in-the-night adequate as the germinating and organizing symbol for *Romeo and Juliet*. The theme of love, which he expands in other keys in plays before and after, remains central, though now it is to be idealized in all seriousness. Yet since the dark shades of hate are here little more than the touches of an artist designed to set off the brilliant lightning flash of passion, *Romeo and Juliet* shows less the tragedy than the pathos of pure love: "So quick bright things come to confusion!"

The school of love is still in session. The hero is still fickle, the heroine constant. Romeo's moonstruck calf-love for Rosaline must be laughed out of him by his friends Benvolio and Mercutio, by his guide Friar Laurence, and by his own true love. But since Rosaline is so cool that beauty itself is "starved with her severity," she is easily forgotten. She is no more than a name that proves Romeo an apt pupil from the start, a young man who can mint conceits, imagine the tears of fickle love as "transparent heretics," and cope with the best of witlings in defining his fashionable passion in a rain of paradoxes: "Feather of lead, bright smoke, cold fire, sick health!" Once "Romeo is belov'd, and loves again," the mutual attraction is so strong that any further twitting of his fickleness is wasted.

Even more obvious, in this play love becomes the teacher of society. Shakespeare was never more patently the schoolmaster than in his repeated moralizing that love must destroy hate: The prologue tells us that the misadventured piteous overthrows of the two lovers bury their parents' strife. Nothing could remove the continuance of their parents' rage except their children's end. The moral lesson is so shaped formally that it becomes the main theme of the drama: the opening scene stops the bitter feud temporarily; the middle act results in two deaths and the separation of the lovers when murderous quarreling breaks out again; the closing scene offers the sacrifice of innocents to wipe out in blood the cursed strife of the old partisans. Church and state combine at the end to arraign the hate-filled families. The Friar presents himself "both to impeach and purge." And the Prince of Verona speaks the ironic moral:

> Capulet, Montague,
> See what a scourge is laid upon your hate,
> That heaven finds means to kill your joys with love!

"All are punish'd." Yet the houses are reconciled in clasped hands, and golden statues shall rise as memorials to these "Poor sacrifices of our enmity!" The universe is guided by "the rigour of severest law"; and Time works inevitably "to wrong the wronger till he render right." Insofar as this play is a tragedy of fate—and Shakespeare sets up dozens of signposts pointing toward the foregone moral conclusion—all accidents and events work toward the final sacrifice. Romeo and Juliet are puppets, since the moral punishment of the raging clans becomes more powerful in proportion to the innocence and helplessness of the sacrifices. In no other play does Shakespeare envisage a general moral order operating with such inhuman, mechanical severity.

On the surface, social evil is castigated and purged by "Fate," which is an extra-human moral order. Yet in contrast to this often declared thesis, and by no means reconciled with it, Shakespeare intrudes a line of thinking which was to become central in his serious philosophy: that the causes of tragedy lie in the sufferers themselves. The doctrines of individual responsibility and of fate as a social Nemesis offer divergent motivations: this play may fail as serious tragedy because Shakespeare blurs the focus and never makes up his mind entirely as to who is being punished, and for what reason. Later he learned to carry differing hypotheses simultaneously, to suggest complex contradictory interactions convincingly; but that is not the effect of the double moral motivations in *Romeo and Juliet*.

The dangerous fault of the two lovers is their extreme rashness. The Friar chides his protégé's sudden haste: "Wisely, and slow. They stumble that run fast." He has rebuked him earlier "for doting, not for loving." And even in a love affair which he approves he will counsel Romeo to

> Love moderately: long love doth so;
> Too swift arrives as tardy as too slow.

The explosive force of pure passion throughout the play he casts in its characteristic imagery:

> These violent delights have violent ends
> And in their triumph die, like fire and powder,
> Which, as they kiss, consume. (II, vi, 9–11)

Juliet, too, is uneasily aware of what may be their fault:

> I have no joy of this contract to-night.
> It is too rash, too unadvis'd, too sudden;
> Too like the lightning, which doth cease to be
> Ere one can say 'It lightens.' (II, ii, 117–20)

If the theme of personal responsibility were not drowned out by the theme of fate, it might be argued that the lovers' deaths in the tomb are caused by Romeo's sudden decision to buy poison, and again by his immediate suicide when he mistakes Juliet's sleep for death. But this is quibbling with destiny.

It is not quibbling to point out Shakespeare's emphasis on their surging wrong-headed impulses midway in the drama, so much more cunningly wrought and convincing than the moral tags. Juliet, when she hears that her husband has killed her cousin Tybalt, at once breaks out in a paradoxical curse twelve times illustrated: "O serpent heart, hid with a flow'ring face!" True, she soon veers back to her loyalty, but fast running has led to stumbling at the start. In the preceding scene, Romeo has banished "respective lenity" to heaven and has embraced "fire-ey'd fury" to kill Tybalt. And in the succeeding scene, Romeo's passion turns him hysterical. He has become a "fond mad man," who grovels on the floor of the Friar's cell, weeping and blubbering, who is drawn to his feet by the nurse's words—"Stand up, stand up! Stand, an you be a man"—only to unsheathe his dagger to kill himself, and who is finally restored to his senses by the Friar's bitterest as well as his most powerful adjurations. He has shown "the unreasonable fury of a beast"; he has betrayed the form of man; his spirit

> Like powder in a skilless soldier's flask,
> Is set afire by thine own ignorance.

No less than in the hatred of brawling houses, then, "unreasonable fury" may be shown in love. And Shakespeare's own sounder moral sense answers the philosophy of this so-called "tragedy of fate" in the Friar's direct statement:

> Why railest thou on thy birth, the heaven, and earth?
> Since birth and heaven and earth, all three do meet
> In thee at once; which thou at once wouldst lose.

Man cannot evade his pilotage by proclaiming himself "fortune's fool."

Such are the moralizings in this play. They protest too much in words, attest too little in experience. The actual ethical energy of the drama resides in its realization of the purity and intensity of ideal love. Here there is no swerving. Both Romeo and Juliet are wholly devoted to their overpowering discovery: from the religious imagery of the wooing to the feasting imagery of the

Capulet vault, when Romeo's wit plays its "lightning before death," the power of love is idealized; and true love, as though it were a hyphenated compound, echoes through the play.[7]

Shakespeare has found skill adequate to his ambition. Nothing but the finest part of pure love inhabits his scenes of romantic enchantment—the courtship at the ball, the moonlit wooing, the bridal night. He has intensified its purity by contrasting it with Romeo's first posings, with Capulet's bargainings and tantrums, with Mercutio's bawdry, with the Friar's benign philosophizing, and with the nurse's loose opportunism. He has shown that love makes lovers fearless. He sings its hymn in Juliet's epithalamium; and consecrates it as rising above life, in the successive draughts, of sleep and of death, which each lover drinks to the other. His favorite theme of Death the Bridegroom he has introduced when the lean abhorred monster, in Romeo's imaginings, keeps Juliet "in dark to be his paramour."

Above all, he has brought out the pathos of love by violent contrasts. Time hurries all things away, and in the lightning imagery the kiss and the consummation are as fire and powder. Frail love, surrounded by disasters, becomes a thing of light in blackness, itself "like a rich jewel in an Ethiop's ear." All is loneliness: Juliet is deserted by her father, then by her mother, then by her nurse, until she is left only with the power to die, or to consign herself to the horrible vault. Romeo is exiled—and indeed through the middle scenes "banished! banished!" beats like a pulse.[8] Desperate and exiled, love knows only enemies, ranging from the vulgar nurse to "love-devouring death" itself.

The secret of the play is that the deaths of the lovers are *not* the result of the hatred between the houses, nor of any other cause except love itself, which seeks in death its own restoring cordial. Love conquers death even more surely than it conquers hate. It sweeps aside all accidents, so that fate itself seems powerless. Time is conquered, in that first stirring of a belief that Shakespeare came later to trust completely: that the intensity of an emotion towers above its temporal duration or success. Shakespeare's moral measurements are to be qualitative, not quantitative. Romeo says in the second act:

> But come what sorrow can,
> It cannot countervail the exchange of joy
> That one short minute gives me in her sight.

And when he has indeed experienced such sorrow, in exile, at Mantua, he turns to his happy, flattering dream:

> I dreamt my lady came and found me dead
> (Strange dream that gives a dead man leave to think!)
> And breath'd such life with kisses in my lips
> That I reviv'd and was an emperor. (V, i, 6–9)

The dream is closer to truth than to dramatic irony. For the intensity of their single-souled impulse has turned their passion into a death-devouring love. Their life is in their kisses, and Juliet turns to Romeo's murdered lips for a restorative. The suicidal weapon is a "happy dagger," wedding the lovers to eternity. Man's deeper instincts play strange juggleries in attaining truth beyond the reach of metaphysics, so that there is a mysterious authenticity in Romeo's phrase "a triumphant grave." From the time he hears of Juliet's death, all his actions in this world are those of "a dead man" until he can reaffirm his marriage to Juliet, this time with no possible separation, by drinking the poison cup. The sense of triumph descends upon the play from a love so straight, so simple, and so certain that its very bravery transforms death and time and hatred—yes, and the accidents of Fate—into insubstantial shadows. The quick bright things remain shining and alive.

THE MERCHANT OF VENICE

If *Romeo and Juliet* considers the conflict between ideal romantic love and society, culminating in the victory of love over the world, *The Merchant of Venice* imagines the triumph of ideal love within the social framework. In one sense, then, the comedy of Portia and Bassanio is more serious than the "tragedy" of Romeo and Juliet, since any philosophy that reconciles significant opposites is ultimately more comprehensive and responsible than a philosophy that exalts one mode of life at the expense of another. The sweet gravity of this play crowns the second stage in Shakespeare's journey—the period in which he acts as eloquent and smiling tutor in that subject which he first made his own. *The Merchant of Venice* sums up with certainty and authority the principles which he had so far advanced, sometimes tentatively, sometimes in over-statements. Now that he accepts them as sure, he need no longer state them, so that the succeeding Golden Comedies, his greatest in the genre, exist as pure art, rather than as art pleasingly mixed with moral tags.

Experience replaces doctrine. That this constitutes a higher form of ethics we have on the authority of Aristotle: the truly virtuous man is not the man who constrains rebellious passion to obey his reason, but the man who, through habit and long experience, finds his highest convictions and his instincts in accord. This will be the spirit that informs *Much Ado About Nothing, As You Like It,* and *Twelfth Night,* and that finds its first unforced expression in *The Merchant of Venice.* For this period, at least, Shakespeare has made himself into a natural Aristotelian, and flowingly preaches the doctrine of the mean.[9]

Nor is the relativity in Aristotle's ethics slighted—the belief that each moral act must be separately judged in relation to its surroundings and its agent. It is Portia, that model Aristotelian, who observes:

> Nothing is good, I see, without respect. . . .
> How many things by season season'd are
> To their right praise and true perfection! (V, i, 99, 107–8)

She has a comprehensive and balanced spirit. On minor matters she is perfectly willing to help fate choose her suitor, even laughingly ordering her maid to set Rhenish wine on the wrong casket in order to mislead the young German wooer. But when it is a question of Bassanio, she will not let desire cloud her deep integrity, her justice to herself:

I could teach you
How to choose right, but then I am forsworn.
So will I never be; so may you miss me;
But if you do, you'll make me wish a sin—
That I had been forsworn. Beshrow your eyes!

No wonder, then, that when she offers herself to Bassanio, she does not offer him what she would like to be, but, in her clear-eyed temperament, what she is: "an unlesson'd girl, unschool'd, unpractis'd"; but happily young enough and intelligent enough to learn, committing a gentle spirit to "her lord, her governor, her king." Only the "wise, fair, and true" should be worshipped in a "constant soul," and Portia well merits the praises, "past all expressing," of Jessica or of Mrs. Jamison.

Yet even in Portia—and certainly in others—Shakespeare is fully aware of the soul's warfare between reason and passion. Launcelot Gobbo carries on a long and funny debate between his conscience and the fiend. Conscience tells him not to budge from his master Shylock, but "The fiend gives the more friendly counsel," and he runs away to Bassanio. Gobbo's running away is not the only instance in Shakespeare in which instinct is sounder than preaching; part of his moral creed makes instinct more friendly, and often more true, than the puritanical inner check that finds delight only in denial. In this conflict between the reasonable and the romantic, there is little doubt where Bassanio stands. He chooses the lead casket without hesitation or reserve, because his natural sympathy responds to its motto: "Who chooseth me must give and hazard all he hath." Bassanio is almost pure instinct: in the ecstasy of success, "Only my blood speaks to you in my veins," and his confused feelings have turned "to a wild of nothing, save of joy, Express'd and not express'd."

The caskets in themselves offer a moral philosophy in symbolic action, and in the rejection of the gold and silver, Shakespeare makes clear that he will base no system on popular opinion alone, nor on outward shows, nor on pharisaical satisfaction in one's own merit. He is not fond of people who "assume desert." Already he displays an instinctive distrust of cunning,[10] of virtue founded

upon the letter of the law, and of deliberate rationalizing. Even
Portia expresses this distaste:

> O, these deliberate fools! When they do choose,
> They have the wisdom by their wit to lose. (II, ix, 80–1)

And earlier: "Too long a pause for that which you find there."

The impulsive and reckless Bassanio is nearer the truth, for love
is generous. Portia's spirit embraces this aspect, too. Though she
is witty, practical, aware of obligations to the world and society,
self-critical, and not above shady jests, she feels fully the overmastering power of love. At the first moment of Bassanio's fortunate choosing, love crowds all other passions from her heart—
fear, jealousy, doubtful thoughts, and "rash-embrac'd despair."
For her lover—not for herself alone—she would willingly mul-
tiply superlatives and exceed excess "in virtues, beauties, livings,
friends." That this is more than mere verbal display, the immediately ensuing action makes plain. Her bounty is boundless,
and on her wedding day she banishes her husband from her bed
until he has freed his friend. His people shall be her people. Lorenzo, who says so many good things in the play, is aware that
Portia has "a noble and a true conceit Of godlike amity, which
appears most strongly In bearing thus the absence of your lord."
Portia in her reply, though she speaks of proportion, reveals also
the liberality of love—Aristotle's Magnificence or Magnanimity
in chivalric terms:

> in companions
> That do converse and waste the time together,
> Whose souls do bear an egal yoke of love,
> There must be needs a like proportion
> Of lineaments, of manners, and of spirit;
> Which makes me think that this Antonio,
> Being the bosom lover of my lord,
> Must needs be like my lord. (III, iv, 11–8)

In freeing Antonio, therefore, she says that she is but "purchasing
the semblance of my soul." So well are generosity and a sense of

proportion mixed in her own nature that she immediately cuts off such high metaphysics to return to the world of action:

> This comes too near the praising of myself.
> Therefore no more of it.

Love, therefore, though it gains its fire from the exalted communion between two human beings, now widens its sphere. We may overlook the ring plot at the close, since apart from its joyous marital teasing, its sole wifely lesson to husbands might be the advice not to promise more than they can perform. But the pound-of-flesh plot looms large. What is the place of love in a lawcourt? In what sense can Shakespeare accept Browning's "All's love, yet all's law"?

Here there are no quick judgments. The raw materials for the law are human beings; and how can their motives, assertions, actions, and appearances be certainly distinguished? The casket plot alone should serve as warning not to mistake seeming for reality.[11] Bassanio and Antonio—even Gratiano and Arragon—speak of the differences between semblance and substance, and the difficulties even the wisest may encounter among such cunning shows.[12]

But if judgment should be slow because truth and appearance are so confused, it should also be circumspect because various casts of mind cannot fairly be judged by a single personal standard. Temperaments cannot be explained: when Solanio seeks the motives for Antonio's sadness, he is forced back upon the description that Antonio is sad because he is not merry. "By two-headed Janus," he says—a god whose power Shakespeare seriously contemplated—"Nature hath fram'd strange fellows in her time"; and the laughing parrots and vinegar-faced fellows must be taken as they come. Shylock will not answer for his humor of hate— "So can I give no reason, nor I will not." Nevertheless, his certain loathing remains as instinctive as some men's reasonless aversions to pigs, or cats, or bagpipes. "Live and let live" must be the social rule in a world of deep-rooted, irrational, antagonistic personalities, for likings and loathings depend on the mere moods of "affection, Mistress of passion." Society must nurture tolerance if it is to continue. Hatred alone cannot be tolerated, since it destroys toleration itself; and Shylock must be punished, immediately and in the terms he understands, for attempting to amalgamate his personal selfish virulence with the impersonal law of the state. Malice must not bear down the social order. Punishment must be reserved for those who judge with rigidity and personal passion.

But most important of all Shakespeare's speculations about suspended judgment is his belief that the judge himself may be in part a culprit. "To offend and judge are distinct offices And of opposed natures." This sharp, clear saying of Portia's is more an apothegm for the whole play than a characteristic remark relevant to the situation in which it occurs. Man's nature is dual: if he acts solely as offender or as judge, his reckless despair or his fanatical righteousness will be punished. He must acknowledge his own complexity, and allow it to develop naturally. The healthy man is aware of himself, if not constantly self-critical. Something of the actor or the poseur, moreover, exists in each one of us except the simplest souls. Antonio realizes this in himself and others, and holds "the world but as the world"—"A stage, where every man must play a part, And mine a sad one." And Portia, even in herself, is conscious of the great gap between virtuous contemplation and action:

If to do were as easy as to know what were good to do, chapels had been churches, and poor men's cottages princes' palaces. It is a good divine that follows his own instructions. I can easier teach twenty what were good to be done than be one of the twenty to follow mine own teaching. The brain may devise laws for the blood, but a hot temper leaps o'er a cold decree. (I, ii, 13–21)

Out of this humble fellowship in human fallibility flowers the famous eloquence of the trial scene. Love has expanded into a social doctrine, and in arguments firmly based on Christian teaching, a man becomes his sinful brother's keeper through his own sympathy, so that moral strength springs from acknowledgment of one's own weakness. Justice and mercy, the Old Testament and the New Testament, fight out once more their ancient battle, and the plea is for the freedom of love, not for the compulsion of passion. This social or cosmic love, though it is "mightiest in the mightiest," is beyond the dread and fear of kings:

> Mercy is above this sceptred sway;
> It is enthroned in the heart of kings,
> It is an attribute to God himself;
> . . . in the course of justice, none of us
> Should see salvation. We do pray for mercy,
> And that same prayer doth teach us all to render
> The deeds of mercy.[13] (IV, i, 193–5, 199–202)

As an artist, Shakespeare has by this time learned to cast his moral ideas in dramatic mold. Perhaps his finest, most completely realized, dramatic invention up through the writing of *The Merchant of Venice* is the figure of Shylock. Nothing should delight the shade of Shakespeare more than the endless warfare between pedant and sentimentalist as to whether Shylock is a stage villain or a wronged outcast who merits our sympathy. If the contest were ever finally settled, so much the worse for Shakespeare's art! For in Shylock, realized with the illusion of living, Shakespeare's conception of suspended or divided moral judgment walks and speaks.

The balanced and triumphantly organized themes, counter-themes, and plots move to a close; and the ideal of a harmoniously comprehensive virtue—reason reconciled with generosity, common sense with warm personal passion—finds its final perfect symbol in the moonlit and melodious garden of the lovers. Music can, for the time, change man's nature; Paradise may be taken in through the ear; and if he lacks responsiveness to the proportions that make music, man may not be saved. Mortals are condemned to "this muddy vesture of decay," but heaven breaks in at times through the "concord of sweet sounds," and then men know: "Such harmony is in immortal souls."

The muddy vesture in this play is the world of commerce. Pacts, agreements, bonds, promises, bargains, oaths, terms, contracts, clerks and merchants fill the dialogue and crowd the stage.

In a negative sense, Shylock is the merchant. In a more positive sense, Antonio deserves the titular rôle, and, since "he only loves the world for" Bassanio, he proves himself a master at trafficking through his willingness to lay down his life for his friend. In a more esoteric sense (and Shakespeare was not averse to emblems), the great argosies of the play are those that venture forth to possess love. The merchant who "must give and hazard all he hath" is Bassanio. There are others besides Bassanio: Antonio, of course, or Jessica and Lorenzo, or Gratiano and Nerissa. Or Portia. The Golcondas and El Dorados they discover surpass all.the "gaudy gold, Hard food for Midas" that the Venetian quays can offer. Gratiano speaks for himself and his friend Bassanio when he says:

> We are the Jasons, we have won the Fleece.

Shakespeare the poet has now learned the more specialized art of the poetic dramatist: how to transmute his ideas into actions, symbols, images, and complex human characterizations. "I think," remarks Lorenzo, "the best grace of wit will shortly turn into silence." Increasingly, in the plays that were to come, Shakespeare employs the grace of his wit to turn his moral convictions, not into silence, but into those imitations of human actions that constitute drama. He knows the secret for making an idea walk like a man. In the beginning was the word, and out of the word, guided by love, he is creating his own world of images.

CHAPTER THREE

The Garden of Eden

SHAKESPEARE had first learned to express, and never lost his delight in expressing, the beauty of English countrysides and the warmth of English hearths. Compared with such contemporaries as Marlowe, Spenser and Sidney, Shakespeare in his earthiness and his naturalism startles us again and again. Even when he writes in their style, as in *Venus and Adonis*, high convention often crumbles. The gorgeous palaces of antiquity dissolve, and we see poor trembling Wat the hare, scenting the hounds from some far hill, or we hear shrill-tongued tapsters. Shakespeare, as if foreknowing and disapproving the Baconian theory, seems bent on proving in every image that his works were written by one who had been a country boy at Stratford, living next door to the butcher, taught in the local school, watching the birds and animals of the fields and woods, knowing the old tales of taverns and firesides. His scene is England; Robin Goodfellow inhabits near "Athens"; and in the world of "Greece" we hear that

> The fold stands empty in the drowned field . . .
> The nine men's morris is fill'd up with mud.
>   (*Midsummer Night's Dream*, II, i, 96, 98)

The first moral act that Shakespeare's art suggests is one of acceptance. He is neither falsely proud nor falsely humble, and he will build on things as they are.

The second act is the conscious preaching of the doctrine of love. Love he realizes as dangerous energy, capricious because it works through kindled human emotions, yet capable of exalting, of discovering hidden ore and refining it into the purest and most lasting gold of the spirit. Love is a going out from one's self; and in *The Merchant of Venice* its liberality begins to transcend selfish interests.

This generous, expansive spirit of love dominates and directs the development of Shakespeare's moral speculation as reflected in his writings.[1] He moves steadily toward a greater comprehensiveness and a more perfect reconciliation. Purists in all ages have reprimanded him for the mixture of *genres*. That he did mix all modes of living is incontrovertible; evidently he found little interest, or little reality, in rigidly treating a single aspect of existence. Chastity to him was unfruitful, in art as well as in "breed." Nor could anything be valued in a void; contrasts, surroundings, "respect" in the sense of relationships, were essentials in arriving at any true judgment of worth.

Rather than speak of the mixture of the *genres* in Shakespeare, it would be more accurate to speak of their wedding. In the period of his development when he was writing his purest comedies and his best English history plays, this spirit of love urges him repeatedly toward reconciliations of his highest hopes for what man may be with his widest experiences of what man is. *Much Ado About Nothing* is the wedding of love and humor; *As You Like It* is the wedding of love and nature; *Twelfth Night* is the wedding of love and music, the final harmony. And each stage in this progress assumes and assimilates the unions that have gone before.

The domiciling of romance in the real world had long been Shakespeare's task. *The Two Gentlemen of Verona* was as close to failure as he permitted himself to come. *Love's Labour's Lost* tried to mix romance with high-bred wit, but this is merely to marry two somewhat artificial and conventional worlds. *A Mid-*

summer Night's Dream hardly takes its high-born figures as flesh and blood. All three of these plays introduce vulgar characters sketched in realistic if exaggerated fashion, as if—the argument of the dramatist might run—the audience must believe in high romantic lovers because they rub elbows with Launce, with Costard and Jaquenetta the kitchen wench, and with Bottom the weaver. But essentially these characters are juxtaposed, not related, to the central figures.

Romeo and Juliet dares again to treat pure passion. This time Shakespeare is more successful, because such figures as Old Capulet and Mercutio, existing in their own right and their own moods, help shape the destiny of the two lovers. In *The Merchant of Venice* Shakespeare takes the important step of wedding the two worlds of romance and reality in a single mind. He had tried it previously in Berowne. Belmont is a withdrawn, aristocratic, protected world. Nevertheless its own high chivalric code of honor and sentiment ties it to the markets and the tribunals of Venice; and Portia is equally at home in the court of love and the court of law.

MUCH ADO ABOUT NOTHING

The spirit of the farces, *The Taming of the Shrew* and *The Merry Wives of Windsor,* most nearly parallels the approach to romantic love in *Much Ado About Nothing.* Like them, this play is written with more than a dash of prosaic common sense.[2] Portia's real home had been in the gardens and galleries of Belmont, from which she sallies forth into the world of action like a feminine and effective Don Quixote. But in *Much Ado About Nothing* Shakespeare's sympathy from the beginning lies with the hard-headed and sharp-tongued Benedick and Beatrice. The play constitutes his severest criticism to date of the weaknesses lying in romantic love. He takes as his main plot a highly fanciful story—what could be more romantic than a crucial scene in which a lady swoons into supposed death upon hearing her honor falsely traduced by her lover at the altar? Yet the lady Hero, shadowy and almost silent, is strangely ineffective, the villain is little more than a conventional malcontent, and Shakespeare is satisfied to develop in a few fine touches the weak impulses of his smart young gentleman Claudio.[3]

So full of tricks is fancy, that Claudio in his melodramatic scene of accusation, rails against the "cunning sin" and "savage sensuality" of his Hero, who is as modest, chaste, and sincere in reality as he accuses her of being only in "exterior shows." He wilfully makes over the world to his own mistaken misogyny:

> On my eyelids shall conjecture hang,
> To turn all beauty into thoughts of harm,
> And never shall it more be gracious. (IV, i, 107–9)

Before he is forgiven and restored to his happiness, the Friar insists that the crime must be purged and punished in the place where it was committed—Claudio's own mind. Slander must change to remorse.

> Th' idea of her life shall sweetly creep
> Into his study of imagination, . . .
> Into the eye and prospect of his soul . . .
>   Then shall he mourn . . .
> And wish he had not so accused her.

The reconciliation scene is as melodramatic as the denunciation. It too plays with the paradoxes of true love that transcends, or runs counter to, this world of shadows. The resurrected Hero presents the truth as a conceit:

> And when I liv'd I was your other wife;
> And when you lov'd you were my other husband. (V, iv, 60–1)

Leonato enforces love's transcendence: "She died, my lord, but whiles her slander liv'd." And the Friar reaffirms the joy and the remorse before the miraculous grace of love that will not die: "Meantime let wonder seem familiar."

The trouble is that in the main plot wonder does not seem familiar enough. The operatic situations and the ill-developed or poorly motivated characters are not convincing. Shakespeare rescues them through his favorites, Benedick and Beatrice. The denunciation scene turns from verse to prose, from melodrama to drama, when the stage is left to the two lovers and Benedick asks the question that shows again Shakespeare's dramatic use of silence: "Lady Beatrice, have you wept all this while?" She does not weep much longer, nor does she allow Benedick to fall into conventional vows of love. When he protests: "Bid me do anything for thee," she answers in two words: "Kill Claudio." [4] As she thinks of Claudio, her bitter eloquence pronounces a moral judgment not only on his blindness but on the unnecessary cruelty of his procedure:

> O that I were a man! What? bear her in hand until they come to take hands, and then with public accusation, uncover'd slander, unmitigated rancour—O God, that I were a man! I would eat his heart in the market place. (IV, i, 305–9)

Mere words are useless. When Benedick swears "By this hand, I love thee," Beatrice retorts: "Use it for my love some other way than swearing by it." And Benedick replies with equal economy: "Enough, I am engag'd, I will challenge him." Actions will speak, and "As you hear of me, so think of me." Benedick has had to choose between loyalty to Claudio and love for Beatrice. The greater love eclipses the smaller, and Benedick acts contrary to the presented evidence, on the strength of his trust in Beatrice's loyal love. Faith begets faith. He has asked but one question: "Think you *in your soul* the Count Claudio hath wrong'd her?" She answers: "Yea, as sure as I have a thought or a soul." And the debate in his mind has been decided in favor of Beatrice.

This is serious matter for comedy. But Shakespeare had long felt restive at the thought of mere manners passing for sound coin. In the court of love, there had been too much courtliness and courtesy, not enough love. This is evident in Berowne's renunciation of "taffeta phrases, silken terms precise," as well as in the portrayal of the villain Tybalt in *Romeo and Juliet* as one of "these antic, lisping, affecting fantasticoes—these new tuners of accent!" Portia herself waxes sarcastic against the tribe of immature swaggerers and the "thousand raw tricks of these bragging Jacks." And Beatrice showers vitriol on such courageous captains of compliment:

> But manhood is melted into cursies, valour into compliment, and men are only turn'd into tongue, and trim ones too. He is now as valiant as Hercules that only tells a lie, and swears it. (IV, i, 320–4)

Old Antonio, uncle to Beatrice and Hero, grieving at the younger generation, carries on the tongue-lashing of these "Boys, apes, braggarts, Jacks, milksops!" "I know them," he says:

> I know them, yea,
> And what they weigh, even to the utmost scruple,
> Scambling, outfacing, fashion-monging boys,
> That lie and cog and flout, deprave and slander,
> Go anticly, show outward hideousness,
> And speak off half a dozen dang'rous words,
> How they might hurt their enemies, if they durst;
> And this is all. (V, i, 92–9)

Why has Shakespeare taken such an antipathy to the vain young slanderers, the hot-headed lying Jacks of which Tybalt, and Claudio in *Much Ado*, show possible varieties? In part because he loathed particularly those evil elements that base their hostile actions on unfounded suspicion or on nothing whatever. Jealousy and slander he viewed with special aversion, for how can chastity and integrity oppose them? They mock our eyes with air. Of the two, slander may be the more sordid, since jealousy at least springs from misguided passion, whereas slander is purely malicious, destructive, and irresponsible. Who steals my purse steals trash; and outlaws are not such bad fellows, as *The Two Gentlemen of Verona* and *As You Like It* testify. But the slanderers, almost alone among Shakespeare's sinners, are nearly unforgivable; and Shakespeare, like Spenser, treats with revulsion the Blatant Beast whose myriad tongues wound for sheer spite. In the plays with political implications, of course, slander becomes even more criminal than in the dramas of personal fortune.

Partly Shakespeare is bitter against the young swaggering slanderers out of his usual contempt for pretension in any form. And partly he seems to have developed, with considerable deliberation, a distrust for the cocksureness of callow youth. He works himself into a rather curious position: the smooth, privileged young men are too young to know what they are talking about; on the other hand, old age with its wise saws is impotent in convincing anybody. There seems little left for Shakespeare to acknowledge as a principle for conduct except Poor Richard's adage, "Experience keeps a dear school, but fools will learn in no other." Men's passions make all of them fools, incapable of accepting any sage advice or profiting from any hard-won experience except their own. Let us take a formally developed illustration. When old Leonato is grieving for his daughter Hero's shame, his yet older brother Antonio admonishes him:

> If you go on thus, you will kill yourself,
> And 'tis not wisdom thus to second grief
> Against yourself. (V, i, 1–3)

Leonato answers in a thirty-line speech, "I pray thee cease thy counsel," the gist of which is that no one can console him except a comforter "whose wrongs do suit with mine," that no man can patch his grief with a few proverbs, that only those who do not feel grief mouth comfortable counsel, that aches cannot be charmed with air, nor agony with words. He ends with certainty:

> No, no! 'Tis all men's office to speak patience
> To those that wring under the load of sorrow,
> But no man's virtue nor sufficiency
> To be so moral when he shall endure
> The like himself. Therefore give me no counsel.
> My griefs cry louder than advertisement.

And old brother Antonio answers with too much truth: "Therein do men from children nothing differ." Knowledge of this lamentable fact in human behavior is not the monopoly of the old men. Benedick has said earlier in the play: "Well, every one can master a grief but he that has it." And Romeo had answered the

Friar's soothing wisdom in some irritation: "Thou canst not speak of that thou dost not feel." [5]

To sum it up, Shakespeare is no believer in the schoolroom. Copybook maxims, admirable as they may be, are ineffective. The only school is experience, and axioms are proved upon the pulses. Believing this, Shakespeare finds the drama a most excellent moral instrument, since in the drama characters reach conclusions by putting their various conflicting beliefs into action. Their passions and philosophies are forced to work out practicable solutions, in conflict with a larger world and with unsympathetic alien forces or personalities. The audience may profit vicariously from the display of life in action. This belief, so slowly affirmed, accounts for the greater soundness and sanity of Shakespeare's handling of love in the Golden Comedies. Romantic love, in the characters that interest him in *Much Ado About Nothing*, is not to be a doctrine promulgated to puppet lovers and forced upon them. Benedick and Beatrice will fight it to the last gasp. They take their stand against sentimentality, and carry on the war between the sexes with gusto.

The main interest of the play, then, starts in the world of common sense. Raillery and wit will protect light hearts. "There is measure in everything," says Beatrice, and lest that remark on moderation sound immoderately serious, she makes it into a pun and dances out her conviction. The lovers are too clear-eyed not to be self-critical. When Beatrice overhears her disdain, scornful wit, and self-endearment exaggerated, she abandons them. "Contempt, farewell! and maiden pride, adieu!" And when Benedick also overhears a conversation on his character—that he will scorn Beatrice's love, since he "hath a contemptible spirit"—he decides to forsake "quips and sentences and these paper bullets of the brain," because, he says, "I must not seem proud. Happy are they that hear their detractions and can put them to mending." Part of this, of course, is not the result of the lovers' good resolutions, but of their instinctive attraction toward each other. "Good Lord, for alliance!" cries Beatrice, as she watches Claudio and Hero making love, and there is a touch of envy and self-pity in her jest:

"Thus goes every one to the world but I. . . . I may sit in a corner and cry 'Heigh-ho for a husband!' "

"Alliance," then, catches these two independent spirits, who
have too much good sense to resist nature. Leonato in his passion
of grief had asserted:

> I will be flesh and blood;
> For there was never yet philosopher
> That could endure the toothache patiently.

Now Benedick feels the pangs of love, and when his friends twit
him on his sadness, he replies: "I have the toothache." They ascribe
it to love and suggest a remedy, but Benedick already knows well
that "Yet is this no charm for the toothache."

To himself, he will not deny the effects and the power of love.
Yet he will try to keep it in proportion through humor:

> Leander the good swimmer, Troilus the first employer of
> panders, and a whole book full of these quondam carpet-
> mongers, whose names yet run smoothly in the even road of
> a blank verse—why, they were never so truly turn'd over
> and over as my poor self in love. (V, ii, 30–6)

He has too much respect for his genuine feelings to transform
them into fashionable conventions; he "cannot woo in festival
terms," and when he looks for rhymes for "lady," "scorn," and
"school," he can only come out with "baby," "horn," and "fool."
Sentiment—even when it is experienced directly—is to be kept in
its place by anti-sentiment.

His sincerity is best shown in that excellently conceived dramatic scene of his challenge to Claudio. Here we have dramatic
reversal of moods, for the perpetual giber Benedick is now in
deadly earnest—"You have among you kill'd a sweet and innocent
lady"—and his friends Pedro and Claudio are uneasily jesting
against his estrangement and their own bad consciences. In critical
moments Benedick controls both his emotion and his wit; their
interaction protects him at once against the affectations of intellect and the extreme sallies of passion.

The integrity and sincerity of his love, based so broadly, make him in the end impervious to mockery, and it is "Benedick, the married man" who, after kissing Beatrice heartily, replies in all surety: "I'll tell thee what, Prince: a college of wit-crackers cannot flout me out of my humour," who demands music and dancing, and who advises Pedro: "Prince, thou art sad. Get thee a wife!" In the wedding of Benedick and Beatrice, humor has been married to love on both sides of the family. Since humor presupposes a greater consciousness of the world and of one's self, the wedding promises more stability and happiness than in any of Shakespeare's previous imaginings. "Man is a giddy thing," says Benedick, "and this is my conclusion." Man is less giddy, surer in his moral sense, in direct proportion to his awareness of his own giddiness.

AS YOU LIKE IT

The harmony in *As You Like It* and *Twelfth Night* is masterful and assured. We are never made conscious that such clear and easy interweaving of melodies required years of practice. The heroines Rosalind and Viola know the sure secrets of love, their humor and sense checking the aberrations and excesses of Orlando and Duke Orsino, and of romantic love itself. Their ideal love is so certain and so rewarding that even the most delicate affection may be laughed at without harm to its nature, while the plays as wholes take every opportunity to play pleasant variations on the theme, from high comedy to grotesquerie. Since his belief is so firmly based on flesh and blood, in *As You Like It* Shakespeare allows his smiling realization of human potentialities to create a thornless garden. The forest is a simple, self-sustaining, out-of-doors domain, and its spirit lives in the famous words: "They fleet the time carelessly as they did in the golden world."

Any affectation or eccentricity, though immediately noticeable, becomes amusing; yet the goodness of human nature is so certain that men do not need sharp satire to defend them. The villains, having served their purpose in showing the heroes unafraid, are cardboard ogres, and at any crucial instant fold up like paper dolls. Antonio's genuine melancholy in Venice would lose its meaning in the Forest of Arden, and the melancholy Jaques becomes a laughable eccentric, who to his knowing companions is the greatest fool in the forest. Touchstone baits Jaques' humor by lugubrious speculations on time, and Shakespeare is working toward his most ironical inversions in Jaques' taking Touchstone for the true fool: "That fools should be so deep contemplative!"

Shakespeare was always skeptical of the best generalizations of philosophy; at this time, therefore, a philosophy so shakily founded as to misprize the human race rouses him to an earnestness hardly in keeping with the play. Jaques, whenever he finds a listener, is willing to lash out with the whips of the professional satirist and cynic:

> Give me leave
> To speak my mind, and I will through and through
> Cleanse the foul body of th' infected world,
> If they will patiently receive my medicine. (II, vii, 58–61)

The Duke replies sharply in the familiar Shakespearean vein, that misanthropy frequently may show only the misanthropist diseased:

> Most mischievous foul sin, in chiding sin.
> For thou thyself hast been a libertine,
> As sensual as the brutish sting itself.[6]

Jaques crows back with the threadbare old argument of the satirists, that in reproving pride, lechery, avarice, baseness and folly, he hurts no one but an actual sinner, so that the Duke's reproof of Jaques is an admission of the Duke's guilt. By one of Shakespeare's characteristic juxtapositions, Jaques' appraisal of the sourness of human nature is immediately disproved in action. His disquisition is interrupted by the entrance of the exiled Orlando, sword in hand, rude, harsh, and desperate. Orlando's motive, however, is to get food for his fainting old servant Adam, whom Aeneas-like he has even borne on his back. The demeanor of the Duke and his followers at once reduces Orlando to gentleness, and the scene changes into an antiphony praising gentleness and "sacred pity." "Let gentleness my strong enforcement be." The answer of this play is:

> Your gentleness shall force
> More than your force move us to gentleness.[7]

Jaques' ill-founded moping is not the only affectation Shakespeare finds funny. Phebe's scorn, and the whole artificial tradition of pastoral romance, merits an answering scorn. Misprized love, and the misprizing loved one, are both silly in Arden. Woman's fickleness, her conflicting judgments, and her bold-coy reversals in words of her true feelings, provoke smiles not only in Phebe's uncritical musings but in Rosalind's. Moderation and temperance keep the sun shining over the forest, and as for either too much melancholy or too much mirth, Rosalind passes judgment: "Those that are in extremity of either are abominable fellows." The same judgment holds for love: "Come, come, you are a fool, And turn'd into the extremity of love." Love, too, must be seen in proper perspective in this poor world, which is almost six thousand years old yet in which never yet has man died in a love cause. "Men have died from time to time, and worms have eaten them, but not for love." The only possible antitoxin against Cupid's fever-tipped dart is a full awareness of the disease. Chanting love's symptoms in quartette can be made into a pleasant game, as the lovers find when Phebe asks Silvius "what 'tis to love":

SILVIUS: It is to be all made of sighs and tears;
              And so am I for Phebe.
PHEBE: And I for Ganymede.
ORLANDO: And I for Rosalind.
ROSALIND: And I for no woman. (V, iii, 90–4)

With appropriate interruptions from his sympathetic chorus, Silvius continues his anatomy:

> It is to be all made of faith and service . . .
> It is to be all made of fantasy,
> All made of passion, and all made of wishes,
> All adoration, duty, and observance,

All humbleness, all patience, and impatience,
All purity, all trial, all obedience . . .

And remembering moderation, Rosalind breaks up such delighted devotions with: "Pray you, no more of this; 'tis like the howling of Irish wolves against the moon."

Touchstone, too, keeps the salt of earth in this midsummer day's dream. He proves a touchstone for every affectation, and though he must have his wench Audrey by marriage or mock-marriage, he knows her to be "a poor thing but mine own." Mooncalf maunderings and useless speculations cannot go far afield when Touchstone is around, and there is hardly a funnier irrelevance in all of Shakespeare than when Touchstone breaks into the middle of his own explanation of the seven causes of quarreling with "Bear your body more seeming, Audrey!" We can place reliance upon Shakespeare's sense of moral responsibility because in spite of his most vivid imaginings he knows that he is always in the theatre.[8] Realizing this as essential fact, he can afford to propose hypotheses. "Your If is the only peacemaker," says Touchstone. "Much virtue in If."

The "If" that Shakespeare ventures in *As You Like It* is the Forest of Arden itself. The forest is not to be found in geographies, nor traced to his maternal ancestry. Yet he will lavish his matured descriptive skill to fill it full of greenwood trees and deer and merry foresters and brawling brooks and oaks and sweet birds and sunlight. The play is a great idyl of natural beauty, wagering all on the assumption that such a smiling setting, "exempt from public haunt," will bring out the gold in human nature. Its symbol is not man weeping in useless sympathy for a stricken deer (which amuses the lords of the forest), but man in needful action—the doe giving food to its fawn (II, vii, 128–9). "Old custom makes this life most sweet," and the co-mates in the forest are exiled into happiness. "The constant service of the antique world, When service sweat for duty, not for meed!" finds its natural place there. And though in the world outside the forest Orlando may lament

                              the fashion of these times,
                   Where none will sweat but for promotion,
                   And having that, do choke their service up
                   Even with the having,

yet "It is not so with *thee*." Love has created out of itself an Eden
of loyalty, gentleness, self-forgetfulness, courtesy, harmony, and
laughter. Nature is good, and good nature is natural. The picture
may be only a picture, consciously set in a frame of sterner facts.
Envy touches it lightly. Only in the shadowy, easily reformable
characters of Oliver and Duke Frederick, motivated as were Richard III and Don John before them, may one glimpse: "But, O,
how bitter a thing it is to look into happiness through another
man's eyes!" If the Forest of Arden is no more than an If, it is
at least an If hazarded with the most liberal gladness.

                              TWELFTH NIGHT

   If it is possible, *Twelfth Night* goes even further than *As You
Like It* in the idealization of love. Shakespeare never surpassed
the scenes between Viola and Orsino, or between Viola and
Olivia, in the lively and sensitive conversation of pleasant and
gently nurtured young men and women. If Rosalind's humor
keeps her love from extremes, Viola's unassuming fidelity sets the
seal upon hers. It is so perfectly proportioned, so much of the
purest essence of what love ought to be, that in comparison even
the fine natures of the Duke and Olivia seem unformed, as though
they were yet young and new in that emotion which in Viola was
a natural instinct. Orlando in *As You Like It* is much preoccupied
with gentility and good manners, and their relation to birth, edu-
cation, position, and riches. But Viola is gentleness in action.
There is no more to be argued or learned or said. The melancholy
which is so mysteriously associated with love, which Shakespeare
smiles at in his lovers sighing like furnaces, which seems almost an
affectation in the early Romeo and Duke Orsino and even in
Antonio in *The Merchant of Venice*, is transmuted in Viola into

pathos and tenderness. The quintessence of love, in which the personal fever or madness has been refined into noble sympathy, is close to that charity which Paul exalts in his letter to the Corinthians.[9] In Viola, this conception is realized with all the complexity possible to developed dramatic art. It is not fossilized in a few wise sayings, in formal soliloquies, or in the neat opinions of others. The finest ideals live in persons, not in copybooks. Shakespeare's power to present moral ideas—and if charity is not a moral idea, where is one to be found?—is now so subtle and comprehensively *dramatic* that to summarize adequately Viola's spirit would be to reproduce all the scenes in which she appears— or better, to produce the play. Her "soft and tender breeding" shows in her every action, but most, of course, in her wooing Olivia for Orsino as, she tells her, "your servant's servant," loyal to her master against her own true love. She must therefore seem scornful to Olivia while she pities her—"Poor lady, she were better love a dream!"—and loyal to Orsino's passion in her own silence and obedience, so that true love is seen not in tears, but "smiling at grief. Was not this love indeed?" With something of the unmixed innocence of Desdemona, who believes that unchaste women must be mere fictions, Viola holds that pity is common and natural enough to all men: "for 'tis a vulgar proof That very oft we pity enemies."

The melancholy that touches the gentle scenes of this play is rarely directly expressed, yet it manages to make the lovers in *Much Ado* seem almost boisterous in comparison, and those in *As You Like It* appear pert. It is the Keatsian melancholy, that "dwells with beauty, beauty that must die." "Women are as roses," says the Duke, and Viola answers:

> And so they are; alas, that they are so!
> To die, even when they to perfection grow! (II, iv, 41-2)

With this play Shakespeare touches the pinnacles of romantic love, after a long and arduous ascent. Never again does he repeat the theme in the same key. There is about it the merest trace of that melancholy evanescence of an ideal achieved, like the sadness that is part of the beauty on the faintly smiling face of Giorgione's sleeping Venus.

Such effects must have their symbol and embodiment, which Shakespeare here secures through the music that fills the play from the first line—"If music be the food of love, play on"—to the song that ends the play "With hey, ho, the wind and the rain." The artifice and ambition of *Love's Labour's Lost*, written just a few years before, are far from the simplicity and sincerity to which this play returns as if it were going home. The wedding of love to simple nature is celebrated again in the praise accorded to one of the sad songs that is sung:

> it is old and plain.
> The spinsters and the knitters in the sun,
> And the free maids that weave their thread with bones,
> Do use to chant it. It is silly sooth,
> And dallies with the innocence of love
> Like the old age. (II, iv, 44-9)

Music is the perfect symbol for this exalted theme of love, as is seen in Viola's comment: "It gives a very echo to the seat Where Love is thron'd," and in the Duke's reply: "Thou dost speak masterly."

Harmony achieved through unselfish love—how all the Golden Comedies point to that as the moral ideal! "Shakespeare wrote his comedies merely to please." Critics may well say so, for Shakespeare himself said it often enough in his epilogues.[10] Yet it is a false deduction that therefore they contain no moral beliefs. What if Shakespeare found his moral convictions were themselves delightful? Is it not striking that his comedies in their main plots are filled with self-sacrificing actions, which are rewarded by contentment, though they were not undertaken for reward? Antonio throws his life down, like a coin, to aid Bassanio's love. Beatrice's trust in Hero is such as to flare like lightning against all accusers. Benedick abandons his mockery long enough to champion Beatrice's loyalty and Hero's innocence, in a challenge,

painful to him, which places his sense of justice above his friendship. In a play during which estates are given away for shepherd's
cots, and dukedoms traded for hermitages, Celia deserts her
birthright to follow into exile her Rosalind, because "thou and I
am one." Touchstone follows his mistress Celia, who knows
that "He'll go along o'er the wide world with me." Adam leaves
the family house with Orlando, to "follow thee To the last gasp
with truth and loyalty"; and as Orlando says "We'll go along
together," it would seem that renunciation has become holiday,
and that following one's loyalties is more rewarding than holding
to one's own selfish interests. The world is wrong, the Forest of
Arden right.

> Now go we in content
> To liberty, and not to banishment. (I, iii, 139–40)

Liberty and liberality of spirit are one in *Twelfth Night*. Antonio gives away not only his purse but almost his life out of love
for Sebastian. Presenting the lesson in reverse, the subplot becomes serious only because anyone who is "sick of self-love"
(that dark room and that prison) must be given a curative. And
Viola's love which endureth all things is so strong that she will
not place her own affection above the fondnesses of her lord
Orsino. Yet none of these sacrificing actions is taken out of a
sense of sour-faced duty. Those who are "generous, guiltless, and
of free disposition" will not make cannon bullets out of birdbolts.
Generosity can create its lucky kingdom, in which it is both
delightful and natural that Sebastian, shipwrecked and unknown,
may be wooed and wed by the richest and most beautiful lady in
all Illyria. Though these ideal empires of the mind are founded
upon an If, they remain spacious states where to be good is to be
happy, where instinct sings harmony with conscience.

TOWARD A THEORY OF THE STATE

To what extent does Shakespeare's glad acceptance of the world
shape his political thought at this time? England, the precious
stone set in the silver sea, is a part of the ideal empire of the mind,

and is naturally affected by its climate. After his first tetralogy on English history (*Henry VI*, 1, 2, and 3, *Richard III*), which rode out the tempest of the civil Wars of the Roses, his second tetralogy (*Richard II*, *Henry IV*, 1 and 2, *Henry V*), quite in keeping with his temper at the time, constructs an ideal commonwealth, building Jerusalem in England's green and pleasant land. Yet since this glorious structure is also founded, though slowly, on an If, and therefore represents no more than a possible vision of past or future, in the four plays on ancient history (*Julius Caesar, Troilus and Cressida, Antony and Cleopatra, Coriolanus*) Shakespeare finally turns in his political thought to more complicated, unimpassioned, and ambiguous thinking, neither so crudely and materialistically motivated as the first English tetralogy, nor so fervently optimistic as the second.

KING JOHN

The isolated play of *King John* serves as prologue to the swelling theme of a triumphant England. It is a restless play, as if it marked the crossroads of many moods and styles in Shakespeare's development. The verse is as formal and regular as in *Love's Labour's Lost* or *Richard II*. Yet the plot is not equally formalized, and historical judgments are rarely developed to conclusions. On the other hand, Shakespeare uses historical situations in order to set up personal dilemmas, in which characters must make a tragic choice between alternatives clearly balanced and stated. The ideal of a united England glimmers but faintly. More memorable are the mad cursings of the bereaved Constance, that lineal descendant (in Shakespeare's art, not in history) of the bitter old Queen Margaret of the Henry VI plays. More memorable also is the pathos of the young Prince Arthur, whose sweet volubility and unboylike forgivingness leads Shakespeare, for perhaps the only time in his career, into sentimentality.

This pathos is intensified, or rendered more implausible, by the hard world around the young prince. The citizens of Angiers will yield their town only to the winner, acknowledging that success constitutes legitimacy. France's claims against England will be abandoned when a projected marriage holds out more profitable opportunities. Self-seeking opportunism, the eye for the main chance, is personified as "that same purpose-changer, that sly devil, That smooth-fac'd gentleman, tickling Commodity." And the speaker who sees so clearly the motivations of the faithless and the cheaters, interrupts his own diatribe to remark: "And why rail I on this Commodity? But for because he hath not woo'd me yet." For a moment King John seems to stand for an independent commonwealth against the power of Rome as he vows that "no Italian priest Shall tithe or toll in our dominions,"—until we learn that he intends to use the rich ecclesiastical foundations merely as convenient cashboxes and coffers: "The fat ribs of peace Must by the hungry now be fed upon." On the other hand, the Papal legate Pandulph develops in leisurely logic the conception of ultimate values, warning his pupil to "arm thy constant and thy nobler parts Against these giddy loose suggestions," and counselling a firm-souled integrity that may stand against "in thyself rebellion to thyself." Action, nevertheless, proves Pandulph's morally unassailable arguments to be special pleading. In a succeeding scene of the same act, this fine philosopher scorns the Dauphin for failing to see the new pattern which Commodity may make of the latest turn of the kaleidoscope of policy; he scoffs at him for not grasping a new opportunity for personal advancement: "How green you are and fresh in this old world!" The nobles, both French and English, change sides at will; and the play huddles up its end in a series of yieldings, in which the defeated bow to the defeated and dying.

Opposed to this mad mixture of selfish, ephemeral, fearful, greedy striving is the one figure of Philip Faulconbridge, nephew of King John and bastard son of Richard Coeur de Lion. He is one of Shakespeare's important experiments. The senseless *Realpolitik* is to be judged *dramatically*—that is, not by wise comments and political adages, but by juxtaposing the free spirit of "a good blunt fellow" next to all the conventions of the chronicles, the romances, the politicians, and the Machiavellians. The invention will be developed even more fully in the person of Falstaff. Philip the Bastard is blood-brother to Berowne—Philip playing his wit, bluntness and surface cynicism on society and the state, Berowne exercising the same instruments on romantic courtly love and affectations. The moral drama of *King John,* therefore, is the conflict between convention and hypocrisy on the one hand, and clear-eyed humorous reality on the other. It is as if a boon companion whom Shakespeare admired had journeyed almost four hundred years back into the past, to comment from the stage on ancient action in a manner that all contemporaries could understand.

As a moral commentator, the Bastard's great strength is his self-awareness. This manifests itself in his humor and his forthrightness. It is he who not only rails against self-seeking compromises and gainful "Commodity," but is simultaneously aware that he himself may fall a prey to them. His action, rather than his words, shows that he places honor above material possessions: he gives up his estate rather than deny Coeur de Lion as his father. "Brother, take you my land, I'll take my chance." Yet he is humorously aware, even when he makes his decision, of the tricks and affectations of "worshipful society," and evaluates his being knighted in terms that show him in no danger of turning into a straw nobleman:

> A foot of honour better than I was,
> But many a many foot of land the worse!

Though he will not practice to deceive, he means to look at the world sharply in order to avoid deceit.

> For he is but a bastard to the time
> That doth not smack of observation—
> And so am I, whether I smack or no. (I, i, 207–9)

Observation, then, and the weighing of all possibilities, is to be the safest road to true judgment.[11] This is strikingly borne out in the ironically accidental death of the young Prince Arthur after he has won his vile-visaged would-be murderer Hubert to compassion. The other lords accuse Hubert in high-astounding terms. The Bastard is a better judge that even hideous appearances may be deceitful. He stops a violent and mistaken vengeance in a line much admired in its variant in *Othello:* "Your sword is bright, sir; put it up again." And later he adds in his own idiom:

> Put up thy sword betime,
> Or I'll so maul you and your toasting iron
> That you shall think the devil is come from hell. (IV, iii, 98–100)

Irony and the deliberate understatement of emotion keep him from sentimental hysteria even over the body of the young prince: "Here's a good world! Knew you of this fair work?" Though he feels that he may lose his way "Among the thorns and dangers of this world," though in the death of Arthur "The life, the right, and truth of all this realm Is fled to heaven," and though dogged war is now bristling over the bare-picked bone of majesty, significantly his immediate decision is to support the king, as he has always done in the past, among the thousand businesses that threaten the destruction of the state.

The Bastard, in his practical wisdom, shows a genuine respect for that which exists, defending the integrity of the present order against all theories, specious or valid, including his own; and determined to set the whole above any of its parts.[12] It is he who unites for a moment the warring French and British forces against Angiers, when its citizens refuse to acknowledge the authority of either. He, no less than Salisbury, laments the disfiguring of "the antique and well-noted face Of plain old form," and suspects truth when it is decked in "so new a fashion'd robe." Tradition and authority are the needed grounds for moral order, and they can be maintained only through obedience to their symbol. This symbol is no other than the king.

King John is not superhuman. His vices, unlike Richard III's, waver into mere velleities. Even the king must leave "the soul's frail dwelling house." He uses his voice, "the organ-pipe of frailty," in last awareness of the "one thread, one little hair" on which his life hangs, knowing that in one swift moment "all this thou seest is but a clod, And module [= little image] of confounded royalty." The new King Henry acknowledges the awful symbol of sovereignty as the foundation of all stability:

> What surety of the world, what hope, what stay,
> When this was now a king, and now is clay? (V, vii, 68–9)

The king is mortal and weak; but he is also the enduring image, whose subjects "calmly run on in obedience Even to our ocean, to our great King John." The individual and the state are in conflict; action and ideals; the part and the whole. In this struggle, in order to preserve a stability without which right and wrong are meaningless, Shakespeare takes a stand. With hesitation and misgivings—fully aware of what may be said on the other side, and, indeed, saying it himself—in this rather inchoate play he gives his allegiance to the king. Fealty does not depend upon the person of the king, whose human fallibilities are inexorably magnified by the curse of power; allegiance depends upon the kingly office. The king, then, becomes one of Shakespeare's first serious symbols. He adopts it because without this emblem of authority to which loyalty may attach itself, he has found political thinking to be a tale told by an idiot.

RICHARD II

Considered as a political allegory, *Richard II* is constructed with admirable clarity. Shakespeare proportions this political study with a surety lacking in *King John*. In this history play he first finds the way to present a serious problem. The method might be described as the setting up of a dramatic conflict between two points of view, each of which has strengths and weaknesses. In this play the basic conflict is between the conceptions of Richard and Bolingbroke as men and as rulers.

As a man Richard has charm, fire, sensitivity, and imagination. But he is also—and how much of this fault may be attributed to the loneliness of power?—headstrong, inconsiderate, and unjust, believing that his will is the sole right. His weakness as a man, therefore, springs at least in part from a narrow interpretation of the divine right of kings—that his right to do as he pleases cannot be questioned. Since this flaw in his character is fatal both to himself and England, it is evident that Shakespeare does not accept such a conception of divine right.

As a ruler he is unbelievably bad. Every action is a mistake. He shows himself ineffectual and capricious in his handling of the quarrel between Bolingbroke and Mowbray at the outset. He weakens his party by banishing his defender Mowbray. Instead of making his antagonist Bolingbroke into either a friend or a dead man, he banishes him as well. He confiscates without a shadow of justice his uncle Gaunt's estates, and thereby not only gives Gaunt's son Bolingbroke a lawful grievance, but also alienates all who possess estates under his arbitrary power. He leaves England for Ireland in time of crisis, and returns to find his land in rebellion. He acts as his own worst enemy in throwing away his crown for the pleasure of a melodramatic tantrum.

But he had been the rightful king of England.

Bolingbroke, on the other hand, the usurping King Henry IV, never makes a mistake on his march to power. He knows when to be bold or cautious, ruthless or forgiving. Though he may be cold and politic, he is politic enough to know that honesty is the best policy, and he is not without a conscience. He is an admirably efficient ruler.

But he is not the rightful king of England. And as a subject he commits the cardinal sin of disobedience.

The querulous old Duke of York, Lord Governor of the realm during Richard's absence, serves as the touchstone figure, balancing between Richard and Henry, setting up his wise adages on the side of Richard and his prudent actions on the side of the efficient self-made king.

Obviously the play is a succession of balances neatly held. If the choice were between a good and a bad monarch, the question would not be worth asking. Nor would it be if the choice were between a lawful monarch and a usurper. It becomes drama be-

cause on one side is ranged arbitrary irresponsibility and the stability of law and ceremony; on the other side good government
based on the principle of insurrection.

Almost as the proof of a mathematical proposition Shakespeare's
conception of the ideal state develops its dual nature: the duty of
the citizen-subject to obey his traditionally constituted and sanc-
tioned government; the duty of the citizen-governor to wield
his power for the good of the state. It is so simple that it has never
been concertedly practised in history.

Of this ideal both Richard and Bolingbroke fall disastrously
short. Each acts from personal passion or for selfish advancement.
The play presents an unrealized Utopia in dramatic form, shot
full of warnings and advice and prophecies and pictures of England as it ought to be and may be. Richard and Bolingbroke become double antagonists in a drama whose tragic hero is bleeding
England.

Richard is fully warned by his uncles. The proud and famous
speech of John of Gaunt on his deathbed is designed to bring the
frivolous Richard to some realization of the magnificent land
which under his rule has made "a shameful conquest of itself." [13]
Richard has become "Landlord of England, not King." And if
Gaunt is unsuccessful in rousing Richard to the glory of his land,
his other uncle York fails likewise, though he is equally serious,
in presenting the glories of his line and blood. Richard is in
danger of proving traitor to that same respect for hallowed tradition and ancestral magnificence on which he founds his claims.
The passion for the past becomes almost religious in this play,
in which Edward's seven sons are "seven vials of his sacred blood
Or seven fair branches springing from one root." Gloucester,
"one flourishing branch," "is hack'd down, and his summer leaves
all faded"; and York, "the last of noble Edward's sons," makes his
desperate attempt to wake Richard to responsibility by calling
up the picture of Richard's father the Black Prince. When that
fails, his plea for justice will have little effect on his nephew,
however important it may be in the clarification of Shakespeare's
political thinking:

Take Hereford's rights away, and take from Time
His charters and his customary rights . . .
If you do wrongfully seize Hereford's rights, . . .
You pluck a thousand dangers on your head,
You lose a thousand well-disposed hearts,
And prick my tender patience to those thoughts
Which honour and allegiance cannot think. (II, i, 195–208)

Richard arrogantly overrides all counsel. King Richard himself is the first traitor to the King of England.

The crimes of the traitorous subject are presented, if it is possible, in even more direful eloquence. In the play itself such dramatic justice is done to Bolingbroke's rightful claims and Richard's faults that the power of Shakespeare's conservative political convictions is not always fully felt. No wrongs can without penalty be redressed by the overthrow of the lawful ruler, for that is to set a part as greater than the whole, and to avenge one wrong by committing the greatest evil of all. Shakespeare, in writing his earlier tetralogy, had been soberly impressed by the century of ills that followed upon Bolingbroke's usurpation. If space permitted, Shakespeare's serious thought might here be represented in right proportions by setting down continuously some pages of the collected warnings and prophecies that spring from meditation on tradition and rebellion.[14] A few of Richard's burning lines must serve:

Tell Bolingbroke, for yon methinks he stands,
That every stride he makes upon my land
Is dangerous treason. He is come to open
The purple testament of bleeding war.
But ere the crown he looks for live in peace,
Ten thousand bloody crowns of mothers' sons
Shall ill become the flower of England's face,
Change the complexion of her maid-pale peace
To scarlet indignation, and bedew
Her pastures' grass with faithful English blood. (III, iii, 91–100)

In such words, England, "this other Eden, demi-paradise," becomes a sentient being. Supporting its "happy breed of men," this little world is at once a social and a geographical entity. Shakespeare's feeling for nature now blends with a feeling for men in nature, somewhat after the manner of Wordsworth's development from the passion for cataracts and mountains toward the expansive response to the still, sad music of humanity. *Richard II* is one long intermittent dirge on a great countryside suffering the "crimson tempest" of civil war, its beauty and valiance laid waste.[15] England is as persistent an image in this play as is the sun of royalty, but the image of England is presented not only through scattered little pictures of parks and tufts of trees and silver rivers and fresh green land and high wild hills; it also moves sentient through its citizens, oysterwench and journeyman, craftsmen and draymen, landlords and rough rug-headed kerns, rich men and ruffians, distaff-women and boys with women's voices, gardeners aware alike of too fast growing sprays and of caterpillars, and the loyal groom of the stable who alone comforts Richard in his last hour. Such deliberate artistry in building by continual little touches is necessary in a play whose real protagonist, England, can enter the action only through the thoughts and descriptions of others.

The doctrine of responsibility toward "this blessed plot, this earth, this realm, this England" has one further refinement. Although the old uncles Gaunt and York hold up the ideal of duty to erring ruler and subject alike, they resemble Philip the Bastard in this: that they will sacrifice both personal preferences and impossible perfection to the stable order which is the best that the world affords. Since the world, though imperfect, is the only world we have, it is better to accept it. In the Shakespearean universe, the uncompromising idealist is not fully responsible, since he endangers existing society, so much greater than himself, for the sake of an ideal which by definition cannot exist. All three men, therefore, make the compromises which the mere process of living requires. In the opening act John of Gaunt counsels the exile of his own son, serving as judge and not as father. His moral decision is clear in his mind, since he is supporting not only existing authority but the ideal of lawful kingship in the person of

Richard, "God's substitute." But in a surprising balanced scene at the end of the play, the other uncle York similarly acts against his own son Aumerle when he reveals his son's treason to the new usurping king. His problem is not easy, since he has himself earlier preached against the "rebellion" that placed Henry on the throne. Yet once the rebellion has succeeded, he must make a painful decision. His choice is for the newly established order. It is highly doubtful whether Shakespeare would have approved of the fairly common stage presentation of the Duke of York as a doddering old Polonius. His active support of the new king is based on a constructive and genuine philosophy, and Shakespeare himself seems behind Henry's admiring tribute to York's loyalty: "Thou sheer, immaculate, and silver fountain!"

No matter how intense or noble, then, may be one's dreams, they are useless or even dangerous unless they are rooted in reality, not pinnacled dim in the intense inane. The final cause of Richard's moral failure is ontological: he does not understand the nature of reality. The play is a succession of situations—how well Shakespeare learned to develop a general conception through varied specific actions!—that show Richard's inability to square circumstances with his own emotional distortion of them. In the first scene, powerless to reconcile his quarreling nobles, he orders them to do what they insist upon doing, and thus sees their disobedience as his own authority: "We were not born to sue, but to command." Gaunt's solemn warnings he interprets as a fit of "age and sullens"; and York's impatient allegiance makes him Lord Governor of England. While Richard imagines himself as sun-king, and constructs armies of glorious angels who fight for him in heavenly pay, he learns that the Welsh, at least, are not to be numbered in such angelic orders. The deaths of his favorites stir him, not to retribution, but to his superb anatomy of melancholy. Confronted by the rebel Bolingbroke, he is at first regal in conjuring up God's armies of pestilence, then hysterically humble in his self-pity, until his image of tears digging his grave compels even Richard to realize that "I talk but idly." And this in a situation where he himself has first brought into the open the dangerous idea of deposition! Richard in his own person is acting out the Bastard's warning:

> This England never did, nor never shall,
> Lie at the proud foot of a conqueror
> But when it first did help to wound itself.
>
> (*King John*, V, vii, 112–4)

Yet in the great scene in Westminster Hall Richard continues to play the wanton with his woes—to make a pretty toy with the idea of Christ and the multiplying nature of Judas, to enact his last will and testament, and peevishly to shatter a mirror because its actual reflection does not do justice to his delusions of grief. The parting with his queen serves merely as a further occasion for embroidering conceits on the theme of sorrow. And at the last, in Pomfret Castle, he may give full rein to his fancy, undistracted by the troublous world, and people the little world of prison with his thoughts. In the world of social action Richard's failure is complete, for the ontology of politics, as the modern debasing of the word "politician" sadly testifies, demands an awareness of possibilities, of the clumsy movement of masses, the seaminess of vain mortals, the multiplicity of motives. Shakespeare's morality continues to demand, in politics as elsewhere, the reconciliation of the imaginative and the real, of art and business, of the individual and society.

HENRY IV, 1 AND 2

As is characteristic of Shakespeare's development, thoughts that were tentative or merely speculative in early versions, become so clear in his later plays that they may be summarized more briefly. In the two parts of *Henry IV*, his political philosophy is entrusted to four major figures: Hotspur, Henry IV, Falstaff, and Prince Hal. To consider each in the simplest terms, Hotspur represents an idealism centered on manly honor and family loyalty. He is a danger to the state because he cannot think in terms of the state, but merely in the restricted modes, however warm and noble they may be, of personal glory.

The king is an efficient instrument, dependable, competent, cool. But worldly success is no god in Shakespeare's thought, or, for that matter, even in Henry's mind. In these plays the mill-stones of justice continue to grind relentlessly in both the inner and the outer worlds. Henry's conscience reproaches him for mur-der—or worse: for the sacrilegious act of overthrowing God's appointed order. Yet with supreme dramatic irony and justice, he is prevented from making a repentant pilgrimage to the Holy Land by the very principle of rebellion which he himself initiated. It had been prophesied that Henry was to die in Jerusalem, but death comes to him in the Jerusalem Chamber in Westminster, those cares of state which he had wilfully taken upon himself still weighing down his pillow with the golden circlet of the heavy crown.

Falstaff has none of the King's worries, none of Hotspur's blaz-ing visions of honor. He is a comfortable materialist, who thinks bravery is the effect of drinking, honor a mere word, death a grim species of grinning, and war an occasion for making corpses and mutilated beggars. But war may also be the making of one's personal fortune, and if one acts confidently on one's belief in gravy, not gravity, one may turn a tavern into a drum, the world into an oyster, and live merrily. The disasters of Hotspur's brittle and dangerous glory, Henry's nibbling conscience, and Falstaff's limited realism show, as the scenes of history follow each other, that none of their philosophies is adequate.

Prince Hal is the seedling of the perfect king. He comprehends them all, admiring Hotspur, respecting his father, roistering with Falstaff. On the fields of chivalry, young Harry rises "from the ground like feathered Mercury" until Hotspur himself is jealous of hearing his praises. By the couch of his dying father, he dedi-cates himself to the cares of state in an obedience taught him by his "most inward true and duteous spirit." In the rooms of the Boar's Head Tavern he bests Falstaff in practical jokes and comes close to leaving even that agile wit breathless.

Prince Harry's comprehensive spirit, as it develops from extrav-agant youth to early assumed responsibility, takes the best from each of these three persons, as if he were purposefully building up for his own use the character of a good ruler, through observation of human personalities. Prince Hal, who has laughingly caricatured Hotspur's foibles, says over his dead body on the field at Shrewsbury in tempered admiration:

> Fare thee well, great heart!
> Ill-weav'd ambition, how much art thou shrunk!
> When that this body did contain a spirit,
> A kingdom for it was too small a bound;
> But now two paces of the vilest earth
> Is room enough. This earth that bears thee dead
> Bears not alive so stout a gentleman. (1, V, iv, 87–93)

And what but a combination of personal liking and impersonal judgment could have inspired his remark over Falstaff, conveniently and discreetly playing dead on the battlefield?

> Poor Jack, farewell!
> I could have better spar'd a better man.

Henry IV himself could not have spoken with a greater knowledge of the heavy duties of governing than his son Harry manifests in the moving scene at the deathbed of his father:

> I spake unto this crown as having sense,
> And thus upbraided it: 'The care on thee depending
> Hath fed upon the body of my father.
> Therefore thou best of gold art worst of gold.' . . .
> Accusing it, I put it on my head,
> To try with it (as with an enemy
> That had before my face murdered my father)
> The quarrel of a true inheritor. . . .
> You won it, wore it, kept it, gave it me. (2, IV, v, 158–222)

From Hotspur a gallant idealism and boldness; from Falstaff gaiety, the shrewd observation of mortal oddities, the study of his companions, the revelling in the common pleasures of life; from his father, a sense of responsibility, temperance, and the power to act. This synthesis is accomplished with no apparent artificiality, but through the interplay of personalities, among which the Prince himself is far from being a passive dummy, as the King's and Warwick's character sketches of him make clear.

More interesting than this development of political ideals by means of character-in-action is their development through the dramatic structure itself. Shakespeare now presents an argument through the succession or juxtaposition of scenes.[16] He channels what looks like a careless stream of consciousness within the straighter banks of imaginative logic. Panoramas and pageants move as thoughts; and connotations prove as clear as denotations, without ever losing the illusion that life, not art, is unfolding.

The structure of the First Part is so simple that it need not detain us. Prince Hal is the vertical support for a pair of scales, in which Hotspur and Falstaff are balanced, until in the battle of Shrewsbury toward which the action points, the Prince remains erect above the bodies of chivalric recklessness and worldly prudence. Passion and porridge are underfoot.

The Second Part is not so obvious. It is more a playing with themes than with actions, more a delicate shifting of proportions to suggest a conclusion. The first scene presents rebellion; juxtaposed in the second scene is Falstaff's rebellion against the authority of the Lord Chief Justice. Rebellion against the state has been blotted out by the fourth act, through the merciless cunning and deceitfully literal promises of Prince John of Lancaster.[17] In the action, the shrewd conscientiousness of Henry IV is neatly split into separate parts between two sons. Prince John, "this same young sober-blooded boy," inherits all of his father's cold calculation, and is alone responsible, without any guilt attaching to his father, for the ignoble legalistic trick that ends the rebellion. Prince Henry inherits his father's conscience. The scenes in which Henry IV figures are artfully colored by a mood of melancholy meditation—on poorest subjects and uneasy crowns, on sleep and conscience, chance and change, time and necessity, "inward wars" and thwarted pilgrimages, on "golden care," on disloyalty and sorrow, on greatness and "forgotten dust," sanctity and guilt, sages, apes and wolves, "indirect crook'd ways" and the fear of God, culminating in the "happiness and peace" of Shakespeare's longest colloquy between father and son, as Henry at last realizes that his heir accepts "this lineal honour" of the crown with the due obedience "which nature, love, and filial tenderness" should pay a father. Like Oedipus at Colonos, Henry IV at his death has been so changed that he seems less a rash defier of justice than the repository, through his acceptance of guilt and suffering, of wisdom.

Falstaff, as is often pointed out, becomes in this play less the king of Eastcheap than an exiled adventurer, who meditates with increasing frequency on change and old age. He meets his Prince Hal once only before the final scene, and even then, he loses him to the wars. The pathos of parting and separation is already suggested when the martial knocking at the door interrupts the Boar's Head banquet and leaves Doll and Mistress Quickly all blubbered in tears. Yet where King Henry IV has said "Are these things then necessities? Then let us meet them like necessities," Falstaff dodges them to the last. The most cunning of all Shakespeare's juxtapositions in this play occurs in the final act. Dovetailed between the scene of the new King Henry's bowing before the Lord Chief Justice, and the scene of the coronation, are two scenes in Gloucestershire and the streets of London. In the latter, the muddy-mouthed Doll and the querulous Quickly are borne off by an officer of the law. And in Shallow's orchard, Falstaff hears that Hal is king, and, seizing any man's horses, rushes off with the shout: "The laws of England are at my commandment. . . . Woe to my Lord Chief Justice!"

But although Falstaff has milked his old acquaintance Shallow of a thousand pounds, on the principle that "the law of nature" makes the young dace fair prey for the old pike, the laws of England are not to be those of favoritism and self-interest. The two scenes that frame Falstaff's exultation [18] persuasively present "the majesty and power of law and justice." The Lord Chief Justice is formally acknowledged as the father of the young king, who promises to stoop to his "well-practis'd wise directions." Yet the rejection of Falstaff is so supremely realized in terms of clashing modes of life that one is inclined to minimize the equal artistry and eloquence with which Shakespeare makes crystal-clear his conceptions of government. In the realm of political morality, there are duties as well as desires. The law of voracious nature must and can be subdued to the rule of law and justice. And as the roused Henry V casts aside his irresponsible dream, those who are his lieutenants in the governing of England may rejoice in "this fair proceeding of the King's."

HENRY V

The metamorphosis has been complete: there is nothing of the wild and witty Prince Hal in the culminating figure of the tetralogy, Henry V. The play belongs to him more entirely than any other of Shakespeare's English chronicles belongs to its titular monarch—with the exception of Richard III, from whom Henry V is separated as far as the poles of the world.

There is no dramatic conflict in *Henry V*. None of his possible foes—a weak citizenry, rebellion at home, enemies abroad—develop any power in the theatre of the mind. The colors have changed to darker tones for the ragtag and bobtail of Eastcheap. "The fat knight with the great belly doublet" is dead, and the others, stealing, drabbing, vaunting, following the lion of England like jackals, end their careers on the gallows, or in hospitals, or ignominiously shamed and stripped of what had once seemed so ridiculously gay and brave.

The old theme of rebellion is nipped in the bud. Such is the spirit of the play that one of the traitors, when he is unmasked, proclaims:

> Never did faithful subject more rejoice
> At the discovery of most dangerous treason
> Than I do at this hour joy o'er myself,
> Prevented from a damned enterprise. (II, ii, 161–4)

So essential is the stability of the state that repentance, which for other crimes leads so easily in Shakespeare to pardon, cannot atone for treason. In condemning the three traitors Scroop, Cambridge, and Grey, the king draws the sharp distinction between his own person, which seeks no revenge, and "our kingdom's safety," which compels him to deliver them to her laws.

As for the French, they are treated unfairly. Shakespeare is as militant as a Communist novelist writing during a war. The audience knows, and the English soldiers guess in their stout hopes, what the outcome of the battle of Agincourt must be. Numbers do not count against quality. Trappings and caparisons make a pitiful show against the "island carrions," the grotesque rags and rust under which beat English hearts. Let the French nobles brag of their steeds, their armor, and their mistresses, or speculate concerning their comrade's cowardice! What else can be expected of the enemies of England? Let the basest of the English, "the rascally, scauld, beggarly, lousy, pragging knave, Pistol," take a French gentleman prisoner! For although Shakespeare does not quite equal Doctor Johnson's mathematical reckoning which proved a few Englishmen the equal of 1,600 Frenchmen, on Saint Crispin's day at Agincourt he comes close.

As a dramatist, Shakespeare should have been ashamed of himself for his shabby handling of the scum, the English traitors, and the foreign foes; he has failed in the moral duty of every dramatist to allow each character full and fair self-defense. But, for one of the few times in his career, he is not writing a drama. He is composing a patriotic hymn. Rather than as a play, *Henry V* might be considered as the greatest advertisement in literature, with this one distinction between the dramatist and the average writer of advertising copy, that Shakespeare here seems to have believed every word that he put to paper. He sets up his cast, warps every character (including his earlier conception of the king himself), and shapes every scene with the one end in view of blazing England's glory, helped by a Muse of fire, on the brightest heaven of invention.

In a sense Shakespeare here writes a Utopia for theatrical presentation. But it is not a Nowhere, for he believes his picture evokes an England that lives in the hearts and hopes and history of his race. To set down the political vision in full would be to reproduce the play. The theme is epic in scope and in aim. All classes are included, from the Archbishop of Canterbury with his historical disquisitions on the laws of succession, to common soldier John Bates, who knows he is the king's subject. The racial strains are formally presented in the English Gower, the Irish Macmorris, the Scots Jamy, and the Welsh Fluellen. England's glory stretches out in time as well as in space, so that the noble deeds of ancestors echo over and over in Henry's speech before Harfleur:

> And you, good yeomen,
> Whose limbs were made in England, show us here
> The mettle of your pasture. (III, i, 25–7)

The power of England is presented in many moods: ceremonious, gentle, implacable, hopeful, long-suffering, imperilled, triumphant. All these weathers of the spirit, this ancestry and history, these strains of blood and classes of society, are centered in the person of the king—who is a trumpet before battle, a watcher with his soldiers in the dark, a discourser on divinity and commonwealth affairs and war and policy, a gamester who wins a kingdom through lenity, a plain king with a good heart, "whose face is not worth sunburning" and who knows no ways to mince it in love when he woos the French princess. He has learned to make "the art and practic part of life" "the mistress to this theoric"; he is "Harry England"; and before the crucial battle, all who are to venture their lives for England, the mean and the gentle, behold "A little touch of Harry in the night."

Henry V is conscious of his heritage of blood—both the blood of his great-grandfather Edward and his great-uncle the Black Prince, who defeated the French

> Whiles his most mighty father on a hill
> Stood smiling to behold his lion's whelp
> Forage in blood of French nobility, (I, ii, 108–10)

and also the blood of Richard shed by his father, which he prays the God of battles to pardon in his own penitence and contrite tears. His actions will preserve only the honest courage of his line, so that new deeds of valor, undertaken for England, may help to

> make her chronicle as rich with praise
> As is the ooze and bottom of the sea
> With sunken wrack and sumless treasuries. (I, ii, 163–5)

The tide of pomp presses heavily upon him. His prayers and exhortations before battle, and his long meditation on that proud dream of kingly Ceremony, show with what full realization he accepts responsibility and public care. Yet sympathy now exists between subjects and ruler, who shows repeatedly in actions and speeches that the "large and ample empery" of ceremony will not in his case change human nature, and that "I think the King is but a man, as I am." He may receive, therefore, with pleasure and candor the compliment paid him by his fellow-Welshman and campaigner Captain Fluellen: "I need not to be ashamed of your Majesty, praised be God, so long as your Majesty is an honest man." Nor does the king flatter the common people because of policy, as his father had done; he mixes with them naturally and observantly, and is not above practical jokes that seem one of his few inheritances from that wraith Prince Hal of Eastcheap. Among the parts he plays without trying is that of his own publicity agent and public relations officer.

In this ideal state, the subject accepts his duties no less than the king. Though it is the king in disguise that reconciles public and private morality when he says to his common soldiers: "Every subject's duty is the King's, but every subject's soul is his own," it is plain John Bates that replies: "I do not desire he should answer for me, and yet I determine to fight lustily for him." Bates had reproved that other soldier Michael Williams for his veteran's skepticism regarding the justice of the English cause, by saying: "We know enough if we know we are the King's subjects." But it is Williams who, aware of the grim and heavy ills of war, nevertheless acknowledges that " 'Tis certain, every man that dies ill, the ill upon his own head—the King is not to answer it." And it is Williams also who quarrels with the disguised king because he feels that holding "a poor and a private displeasure" against a monarch is as foolish as fanning the sun into ice with a peacock's feather. These are the men who, surviving Agincourt, shall be Henry's brothers. The common battle will "gentle their condition." If the king accepts responsibility, the subjects accept allegiance; and the "band of brothers" makes for harmony and proportion in the state. "To disobey were against all proportion of subjection."

The splendor of the state being firmly established on ideals of responsibility and magnanimous thoughts, obedience is no more mechanical, blind, or unwilling than it is at the close of *Paradise Lost*. Indeed, the devout Christian spirit, more marked in *Henry V* than in any other of Shakespeare's plays, seems almost to spring out of thankfulness to God for having created such a perfect political order.

Stability, through obedience to a state which is embodied in a single great-souled responsible ruler, rules the long pageant, from the opening scene which preaches historical precedent, justice, and statecraft, to the epilogue which Shakespeare signs with a *Hic pinxit*, introducing himself into the gigantic historical painting as "Our bending author In little room confining mighty men." The choruses show Shakespeare pleading that the stage is inadequate for epic narrative, and challenge the audience to keep pace in their imaginations with the fiery gallop of the author's Pegasus. Small time has elapsed in the performance "within this wooden O" of the Globe Theatre, "but in that small, most greatly lived This Star of England." The theme of a nation united joyously and confidently in great purposes is expressed in that famous image of the kingdom of the honeybees, "Creatures that by a rule in nature teach The act of order to a peopled kingdom." The centrality and fixity of the ruler is developed in a quadruple comparison:

> As many arrows loosèd several ways
> Come to one mark, as many ways meet in one town,
> As many fresh streams meet in one salt sea,
> As many lines close in the dial's centre;

> So may a thousand actions, once afoot,
> End in one purpose, and be all well borne
> Without defeat. (I, ii, 207–13)

As Shakespeare conceives it, the result is no totalitarian state, but the achieving of variety in unity. The variety is impossible without the underlying unity. The brave realm of this Star of England is the one deliverance in the world of politics from all the sad monotony of chaos. "Many things having full reference To one consent may work contrariously." The government is complex but articulated; it is not a one-celled amorphous amoeba.

> Therefore doth heaven divide
> The state of man in divers functions,
> Setting endeavour in continual motion;
> To which is fixed as an aim or butt
> Obedience. (I, ii, 183–7)

Articulated but complex. Small wonder, then, that in this most hopeful of all his visions of the good state, this patriotic lyric, Shakespeare should turn for a final symbol of harmonious perfection to his beloved music:

> For government, though high, and low, and lower,
> Put into parts, doth keep in one consent,
> Congreeing in a full and natural close,
> Like music. (I, ii, 180–3)

THE JOY OF LIFE: HOW BEAUTEOUS MANKIND IS!

Among the English histories *Henry V* seems a natural and inevitable development analogous to the Golden Comedies that come as the culmination of his comic period. It is, in fact, a Golden History. In both comedy and history the course is the same: the reconciliation of an ideal world, of perfect love or of the perfect state, with reality.[19] The reconciliation, both in romantic comedy and English history, comes from the most venturesome confidence in the goodness of human nature. Shakespeare goes beyond a belief in human perfectibility or progress. The Golden Age is neither in the distant past nor the distant future. Nor is it in far-off Illyria or Athens. It is in England, now. It is within us, waiting for realization in a form perhaps less tangled by Occasion, but nevertheless, immediately and actually realizable by any man of observing eye and sympathetic heart.

Shakespeare's ideas on human relationships, whether the standard is the good of the state or the good of the individual, depend upon a general attitude, which at this time might be described as the easy, trustful, joyous acceptance of human life. This feeling, the supposition on which his characters are formed and his plots shaped, is so instinctive and so rarely formulated that it can hardly be ranked as a moral idea, though it is the foundation on which his more obviously moral ideas rest. In the comedies, the exalted idea of love as sympathy and the charity of human brotherhood, its reconciliation of generosity and worldly common sense, make stiff demands on human nature. Shakespeare assumes not only lovers who love the world more than themselves, but also a world amenable to unselfish action, essentially responsive to the liberality of the spirit. In the histories, the conception of the stable state is no less demanding. It insists that subject and sovereign be responsible agents, conscious of their functions in society, and gladly subordinating their personal wishes to the good of a larger organism.

This attitude of acceptance and trust may be called Shakespeare's comic spirit. How rare it is may be sensed by running over any list of the great comic writers—Aristophanes, Plautus, Terence, Lucian, Apuleius, Molière, La Fontaine, Swift, Pope, Byron, Balzac, Meredith, Shaw. Much of their spirit is satiric, and their comic effects are secured through the manipulation of the sordid, the weak, or even the vicious aspects of our human nature. Relative to their disapproval, Shakespeare's laughter springs from sympathy. He cannot seem to make himself believe that the worst in human nature is more than a foible. He is not so much a reformer as a conciliator. We are all in the same boat. If it is a ship of fools, the merrier for us.

There is little to forgive. In his comedies, it is not the happy endings that are the convention, but the villains. For purposes of plot, Shakespeare is willing to label some characters as wicked and allow them to help carry on the story to the inevitable moment when they discard their misconceptions and blindnesses almost with a sigh of relief. They are the somewhat unwilling grindstones that give brilliance and sharpness to the good characters. How can there be a serious antagonist in *The Comedy of Errors*, for instance, when the ridiculous entanglements of the hero are caused by his twin self? Valentine makes a poor sort of villain, since the other gentleman of Verona and the two heroines are Valentine's especial friends and sympathetic helpers. And in *Love's Labour's Lost*, the farces, *A Midsummer Night's Dream*, and *Twelfth Night*, there are no evil characters; at the wickedest, there are a few harmless butts and some straying individuals who need to be led back to the fold. As for *Much Ado About Nothing* and *As You Like It*, their stories contain, or should contain, some true-blue desperadoes—a usurping duke, a brother with fratricidal impulses, and a professional malcontent eager to destroy the happiness of others through false machinations. What do they matter? It is hard to remember their names, or anything of their characters beyond their usual speedy reformation.

Exceptions, of course, should not be overlooked. The history plays must introduce evil elements with at least the seriousness of the chroniclers, though Shakespeare's drift toward a more comprehensible and hopeful interpretation of statecraft sets him apart from the annalists. The important exceptions are the characters of Tybalt, Shylock, and Falstaff. Tybalt belongs with Don John of Austria in the class of professional trouble-makers—disasters of hate and anger and malice which are fortunately infrequent in human nature, and which must be reformed, killed off, or banished from society. They are anti-social types, the weak offspring of Richard III. Shylock, as we have seen, is Shakespeare's first seriously complete presentation of a somewhat justifiable personal passion unreconciled to the social order.[20] The handling of Shylock's character foreshadows the central moral issue in the tragedies.

The same may be said of the rejection of Falstaff by Henry V. From the political point of view, it is a necessary and reasonable action of which Shakespeare as a social thinker clearly approved. Falstaff is careless, selfish, and irresponsible. But he is far more than that, just as Shakespeare is far more than a political philosopher. From Falstaff's point of view it is fair to ask even a monarch Sir Toby Belch's question: "Dost thou think, because thou art virtuous, there shall be no more cakes and ale?" The world of Falstaff and of Sir Toby, with its fat and merry living, will continue to exist in spite of all ideal lovers and noble kings. The court of love needs its Berownes and Mercutios, the court of England needs its Philip the Bastard and its Falstaff. Not until he has learned from Falstaff the art of common and careless living, not until he has squeezed the great orange dry, can Henry afford to cast off his great companion. Shakespeare's dramatic sympathy carried him instinctively far beyond the conscious moral lesson in citizenship, as is evident in the effectiveness of that climactic scene in which Henry renounces so much of his earlier life. And in the death of Falstaff Shakespeare delivers a Parthian shot and passes another of his suspended judgments when we learn of Falstaff that "The King has kill'd his heart." [21]

At any rate, in action Falstaff must go down because he is in unreformable conflict with society; for in history plays, as in comedy, society supplies the standard. (Tragedy in the Shakespearean sense makes the standard inward and personal.) Yet since society as Shakespeare envisages it is large and tolerant, the most diverse human types may inhabit it without undue friction. "Many things may work contrariously," since they have "full reference to one consent," the consent being Shakespeare's acceptance of a varied world. During the golden decade of the 1590's Shakespeare's embracing of all the world is little short of amazing. Almost without exception he finds all human beings either amusing or admirable or both at once. What would irritate or appall the average person merely makes Shakespeare laugh. The stupidity of Dogberry the constable, which helps toward a catastrophe almost as much as the malice of Don John, Shakespeare finds funny. Characters on the stage (Leonato and the Lord Chief Justice and the Capulets) try to dam the garrulous floods of Dogberry and Mistress Quickly and Juliet's nurse, but Shakespeare lets them run on, for he finds them amusing. Boors and dolts and clowns and poseurs and bumpkins and viragoes and braggarts, idle dreamers and drunkards and blue-nosed puritans and the self-approving—types that fill a mild inferno for those of us who are more finical—are to Shakespeare but parts of God's great gift of wonderful variety. He transmutes them; he turns our sneers into laughs; he unites the censorious, against their primmer judgments, in a warm feeling of brotherhood under Puck's banner: "Lord, what fools these mortals be!"

The open-handed creation of such throngs of gay and noble mortals is Shakespeare's constant moral gesture at this time, showing his instinctive confidence in the goodness of human nature. This glad vitalism carries conviction because it is so obviously unforced. Shakespeare strikes no deliberate attitudes in demonstrating that the mere living of life is good. He does not fall into the combative assertiveness of Browning or Whitman, for it does not occur to him that it is necessary. His gust for life is equal to that of Chaucer or Dickens; his tolerance may be even greater.

Gaiety and love and virtue are infectious. At their merest touch selfishness and blindness melt away. These worlds are presented less as hypotheses than as discoveries; among the many voyages of the Renaissance Shakespeare charts his findings with as much certainty as actual islands might be set down on the "new map with the augmentation of the Indies." Believing so strongly in the triumphant goodness of human nature, Shakespeare might find that any shaking of this stability through doubt would be far more catastrophic than, say, a cynic's turning up new evidence for his cynicism.

But here, at this time, cynicism and satire are harmless; skepticism smiles; tolerance springs from good nature and the knowledge that sense, humor, and sympathy are bound to win. Reconciliation is universal, and society is accepted because it affords opportunities for yet a larger reconciliation. The fiend, as Launcelot Gobbo says, is friendly. The real and the ideal are not at odds, because the real world changes to gold at the mere touch of the ideal. The wider the embrace of love, the greater its ideality. The old Garden of Eden is again at hand. And the paradox of Marvell's praise of solitude is unwoven into the straight and happy statement: Two Paradises 'twere in one, to live in Paradise—together.

CHAPTER FOUR

The Unweeded Garden

INSTINCTIVE hope and trust, coupled with an artist's desire
for clarity, had enabled the young Shakespeare to create simple idyls. Orlando and Rosalind woo in Arden. Cousin Silence,
who was merry once, sings in Justice Shallow's orchard. The
juice of Love-in-idleness melts thwarted passion away. The citizens of England build their golden hive around Henry the Fifth.
The garden is thornless. Or nearly so.

Such pictures, with their implied simple moral judgments, have
something fragile about them. The golden world seems almost an
intimation from childhood, a transient dream of early innocence.
Even in the happy plays, however, more complex appraisals suggest themselves. The first time Prince Hal speaks in soliloquy, he
shows a cool and not endearing appraisal of his drinking companions, an ambitious responsibility that will make him a good
ruler but a dangerous friend. Falstaff on the other hand, that great
Silenus of pleasure, in his first scene turns aside any thoughts of
future justice. "No more of that, Hal, as you love me!" His merriment is pure because he wilfully holds it to the momentary and
the delightful. He is such a genius at good living that he fails in
the good life.

Such double, or balanced, or compensating judgments eventually excite Shakespeare's best thought. A simple answer is not dramatic, for drama implies conflict. Shakespeare's moral perceptions become increasingly dramatic, in the sense that they cannot be set down in didactic saws or lyrical certainties. Yet this complexity, this ambiguity, is not the result of indifference or vagueness. On the contrary, it is a sign of Shakespeare's growing susceptibility to all forms of life, his receptivity, his sensitivity, his imaginative power to live fully in conflicting worlds, to hold in mind simultaneously and impartially warring and incompatible ideas. Shakespeare becomes an Isaac Newton for human emotions, and discovers the law: For every action there is an equal and opposite reaction. Every emotion creates differing or supplementary or opposed emotions, and cannot be fully understood or described without them. Each decision, each course of conduct, generates the possibilities of other decisions and other courses. When he is in this mood, Shakespeare's dominating moral idea seems to be that all judgments are partial; that all action, though it is a necessary part of human life, falls short of ideal contemplation. He sets up whole plays almost as demonstrations in the laboratory of art, to prove the moral value of suspended judgment.

JULIUS CAESAR

Consider the puzzle of *Julius Caesar*. It stands lonely among the bright comedies and English histories of Shakespeare's hopeful decade, written a little before the turn of the century. Critics have not agreed on what the portrayal of Caesar is designed to accomplish; they cannot agree on whether Caesar or Brutus is the hero; they have even felt that the play is two plays patched together—the assassination of Caesar, and the vengeance of Caesar's ghost.

And yet in many ways the playwright shows his surety. The play is finished; it is not a rough sketch or a collaboration or an incompleted draft. It handles famous episodes and tag-lines with thrift and point. It uses rhetoric confidently, in formal balances and responses and repetitions. Above all, contrasting with its magenta orations and set-pieces of description, the usual ground of its diction is bare and unadorned. Shakespeare's conception of the simple virtue of republican Rome is reflected most subtly in his language.[1] The style of *Julius Caesar* stands out from the other plays written about this time, and its austerity in speech remains unmatched until Shakespeare surpasses it in *Coriolanus*.

In its ideas also, the play rests upon certain propositions with which Shakespeare is now so familiar that he assumes them without argument: The overthrow of any stable state is an evil. Power corrupts. Flattery and falsehood may blind responsible leaders.

Why, then, is the play a puzzle? Because in any of those characters or themes which elsewhere Shakespeare treats with glad confidence, there is now an element of self-destruction. Ambiguity devours itself. Every thought gives birth to an afterthought. The pendulum of contrarieties ticks on. The Roman state must be preserved, yet its best preserver must be destroyed. The best preserver, however, is no god; he certainly is more than ambition personified. He has the falling sickness, he loses in physical contests, he changes his mind suddenly, he listens to omens and holds himself superior to them, he does not hesitate to reveal weaknesses such as his deafness. Yet perhaps these are the carelessnesses of a genuinely great man, and perhaps Bernard Shaw borrowed from Shakespeare the notion that Caesar could afford to be above consistency, emulation, and the outward show of perfection. His casualness demonstrates his power. On the other hand, it has been argued that Caesar is here a caricature of greatness; his achievements are in the past, and now his unique and dizzying place in the state corrodes his character. Here is the arbitrary and vacillating tyrant, who ludicrously lauds himself in the third person.

But is it not possible, on the contrary, to think of Caesar as obsessed with the idea of the soul of the state, which he calls "Caesar," making a series of quick appraisals and decisions, and sensitive to all the forces and factions in Rome except care for his own personal safety? He dismisses the soothsayer: should a governor heed portents? He decides not to attend the Senate, at Calpurnia's entreaties: is this not a husband's generous gesture? When Decius presents the problem as a choice between a wife's whims and the business of state, between fear and fortitude, who would have him fail as a ruler to set the state before family comfort? He places the petition of Trebonius ahead of the personal warning of Artemidorus. His last long speech is an eloquent defense of his constancy in statecraft against the flattery of Metellus Cimber, the exhortations of Cassius, Cinna and Decius, and the friendship of Brutus. In his few huddled and hurried appearances, he yet has time for shrewd appraisals of Cassius and Antony, and special glancing words that show how affairs stand between him and Brutus, or Caius Ligarius, or Trebonius, or the unnamed Soothsayer. He listens to everyone, is aware of everyone. Nowhere does Shakespeare make Caesar's sensitivity to opinion clearer than in the account of how popular sentiment caused him, though personally ambitious, to refuse the crown—as if "he was very loath to lay his fingers off it." He swooned after this great refusal, but before he fell down, says Casca, "when he perceiv'd the common herd was glad he refus'd the crown, he pluck'd me ope his doublet and offer'd them his throat to cut."

May not this be a picture of the ideal governor, disregarding his own desires and fears, acting for the good of Rome as he conceives it, speaking the famous "Cowards die many times before their deaths" with the voice of Rome to quell his own personal tremors, and building above his weaknesses the conception of the impersonal Caesar, unshaken, unseduced, unterrified? Unless Caesar is seen as more than a person in this play, then his name should never have been given to a tragedy in which he appears, unghosted, in only three scenes, and speaks in a mere hundred and fifty lines. His body lies in full view on the stage during two scenes, each of which is considerably longer than the sum of the lines Caesar speaks in the entire play. Stage pictures and silence may point a moral.

While that body contained a spirit, Julius Caesar, seeking the action that conserves, made no mistaken moral decisions—with one exception: he believed that Brutus was true.

> Et tu, Brute?—Then fall Caesar!

That line contains more than a personal tragedy of broken loyalties. Caesar's idea of government crumbles when it cannot hold the allegiance of the noble Brutus.

And what of Brutus himself? Here the irony bites deeper, in a play cross-shot with ironies. It is ironical that the practiced statesman Caesar erred in trusting to the noblest. It is more delicately and bitterly ironical that flattery—the sweet words that melt fools, as Caesar described them with such familiar awareness—should cloud the idealism of Brutus. The temptation here is as subtle as that of the last tempter of Thomas Becket in *Murder in the Cathedral;* it takes many forms, though it always appeals to Brutus' better nature. Portia learns from Brutus the secret that contributes to her death by reminding him that she is "a woman that Lord Brutus took to wife." Antony through his kneeling servant appeals to the "noble, wise, valiant, and honest" Brutus; Antony asks no more than "reasons" why the conspirators have murdered Caesar; and Brutus, confident that reason and honor must prevail, basing his own speech before the plebeians on honor, wisdom, judgment, and freedom, trusts Antony's frankness, pledges his word to Antony, and leaves him alone in the Forum, where the words "honorable" and "ambitious" echo until they are indistinguishable. In the most moving scene in the play, the quarrel between Brutus and Cassius in Brutus' tent, the most exquisite flattery is offered by Cassius. "Hated by one he loves, brav'd by his brother," Cassius presents his heart to Brutus. He bares his breast and proffers a dagger: "Strike as thou didst at Caesar." Brutus succumbs, and no more is said of Cassius' itching palm.

The dilemma is unanswerable. If Brutus was right in condoning Cassius' faults, then earlier he was wrong in stabbing Caesar "for justice sake." In the same scene, Brutus is confronted by the ghost of Caesar, a presence that defines itself as "thy evil spirit, Brutus."

It may be that Brutus' evil spirit is his unshakable sense of being always right, as if man could take it upon himself, in the closed circle of his own integrity, to judge and punish other men. There is something of the spiritual sadist and masochist in Brutus: he speaks to Cassius, his brother in blood, of "chastisement"; he publicly affirms, almost with exultation, that "I slew my best lover for the good of Rome"; he says of himself, while grieving for his dead wife, "No man bears sorrow better." In his own conscious mind he is never wrong. He is most human when he forgets his reason and his philosophy, when he moves as a somnambulist, pities the sleeping young boy Lucius, or muses:

> Between the acting of a dreadful thing
> And the first motion, all the interim is
> Like a phantasma or a hideous dream. (II, i, 63–5)

Dread haunts the play, and all good things move toward destruction. Pompey's statua runs blood, and Philippi closes all. Portia is dead, and slumber itself is "murderous." The conspirators are ready for their own deaths immediately after the assassination, and almost in the teeth of triumph at Philippi, Caesar is avenged with the suicidal swords that killed him. Brutus has little to offer but reason and philosophy, as if a well-intentioned deed coolly done were somehow inconclusive and insufficient. The play is shaped to an ambiguous and ironical close, in that the words of praise over the body of Brutus are spoken by the multiple-minded opportunist and orator Antony. In Shakespeare's telling, Caesar's conception of the state is dead, and though Brutus may have been the sole honest and gentle conspirator working for the "common good to all," history goes on under the triumvirs, while Antony and Octavius plan to dispose of Lepidus as a mere property, an empty ass, a barren-spirited fellow.

Where is the center of the play? In no single character. Perhaps it can be sensed in such a glancing, blind remark as that of the plebeian praising Brutus for his bloody deed:

> Let him be Caesar!

Or in Caesar's wounds—"poor poor dumb mouths." Or in Brutus' counselling the assassins to smear their hands and swords in blood and cry "Peace, freedom, and liberty!" Or in the conception of the state, which, as later in *Coriolanus*, finds its best human exemplar overthrown. Or in the mob willing to kill Cinna the poet for bearing the name of a conspirator. Julius Caesar's ghost is liveliest in the quarrel scene between Brutus and Cassius; and throughout the play, in one form or another, through flattery or self-interest or betrayal or desire for power or idealistic theory, the brotherhood of man is murdered.

And this will be the theme in the plays that follow.

Enigmatic as it may be in its total effect, *Julius Caesar* at least contains positive and admirable qualities, so that good things may be said of both the dead Caesar and the dead Brutus. In the four succeeding plays considered in this chapter—*All's Well That Ends Well, Hamlet, Troilus and Cressida,* and *Measure for Measure*—characters worth a funeral oration would be harder to find. They might almost be limited to Hamlet and Hector (who, incidentally, are as dead as Caesar and Brutus when their plays are over). Shakespeare has radically changed his general estimate of human nature.

More than that, he is temporarily neglecting his skill as a dramatist. *Hamlet* is an exception, but not thanks to Shakespeare: for Hamlet was a successful dramatic structure before Shakespeare turned his hand to rewriting the story. In *Hamlet* the motivations of the old story and Shakespeare's new conception of the hero's character fight it out between them, and create a moral tension. Generally in this group of plays, however, Shakespeare abandons his dramatic judgment—that is, his suspended or multiple moral observations on any subject—in favor of intense, personal, lyrical opinions, unbalanced or uncompensated.

These opinions belong to a single family, from the wry to the savage. They ring variations on the theme: "Man delights not me—no, nor woman neither." Three of the four plays are in the fashion of comedies; but the laughter is sarcastic, and the "happy" endings seem an almost shockingly irresponsible and unexpected applying of brakes on the brink of inevitable catastrophes. The good characters are powerless in their goodness, or contain within themselves the seeds of evil. Pain and cruelty are the experiences most fully realized. The dominant and reiterated themes are lust and betrayal, and Shakespeare finds little moral retort to such enemies other than a sharp awareness of their existence.

It is as if Shakespeare were possessed by a demon. His pen runs away with him. The result is the automatic writing of a sufferer, the release and escape of confession, rather than the controlled creation of an artist. The three "problem" comedies are indeed problems: how they can be called comedies or even good actable dramas requires sophistical argument. As plays, they have a long record of popular failure. As the contorted expressions of unknown personal agony, they are perhaps Shakespeare's most brilliant successes.

That such plays could have followed so close upon the heels of the Golden Comedies appears at first incredible. But Shakespeare gives the answer, some years later, in *Timon of Athens*. In Timon he objectifies in a symbolic figure his own earlier moral experience: the great truster in human goodness who, disillusioned, becomes the bitterest misanthrope. Without Shakespeare's earlier and long continued glad confidence in humanity, this agonized revulsion could not have been felt so deeply, this reappraisal and readjustment could not have shattered the plays into cliffs and chasms, like a geologic fault across this cooling, shrinking planet. The careless caring gives way before a care-stricken misprision. The Garden of Eden has become an unweeded garden; and only in gardens are weeds resented. The lilies have festered. The bitterness at the loss is the measure of the love. For it is hard to feel bitter and empty over the loss of something one has never really cared for.

ALL'S WELL THAT ENDS WELL

Following the comedies of the earlier period, *All's Well That
Ends Well* seems the most dejected and pathetic of this group
of plays, for here Shakespeare without conviction goes through
the motions of his earlier successes. After so many roses, this is
the last and faded bloom. In Shakespeare's usual metaphor, the
canker is eating the flower. Or as expressed in this play:

> This thorn
> Doth to our rose of youth rightly belong, (I, iii, 135–6)

and the lines better express the thorn than the rose. Shakespeare
works over his tried devices. Here is the unmasking of a liar, but
the lies are vicious. Here is the heroine unswerving in love, but
true love seems powerless to convert all beholders. Here is the
contrived happy ending, but the contrivance is itself not happy.

Consider in the underplot the baiting of a boaster. Parolles is
no ridiculously bombastic Don Adriano de Armado; he is not the
master of uproarious ceremonies that Falstaff is; he is "a most
notable coward, an infinite and endless liar, an hourly promise-
breaker, the owner of no one good quality." Unlike Falstaff's
essentially harmless inventions, Parolles' lies are treacherous, degrading, and harmful—as Lucio's will be in *Measure for Measure*.
He will gratuitously reveal military secrets, or defame his close
friend and patron to save his own skin. Shakespeare, reassessing
life in lower terms, does not abandon life even in this dead center
of his thought. If life can no longer be exalted into a golden world,
it can at least be maintained. His low characters expound a philosophy of debased vitalism, as if mere existence were its own
argument. "If men could be contented to be what they are," says
Lavatch the Clown, "there were no fear in marriage," for though
young Charbon the Puritan and old Poysam the Papist differ
in religion, they are alike in being cuckolds. The fires of hell may
admittedly burn—but then, says the Clown, "I am a woodland
fellow, sir, that always loved a great fire"; the narrow gate is not
for the many, who, being too chill, will be "for the flow'ry way

that leads to the broad gate and the great fire." [2] Parolles is reduced by fear to his ultimate and only moral value: "My life, sir,
in any case! . . . Let me live, sir, in a dungeon, i' th' stocks, or
anywhere, so I may live." His life having been spared, he resolves
that "simply the thing I am shall make me live." Believing that
"there's place and means for every man alive," he is able to confront his own ignominy with the words: "Parolles, live safest in
shame!" The respectable characters themselves accept the lowest
common denominator of human life, and Lafew, who began the
unmasking of Parolles, at the end takes on the plucked peacock
as a waiting-man and says to him: "Though you are a fool and a
knave, you shall eat."

If, therefore, such a low character as Parolles is willing to
betray the brotherhood of man to save his own neck, a higher
character such as Lafew will affirm the blood brotherhood by
redeeming the renegade, or at least putting up with him.

The propounding of love is left in this comedy almost solely to
the heroine Helena. She is an odd and not altogether attractive
combination of patient Griselda and the ruthless self-made
woman. As a person, Shakespeare does not seem too sure of her.
Tongue-tied at times, at other times she is a young female Polonius
with a varied stock of wisdom.

> Our remedies oft in ourselves do lie,
> Which we ascribe to heaven,

she says at the end of the first scene, though she is quite ready
in the second act to reverse herself by telling the King:

> But most it is presumption in us when
> The help of heaven we count the act of men. (II, i, 154-5)

In snaring her husband she alternates between the rôles of aggres-
sive huntress and passive martyr.

But if she fails as a dramatic character, at least she offers Shakespeare a mouthpiece for the theme of despised love, perhaps his
principal interest in the story. Deliberately he sets up situations
so dark, so despairing, that in contrast her brave words of love

jet like bright fountains of hope.[3] Love for her is an ever-fixèd
mark which tempests cannot shake. It distorts the truth for the
sake of its own salvation, so that Helena speaks of herself as "too
mean to have her name repeated" and of the blind, proud, unnecessarily cruel boy she loves as "a bright particular star" whose
every feature is drawn in her heart's table. In the "dreadful sentence" of Bertram's letter of desertion after their marriage, refusing to return to France while his wife is there, love scores its
miracle: Helena's first wistful thought is for her husband:

> Poor lord! is 't I
> That chase thee from thy country and expose
> Those tender limbs of thine to the event
> Of the none-sparing war? (III, ii, 105–8)

And in the spirit of the sonnet, "No longer mourn for me when
I am dead,"—indeed, in the form of a sonnet—she takes it upon
herself, poor thief, to steal away into exile and death:

> He is too good and fair for death and me;
> Whom I myself embrace to set him free. (III, iv, 16–7)

Love cannot go farther as a self-creative force, independent of
its object. Yet Helena, though she is never bitter, is at least poignantly aware that her love is unrequited:

> I know I love in vain, strive against hope;
> Yet in this captious and intenible sieve
> I still pour in the waters of my love
> And lack not to lose still. Thus, Indian-like,
> Religious in mine error, I adore
> The sun, that looks upon his worshipper
> But knows of him no more. (I, iii, 207–13)

The image of love boundless as the sea has changed to the image
of the sieve. And it may be true also that when she rejects one
of the young French lords as a prospective husband because he is
"too young, too happy, and too good," Helena is aware that her
bright particular star is above reproach only in the idolatry of love.
    Believing her dead, the King of France recites "sweet Helen's
knell" in words that show man the destroyer of love:

> But love that comes too late,
> Like a remorseful pardon slowly carried,
> To the great sender turns a sour offence,
> Crying, 'That's good that's gone.' Our rash faults
> Make trivial price of serious things we have,
> Not knowing them until we know their grave.
> Oft our displeasures, to ourselves unjust,
> Destroy our friends, and after weep their dust;
> Our own love, waking, cries to see what's done,
> While shameful hate sleeps out the afternoon. (V, iii, 57–66)

Sweet Helen's knell comes in the final scene. The old king, after delivering it, immediately says: "And now forget her," and turns to the business of finding Bertram a second wife, with the full consent of Bertram's old mother the Countess of Rossillion, and of the wise old lord Lafew, who offers his daughter as candidate. The trio of wise elders is determined to abide by the King's words: "I have forgiven and forgotten all," and to patch up the action to a hasty end. Yet when Bertram produces a ring for Lafew's daughter, the ring is Helena's; and suspicion, fear, falsehood, treachery, and hate are back in the minds of the old aristocrats. This sudden reversal Shakespeare employs, as he had learned to do, to teach the erring characters melodramatic lessons. But here he goes out of his way to befoul and debase his hero Bertram. Bertram lies about the ring. He is confronted by Diana, whose virginity he thinks he has purchased. He blackens her character to save his own. Parolles is summoned, and in the midst of his own lies Bertram shudders away from his dishonorable lying former friend. Shakespeare delights in revealing his hero's every weakness, and when in the last disclosure Helena herself is discovered alive, she seems to be, in her own words, "the shadow of a wife, the name and not the thing." Trapped by his own wife's cunning, caught *flagrante delicto* by Helena's trickery, Bertram yields to wedded bliss in a most unconvincing and mockingly hollow couplet:

> If she, my liege, can make me know this clearly,
> I'll love her dearly—ever, ever dearly.

As a play, *All's Well* is the poorest that Shakespeare had written since *The Two Gentlemen of Verona*. He seems here to have used earlier work of his own as a palimpsest on which he could jot down maturer speculations on subjects that held his interest. He has much to say on virtue, nature, honor, and the death of fathers. His old aristocrats—the bluff Lafew, the detached King of France, the wise and tender Dowager Countess of Rossillion— set forth some of his ripest, if disillusioned, thoughts.[4] He plays, too, with ambiguous judgments, particularly with those where reason and desire are given equal sway.[5] But the principal counterpoising in the play is love set against lust and virginity. The theme of lust is framed in action and in myriads of glancing speeches; in contrast virginity is given what amounts to a long formal essay. Shakespeare—or Parolles, with Helena listening and not averse—will have none of it. He does not exalt with Milton "the sage and serious doctrine of virginity," but finds it rather "like one of our French wither'd pears: it looks ill, it eats drily." Virginity offends against nature; it is "made of self-love, which is the most inhibited sin in the canon." Such an opinion squares with the larger pattern of Shakespeare's thought. The purity of any idea or ideal inhibits that idea. Lacking relationships and "respect," no idea, not even the finest, is worthy of this complex world. In all of Shakespeare, perhaps the most characteristic moral observation—and it, too, holds that purity is not faithful to experience— is to be found in this play:

The web of our life is of a mingled yarn, good and ill together. Our virtues would be proud if our faults whipp'd them not, and our crimes would despair if they were not cherish'd by our virtues. (IV, iii, 83–7)

All's Well fails as a play because its central idea of misprized love possibly rewarded is itself too virginal, too lyrical. As a whole it is not related to the world—or to any possible world—as faithfully as are some of its individual thoughts. It was written by "a shrewd knave and an unhappy." If we cannot pluck out the heart of Hamlet's mystery, at least the Dowager Countess discovered the secret of Helena, silent in her love for Bertram:

> Now I see
> The myst'ry of your loneliness and find
> Your salt tears' head.

HAMLET

So much that is good has been written about *Hamlet* that we tend to take the play for granted, as an old friend. We are aware with Goethe that Hamlet is a frail instrument, and with Coleridge that Hamlet thinks too much. We may even adapt Coleridge's confession and believe that there is a bit of Hamlet in each of us. We may believe that his mission was beset with physical difficulties, that the secret of the play lies in Hamlet's disillusioned relationship with his mother, that Hamlet believes or does not believe in the ghost, that the Elizabethans would have felt the ghost might be the devil's agent, and that the play is tinged by contemporary events—the death of Essex and the old age of Elizabeth—so that it reflects the end of glory. Any or all of these ideas, and more, may be assumed. Yet the best criticisms have always left to the play a mystery beyond the reach of analysis.

Considered simply as a fragment in Shakespeare's artistic career, however, *Hamlet* becomes less mysterious. The approach in these pages is based on the simple assumption that *Hamlet* has ancestors.

There are, first of all, the earlier versions of the story in Saxo Grammaticus and Belleforest and Kyd. These give it a crude march and drive that is no part of the character of the Hamlet we know, and account in large measure for the success of *Hamlet* on the stage. Much of the speculation on *Hamlet* is framed as if one of these inferior storytellers or playwrights had written Shakespeare's tragedy. For instance, what could be more irrelevant to Shakespeare's character than the question: "Why did Hamlet procrastinate?" The question is germane if we are thinking of the conventions of the earlier stories or of the tragedy of revenge. When your uncle kills your father, forthwith you kill your uncle. It is as simple as that. But Shakespeare follows his usual course. Deliberately, here as elsewhere, he poses himself the question: How would conceivable characters act if they were placed in artificial situations? One of his abiding moral principles is that the dignity and complexity of human life as it is actually lived must not be explained away by infantile simplicity and storybook motivations. Only those who are quick and certain uncle-killers themselves need chide Hamlet for his deliberation. Shakespeare, on the other hand, keeps his moral intuitions sound and complete by setting a judge to judge a judge, with other judges above them. In this play, the mechanical morality of the old revenge story is judged by handing it over to a complex contemporary human being as hero; the hero judges his own actions, and is in turn judged by other characters and by the disposition of the whole drama.

Shakespeare consciously strives to set Hamlet up as an actual man, not as a character in a play. Hamlet speaks at great length about the visiting players, so that his comments may show that he is no part of the play-world. He upbraids himself by contrasting his inaction, though he has the motive and the cue for passion, with the player's tears at a fiction, a dream. Much as Hotspur had derided poetry while magnificently using all of its devices, so Hamlet contemptuously recites doggerel and asks his friend if his performance would not get him a fellowship in a cry of players. The situations of Hotspur and Hamlet are not alike, but the effect of their derision is the same: to create the belief that neither one is a mincing poet or a mere play-actor, that both are independent of their creator, since they mock at his tricks. Best of all is the contrast between the stilted archaic speech of the players in Herod's and Cambyses' vein, and the sharp, supple, actual speech of Denmark's court. Shakespeare is building his illusion that the events are important because they are happening, not merely being staged. He is imparting reality by scoffing at poetic or dramatic conventions while he uses them.

The old ancestral stories Shakespeare ties together in a tighter, more fully motivated plot. In view of this craftsmanship, he can hardly have been unaware of his inclusion of inherited elements that are incompatible in his new play. Take the ghost and the feigned madness. In Saxo's story, the murder of the king was public, and Hamlet, witnessing it, did well to feign madness in order to avoid being killed as a possible avenger of his father. But when Kyd supposedly introduced a ghost in the lost play on the Hamlet theme, the ghost could be given a genuine rôle in the plot only if he appeared to inform his son of a secret murder. If the murder is open, there is no need for a ghost; if the murder is secret, there is no need to pretend madness. Yet ghost and madness, Shakespeare keeps them both. They intensify his themes: the majesty of Denmark being now buried, ghastly nobility must rise from the charnelhouse; a world of traitors must be exposed in hysterical revulsion.

But here we are verging upon other forebears than the versions of the Hamlet story. We are considering Shakespeare's own precedent thoughts as expressed in his earlier plays. Some of the vitality of the tragedy springs from Shakespeare's identification of himself with Hamlet. Of course, this identification is not crude or literal. Working as a dramatist, Shakespeare knows that his job is merely to motivate fully and convincingly situations and characters not his own. But Hamlet's character is illuminated by the sympathetic projection of Shakespeare's feelings at this particular stage in his career.

This tragedy is impregnated with the intuitions of the bitter comedies that surround it—the death of something noble, the powerlessness of the good or the rational, the decay of that which was beautiful, the betrayal of trust, the savage insurgence of the base. Shakespeare had lost his belief in the building world of the English histories; the bright hope of the confident comedies had become clouded and overcast. Symbols for Shakespeare's brooding exist in Hamlet's situation: the majesty of the state murdered; the loyal, tender, loving queen debauched. The early positive ideas Shakespeare now consciously accepts as illusions—and on what is Hamlet's bitter cynicism based if not on his disillusioned idealism?

At any rate, in Hamlet's actual world Hyperion is replaced by a satyr. Nobility is dead. Can it be recaptured mentally? Not entirely, for the world is too strong for it. "O God, I could be bounded in a nutshell," says Hamlet, "and count myself a king of infinite space, were it not that I have bad dreams." But Denmark is a prison, and Hamlet's every soaring thought toward infinite space is cut down by the characters or events that mesh him round. The world entangling him authenticates his bad dreams—never his momentary hopes. His unvoiced suspicion of Claudius is changed by his father's ghost into dark knowledge. Going to Ophelia's chamber for possible comfort and understanding, he sees her affection turn to fright, to silence; finally, as she surrenders his love letters to be read aloud at court and acts as cat's-paw for the king, she is allied with betrayal. His schoolfellows Rosencrantz and Guildenstern, whom he receives at first in careless comradeship, become sponges in the king's mouth. Polonius, that purveyor of wisdom for any occasion (though in practice he invariably suspects the good and trusts the evil), is true to his own self, false to no man, only in death—a wretched, rash, intruding fool. Laertes accepts Hamlet's offered love and says he will not wrong it: then he selects the poisoned foil. As for Hamlet's mother, even at the beginning of the action, her conduct has placed her in her son's mind as lower than an unreasoning beast. Who around him of any importance except Horatio does not add to the nightmare?

What shall be the moral attitude of the hero? In part, as Hamlet's characteristic posture in half of his soliloquies best shows, he must reflect the desperate stoicism which brims over in the plays of this period. Admit, accept, endure. Augury is defied, destiny is bitterly acknowledged, and a passive readiness is all. The heart breaks, while one keeps silence.

If this were all of Hamlet, if he were a Brutus, or if he were merely the thinker which he is so widely famed to be, this partial explanation would be the whole one. But Hamlet is far more a man of nerves than a man of thought, and indeed, his nervous bursts of action explain his periods of thought and inaction. His mother and his creator are aware of his makeup, even if he himself is not.[6] He can no more hold his tongue than he can control his emotions. Here Shakespeare avails himself brilliantly of the device of assumed madness. In the plot it serves no rational purpose, since the murder of King Hamlet was unwitnessed; and far from allaying Claudius' suspicions, it arouses them. Psychologically, however, the grim pressures in Denmark may well lead to madness. Closer than kin and less than kind, the interlocked houses crowd together and destroy each other, until repressed and conflicting emotions give way to madness and suicide. But Ophelia is weaker than Hamlet, whose darting mind plays with the possibilities and not the fact of madness. For him, the antic disposition affords a vent for tortured feelings. His madness is merely the expression of unpalatable truths, and Hamlet is no more mad than the Fool in *Lear*, or is mad in the same wry and bitter fashion. To the world, accustomed to convention and the social lie, such brutal frankness may seem insanity. Hamlet's madness is most evident in the presence of his enemies, where its imaginative intensity and glancing allusiveness keep them from seeing that he never deviates from truth. But it is merely a device that allows him to give rein to his tongue and emotions, while protecting his secret in a hostile country. To call Hamlet's madness "assumed" is perhaps as inaccurate as to call it madness: carried away by the same ironic flights before his friends, Hamlet is reproached by Horatio for "wild and whirling words." Carried away again by sadistic ecstasy in his mother's chamber, Hamlet is reproached by the ghost. The ghost, who bids Hamlet step between Gertrude and her fighting soul, may be Shakespeare's indirect judgment that the righteous purity and intense preaching of even such a lonely and sensitive soul as Hamlet's is a species of moral madness. As for King Claudius, he learns quickly that Hamlet's odd disposition is pointed to a single end. Again like the Fool in *Lear*, Hamlet is a hunter of consciences, a walking Nemesis. His remarks to the King become more and more flagrant and flaunting, until the disguise seems hardly worth the candle as the two are drawn closer together in the terrible intimacy of their knowledge.

The outlet of madness or hysteria is doubly necessary to this man of nerves because he is also a man without faith. He is incapable of any recuperative action—for how can the past be obliterated, his father restored, his mother purified? What does he consistently believe through the play? Only that the reigning power is evil. He trusts and doubts the ghost. He mistrusts and trusts his mother. In one soliloquy he refrains from suicide because of the Christian commandment, yet in another he shows himself agnostic. In a single scene he tells Ophelia "I did love you once" (the young lover in King Hamlet's happy court) and "I loved you not" (the avenger who knows all women frail). An abyss gapes between his past and present circumstances, between life as he would have it and life as it forces itself upon him.

It is not generally true that thought weakens resolution or that consciousness makes us cowards. But it is true for Hamlet, because his lack of faith makes his thought pale and sickly. He cannot act positively and rationally, because his trust is dead and his reason leads him only to despair. He can analyze how a dram of evil quenches all noble substance; or how reason is broken down, a man of noblest character destroyed, because of some one "vicious mole of nature" in him. But his unbelief cannot imagine positive salvation. He generalizes concerning "reason" on the basis of his own negative emotions, and inverts Portia's image of the candle shining in the night: to Hamlet a little blotch of evil can infect the world with darkness.

His only assuagement, as his unbelief acts upon his lacerated nerves, is to destroy. Here there is no compromise, no reconciliation. Hurt by his mother's weakness, he will allow Ophelia no quarter, but will cast her off, in an invective against all women, before she too can hurt him further. He will cleave his mother's heart in twain. He will be merciless against himself in soliloquies, those keen whippings of self-loathing, and will describe himself in bitter truth, and the world with him, in words that etch their poison on the mind of the girl he loves:

I could accuse me of such things that it were better my mother had not borne me. I am very proud, revengeful, ambitious; with more offences at my beck than I have thoughts to put them in, imagination to give them shape, or time to act them in. What should such fellows as I do, crawling between earth and heaven? We are arrant knaves all; believe none of us. (III, i, 124–33)

In the rough-grown grove of the world he has discovered, and has roused within himself, "cave-keeping evils that obscurely sleep." In such destruction, his death-warrant against Rosencrantz and Guildenstern seems but a trivial flicking of noxious insects, comparable to Wotan's contemptuous "Geh!" that drops Hunding dead amid greater tragedies. Hamlet is responsible for seven deaths, and in his bitterness, hopelessness, and indecision, almost gladly responsible. "It were better my mother had not borne me." And therefore he proceeds, ready for catastrophe and aiding it, torturing others because he himself is tortured, until the final slaughters come as a relief among the instruments of torture that fill the doomed prison of Denmark, from which there is no escape but death.

Even in this most desperate period of Shakespeare's thought, however, gloom does not obscure the whole picture. There are positive elements. King Claudius is not so lost as not to feel guilt. The Queen in her last gesture sides with Hamlet against the King's treachery, and reunites herself with her son—"O my dear Hamlet!" She has been weak rather than wicked. The ghost—it is a part Shakespeare himself is supposed to have played—returns to protect the woman who has betrayed him and is married to his murderer, so that again love triumphs over faithlessness and even over the grave. Above all, a triumvirate of young men shoulders moral responsibilities: Fortinbras, soldierly, efficient, with a conventional sense of right and wrong, who is left at the end to carry on the state; Horatio, whose unshakable loyalty culminates in the attempt to follow his friend in death; and Hamlet himself, whose convulsive irreconcilement marks at least his determination never to compromise with evil, nor to exculpate his own faults. He had wished at the beginning for death; he had

wished for the strength also to carry out his cursed duty of avenging his father. At the end, both of his desires are fulfilled; and to
that extent, even this tragedy ends in triumph.

In the light of Shakespeare's whole career, this play seems
touched with a transient and mysterious pathos. There are sweet
bells, but they jangle harshly. In Ophelia's description, in Horatio's farewell, we catch what Hamlet was and what he might have
been. But not in Denmark. Not in this realized state, where from
beginning to end the best that can happen to the sweet Prince
is to dissolve into a dew, to find the quiet of the grave. Felicity
is rest, and the rest is silence, in a world where to wake is to
have bad dreams, and where so much sweetness has been overlaid
with so much that is weary and flat and rank and gross.

TROILUS AND CRESSIDA

Though it is more actable than its infrequent performances
would suggest, *Troilus and Cressida* is not a good stage-play in
comparison with the usual Shakespearean product. Three causes
for its failure in dramatic appeal might be suggested. For one
thing, it has two subjects—statecraft and betrayed love—which
Shakespeare cannot tie together. The plot has no central drive, no
consistent argument. Second, both subjects trail off painfully.
Passive suffering, Yeats has said, is no theme for tragedy. Still
less, then, is it a theme for comedy, if indeed this odd play can
be assigned to any form. (The editors of the First Folio, after some
second thoughts, placed it between the histories and the tragedies.)
The theme of war ends in the accidental, hasty, surprisingly motivated, and shameful death of Hector. The theme of lechery ends
in Troilus' learning that lightness is stronger than loyalty; yet
this knowledge leaves him powerless to settle upon either a stable
philosophy or course of action. Third, several long scenes are
ruminative debates that are scarcely good drama; sometimes they
lead to decisions, but the decisions either do not follow from the
arguments (II, ii), or do not cause the ensuing action (I, iii; III, ii).

Shakespeare, again placing his personal thoughts and interests above his dramatic skill, is amusing himself by writing a closet drama.[7] Few among his plays contain mature reflections in greater quantity or of higher quality. The work is neither hasty nor rough. Yet if a search is made for the organizing *theme* that informs the writing, no better idea can be found than that the worst contaminates and overthrows the best. In bitter irony and self-contempt, Shakespeare builds up his finest thoughts only in order to tear them down. The high thoughts are there in abundance, but their validity is repeatedly befouled by the action. The Homeric Grecians and Trojans, whom Chapman had so lately given in English to the Elizabethans, are here presented cynically and satirically as base cowards and traitors and railers and headstrong beasts. The spirit of epic and romance that Spenser had celebrated in the *Faerie Queen*—"Fierce wars and faithful loves shall moralize my song"—is degraded. The war itself, as Ulysses sees it, is a waste of lives to avenge a cuckold upon a strumpet:

> O deadly gall, and theme of all our scorns,
> For which we lose our heads to gild his horns!

And the faithful loves? With Cressida in the title rôle? Hear Thersites mock Spenser: "Lechery, lechery! still wars and lechery! Nothing else holds fashion. A burning devil take them!" The iron in his spirit, Shakespeare will make himself into a dramatic Polonius, full of wise saws, and will kill himself off as a wretched fool.

The play, then, has a thematic—almost a mathematic—unity. The thesis is constructive reason, the antithesis is destructive will. But since will overpowers reason, there is no synthesis, no reconciliation. The five acts expand at large the conflicting themes of Hamlet's meditation: "What a piece of work is a man! how noble in reason! And yet to me what is this quintessence of dust?"

Shakespeare uses the form of the drama to carry his over-all judgments upon such topics as honor, authority and subordination, nature, truth, love, and value. It is not so much that ideas are in conflict, leading to characteristic double judgments—although Thersites curses the ambiguity of thought: "A plague of

opinion! A man may wear it on both sides like a leather jerkin."
Rather, judgments are rendered dramatically, indirectly: idealistic
reason is destroyed by actual practice; brave speeches are answered by base actions.[8] Troilus, who has witnessed his betrayal
by Cressida, throws her love letter to the wind almost in Hamlet's
phrase: "Words, words, mere words, no matter from the heart."

In analyzing *Troilus and Cressida*, therefore, this theorem of
thought that passes for a play,[9] the best method will be to survey
the theses advanced on the two subjects of statecraft and love, and
then to consider their antithetical destruction in action.

The Greeks are first seen in a time of checks and disasters.
Agamemnon immediately rationalizes "the protractive trials of
great Jove" in a long argument that would equally well explain
why tragedy is a worthier moral instrument than comedy or
naturalism. Such trials are designed

> To find persistive constancy in men;
> The fineness of which metal is not found
> In Fortune's love. (I, iii, 21–3)

The bold, the wise, the artist, the man rich in virtue, can be certainly discovered only in the wind and tempest of Fortune's
frown. The old sage Nestor responds antiphonally to Agamemnon's sentiments in a speech almost as long, holding that

> In the reproof of chance
> Lies the true proof of men.

Ulysses, however, seeks beyond fortune and chance for causes.
He finds the Grecian ills due to insubordination, lack of respect,
disdain for tradition. His famous speech on "degree" holds that
all stability rests upon reverence for an accepted hierarchy—the
idea of the gradations in nature that one finds in Thomas Aquinas,
or of the ascending and expanding stages in Dante, or of the great
chain of being in any of its forms from Plato to Pope.

> Take but degree away, . . .
> Then everything includes itself in power,

Power into will, will into appetite;
And appetite, an universal wolf,
So doubly seconded with will and power,
Must make perforce an universal prey,
And last eat up himself.

As a practical man, Ulysses has definite plans for restoring right-ful rule by manipulating its principal opponents, Achilles and his parasite Patroclus, and Ajax. Out of these plans grows his equally famous speech on honor, in which he eloquently per-suades Achilles that only through constant effort are honor and virtue kept bright. His words are just effective enough to con-vince Achilles that out of curiosity at least, he should invite the unarmed Hector to his tent.

The Trojans in council are seen for the first time debating the surrender of Helen to the Greeks. Here Troilus, who had earlier said that Helen's fairness was too starved a subject to command his fighting sword, is inflamed to defend her on grounds of honor, valor, constancy, and pride. He greatly finds quarrel in a straw. As for reason—

> Reason and respect
> Make livers pale and lustihood deject. (II, ii, 49-50)

He holds the romantic notion of "What is aught but as 'tis valu'd?" against his brother Hector's claim that "Value dwells not in particular will." Hector maintains that Helen is not worth the cost in Trojan lives, that the law of nature owes a wife to her husband, that "these moral laws of nature and of nations" call for Helen's return to Menelaus, and that a persistence in wrong does not excuse the wrong. He reproves Paris and Troilus for speaking in hot passion, "not much Unlike young men, whom Aristotle thought Unfit to hear moral philosophy." [10]

The conception of value, which Troilus and Hector here de-bate, is taken up again in the third scene of the third act, where Ulysses and—surprisingly—Achilles accept Hector's social judg-ment. Ulysses states it in two lines that form the permanent basis of Shakespeare's moral thought:

> no man is the lord of anything . . .
> Till he communicate his parts to others.

The idea of action becoming virtue only in a social context, reflected back from others, is embellished in various images—of an arch reverberating the voice, of a steel gate rendering back the sun's rays and heat, and (in Achilles' words) of the eye, though it is the organ of vision, not seeing itself until reflected in other eyes or mirrors:

> For speculation turns not to itself
> Till it hath travell'd, and is mirror'd there
> Where it may see itself.

It is given most extended form, in this careful philosophical colloquy, in a further image of reflected warmth. Ulysses says:

> A strange fellow here
> Writes me, that man—how dearly ever parted,
> How much in having, or without or in—
> Cannot make boast to have that which he hath,
> Nor feels not what he owes, but by reflection;
> As when his virtues, aiming upon others,
> Heat them, and they retort that heat again
> To the first giver.[11]

Achilles observes of the idea, "This is not strange at all," and Ulysses replies: "I do not strain at the position. It is familiar." Shakespeare finds the idea familiar because he has turned it over so often in his thought. He anticipated by a century and a half what the economist Adam Smith considered his masterpiece, the *Theory of Moral Sentiments*. Merit, value, worth, virtue, depend upon the reception and opinions of society. This idea might seem more natural to a dramatic than to a lyric poet. It forms a classical thread in Shakespeare's romantic thought.

If Ulysses is the principal voice of statecraft in this play, Hector is not only a voice, but a shining example-in-action of honor in war and government. A complete scene revolves around his decision to go forth in fatal fight in order to uphold "the faith of

valour" and the Trojan cause, in spite of the entreaties of Andromache and Priam and the dire bodings of Cassandra. When in
battle Achilles is disarmed, Hector will not kill an unarmed man.[12]
And Homer's epic world lives again, colored by Shakespeare's
own meditations on the pathos of time, and by Renaissance
chivalry at its highest, in Agamemnon's greeting of his enemy
Hector:

> What's past and what's to come is strew'd with husks
> And formless ruin of oblivion;
> But in this extant moment, faith and troth,
> Strain'd purely from all hollow bias-drawing,
> Bids thee with most divine integrity
> From heart of very heart, great Hector, welcome.
>   (IV, v, 166–71)

The play, indeed, contains more general appraisals of what
constitutes human perfection than perhaps any other of Shakespeare's works. Pandarus finds that birth, beauty, good shape,
discourse, manhood, learning, gentleness, virtue, youth, and liberality are the spice and salt that season a man. Agamemnon, seeking the qualities of a good man, finds him to be strong, valiant,
wise, noble, gentle, and—is not a governor speaking?—tractable.
Ulysses describes an ideal Troilus as a true knight, matchless, firm
of word, active, slow to anger and soon calmed, open and free
of heart and hand, his judgment and sense of fitness equal to his
bounty, manly, and determined. In more general terms, he anato-
mizes virtue into her parts: "beauty, wit, high birth, vigour of
bone, desert in service, love, friendship, charity." [13]

Love, the other great theme of the play, is positively exalted,
though rarely in scenes or passages that do not contain skeptical
or negative elements. Written midway between Shakespeare's
other two plays whose man-and-woman titles dedicate them to
love, *Troilus and Cressida* is far more sophisticated and complex
than *Romeo and Juliet*, as it is more frenetic and unbalanced than
Antony and Cleopatra (which nevertheless could not have been
written without these earlier artistic experiences). Troilus' adora-

tion of Cressida's hand, though it is hectic and overwrought, makes Romeo's description of Juliet's hand appear callow and prosaic. Love is infinite, eternally constant, plain and simple, and trusting.[14] Troilus describes himself in the spirit of happy comedies:

> I am as true as truth's simplicity
> And simpler than the infancy of truth. (III, ii, 176–7)

Through most of the fourth scene of the fourth act the word "truth" sounds like a steady ground-bass. Shakespeare has shaped the word to his own meaning. Truth does not gain its value from the intellect, but from the emotions. It is the infinite confidence and constancy of love, admitting no qualification, and creating an answering truth in the beloved by its sheer intensity. It is a kind of "godly jealousy" that compels Troilus to say:

> I will throw my glove to Death himself
> That there's no maculation in thy heart.

True love is so strong that it will deny experience and build a heaven in hell's despite:

> This she? No, this is Diomed's Cressida!
> If beauty have a soul, this is not she.

Love the great alchemist converts the base evidence of the senses into trust and hope:

> there is a credence in my heart,
> An esperance so obstinately strong,
> That doth invert th' attest of eyes and ears,
> As if those organs were deceptious functions,
> Created only to calumniate. (V, ii, 120–4)

Love is so strong that Dante's conception of

> The love that moves the sun and the other stars

is translated into Shakespearean human terms as the force that binds all things together in its noble gravity:

> Time, force and death,
> Do to this body what extremes you can,

But the strong base and building of my love
Is as the very centre of the earth,
Drawing all things to it. (IV, ii, 107–11)

Yet these unqualified affirmations of love are poisoned by circumstances. Among the last three quotations, two are spoken
by Troilus as he witnesses his betrayal. The third is Cressida's!

Undying love is negated by the very plot. This is so flagrantly
obvious that any speech on love in a play about Cressida will seem
ironical. How may Troilus dare hope for a constancy

Outliving beauties outward, with a mind
That doth renew swifter than blood decays?

He himself relishes outward beauties too keenly, crushing them on
his palate in gustatory images of impatient desire. Pandarus tempts
Troilus with sensuous comparisons between Helen's and Cressida's fairness, or with Cressida's blushings and short-drawn
breaths; he whets Cressida's jealousy by describing Helen stroking
Troilus' face, by suggesting that Helen would trade Paris for
Troilus. His pandering is unnecessary. The noble advice in this
play is disregarded, while advice to sharpen appetite is a waste of
words. Troilus is already whirled round with giddy expectation.
Cressida, a convert before Pandarus preaches his tickling sermons,
reveals in soliloquy that her reluctance is calculated to tantalize
the unsatisfied Troilus. Sensual clogs soil the overflowing generosity of love that Shakespeare celebrates in other plays. In *Troilus*,
the infinity of love—Juliet's "My bounty is as boundless as the
sea," or Cleopatra's "Eternity was in our lips and eyes"—is made
monstrous and tortured by man's limitations. "This is the mon-
struosity in love, lady," says Troilus to Cressida, "that the will is
infinite and the execution confin'd, that the desire is boundless and
the act a slave to limit."

Of the four women in the play, Cassandra is a mad prophetess
whose warnings are unheeded; and the dutiful Andromache,
powerless to sway her husband, withdraws in silence at Hector's
reproach. The other two, best described in Ulysses' contemptuous words, are "sluttish spoils of opportunity And daughters of

the game!" In Helen's one extended appearance, her entrance is graced by the description, "the mortal Venus, the heart-blood of beauty, love's invisible soul," and her exit by the tribute: "Sweet, above thought I love thee!" But again the action mars the mental illusions. What should have been the court of beauty is presented as a boudoir of chitchat and gossip—"My niece is horribly in love with a thing you have, sweet queen"—in which the main action is Helen's teasing Pandarus to sing a bawdy song, and in which her general observations rise no higher than "To make a sweet lady sad is a sour offence," and "This love will undo us all. O Cupid, Cupid, Cupid!" Superficiality and lightness here run in such rippling shallows that the repeated words "fair" and "sweet" begin to cloy. Whatever her beauty might do, Helen's wits and heart could not have launched a paper boat.

Love's very shallowness—as mobile as Phaedria's dancing bark—increases its pain in the world of serious action. Troilus' realization of the pangs of parting is at least as intense a love-poem as any of Romeo's ecstasies. Yet now Shakespeare is cynically insistent that the treachery of love be faced openly. He dwells formally on Cressida's oath that she will never be false. Troilus forces himself to take hideous note of his betrayal. His frantic speech is Shakespeare's direct renunciation at this time of his earlier conception of love. Poignant and pure emotion can no longer shape the world to its own pattern. With a great effort of the will, Troilus sets down this lesson, these instances, in the tablets of his brain. His conviction that faith and hope can invert the testimony of his eyes and ears must yield now to bitter reality. His heaven has become a garbage heap. The truth of his love must be denied, and denied again:

> Instance, O instance! strong as Pluto's gates:
> Cressid is mine, tied with the bonds of heaven.
> Instance, O instance! strong as heaven itself:
> The bonds of heaven are slipp'd, dissolv'd, and loos'd;
> And with another knot, five-finger-tied,
> The fractions of her faith, orts of her love,

The fragments, scraps, the bits, and greasy relics
Of her o'ereaten faith, are given to Diomed. (V, ii, 153–60)

Love in this play has had within it from the beginning the seeds
of its own decay. More as a moralist than a dramatist, Shakespeare
has his hero express a hope to "wallow in the lily beds" of his
desire. Troilus describes his emotion in terms of giddiness, of
the banquet of an ecstatic gourmet, of a fever. There is a corrup-
tion in outward beauty; of the fair virtues of high courtesy he
may say:

in each grace of these
There lurks a still and dumb-discoursive devil
That tempts most cunningly. (IV, iv, 91–3)

Love may overleap itself in its very intensity and fall on the
other side. As "sometimes we are devils to ourselves," love itself
may become "a virtuous sin." Cressida says: "My love admits no
qualifying dross" (as, say, Viola's love was qualified by self-
sacrifice, or Rosalind's by humor). "Why tell you me of moderation?" Nor can Troilus moderate or qualify "love's thrice-
repured nectar." Purity itself emerges as an enemy dangerous
in its intensity. "Cressid, I love thee in so strain'd a purity," cries
Troilus—that the angry gods are taking her from him. And Troilus becomes love's wilful martyr because he has mistaken his
passion for the whole of existence. All else is excluded in this
obsessive purity. Qualifying "degree" is lost, and if reason is to
be allowed in this burning sensual world, "Let's shut our gates and
sleep." Troilus wonders despairingly "if there be rule in unity
itself." But he himself insists on setting up as his rule a pure part
for the complex whole. In the play's imagery of feeding, Troilus
eats himself up.

The great lessons of statecraft also, envisaging "the unity and
married calm of states," are denied by the action. Nestor and
Ulysses are spared from the slavery of the others because they at
least are acting for a good outside themselves. But "that stale old
mouse-eaten dry cheese, Nestor, and that same dog-fox, Ulysses"

are too world-worn to trust to wise precepts. More effective in moving to action than their moralizings is the contempt of the oblivious princes before Achilles' tent, or the glozing flattery heaped upon Ajax, until the bloated giant says in all complacency: "I do hate a proud man as I hate the engend'ring of toads." Thersites is clear-eyed in seeing that the two wise men yoke Ajax and Achilles like draught oxen and make them plough up the wars. Hector himself acts contrary to reason. After building up an uncontroverted case for the return of Helen to the Greeks, he immediately adds:

> This in way of truth. Yet ne'ertheless,
> My sprightly brethren, I propend to you
> In resolution to keep Helen still. (II, ii, 189–91)

Out of character, this reversal is as cynically startling a triumph of will over reason as any in the play.

Not only wisdom and reason, but honor, chivalry, and the ordered rule of the state are debased, rendered powerless, or destroyed. Achilles sees that honor in this world does not so much depend upon a man himself as upon "place, riches, and favour, Prizes of accident as oft as merit," so that man rises or falls by chance. "But 'tis not so with me," he thinks. "Fortune and I are friends." Since he is a blackguard, in this play his proud luck happens to hold. Hector for honor's sake goes to the field of battle and to his death. Achilles, in contrived contrast, is not moved to positive action by Ulysses' praise of honor and emulation. He refrains from battle because of a message from his mistress in the enemy's camp—a cynical balancing against Hector's painful rejection of his wife's pleadings because his honor is even dearer. And when Achilles does fight, it is in anger over Patroclus' death, not for the good of the Greeks. Hector having been welcomed as a guest in the Grecian camp, Achilles addresses him insultingly in the third person and surveys him as coolly as a meat-carver: "In which part of his body shall I destroy him?" Selfish brutal force, Achilles is indeed what Thersites calls him: "thou picture of what thou seem'st, and idol of idiot-worshippers."

Shakespeare is uncompromising in his savagery in the fifth act, which begins by compelling Troilus to watch every detail of his betrayal, and ends in a quick succession of slaughter-scenes and the echoing choruses, "Hector is slain." The monstrous shaping is wilful. The vile shall live and have the last word. Pandarus in the epilogue shall bequeath his diseases to brethren and sisters of the hold-door trade. Hector shall accede to the spirit of the ending, and when Thersites describes himself as "a rascal, a scurvy railing knave, a very filthy rogue," shall reply: "I do believe thee. Live." Hector, who had refused to fight the disarmed Achilles, shall be ringed round by Achilles and his Myrmidons, and, unarmed himself, empaled upon their weapons. "The sweet warman is dead and rotten." "The dragon wing of night o'erspreads the earth," and Troilus in his suffering shall call upon the gods to smite all Troy, "and linger not our sure destructions on!"

The answer of events and character to wisdom and hope makes this play in the end a tale told by an idiot. In no other play of Shakespeare's would Thersites have proved a fit chorus, for even Apemantus in *Timon* speaks less aptly to the point. "All the argument is a whore and a cuckold." The argument, nevertheless, is seen clearly. True love and the ordered state, peaceful commerce and brotherhoods in cities, are envisaged far off, and like a dream. This is the time of discord. Proportion, order, and custom are not observed. The rule of unity is broken by hysterical will and greedy aggrandizement.

> Frights, changes, horrors
> Divert and crack, rend and deracinate.

The enemy, in the small and the great worlds, is gluttony. And appetite, an universal wolf, at last eats up itself.

MEASURE FOR MEASURE

The moral intuition illustrated in the character of Troilus—that a passion or an ideal may be so dangerously pure and intense as to destroy its own beauty and its own use—is made clearer in

Measure for Measure, and forms, in the moral development of Angelo and Isabella, the main drift of the serious thought. With the exception of *The Tempest,* this is Shakespeare's only play in which a character is allowed to play God. The Duke Vincentio is in complete control, directing all events, knowing the consequences of each person's actions, meting out deserts, and aware, like divinity, of unspoken thoughts and instincts. His rôle as an omniscient and unerring force keeps him from being convincing as a character, and tends to turn the drama into a morality play. Or into a "problem" play in which this Duke of dark corners sets a number of problems as experiments which various characters must work out for their own salvation. The Duke prefers the laboratory to the lecture-room. Shakespeare returns to his convictions that experience is the best teacher; that painful experience may be deliberately intensified in order to assure a clearer acknowledgment of error; that realization, remorse, repentance, and a change of heart are inevitable steps in moral betterment; and that only the careless and the stupid, since they lack the heart or brain that divides men from beasts, are beyond recovery.

As with the other comedies of this period of dead center, the play fails as a stage-play because it does not fully translate into credible drama Shakespeare's strong temporary predilections for moral philosophy. The prying and tampering of the Duke arouses some incredulity and resentment when he is considered as a human character. Yet considered as the king-piece in a moral game of chess, his power and impregnable calm is justifiable. His philosophic rôle is forgotten if the play is viewed dramatically as a tragedy with an incompatible comic ending tacked on. After the great clean-up campaign, the disappointed audience is hardly left with a bigger and better Vienna. Raw human nature has not been changed, the brothels still concoct their unsavory stews, and the only difference might appear to be that the two finest natures have "become much more the better for being a little bad." It is not easy for the common reader, and it may not have been easy for Shakespeare, to accept disillusioned laxity and over-ripe tolerance as final answers to emotional struggles and conflicting ideals. In this first major crisis in his writing career, Shakespeare has marked down all his goods and is selling them at a loss. His sense of mercy and forgiveness seems based on the desperate belief that the human materials he is working with are in the main shoddy and flimsy.

This extensive tract on morality—and it is his only play, with the exception of *All's Well That Ends Well,* that contains a moral judgment in the title—was written when Shakespeare's intellect was at its most active, though his ethical sense was not at its most certain. As such, it constructs simultaneous fugues on various themes conceived in terms of dramatic conflict: order versus disorder; humility versus pride in power; courageous spirit versus fearful death; clemency versus law; chastity versus animal instinct. Almost all of these fugues resolve themselves at the close into an ascendancy of the better element maintained by an acknowledgment and acceptance of the worse.

The play opens and closes on the theme of order in government. The Duke will not discourse with Escalus on the properties of government, the nature of his people, Vienna's institutions, or common justice, for in courtly humility he acknowledges that Escalus' science exceeds his own opinions. Vienna needs reform. Again in humility—almost in the confessional, if the play were not so drenched with irony—he admits to a holy friar that with his express knowledge the strict laws have long been sleeping, that

> liberty plucks justice by the nose;
> The baby beats the nurse, and quite athwart
> Goes all decorum, (I, iii, 29–31)

and that it was his fault to give the people scope. He is aware that

> we bid this be done
> When evil deeds have their permissive pass
> And not the punishment.

But also he is aware that politics is the art of compromise, the perpetual settling upon a lesser evil; and when he resumes the government at the end of the play, he imposes no impossible amendments upon frail human nature. He is stern in his punishment of only one character—Lucio. That "fantastic" libertine has accused the Duke of the vice of lechery which, though the Duke is free from it, he nevertheless tolerates in others. It is a malicious charge, not only untrue, but levelled against the authority of the state. Therefore Lucio is married to a punk, for "slandering a prince deserves it." As envisaged in *Troilus and Cressida*, "the specialty of rule" must be preserved, and order in the state must begin with a respect for authority.

But may not authority turn into tyranny simply because it cannot be gainsaid? If Lucio as citizen fails in his respect for the governor, may not Angelo as governor fail in his regard for the subjects? The Duke knows that power corrupts, offering unhampered means to gratify native bents. He knows that in Angelo are the seeds of hypocrisy and self-righteousness. He cites as his last reason for turning over the state to Angelo the desire to observe the effects of power upon him:

> hence shall we see,
> If power change purpose, what our seemers be.

He cannot believe that his puritanical deputy knows his own weaknesses and passions, or that ignorance of them gives him safety and wholeness:

> Lord Angelo is precise,
> Stands at a guard with envy, scarce confesses
> That his blood flows or that his appetite
> Is more to bread than stone.

Angelo must find out for himself the "cunning enemy" within him, though the Duke knows it already. There is something frightening about the suave irony with which the Duke first addresses Angelo. Knowing as he does that Angelo has broken off his engagement with Mariana by giving a false, self-righteous reason, he nevertheless says:

> Angelo,
> There is a kind of character in thy life
> That to th' observer doth thy history
> Fully unfold.

And Angelo, with the rash confidence of the untried idealist, insists:

> Let there be some more test made of my metal
> Before so noble and so great a figure
> Be stamp'd upon it.[15]

Angelo as governor proceeds, then, to enforce the laws in such manner as to his soul seems good. Having no doubts of his own worth, he becomes in truth "the demigod, Authority." So extreme and inflexible is his thinking, that when at length he is shaken by inner convulsions to use power to slake his own appetites, habit still holds him to an uncompromising course. Since his thought has known no temporizing or qualification, there is no choice but for the complete saint to become the complete villain. Isabella threatens to tell the world what man he is, but he replies:

> Who will believe thee, Isabel?
> My unsoil'd name, th' austereness of my life,
> My vouch against you, and my place i' th' state
> Will so your accusation overweigh
> That you shall stifle in your own report
> And smell of calumny. I have begun,
> And now I give my sensual race the rein. (II, iv, 154–60)

He has too little observed the mottlings and marblings of good and evil to make a compromise, and power itself has been the instrument for enlarging both his aspirations and his degradation. He is the perfect doctrinaire and fanatic, who has never known, as the Duke knew, or as Hector states, that

> modest doubt is call'd
> The beacon of the wise, the tent [= probe] that searches
> To th' bottom of the worst. (*Troilus and Cressida*, II, ii, 15–7)

Of all the counterpointed themes in the play, none is handled with more complexity than that of the attitude toward death. The horror of vital instinct in the presence of death, the acceptance of death by reason, the transcendence of death through spirit, even the contempt of death because of ignorance, are all presented. Barnardine never performs his one function in the plot of the play, because he represents so well this last motif of insentience that Shakespeare cannot bear to kill him off. Drunk and in prison, he will not be coaxed to his own execution. "I am sleepy," he says. "I will not consent to die this day, that's certain." In contrast, Claudio's sensitive shrinking from death taxes all of the Duke's eloquence. Vincentio, disguised as a friar, reasons at length on the inconsequentiality of life, which should make death welcome. Superficially, Claudio learns this stoical philosophy, thanks his mentor, and says in somewhat unconvincing paradox:

> To sue to live, I find I seek to die;
> And seeking death, find life. Let it come on.

Yet instinct is more powerful, and when in the same scene he learns that there is a way to escape the grave, he breaks out in the shuddering speech

> Ay, but to die, and go we know not where . . .

which surpasses in horror any of Hamlet's broodings about death, and which lingered in Doctor Johnson's mind on his deathbed. His sister is revolted by Claudio's abject fear, for to a mind as certain of its values as is Isabella's, death is of little importance, and one can believe her when she says:

> O, were it but my life,
> I'd throw it down for your deliverance
> As frankly as a pin. (III, i, 104–6)

This is the attitude toward death in the great tragedies, where spiritual values outweigh a mere continued existence. But it is hardly felt as a certainty in this ambiguous play, where death places the seal on no final decisions. The attitude here is rather that of all the plays of this period—that wise reasoning seldom influences action.

Yet in one almost accidental connection with the subject of fronting death, Shakespeare shows that he has discovered a deep secret of human nature. "Be absolute for death," the Duke says. "Either death or life shall thereby be the sweeter." Knowing that death is inevitable, Claudio can be made to face it. The uncertainties of living or dying constitute the torture. And therefore, after Claudio's lacerating interview with his sister, the Duke shows his subtlest ministration to sick souls in his immediate counsel to Claudio. Angelo's proposal to Isabella is a ruse, he says. "Therefore prepare yourself to death. Do not satisfy your resolution with hopes that are fallible. To-morrow you must die. Go to your knees and make ready." And Claudio is quieted.[16]

Though it is less a moral idea than a rare gift of mind, Shakespeare's compassion for all living things makes him close kin to Francis of Assisi. Barnardine has already been mentioned, whom Shakespeare could not kill off though he figures in the plot solely to furnish a substitute dead body. The very insects rouse Shakespeare's sympathy:

> And the poor beetle that we tread upon,
> In corporal sufferance finds a pang as great
> As when a giant dies. (III, i, 79–81)

Hamlet's most callous and casual remarks over Polonius' dead body are tempered with a pathos which he cannot throttle in his rôle of professional avenger. His "farewell" to the wretched fool does not sound perfunctory, and in death he sees this counsellor as "most still, most secret, and most grave." Compassion extends even to ghosts—"Rest, rest, perturbed spirit!" And there is dignity in the answer of Pompey Bum, grilled by the law as to his profession of bawd in the Vienna brothels: "Truly, sir, I am a poor fellow that would live." The mere shouldering of existence, as well as the common potentialities for corporal or mental suffering, Shakespeare conceives as a bond between men. The sadism and denial that are present in the plays of this bitter period appear far more painful in Shakespeare than in twentieth-century existentialists and naturalists. For to Shakespeare they violated the order of nature.

Society must create and respect a social order of its own, if chaos is not to come again. What should be man's attitude toward man-made law? Angelo is its great defender. He radiates the zealous conviction that the impersonal enforcement of the laws is not only justice but mercy, since it gives to all persons the greatest possible safety and certainty. His arguments are fully and dramatically advanced in one of the great persuasion scenes which show their author at the height of his power.[17] He has a worthy opponent in Isabella, who as her brother Claudio says, has a prosperous art when she will play with reason and discourse. Her arguments are resourceful and varied. Let the fault and not the actor be condemned, she says. Merciful heaven will pardon mortal mercy. The greatest grace of power and ceremony is unforced forgiveness. God, because of the vicarious atonement of Christ, has not in strict judgment penalized man for original sin. The sudden and unexpected enforcement of a sleeping law works an injustice upon the first culprits it catches. Pity has the simplicity of truth, while the sheer exercise of giant strength is tyranny. The authority of man, his apish pride urging him to outthunder Jove, may lead him through ignorance to fantastically criminal judgments against his fellows. Personal judgments, striving toward unrealizable impersonality, are dangerous, since all men are not alike. Yet men are alike in one respect: their common fallibility. Against pride, ignorance, narrowness, and the sheer exercise of power in judging, there is one saving medicine: the awareness in the judge's own bosom of human weakness in the judge.

These are Isabella's arguments for clemency. They are based on the great example of Christ's mercy, on the Biblical precept of "Judge not, that ye be not judged," on the Aristotelian concept that every moral judgment must be unique—"We cannot weigh our brother with ourself"—and on the Shakespearean intuition of common mortal weakness.

Angelo is inflamed to defend his strict ideal. The condemning of a fault while sparing its actor makes justice a travesty and a cipher. Angelo's reverence for the law is such that he would condemn his kinsman, brother, or son: personal considerations must not destroy the structure of justice. Rigid, equal, and prompt enforcement of the laws is the sole means to suppress crime and to minimize future crimes before they arise:

> The law hath not been dead, though it hath slept.
> Those many had not dar'd to do that evil
> If that the first that did th' edict infringe
> Had answer'd for his deed.

And as for pity—

> I show it most of all when I show justice;
> For then I pity those I do not know.

Angelo's conception of impersonal pity—of making a painful decision in the case of one man in order to better the lives of unknown multitudes—is coldly noble. To a moralist of the cast of mind of a Brutus or an Angelo, its arguments are unanswerable. Isabella's own high idealism, in fact, squares with Angelo's arguments. Forced against her will to plead for her brother, she had begun by admitting: "There is a vice that most I do abhor And most desire should meet the blow of justice." Hearing Angelo's first argument, she had exclaimed "O just but severe law!" and had been prepared to give up her intercession.

It is one of Shakespeare's neatest observations on the mixed morals of the world that the sensual, loosely malicious, lawbreaking but warm-hearted Lucio repeatedly urges Isabella to further trials. If it were not for this unprincipled rake, the two idealists would have killed Claudio between them. Quite in keeping with the spirit of these plays also, Angelo's high inflexibility is not changed by Isabella's higher spirit of mercy, but by the sudden rise of his own lust. Instinct cannot be bottled up, and may have its own moral indignation: "Why, what a ruthless thing is this in him, for the rebellion of a codpiece to take away the life of a man!" The lax world of careless pleasure condemns Angelo as unnatural: "This ungenitur'd agent will unpeople the province with continency. Sparrows must not build in his house-eaves, because they are lecherous." And Lucio's moral sketch of Angelo is based on his own knockabout experience: "A little more lenity to lechery would do no harm in him. Something too crabbed that way."

Lucio's morals win the day. When Isabella asks Angelo to

> Go to your bosom,
> Knock there, and ask your heart what it doth know
> That's like my brother's fault,

Angelo knows in his mind that she speaks such sense that his sense breeds with it. She offers him a bribe, and in the bitter dramatic irony of the play Angelo mistakes her virginal prayers for the sensual bribe of her body. "Heaven keep your honour safe!" she says in departing. But Angelo's honor is already lost to heaven and to himself, a carpet in hell for devils to walk on.

The clear purity of Angelo's mind, as he would have it, cannot temporize with temptation. He has no place for it, for he has never been willing to understand or to admit weakness:

> Ever till now,
> When men were fond, I smil'd, and wond'red how.

In his great tragic soliloquy, therefore, he wrestles with the devil and is at once overthrown. Shakespeare is certain that the worsting of a strict idealism, which by nature disregards mixed experience, can result in no compromise but only in its opposite vice or cynicism. Once his principles are shattered, Angelo's habitual intransigence leads him further in villainy than Lucio, for instance, could have conceived or executed. Angelo becomes the consistent sensualist, using his authority to aid his depredations, and his good name to mask them. Murder, treachery, and perjury preserve the bright repute of which habitually he was so proud, and foster the lust which he realizes in horror he cannot control. Like Troilus, Angelo catches fever from the burning intensity of his own ideals, and virtue nourishes a vicious offspring. The last twist of the knife, in his revulsion against himself, comes when he learns that the "cunning enemy" within him feeds upon virtue itself. He is contorted with the desire to have power over virtue through degrading it:

> What dost thou? or what art thou, Angelo?
> Dost thou desire her foully for those things
> That make her good? . . .
> O cunning enemy, that, to catch a saint,
> With saints dost bait thy hook! (II, ii, 173–5, 180–1)

The Duke, of course, could have spared Angelo all this turmoil. But how, save through experience, could the man whose blood was very snowbroth have learned for himself that "Blood, thou art blood!" and that "We are all frail"? Angelo's mental sufferings are allowed to continue without interference.[18] His willed deeds also, though the Duke thwarts them, seem to him to have been carried out. In the long judgment-scene that fills the last act, therefore, he is shamed in public to the bottom of shame, as one by one "these black masks" are stripped from him. Yet the evil acts of his will have been shaped by a greater power to contrary goods: in his own mind, he has deflowered a maid—but she is actually Mariana, his affianced wife. He has broken his word and had Claudio executed—yet Claudio lives. Here is manipulated mercy, marshalled in order that apparent cruelty may prove to be kindness, in the reform of the convinced and convicted sinner. Three times, before the purposed revelation, the Duke melodramatically enforces the lesson of impassive avenging justice:

> We do condemn thee to the very block
> Where Claudio stoop'd to death, and with like haste.
> Away with him!

> You do but lose your labour.
> Away with him to death!

> He dies for Claudio's death.

Once Angelo has been relieved from the intolerable burden of masking his guilt, he rises to something of his former stature in

repentance and self-judgment: characteristically he will not ask
mercy even for himself. To the sympathetic Escalus he says:

> I am sorry that such sorrow I procure;
> And so deep sticks it in my penitent heart
> That I crave death more willingly than mercy.
> 'Tis my deserving, and I do entreat it.

To such a character, deepened and humanized by his experience,
the Duke may safely say: "Well, Angelo, your evil quits you
well," where one cannot tell in its mocking, reproving, and forgiving context whether the verb "quits" means to reward, to take
leave of, to acquit, or all three at once.

Angelo's error and reform are easy to see. More important and
more cunning is Shakespeare's (or the Duke's) treatment of Isabella. In her youth there is a prone and speechless dialect such
as moves men. She is esteemed even by the lewd to be a thing
enskied and sainted, an immortal spirit. Her virginal fire blazes
intensely, and rather than yield her body up to shame,

> Th' impression of keen whips I'ld wear as rubies,
> And strip myself to death as to a bed
> That longings have been sick for.

Yet she, no less than the Duke himself, must abandon the life removed which each has ever loved, for the responsibilities and
relationships of society. Called away from the cloisters of the
votaries of Saint Clare, she is compelled to extenuate the very
vice which is most alien to her own nature. Blood-ties war with
purity in her own mind, as she argues for tolerance of her brother's
incontinence,

> For which I would not plead, but that I must;
> For which I must not plead, but that I am
> At war 'twixt will and will not.

In the battle between lust and chastity that is fought out in
this play, Shakespeare supports neither the libertine nor the
snow-maiden. He holds the balance even. If he admires Isabella's
eager conviction, he can also find fun in the gutters and jails of

Vienna among the bawds and tapsters and dissolute prisoners and fantastics and foolish gentlemen. Though Angelo is impatient at stories that last out a winter night in Russia, his fellow-deputy Escalus listens tolerantly as the low characters tell out to the end their accounts of trivialities, of weaknesses and whorings and quarrels, with Elbow the simple constable acting out in miniature Angelo's authority. The world and the flesh will not be whipped out of them, and have in fact contributed to their warmth and good nature. And though Pompey Bum will be subservient to authority, he knows in his own mind that for all the good counsel that may be given him, "I shall follow it as the flesh and fortune shall better determine." The height of Pompey's reasoning is that the trade of being a bawd would be lawful if the law would allow it.

If the low people are incorrigible simply because they are content to remain low, the higher characters view lust as a dangerous opponent. Isabella's purity guards her own person against the cunning enemy, though Angelo's rigidity and fanaticism are powerless to protect him. The impulsive Claudio, even in prison, is aware of the peril of allowing too much liberty to the devil within us.

> Our natures do pursue,
> Like rats that ravin down their proper bane,
> A thirsty evil, and when we drink, we die. (I, ii, 132–4)

Man must learn to live with the thirsty evil that is by nature within himself and others. The Duke bends all his powers to the task of teaching Isabella this lesson. At the beginning of the play, she finds sensual weakness so repulsive that of her own accord she would have given over the fight for her brother's life, though he sinned merely against the letter of the law and not its spirit. In the middle of the play, still mindful only of her own chastity, she cannot extenuate in any degree Claudio's ignoble pleading to remain alive. Instead, she calls him beast, coward, wretch, and shameless bastard. To a brother condemned to die she says in cold anger:

> Die, perish! Might but my bending down
> Reprieve thee from thy fate, it should proceed.
> I'll pray a thousand prayers for thy death,
> No word to save thee. (III, i, 144–7)

Prayer was not given to man for such hateful purposes, not even in the good cause of personal chastity. The Duke works upon her and teaches her compromise, so that she aids in the plot to substitute Mariana for herself in the assignation with Angelo. She is learning to allow weakness in others, when her own virtue is not at stake. But noble as her position is—"I have spirit to do anything that appears not foul in the truth of my spirit"—she acts within the closed circle of her own pure convictions, more from a sense of duty and principle than from human sympathy.

The Duke reserves his great trial of her altered nature for the last act. He does not allow her to learn that her brother is alive.

> I will keep her ignorant of her good,
> To make her heavenly comforts of despair
> When it is least expected. (IV, iii, 113–5)

The last act is not extraneous. Full of melodramatic reversals and ironies and discoveries, it has been carefully calculated from the beginning. It is a judgment, but even more it is a trial. Isabella in her youthful righteousness and anger loudly pleads for "justice, justice, justice, justice!" But she charges Angelo in vain, and the Duke in his lessoning gives Angelo wormwood to drink—"his integrity stands without blemish"—and says of Isabella: "To prison with her!" Righteousness itself seems powerless. The friar Peter accuses her, and she is led off under guards while the Duke turns the trial over to Angelo himself to be judge of his own cause. As the Duke in his own person leaves the stage, the play relaxes to prose, and before the succeeding movement is over, Escalus himself is willing to second the stern hypocrite Angelo against the combined testimony of Isabella, Mariana, and the Duke disguised as friar. Let the villainous friar and the two trollops be led away to prison! In the scuffle that ensues (where ironically Lucio acts as Angelo's master-at-arms), the Duke stands unmasked and Angelo confesses his shame.

But the Duke's kind complots still remain in part secret, for Isabella's spiritual trial and victory yet lie before her as the most important lesson of the play. Addressing Isabella herself, the Duke makes her directly aware of Angelo's sins—the double violation of sacred chastity, and of promise-breach on which her brother's life depended.

> The very mercy of the law cries out . . .
> 'An Angelo for Claudio! death for death!' . . .
> Like doth quit like, and Measure still for Measure.

He proceeds in his judgments to follow out the title of the play. Mariana pleads in vain. He judges again that Angelo must die. In desperation Mariana turns to her fellow-woman, but the Duke says to them both:

> *Against all sense* you do importune her.
> Should she kneel down in mercy of this fact,
> Her brother's ghost his paved bed would break
> And take her hence in horror.

In the rôle of impassive, reasonable justicer, he disregards Mariana's anguished plea that "They say best men are moulded out of faults," and for the third time lays down the letter of the Mosaic law.

Isabella kneels. It is the culminating gesture of the play. Against all sense, against her personal and familial affections, most of all, against her own high standards of purity, she kneels to a higher quality of clemency firmly based on human sympathy. In pleading for the life of one who would have wronged her and who she still thinks has murdered her brother, perhaps Isabella's greatest sacrifice may be that she is forced to sully her argument with legalistic and even contradictory reasonings. She begs that Angelo's good intents be remembered, but that his bad intents, since in fact they miscarried, be forgotten. Her own intent is unmistakable, and so is Shakespeare's. Her pure anger and hate against her own brother in the middle act has now been turned to a prayer that her enemy be pardoned. Her cold and lonely fire she forces into the words of forgiveness of trespasses. It is a lesson in painful growth, and she speaks not a word more to the end of the play. Shakespeare's silences again are eloquent.

Isabella's kneeling leads to the free pardon of repented infirmities, through Isabella's own free realization that in this naughty world such pardon is a moral need. The work is less a drama than a moral demonstration. To the extent that we have felt Isabella to be a real person, we are touched to see her torn and stretched to fit a larger pattern alien to her own nature.

The play ends with four marriages or hints of marriages. Yet the tune is hardly that of the merry wedding bells of the earlier comedies. Chastity, that lonesome and unsocial virtue, has been revealed as dangerously cold. Concupiscence is a cunning devil, more dangerous and far more prevalent in Vienna than chastity. If there are to be weddings, they are now taken in a graver spirit, with full awareness of the thirsty evil of man's nature. The ideal is "married chastity," which Shakespeare had celebrated in "The Phoenix and the Turtle," the most thoughtfully wrought of all his lyrics, written during this period. Yet Shakespeare's responsible heroes know that such ideals are unrealizable, and their nearest approximations are moulded out of faults. If the moral thought of *Measure for Measure* is more positive than that of the other plays of the dark period, it is nevertheless gloomy enough. We must learn to live with our cunning devils, and the principal moral action of the play is to teach the two idealists, Angelo and Isabella, to square their best thoughts and hopes with practicable existence in a world that cannot be ignored. The title, as the Duke's words and actions make clear time and again, is ironical. The Old Testament morality of an eye for an eye is, in Shakespeare's thought, not measured, but extreme. The title hits closer to the actual play if it is taken as a praising of the Aristotelian mean. Moderation and immoderation are frequent themes, and the hope for man is that measured or temperate action may meet with a like response.

Measure for Measure concludes this period of despair and unrest in Shakespeare's career as an artist. At this turning point it
may be fitting to call attention to the device of symbolism which
Shakespeare uses increasingly from now on, and to a consequent
further limitation of this book. To write on Shakespeare's moral
ideas is to translate them, for purposes of scrutiny, into another
medium. Shakespeare's mode is dramatic, not expository or systematic. Moral ideas for him are always embodied in persons and
actions. Though this book, with some sacrifice of a consistent
style, holds closely to his actual or paraphrased words, and though
it treats his created images as if they were people, the full and
precise impact of his ideas is realizable, of course, only in the
productions or the imaginative readings of his plays. Yet if it is
difficult to discuss his dramatic presentations in connected prose,
it is equally difficult to translate his symbols. A word or idea loses
many of its precise meanings when it is taken out of the rich,
complex, leisurely context of a long drama.

Measure for Measure is a morality play, and its characters take
on added interest from seeming to represent abstract qualities in
addition to counterfeiting human persons. This does not mean
that we should play the naïve game of calling Isabella Chastity,
Claudio Impulse or Instinct, and Angelo Law. How ridiculous
such a game would be may be seen by trying to give a name to the
Duke Vincentio. Is he the Conqueror, as his name suggests? Or
Mercy? Or Temperance? Or Rule? Or Tolerance? Or Experience? Or as some would have it, the spirit of the New Testament?
Nevertheless, Shakespeare, with his ranging speculative mind and
his constant experimenting with the possibilities of verbal expression, was not above playing this game with his subtle self. One of
his tricks of style is to invent mottos—emblems as brief, compact,
and often enigmatic as the posy in a ring.[19] Furthermore, he delighted in writing his gnomic sayings in couplets so stiff and
stilted and archaic that critics have formed the habit of uneasily
attributing them to someone else. Another of his tricks of style
is the repetition of a word, sometimes with "turns" or almost seri-

ous puns that expand and change its meaning; or even more subtly, the development of a theme or idea with variations, allowing new contexts and situations to complicate its significance. In his later plays, he uses repeated words and themes almost as motifs in music, and their symbolism is quite beyond translation into analytical prose.

As a hint, however, and after this long preamble, let us consider merely one idea in *Measure for Measure* by which he gives extension to the character of the Duke of Vienna. The idea is that of grace. Angelo first speaks to the Duke as "always obedient to your Grace's will." Though neither Angelo nor someone who had not previously read the play can know it, the idea is already ironical, for Angelo neither possesses, nor is sympathetic toward, the quality of grace. As the play develops, speech after speech may be read in a double context. It is almost as if Shakespeare were aware of the medieval four-fold meanings of Holy Writ, and were himself writing anagogically, with spiritual import back of literal and allegorical and moral meanings. Or it is as if he were Franz Kafka dramatizing some of the ideas in *The Castle. Measure for Measure* is an experiment in suggestion, the closest Shakespeare comes to embodying divinity. The Duke describes himself:

> I have on Angelo impos'd the office,
> Who may in th' ambush of my name strike home,
> And yet my nature never in the fight
> To do it slander. (I, iii, 40–3)

And Lucio says of the Duke (though Lucio must speak out of character to say it):

> we do learn
> By those that know the very nerves of state,
> His givings-out were of an infinite distance
> From his true-meant design. (I, iv, 52–5)

And the Duke again, after winning repentance from Claudio's affianced Juliet: "There rest. . . . Grace go with you! Benedicite!" [20] The Duke in soliloquy ends the third act in couplets that ally his power with heaven:

He who the sword of heaven will bear
Should be as holy as severe;
Pattern in himself to know,
Grace to stand, and virtue go.

In the fifth act, he becomes more than human, and whatever is said of him for the benefit of the action has overtones also if he is considered as "grace": "Is the Duke gone? Then is your cause gone too." He speaks these words himself, for he can make riddles on his duplicity. Disguised as the friar, he says of the Duke: "His subject am I not, Nor here provincial. My business in this state Made me a looker-on here in Vienna." Angelo, as he takes on, like Oedipus, the questioning that will reveal his own guilt, is aware of some unknown power:

I do perceive
These poor informal women are no more
But instruments of some more mightier member
That sets them on. Let me have way, my lord,
To find this practice out.

And when Angelo's inquisition has resulted in the revelation of his Grace the Duke himself, Angelo can only say:

I perceive your Grace, like pow'r divine
Hath look'd upon my passes! . . .
Immediate sentence then, and sequent death,
Is all the grace I beg.

In his plays, Shakespeare never speaks more seriously of the Christian future life than in the Duke's judgment on Barnardine:

Sirrah, thou art said to have a stubborn soul
That apprehends no further than this world,
And squar'st thy life according. *Thou'rt condemn'd.*
But, for those *earthly* faults, I quit them all,
And pray thee take this mercy to provide
For better times to come.

In their cumulative effect of symbolism, the play is full of lines that elusively suggest the Christian hope, as in the Duke's:

Look, th' unfolding star calls up the shepherd.

Vincentio, then, is more than a human Duke of Vienna. He is a power, an influence, knowing the thoughts of all, and knowing how their agonies may find solution and rest. If he were a common mortal tampering with the lives of other mortals, Shakespeare could not have given him such irresistible beneficence. He speaks of what he represents in the third person, as if he himself were a mere instrument. He is grace beyond the reach of dramatic art, a hint of the Christian mystery which makes "heavenly comforts of despair when it is least expected." When he says to Isabella

for your lovely sake,
Give me your hand and say you will be mine,

we are not witnessing the perfunctory happy ending of a bitter comedy, but the acceptance of a pure human aspiration by a more than mortal power.

Though he gives less attention to writing actable plays, Shakespeare devotes as much skill and thought to picturing the unweeded garden through which for some years he walked as he had devoted to his earlier and happier creations. If fewer people care to walk in the unweeded garden, it is because they choose to ignore one aspect of human experience, when things rank and gross in nature possess it merely. The picture, of course, is partial—only one mood or station in Shakespeare's development. Shakespeare does not avoid smelling the lilies that fester; he does not avoid unpleasant reality for the sake of comfort. In fact, he finds relief in intensifying his apprehension of imperfection, weakness, and evil.

The old elements are there, but the wheel of Fortune has turned, and everything is viewed from the other side of the circle. Evil, which had been powerless to hurt in the comedies, and which had gradually faded out of the history plays, is now seen as a strong, sharp reality, while the good in man is powerless. Weakness is the common denominator for all men. The state falls to pieces, or persists thinly after dangerous quakes and cataclysms.

The specialty of rule is neglected, so that the selfish and the brutal rise up. The baser conquers the better: Achilles overcomes Hector, Diomed supplants Troilus, Claudius reigns in the place of the brother he has murdered. The foul-mouthed railer, the squealer, the goatish "poor fellow that would live," the panderer—these live on; but Caesar and Brutus and King Hamlet and Hector and the noble fathers in *All's Well*—these are dead. Lecherers and traitors are of necessity forgiven, else the world would speedily be unpeopled. Some of the plays end "happily," or at least in a quiescence after fever, a period of recuperative order. But the forgiveness of faults is close to a tolerance born of despair and exhaustion; and stability seems a temporary hour of rest after the weak and wicked are shocked for a moment by the consequences of their actions.

In the most intensely realized scenes, even the best characters yield to ignoble instinct, and brightness falls from the air. The idealistic Brutus is moved unknowing by the whisper of flattery; Hamlet gashes others and himself in his desperation; Bertram thrives on mental cruelty; Hector's wisdom bows to Troilus' proud, passionate, vengeful "honor"; philosophical resignation in Claudio turns to heart-shaking fear; justice in Angelo becomes lust; and sisterly sympathy in Isabella flames into a cold excommunicating anger that masks as most chaste virtue. Brutus, Hamlet, Helena, Troilus, Angelo wound themselves, almost as masochists.

Love becomes a garden for desecration and monstrosities—Gertrude and Claudius, the mad Ophelia, Cressida and Diomed, Helen and Paris, Bertram and Diana, Angelo and his midnight mistress—yes, and Lavatch and Isbel the woman, Lucio and Kate Keepdown, Pandarus and Pompey Bum and Froth and Mistress Overdone and Abhorson the executioner and all the little flies about the syrup, Masters Rash, Caper, young Dizie, Deepvow, Copperspur, Starvelackey, Dropheir, Forthright, Shoetie, wild Halfcan, "all great doers in our trade." What remains for such good wives as Andromache and Portia but to keep silent or die? Of the main love affairs and marriages that take place in these plays, one is adulterous, one is broken off by a prying father and results in madness and suicide, a hard-won mistress is lost to a man contemptuous of all women, four are solemnized because of previous sexual intercourse, and one is convincing only if taken on the symbolic level.

Disguise in love had been a happy game in the early comedies, the better to display the gallantry of the young lords of Navarre, the wit of Rosalind, the wifely devotion of Portia, or the tender renunciation of Viola. But here, in *All's Well* and *Measure for Measure*, it is a trick to lure lustful men into a trap, and the dark of night shrouds the rats that ravin down their proper bane. In all these plays, every character treads upon the quicksands of deceit, and even the happy conclusions are patched up by lies.

The canker eats up the rose. Unity and brotherhood are broken, beauty and love destroyed. In the earlier comedies, Sylvia is wise and fair, and all our swains commend her. Now a dejected Mariana hears a song at the moated grange: lips are forsworn; eyes mislead; kisses, though the seals of love, are sealed in vain. The lover and his lass, that once o'er the green cornfield did pass, now walk in an unweeded garden, and hear Ophelia's song of Saint Valentine's day, or Pandarus' tickling ditty of "ha! ha! he!" The wise Ulysses knows: "This place is dangerous, The time right deadly. I beseech you go."

This is not a ship of fools, but worse. It is a great prison-ship, where the galley-slaves at the oars are pale husks of enervated virtues, cruel fanatics, stinking whoremongers, frail pieces of femininity, surly brutes, hysterical weaklings, scurvy railing knaves, butchers, lecherers, hypocrites, sadists, and traitors. Its destination is not even made certain by sure destruction. The injurious gods may wish to respite us "a life whose very comfort is still a dying horror."

Is this a true image of human life, not a complete but a true image? If it is not, then Shakespeare knows less of nature than generations have given him credit for. "Put not yourself into amazement how these things should be. All difficulties are but easy when they are known." Without this dark image of horror, which persisted in his mind for years, Shakespeare would never have been competent to write the great tragedies.

CHAPTER FIVE

The Dark Tower

TO SPEAK of Shakespeare's moral ideas when he is at the height both of his emotional and dramatic powers is a baffling attempt at paraphrase. In the first place, are we speaking of emotion, or will, or conscience, or intellect? In Shakespeare's thought they tend to merge with each other and operate in harmony, except in those characters where an inner conflict constitutes in itself a moral flaw. In the second place, Shakespeare has grown aware that ethical conviction is a part of every human action—the awareness itself constitutes a basic ethical conviction of his own—and in consequence neat moral tags, set apart and pointed at with arrows, cannot easily contain convincing truths.[1] When they occur, to crystallize or sum up an experience, he clothes them in emblematic and Delphic language, so that their overtones and suggestions reverberate. Sometimes he will formulate an idea as a simple character—Belch, Shallow, Miranda—but this is not usual; and when such ideas-or-characters occur they are hypotheses that work out their meanings in conflict with other hypotheses, and are given validity by relationships to other thoughts. His moral awareness is expressed less through articulated ideas than through intuitions, or instincts based on experience, or speculations, or assumptions, or actions taken by unique and complete individuals in particular circumstances because their characters make other actions improbable.

In the third place, Shakespeare's dramatic skill makes it increasingly difficult to distil pure moral ideas from his plays. In the attempt, something of their essential quality departs, and the observations of this chapter are inadequate until they have been restored to their actual life in the drama. For Shakespeare dealt with men in action. He had mastered triumphantly the playwright's skill of embodying his thought. The succeeding chapters, then, must of necessity talk of ideas as if they were people, and people as if they were ideas. It must nevertheless be remembered that although Shakespeare's thought is incarnate in his imagined personalities, almost none of his characters (and the exceptions are minor figures) can be held to one simple conception or trait. His theory of art, moreover, was naturalistic; so that since men seldom talk like systematic moralists or analytic philosophers, his characters seldom talk so either.

Although we may admit that Shakespeare's characters usually do not explain themselves with blunt directness, as do Dryden's or Corneille's, and that his plays do not contain formal choruses that comment on and judge the action from a position apart, as in classical drama, nevertheless Shakespeare was conscious of his art. Form explains content. More precisely—it is his naturalistic theory at work again, which he held most surely and practiced most successfully while he was at the height of his powers—form and content are inseparable in his drama as they are in life. Not only, then, in the characters that give the illusion of breathing, but also in the plotting, the proportions, the repetitions and contrasts, the echoes in foreshadowing and retrospect, the developing movements and the firm controlling structures, the resolutions that have been present from the beginnings, the gradual expansion, the deliberate unfolding of theme, the shaping toward a conclusion—in all of the devices of technique and form his moral thought is implicated and made to shine. Shakespeare brooded over his statement, "The end crowns all." In the light of his dramatic work, it is difficult to decide whether "end" is better taken as the formal conclusion of the plot, or the moral purpose of the playwright.

In the period of the tragedies of *Othello*, *Lear*, and *Macbeth*, Shakespeare's thought is as certain and complete as his art. The thought cannot satisfactorily be extracted or paraphrased, merely because it is implicit, not explicit. Its complex fidelity to experience resists the expositor and the anatomist.

In comparison with the great tragedies, all of Shakespeare's earlier plays appear partial in their outlook. The symphony of his career now shows in retrospect that two complete and contrasting movements have been played to conclusion. In the first, he gradually attained and expressed his unquestioning confidence and trust in man's godlike qualities and possibilities. The second movement, in sudden clashing contrast, shatters such smiling and harmonious consort with cacophony and discord. It is a dance of death and the devils, in which the dominant repeated images are of disease and decease, gluttony and animality and disorder. A surgeon probes festering mortality, only to find that a dram of evil quenches all noble substance, that some vicious mole of nature corrupts, through one defect, man's purest grace and infinite virtue.

The first movement lacks ultimate greatness because of its innocence of evil. The second, which so cunningly and knowingly explores the base and the cruel, fails because of its bitter despair of man. Now the great third movement swells up, seeing man open-eyed; at once involved in and above his destiny; giving, sympathizing and controlling; and rising to the tragic view in the simultaneous awareness of man's almost infinite weaknesses and infinite possibilities.

The informing moral certainty of this period is that man creates his fate. Shakespeare had played with the idea earlier, and selected examples might show that the fault lies not in our stars but in ourselves. But in the earlier comedies and tragedies, the order of the world is given, and men fit into the pattern of propitious or malignant planets; in the plays of the dark period, though evil works freely in man, his power for good is atrophied, and the characteristic figures of Hamlet, Troilus, and Angelo struggle in vain until chance or an outside power, if they are to be released at all, sets them free. Hamlet's impotence leads to a sluggish determinism: "If it be now, 'tis not to come; if it be not to come, it will be now. . . . But it is no matter." But when he writes the later tragedies, Shakespeare knows, to change Emerson's motto, that fate is the shadow of a man, and not even Iago or Edmund blames his actions on the universe—or on our modern equivalents for fate: heredity and environment, glands and the economic order.

That haunting line spoken by the Duke of Vienna, "Look, th' unfolding star calls up the shepherd," implies that the gradual revelation of dawning light wakens a protector, and that the sheep, whether in their homely folds or in a brighter and wider world, are watched by their pastor. Now Shakespeare abandons for a time the gracious Christian hint, and in his deepest thought, the sheep become their own shepherds.

OTHELLO

In his dramatic work, Shakespeare comprehends all of nature and man, but almost completely ignores anything beyond or above man. Whether because he did not know, or doubted, or felt that the matter was outside the limits of the dramatic art of his time, when it comes to thoughts of God he is at one with Mistress Quickly: "I hop'd there was no need to trouble himself with any such thoughts yet." His thought remains consistently within the confines of humanity. The Seven Deadly Sins will not be accepted categorically, but observed as they strike his own experience. In the warmth of his magnanimous nature, Avarice and Envy (in spite of Shylock and Iago) are too limited and cold to merit his full attention. To his generous instinct (and again in spite of Lear and Coriolanus), Anger appears a natural excess, which like Gluttony may often be little more than a harmless or amusing foible. The hierarchy of men might almost be set up by considering how far each overcomes spiritual sloth, but Sloth is universal, and—perhaps it can be said without disrespect— alternates with Anger in Shakespeare himself, to upset the moral balance of his writings in the dark period. As for Pride, Shakespeare is aware of it in all of its forms, from the ludicrous to the cancerous. Choosing as he pleases among the Deadly Sins and the Ten Commandments, he goes further and sets up vices of his own: faithlessness above all, or fanaticism, or slander.

Yet his parade of the vices is neither so ordered nor so complete as that to be found in Dante's *Inferno*. The colder vices of the intellect, or man's rebellions against divinity, do not much interest him. Dante and Shakespeare are agreed on one point: in consigning to the lowest circle of Hell the traitors, those who strike against the divine order of love that binds the world and all its manifestations together in unity and stability.[2]

They are agreed also that love moves the world. Shakespeare's portrayal of the vices is less varied than Dante's because his conception of love is more limited: in Shakespeare love always exists in, or grows from, a personal relation between human beings. Such human love authenticates individual virtue, gives meaning to the brotherhood of man, makes possible society, the state, even learning and the arts, and is the guerdon that rewards fair living. This humanized conception of love, narrower than Dante's, and building on mortal materials whose frailty could not be denied, explains Shakespeare's extraordinary preoccupation with the last of the deadly sins (and to Dante one of the least)—the sin of Lust. Shakespeare sees it as the enemy and travesty of love, the destroyer of faith and brotherhood, the lechery that eats up itself in neverending torment, a disease compounded of gluttony and pride and selfishness. In one sense the Ahriman and Ormazd of his moral cosmos are lust and love, which show themselves at times in other forms: destruction and hope, hatred and charity, the desire for domination and the desire for integration, power and abnegation, cruelty and conciliation, brute matter and spirit, the burning heat and the calm light, the canker and the rose, discord and music, chaos and cosmos, death as a fever's end and death as union. In the mystery of sex, Shakespeare's moral thought expands one of its great metaphors in endless variations, and a single play will view the same subject-material as the old black ram tupping the white ewe or "I saw Othello's visage in his mind," as the monstrous beast with two backs or as freedom and bounty between two spirits.

Quite in line with his progression, therefore, after taking sex as a principal material in the four preceding plays of *All's Well That Ends Well, Hamlet, Troilus and Cressida,* and *Measure for Measure* (and indeed in the comedies before them), he uses sexual jealousy and exaltation to display in *Othello* his first comprehensive and unwavering mastery of the love-lust motive.

The following analysis does not assume that Shakespeare constructed his mature plays synthetically. Probably he did not. What it does assume is that his guiding thoughts were so clear and certain that they afford the materials for such analysis, whether they took shape in the play through conscious formula or instinctive tact. It assumes also that the value of the moral ideas lies less in their novelty (for an idiosyncratic morality is probably a false one) than in that full concrete actualization that carries the conviction of witnessed truth.

Consciously or unconsciously, Shakespeare changes the original story in Cinthio always toward brighter moral illumination. Four points in the earlier story might be mentioned. (1) In Cinthio, Iago is given conventional motives that to some extent justify his enmity. (2) Iago is a family man whose small child helps him to steal the handkerchief. (3) Iago murders Desdemona at Othello's command. (4) Emilia is aware throughout of her husband's villainy, and in fact tells Cinthio's story. As the rest of this discussion should make clear, each change increases the moral significance and coherence of Shakespeare's tragedy. If such shaping is thoughtless, then we are forced to conclude that Shakespeare's instinct is the luckiest among all literary artists.

A more demonstrable conclusion, however, is that Shakespeare gave the drama deliberate form. One of his purposeful designs was to conceal his art. Close analysis establishes this rule: The structures of Shakespeare's plays indirectly enforce, or even create, moral significance. This is true not only in the larger patterns but in the minute devices of verbal technique. Particularly cunning is his development of an idea naturally—in divided and casual and partial observations—rather than as a set sermon.

"Goats and monkeys!" Othello exclaims, as he precipitately leaves the stage after striking Desdemona. But no one except the ambassadors on the stage can mistake this ejaculation for mere madness. The lecherous animality of Othello's suspicions has been prepared for: Othello has said that when he turns his soul to jealousy, let him be exchanged for a goat; Iago has said that the actual witnessing of the copulation of deceitful mortals is impossible even when they are prime as goats, hot as monkeys; in another action which Othello overhears, Cassio varies the idea by calling his light mistress a monkey.

In the great persuasion scene that poisons Othello's mind, Iago blames himself for voicing his doubts, "for too much loving you," and Othello replies: "I am bound to thee for ever." This horrible and ironical truth is reinforced a quarter of an hour later, in the last line of the scene: Othello, kneeling, has vowed revenge; and Iago, also kneeling, has seconded the vow, rising to his feet as Othello's proclaimed lieutenant. His last words are: "I am your own for ever."

The same idea is fitted to differing circumstances. "Put money in thy purse!" Iago ten times repeats to Roderigo—for to Iago the material world is the real world, and money buys anything. When the dishonored Cassio laments that he is hurt past all surgery in having lost his reputation, Iago sarcastically reproaches him with: "As I am an honest man, I thought you had receiv'd some bodily wound. There is more sense in that than in reputation." These earlier scenes add the last rich drop of gall in Iago's comforting sermon to Othello:

> Who steals my purse steals trash; . . .
> But he that filches from me my good name
> Robs me of that which not enriches him
> And makes me poor indeed.

The idea has been made three-dimensional; and the final situation, now that we know Iago's real thoughts, has proceeded through the looking-glass into a further dimension where words mean the opposite of what they say.

The same image may be used for contrasting emotions. Excess of feeling stops Othello's heart. Reunited to Desdemona after the storm, he says:

> I cannot speak enough of this content;
> It stops me here; it is too much of joy.

Yet lost to her in his certainty of her faithlessness, deciding that she shall not live, he says: "No, my heart is turn'd to stone. I strike it, and it hurts my hand." And finally, in the fatal bedchamber, the two opposed ideas of holiness and murder combine with a recurrence of the same image:

> thou dost stone my heart,
> And mak'st me call what I intend to do
> A murther, which I thought a sacrifice.[3]

An idea finds its image, the image is repeated and tied to other images or contrasted with them, until the clusters and chains and oppositions are rich with suggestion. The images of heaven and hell are dominant in this play even more than in *Measure for Measure*, from conventional references up the whole scale to Othello's vengeful vow "by yon marble heaven," or his almost religious meditation overheard by "you chaste stars!" or his unexpected, dazed staring at Iago's feet to see if they are cleft hoofs:

> I look down towards his feet—but that's a fable.
> If that thou be'st a devil, I cannot kill thee.

Appetite, the universal wolf that last eats up itself in *Troilus and Cressida*, becomes here the "green-ey'd monster, which doth mock the meat it feeds on," the "monster begot upon itself, born on itself." The images of the monster "too hideous to be shown," of poison, of magic and charms, of fire, could be illustrated in a whole chapter. They serve to make jealousy not a moral counter but a *lived experience*.[4]

Often an image on one man's lips is caught up with multiplied impact at a later point. Iago says to himself in the middle of the play:

> The Moor already changes with my poison.
> Dangerous conceits are in their natures poisons
> Which at the first are scarce found to distaste,
> But with a little act upon the blood
> Burn like the mines of sulphur.

At the end the burning suffocation of the pit returns in the images of Othello's realization of his crime:

> Whip me, ye devils,
> From the possession of this heavenly sight!
> Blow me about in winds! roast me in sulphur!
> Wash me in steep-down gulfs of liquid fire!

Perdition has caught his soul.

Shakespeare's planting of an idea is as cautious and cunning in its plotting as is Iago's. Where did we first hear such words as Iago speaks to Othello in the temptation scene? "Look to 't. . . . She did deceive her father, marrying you." They echo the bitter counsel of Desdemona's father in the first act:

> Look to her, Moor, if thou hast eyes to see.
> She has deceiv'd her father, and may thee.[5]

The caustic words of Desdemona's father, that first dashing of Othello's confidence, have lingered, or may have lingered, in Othello's mind from the beginning.

"The art of drama is the art of preparation," said Dumas *fils*. How naturally Shakespeare introduces Desdemona's gentle chiding of Othello for refusing to grant her suit in aid of his own friend Cassio!

> I wonder in my soul
> What you could ask me that I should deny
> Or stand so mamm'ring on. (III, iii, 68–70)

She leaves the stage with sweet words whose overtones are ominous: "Be as your fancies teach you. Whate'er you be, I am obedient." Yet the hint is enough to prepare us for her unquestioning obedience in the hideous scene where after striking her and ordering her from his sight, he calls her back obedient—the word is repeated four times—to turn and turn and weep and weep in silence before the shocked ambassadors. Desdemona's obedience—"Look 't be done!"—leads her without retort to a bed, laid with her wedding sheets, that she knows in her soul will be her death-bed.

A spiritual numbness succeeds upon (and also precedes) a dreadful deed, an interim between acting and feeling that is like a phantasm or a hideous dream. Brutus had stated the truth openly; in *Othello* it is twice presented more subtly. When Othello acts out his foul imaginings within their room, addressing Desdemona as that cunning whore of Venice, and quitting Emilia with bawd-money for fulfilling the office opposite to Saint Peter at the gate of hell, Emilia asks her mistress how she does. The answer is as pathetic as any speech in Shakespeare:

> Faith, half asleep.

Desdemona's succeeding speeches are trancelike. Yet even this dramatically realized seizure of a state of the soul is more directly stated than in the scene for which it acts as preparation—Othello's state of mind immediately after he smothers Desdemona. Here he is distracted, forgetful, numbed, alternately brooding upon the meaningless handiwork before him and answering to the knocking at the door.

Deceit enters the play through other characters than Iago, and when innocence or policy falls to lies in little things, how can one be sure of truth in the greater issues? Thus, in a single scene, that turns upon a small web of silk, Emilia lies in saying that she does not know where Desdemona has lost it, Othello lies in asking for it because he has a salt and sorry catarrh, and Desdemona lies in saying that it is not lost. With such preparation, when Emilia tells Othello the blazing truth of Desdemona's honesty and virtue, how can Othello know the face of truth from its mask?

She says enough; yet she's a simple bawd
That cannot say as much. This is a subtle whore,
A closet lock and key of villanous secrets;
And yet she'll kneel and pray; I have seen her do 't.

The play is a portrayal of perdition and chaos, yet the ideas are introduced innocently, smilingly. "Excellent wretch!" Othello says to Desdemona as he yields to her warm sympathy for Cassio,

Perdition catch my soul
But I do love thee! And when I love thee not,
Chaos is come again. (III, iii, 90–2)

The "perdition" of the handkerchief draws forth that one word once more; chaos comes again, represented in action, in the broken phrases that precede Othello's epileptic trance, a scene that is framed structurally by two others that lead Othello (loving her not) in chaotic words to the very brink of uncontrollable seizure.

Othello's end is in his beginning; the start and finish of the play look toward each other; and structure gives the drama its moral certainty. "My life upon her faith!" Othello exclaims in the first act; and in the last, sacrifices his life to a faith Desdemona has never lost. "If it were now to die, 'Twere now to be most happy," he says to Desdemona when they are reunited in perfect love after the storm; and there, for the first time, words are given to the idea that fills his final couplet:

I kiss'd thee ere I kill'd thee. No way but this—
Killing myself, to die upon a kiss.

This extended consideration has been given to technique and structure because the value of Shakespeare's moral ideas comes precisely from the conscious certainty and the deliberate skill with which he gives them convincing forms. The building of the characters that embody his thought is no less deliberate, though he has left less scaffolding and ornament to show the lines of his structure.

Iago is a vision of evil. To make the source of evil plain, to make its destructive effects incontrovertible, Shakespeare endows his character with fine qualities. Iago is consistent, certain, of strong vitality, brave, active, with a close and accurate knowledge of the workings of the human mind. These are all admirable traits, and Shakespeare admires them all. There seems little more to be desired. Iago believes that reason can and should lead the will to action, and that reason and the will control our otherwise wild passions. He says: " 'Tis in ourselves that we are thus or thus. Our bodies are our gardens, to the which our wills are gardeners. . . . The power and corrigible authority . . . lies in our wills. If the balance of our lives had not one scale of reason to poise another of sensuality, the blood and baseness of our natures would conduct us to most prepost'rous conclusions. But we have reason to cool our raging motions, our carnal stings, our unbitted lusts." These are the sentences of a moral philosopher to whose thought few would take exception.

Where, then, is the fault? His glorification of the will and of action for its own sake may seem dangerous: he plumes up his will joyfully; he finds that in his schemes "pleasure and action make the hours seem short." His selfishness is more dangerous. He admires men who do themselves homage. "These fellows have some soul; And such a one do I profess myself." Yet selfishness and pride, though they prevent their possessors from holding a complete view of the world, are in some form necessary for practical action, and may be mixed in the characters of those whom Shakespeare admires.

Actually, Iago is conceived as an outcast from society; and on this sole conception and the reasons for it, Shakespeare builds his image of evil in this play. To do so, Shakespeare carefully strips away any normal or conventional reasons for Iago's hatred. To be sure, Iago mentions enough of them—that he deserves the place given to Cassio, that he loves Desdemona, that he suspects Othello with his wife, or Cassio with his wife. His reasons are too many to be convincing. He introduces them casually, parenthetically, or admits to himself that they are unfounded: "I know not if 't be true; Yet I, for mere suspicion in that kind, Will do as if for surety." His active mind is merely thinking up excuses to decorate a fixed instinct of hate. He says that "It is thought abroad" that Othello and Emilia have abused him; yet knowing the two, we know that the general suspicion is a product of Iago's solitary mind, unfounded jealousy and restlessness gnawing his inwards. "Knowing what I am, I know what she shall be," he says of the spotless Desdemona. Since there is no evidence whatever for any of his imagined reasons for revenge, they all become parts of his disease, which is inner and personal.

He accepts the fact that he is not a part of society, and indeed glories in it. In his own mind, the fact appears reversed: he has cast society out. As Iago sees it, he alone realizes truth and power, and his simple task is to work out his will in terms which dolts and weaklings will act upon. Like a proud stranger in a stupid land, he learns to speak an alien language more fluently than the natives. Dissimulation is for him a mere translation of his actual thoughts into the braying of asses. By a simple perversion of his values, he can make himself understood. When he calls on "Divinity of hell!" we have no lost desperate soul, but a successful man. With the sincerity of William Blake, he inverts heaven and hell, and worships, since he pleases, the devil. Honesty is for knaves who should be whipped, but because the fools are obsequiously shackled to their honesty, Iago will play the ass himself, and seem the most honest of them all. This is not hypocrisy so much as it is a game, the amusement of a clever man among fools.

Remarks that would seem ordinarily to be naïve dramatic writing—compelling a character to damn himself as no one would do in actual life except a professional lost soul—are calculated expressions of Iago's self-satisfaction, delivered in a language where normal values are upside down. When Iago says "The Moor is of a free and open nature," his exact description springs neither from praise nor envy. Free and open, generous and trusting, are merely the translated words in a foreign tongue for what he recognizes as stupidity. Iago makes his contempt for such qualities clear in the lines immediately succeeding:

> That thinks men honest that but seem to be so;
> And will as tenderly be led by th' nose
> As asses are. (I, iii, 406–8)

He does not see his own situation as grovelling or pitiable or sordid or damned. Such lines as: "Knavery's plain face is never seen till us'd," or: "Hell and night Must bring this monstrous birth to the world's light," are exultant. Since his divinity is hell, the black words plume up his will and translate a thought of positive triumph. He is no King Claudius, no Macbeth. Almost alone among Shakespeare's villains, conscience never stirs his mind. If his nature is that of the wolf or the fox, he will appear like a sheep merely to walk among the flock. His god is two-faced Janus.

The play, then, abounds with remarks in double-talk: the language of the sheep used to express the thoughts of the wolf. When the jealous Othello upbraids Iago for casting these tortures upon him, Iago is delighted to say:

> Take note, take note, O world,
> To be direct and honest is not safe.
> I thank you for this profit; and from hence
> I'll love no friend, sith love breeds such offence.

The words are understandable simultaneously in both worlds. In Iago's own wolfish mind, honesty and love are the weaknesses of ignorance. But to Othello in the world of the sheep, Iago's remarks look like the spontaneous indignation of injured friendly frankness.[6] Or again, as Emilia begins to suspect that some villain has devised the abuse of the Moor, Iago is able to answer in the pure speech of Desdemona: "Fie, there is no such man! It is impossible." His greatest triumph in the field of linguistic duplicity comes when he is brought to bay in public inquisition. Questioned as to what he has said to Othello, he answers:

> I told him what I thought, and told no more
> Than what he found himself was apt and true.

This is literal verity in the worlds both of the sheep and the wolf, yet its meaning is different in heaven and hell.

Iago's manipulation of human beings is based on a consistent and sure analysis. To shift and continue the beast metaphor, he is the lone fox who is clever enough to know that "I never found man that knew how to love himself." The world is full of silly gentlemen who either are sheep, weak-willed, credulous, and trusting in their own whiteness, or are goats and monkeys. Man's nature (except for the cunning outcast such as Iago, watching from the thicket) is simply summed up in the ass, the sheep, and the baboon.

He translates these convictions of human animality with deft certainty. In Roderigo, the ass and the baboon are close to the surface, but with a little cleverness they may be brought out in Othello equally well. Cassio, Emilia, and Desdemona are all easily played upon, because they share the flock's weakness of trust—which translated into Iago's thought is the world's name for asinine stupidity. Cassio's sociability and friendliness rise merely from the gregariousness of the stupid herd, while his inability to face or to refuse strong wine is an animal weakness, a raging carnal unbitted lust that his will cannot control but that Iago can turn to advantage. Emilia's confidence in her husband he translates as ignorance; her obedience is another name for fear; at the end, when she has acquired knowledge, he counts on her silence out of terror and self-interest. Like a puppet-master, he twitches the dolls in his improvised play, busy, excited, and removed.

The exile, then, moves through the world but apart from it. Since he is not involved in its life, he can use that life only for his own pleasure. He will play a game—a kind of roulette where he himself spins the wheel, where the one excitement is danger to himself, and where the stakes of the other players are meaningless and worthless to him. This, then, is the secret cause of his evil actions: he is not a part of humanity because he cannot understand in its terms any of its social conceptions. He treats people as objects, as mechanical toys whose clockwork he is familiar with. Endowed with almost all the other admirable qualities, he is disastrously blind to the meaning of good in any form. Completely ignorant as to what love or sacrifice or generosity or spirit or grace might mean, he cuts himself off from men, and uses for his own ends that part of human nature which he knows well. But since he knows only himself, or his own base nature in others, he is tortured continually—"annoyed" might be a better word for his emotional scope—by a phantasmagoria whose motivation is to him sheer silliness. Cassio has a daily beauty in his life that makes Iago ugly; the Moor is of a constant, loving, noble nature. These are the thoughts that explain his hatred, as resentment against injustice, or sexual jealousy, or any of his trumped-up rationalizations, cannot explain it. They show his instinctive unrest before natures he cannot understand. Beauty and nobility are words of irritated contempt in his language, meaningless counters that must be violated into significance. Since his proud reason and solitary will are to him the meaning of life, he will force these puppets, jerking to emotions he finds intolerably ununderstandable, to act out his interpretations and his will. Desdemona's virtue shall be turned to pitch; her own goodness shall make the enmeshing net; she shall be made to kneel in supplication to him; and in an orgasm of triumph, he shall compel Othello to act as his agent for the destruction of the valueless world of noble spirit: "Do it not with poison. Strangle her in her bed, even the bed she hath contaminated." His soul's joy finds absolute delight only in the bending and subjugating of others to his own will. It is a lust of the spirit.

Iago's hideous ignorance of all noble human possibilities is balanced in this tragedy by an antithetical ignorance. The scene is Cyprus after the storm. To beguile the time of anxiety concerning Othello's safety, Desdemona asks her protector to make up little rhymes. It is a scene of waiting, not of action; it serves only to set apart the characters of Iago and Desdemona. His task is to describe woman in all possible combinations of fair and foul, wise and foolish. In the double irony of his honesty, his cynicism folding back upon itself until foul speaking may appear a virtue, Iago degrades woman to the bottom of his own thoughts. They are all frail and lascivious, changing the cod's head for the salmon's tail. The idea of a deserving woman is a fairy story about a person (if ever there were such a person) fit to suckle fools and chronicle small beer.

But Desdemona is not to be taken in by his lame and impotent conclusion. She believes that his debased convictions are the actual fairy stories—old fond paradoxes to make fools laugh in the ale-house. She takes what seems truth to him as the assumed cynicism of the rough camp, which strengthens her trust in Iago's underlying honesty. And in the ignorance of her purity, she turns his revelations aside with a laugh.

Desdemona's purity is her own peril. She is blind to the possibilities of suspicion and jealousy in human nature. In her intercession for Cassio, she acts with such bounteous impulse as even without Iago's prodding might well have roused a questioning in the mind of anyone but a completely trustful lover. In scenes that counterpoise those of Iago's self-revelation, she cannot utter the very word of whore; and trying to conceive a woman that might betray her husband for the whole world, she says: "I do not think there is any such woman." Her heavenly innocence is undeniably a partial blindness; and some admixture of worldliness in her nature might have kept her from the sacrificial bed. In Desdemona and Iago, heaven and hell are purely realized. And though they are a universe apart, they exist simultaneously in the indivisible warp and woof of a single world, so that

> the spacious breadth of this division
> Admits no orifex for a point as subtle
> As Ariachne's broken woof to enter.
> (*Troilus and Cressida*, V, ii, 150–2)

Heaven and hell exist in interaction in Othello's own mind. The terrible middle movement of the play shows the devil in Othello, and there is no need to dwell here on Iago's apt pupil. It is more in proportion to emphasize the pity of what has been destroyed, or to consider whether in the last summing up, nobility has been destroyed at all.

The crumbling of a great man, "he that was Othello," is made almost pathetically vivid—in the famous farewell to his own occupation of glorious war, in the attempt to carry on his duties, to read the letter from Venice or welcome the ambassadors while every word is tormented by repeated goads of suspicion. His very speech and thought crumble into chaotic fragments. Yet resigning his soldiership and statesmanship cannot lessen his personal torment, nor can he hold in concentration to his self-assigned rôle of honor's avenger. The cruelty of the mood in which he flagellates Desdemona as a whore dissolves unexpectedly into intense pathos. He breaks down and weeps, and we learn the last secret of his agony: that he, too, is an exile, an outcast from love. In some place of his soul he could have borne all afflictions, even the scorn of being a cuckold.

> But there where I have garner'd up my heart,
> Where either I must live or bear no life,
> The fountain from the which my current runs
> Or else dries up—to be discarded thence.

And as the rose-lipped cherubim of patience turns its aspect to the grimness of hell, in lines that are almost intolerable he kills the thing he loves:

> O thou weed,
> Who art so lovely fair, and smell'st so sweet
> That the sense aches at thee, would thou hadst ne'er been born!

Tragedy could not have reached such pitch if the heaven that is renounced had not been realized to the utmost. Love, therefore, is presented as the generous communion of soul with soul, unsullied and unshakable.[7] The whole of the first act, which is not suggested in the original story, Shakespeare invents very largely to afford dramatic cause and full scope for the high pleadings of both Othello and Desdemona as they describe their mutual love, so that his romantic nobility and her womanly tenderness meet in "such fair question as soul to soul affordeth," and virtue possesses such "delighted beauty" that it can make a black skin fair.

The first scene of the second act continues to build the high tower. In symbolic foreshadowing of the main action, the lovers

are reunited after "foul and violent tempest." "O my soul's joy!"
Othello exclaims with Desdemona in his arms,

> If after every tempest come such calms,
> May the winds blow till they have waken'd death!
> . . . I fear
> My soul hath her content so absolute
> That not another comfort like to this
> Succeeds in unknown fate.

Iago, looking on, swears to set down the pegs that make such
music. Some Shakespearean music, however, is so nearly celestial
that tampering fingers cannot touch its strings, and of all of the
characters in the play, Desdemona is the only one who could have
said with perfect truth: "I am your own for ever."

Before the destruction of the final tempest, therefore, Shakespeare takes care to reiterate his theme of unalterable love in two
great speeches by Desdemona:

> Unkindness may do much;
> And his unkindness may defeat my life,
> But never taint my love. (IV, ii, 150–64)

Preparing for her deathbed, Desdemona answers Emilia's wish
that she had never seen Othello with:

> So would not I. My love doth so approve him
> That even his stubbornness, his checks, his frowns
> (Prithee unpin me) have grace and favour in them.

Her love is of a charity so rare that it may extend beyond itself,
and even as she and Emilia and Iago speculate as to whether some
villain has led Othello to imagining his home a brothel, Desdemona says: "If any such there be, heaven pardon him!"

It is the steadfast star of her love that prepares us to believe in
her dying victory. Othello may strangle her, but cannot kill her
love. In the final trance she knows herself falsely murdered, yet
guiltless. This is actual truth. But love transcends the actual.
Her ultimate words transmute his cruelty into kindness, and, in
this play of deceits, tell the last lie to protect her murderer and

her lord. "Who hath done this deed?" cries Emilia, and Desde-·
mona answers:

> Nobody—I myself. Farewell.
> Commend me to my kind lord. O, farewell!

Othello himself, though the tides of hell rise once again and
force him to turn a sacrifice into a murder, is near a heavenly
ecstasy in this scene. In the very smothering, he sees himself as "I
that am cruel am yet merciful." And he had entered her chamber
in almost religious brooding. To the chaste stars he must whisper
his cause: that she must die, else she'll betray more men. The
animal body of the super-subtle Venetian must be given to death
in order that her image in his mind, the ideal Desdemona that once
was, may be preserved. Justice and heavenly sorrow fill his
thoughts, and the needful act makes his tears cruel. The weed
has again become a rose, in this cunningest pattern of excelling
nature, and weeping, he kisses her.

> This sorrow's heavenly;
> It strikes where it doth love.

As she wakes, since he would not kill her unprepared spirit, would
not kill her soul, he begs her to repent and reconcile herself to
heaven and grace.

What salvation is there for the honorable murderer? And what
is the instrument that will bring him to self-realization and repentance? The answer lies in Shakespeare's moral convictions
shaping his material. His earlier despair finds new adjustments and
new proportions. Sometimes the changes are minute: Bertram,
and Hamlet, and Angelo, had wilfully or cruelly or coldly forsaken their loves. Now Desdemona in her trancelike waiting recalls the willow song, sung by her mother's maid called Barbara:

> Let nobody blame him; his scorn I approve.

Barbara too had been forsaken, but not deliberately: "He she
lov'd prov'd mad." Sometimes the changes are major: in *Othello*,
as in *Troilus and Cressida*, the hero witnesses his own betrayal.
But the betrayal of Othello is unreal, his own false imaginings

co-operating with Iago's false machinations. Nothing remains to be done but to bring Othello to his senses, to show him that his love is true.

The agent here—and it is the moralist's most significant change in the original story—is the world itself. In the dark plays, the world was imaged almost as incapable of its own reform. It is not so here. No one could deny that Emilia is of a worldly nature. She is coarse, bawdy, practical, fully aware of the world's imperfections and willing to put up with them easily. She need be, in order to live so cheerfully as Iago's wife! Yet he misjudges her, the one error in his master-plan. When she learns for the first time the details that have brought about her mistress's death, not threats, not the fear of death, not hell itself can stop her mouth. If she had remained quiet, she might have been the first lady of Cyprus. Desdemona is dead, and if honor is a mere word, Emilia's truth-telling can do no good to the tragic loading of that bed. But in the swelling tide of the ending, she speaks out in brave rage to defend the chastity and devotion of her mistress—yes, and to brand a destroying lie for what it is, out of sheer common human revulsion. "So come my soul to bliss as I speak true." Her angry revilings, her passionate loyalty to the dead, her fearless blabbing, cost her her life. But the world breathes again.

The crowning movement is the return of Othello to himself. "O thou Othello that wert once so good, What shall be said to thee?" Othello reverts to his honor. His occupation is no longer gone, and the dignity of his last address,

> Soft you! a word or two before you go.
> I have done the state some service, and they know 't,

recalls the soldierly opening before the Venetian councillors:

> Most potent, grave, and reverend signiors,
> My very noble, and approv'd good masters.

He couples in his memory this last act of justice, the killing of himself, with the defence of the state, when in Aleppo he had killed a slanderous Turk. The last images of India and Arabia restore the chivalric hero of romance, and he dies a soldier.

But there is a more important home-coming than the return to his own pride and purposes. It is the return to love. "Where should Othello go?" he asks in his bewilderment. And as he turns toward the death-freighted bed, from the public to the private world, he is no longer an exile. He knows, now, that Desdemona is not and never has been untrue. In that earlier reunion after tempest, when his heart had stopped with joy in the perfect trust and confidence of his love, he had said: "If it were now to die, 'twere now to be most happy." Repentance and retribution cannot dim his final realization, and the killing expires upon a kiss.

The play has been called a domestic tragedy by classifiers using the wrong end of the opera-glass. The category is apt only if one can believe in the domestication of angels and princes. The "divine Desdemona" falls little short of the angelic order; Othello appears as a great soldier who fetches his life and being from men of royal siege; no housewife makes a skillet of his helm; in the foreground, in tempest and war, is the extended empire of Venice; in the background the vast caves and idle deserts of romance. Evil is magnified, unchanging to the last, in an image which Shakespeare never surpasses for uncompromisingly clear and almost abstract analysis. Yet the play is greater and more comprehensive than its individual greatnesses. And justice and love shine forth clearly at the end.

Othello is a play of perdition—of men and women lost and outcast through ignorance. Iago never escapes from the narrow circle of his blindness to all good. He remains the prisoner of his own warped thoughts, a damned slave to the end. Desdemona, in a sense, refuses to accept the reality of evil. But Othello, who has experienced the whole range of moral feeling, from the salt tempests among which he had been lost comes at last to his heart's harbor. He had built an imagined perfection even in his desolation:

> Nay, had she been true,
> If heaven would make me such another world
> Of one entire and perfect chrysolite,
> I 'ld not have sold her for it. (V, ii, 143–6)

There had been an earlier hypothesis—"If after every tempest
come such calms." He learns that his unhoped-for possibility is
the truth, the exiled wanderer returns, and he is safe in haven.

> Here is my journey's end, here is my butt,
> And very seamark of my utmost sail.

LEAR

In the one play of *Lear*, Shakespeare integrated everything of
serious significance that he had come to believe. It repeats and
magnifies earlier ideas, its height and power rolling in like a
seventh wave against the same shores. In its moral universe—and
even in the development and proportioning of its moral ideas—
Lear resembles *Othello*. The main differences are the greater scale
in *Lear*, and—if it can be said of a tragedy that includes also a
greater quantity of evil—its greater positive and active virtue.

Shakespeare's implicit confidence in a world somehow allied
with good is apparent in the structure of his tragedies as well as
his comedies. In his most typical plays, the action leads to the
gradual dispelling of ignorance, the slow brightening of moral
knowledge or wisdom or love, in the minds of principal characters.
This applies, at least in part, even to the plays of the dark period.
At his best, Shakespeare does not base his ethics either upon a
wilful idiosyncrasy (if he can detect it in himself) or upon
ignorance or limitation or exclusion. He can say with Doctor
Johnson: "There is nothing that I would not rather know than
not know." In the comedies it seems more a conviction than a
convention that the increase of knowledge—usually through
young rebels learning the lesson of love—is rewarded in the world
as well as in the spirit. The English histories may not have convinced Shakespeare that the world grows better through time, but
at least he saw a moral pattern in history, and in his own development wrote plays increasingly certain of the possibilities of stable
responsible rule in England. The succeeding plays revealed a split
between the ideal and the real; this knowledge or discovery may
be bitter, and Shakespeare does not attempt to gloss it over. For

a time he finds no rule in unity itself. The dark hypothesis leads him in the tragedies to a new consolidation of ideas: virtue need not be rewarded by a "happy ending" in the actual world—in fact, such a reward might debase virtue to calculated policy. But his moral optimism is so certain that he constructs all his great tragedies on the proposition that the workings of evil as well as of good within the minds of his heroes must leave them better men at the end than at the beginning. Virtue is acquired through experience. And it is inevitably acquired by all except the carelessly ignorant or the wilfully selfish.

The scope of *Lear* surpasses that of *Othello*. If the magnificence of the characters in *Othello*—in purity, in evil, and in the sweep of passion—raises the drama above the domestic tragedy and the naturalistic problem play, it nevertheless turns upon three characters. In *Lear* there are not one, but three, active evil characters; Cordelia as the focus of love attracts many allies as contrasted with Desdemona's one companion; kings and beggars, old men and boys, touch shoulders; and the main action finds a close parallel in the subplot. The purpose and the effect suggest that here is an image of the state of man, not of an island garrison. Though Shakespeare shows more than his casual awareness of the historical sense, *Lear* is not a picture of primitive Britain, and one must think twice to remember that the play is full of wars between nations and rumors of civil wars. For the tragedy is timeless, and man's fate is involved no less surely than in the Garden of Eden.

Yet the movement is that of *Othello*, and characteristically Shakespearean. In *Othello*, Desdemona and Iago represent relatively fixed and unchanging forces that war for Othello's soul. The hero partakes of both their natures. *Lear* is even more formally schematized (though of course in both, the schemes are so artfully presented that the illusion of experienced reality is not lost). It is a war between two worlds of evil and of good, neither capable of changing the other, and each inhabited by characters who—with one startling exception—do not change. Between these worlds, and moved by them both, the figures of Lear and Gloucester play out their parts to a final realization as to which of the worlds is the more powerful. This is a drama of sympathy, but whereas sympathy in the comedies overflowed from the bounty and luck of love, here it rises from bitter wells of human suffering.

And again, Shakespeare changes his sources to express his convictions. Except in its negative aspect as lust, he plays down the symbol of union between man and woman which usually carries his conception of love. Cordelia marries a king (because love even in the tragedies may wield temporal power); but her husband appears simply as a suitor in the opening scene, to whom she never addresses one direct word. Conventional minds found this minimizing of marriage so disconcerting that Shakespeare's play was changed for stage presentation in order that Cordelia and Edgar might marry, and in this altered form held the boards well into the nineteenth century. But the love which Shakespeare here wishes to present is something more universal than sexual union. Nor is it to be rewarded with marriage and long life. Such stage conventions are, of course, mere counters for the expression of mood; but they serve as well as any others to present what seems to have been Shakespeare's conviction: if virtue is to be rewarded by marriage and living happily ever after, then we are not primarily interested in virtue at all, but in marriage and happiness as ends, to which virtue is a convenient means. To put the point in Shakespeare's own words:

> Love's not love
> When it is mingled with regards that stand
> Aloof from th' entire point. (I, i, 241–3)

At any rate, Shakespeare discarded the ending of the original story, in which Cordelia triumphs in battle and Lear is restored to his throne; Shakespeare will have Lear die over the body of his dead Cordelia. What they stand for does not need Shakespeare's protection against worldly unsuccess and the fear of death.

Shakespeare's supreme position depends upon his power over words, his sympathy with and understanding of all sorts of people, the clarity and force of his complex thinking, his ability to fuse his imaginings in presentations accepted as reality, and the health and sanity of his view of life. In short, he is a poet, a dramatist, a thinker, an artist, and a good man. The first two of these five rôles are not our direct concern and may be taken for granted. The last rôle makes his moral ideas, when stated flatly, appear natural and obvious to the point of platitude. As a moralist, his great value lies in the presentation of clear ideas so that they appear as living experience. Dramatic form actualizes inert truisms which everyone can mouth and few can assimilate. Here the rôles of dramatist, thinker, and artist combine; and the complexity of his thought springs in large part from its presentation *indirectly* in the fused image of a single plot, and *brokenly* as one idea is appraised or acted upon by various individuals. All of these elements must keep time, distance, and proportion. His natural temperament must be given free expression; but also the verse must flow in its abounding and apposite images and rhythms; the structure must declare the thought; and numerous seemingly independent characters must not blur the clarity of the central convictions, or weaken them into a chronicle of accidents.

To balance the multifariousness of the dramatic form—a complex of complex individuals—Shakespeare concentrates his thought in a few simple words or ideas, repeated and varied. The animal imagery in *Lear*, for instance, receives standard comment. It is organized around the contemptible or somewhat foolish "small deer"—rat, dog, goose, monkey, eel, worm, hog, sheep, cow, cat, wagtail, fitchew, and ditch-dog—or the beasts of prey: dragon, kite, wolf, bear, vulture, owl, lion, pelican, tiger, fox, serpent, boar. Miss Spurgeon has drawn up a picture of Shakespeare's personality by tabulating his recurrent images. His ideas are also given repeated words and catch-phrases, so that the same tabulating method might help to indicate the moral drift of any play. *Lear*, for example, is filled with words grouped around eyes, hands, the family, clothes, old age, justice, or winter. Iterated words are "nothing," "heart," "gods," "fortune," "necessity," "nature," "monster," and "unnatural." A whole series clusters around "master," "king," and "servant," authority, tyranny, power, slaves, subjects, duty, revolt, and respect. They are set up (often echoing across the distance of the whole play) to re-inforce or to oppose each other: the free man and the slave; or "friend" and "traitor"; or anger, hate, rashness, grouped with one another and arrayed against suffering, shame, patience, blessing, charity, kindness, humility. Any close reader can exemplify all of these ideas in the action of the play. To consider their organized recurrence accidental is to accuse Shakespeare of stuttering.

Yet the scrutiny of minute details in technique, the incidence of such words and their interplay, gradually builds up a picture of the two worlds, one dominated by pride, anger, and heartlessness, the other by humility and patience and sympathy. The play is at once so certain and so subtle that on the one hand the great worlds do not force human action beyond credibility; while on the other hand the diversity of characters does not cloud the implicit outlines of the great worlds of evil and of good. The play is so much a unit, so tightly meshed, that its smallest threads may be seen as connected with the large tapestry of its thought. Open the text at any point, and one can work to the end and the beginning.

Take as an example a moment of comparative relaxation—Kent's soliloquy after he has been put in the stocks and left to his thoughts. It is just before daybreak.

> Good King, that must approve the common saw,
> Thou out of heaven's benediction com'st
> To the warm sun!
> Approach, thou beacon to this under globe,
> That by thy comfortable beams I may
> Peruse this letter. Nothing almost sees miracles
> But misery. I know 'tis from Cordelia,
> Who hath most fortunately been inform'd
> Of my obscured course—and [*reads*] "shall find time
> From this enormous state, seeking to give
> Losses their remedies"—All weary and o'erwatch'd,
> Take vantage, heavy eyes, not to behold
> This shameful lodging.
> Fortune, good night; smile once more, turn thy wheel.
>
> (II, ii, 167–80)

Kent's situation itself is of significance. The theme of bond-age—of Gloucester's corky arms bound fast, of Lear and Cor-delia in the prison—is initiated in Kent's being set in the stocks. Yet though his legs wear cruel garters, his mind is free, and the last line he speaks before he sleeps is one of Shakespeare's most consoling and emotionally balanced prayers. Even the bluff and hot-blooded Kent can practice patience. He can be self-forgetful as well. His first thought is of his master. He notes with pity that the King must experience the common lot. He quotes an old proverb, "Out of heaven's blessing into the warm sun," which to modern ears may sound paradoxical. But the Elizabethans were closer to nature than we, and had no opportunity to patronize her from steam-heated and air-conditioned rooms. Those who felt the winter winds and the warm sun were the beggars and madmen of the roads. And Lear must lose his royal privilege, confirming the common lot of wanderers who live "under the canopy" of the bare sky.

Yet the sun may be warm, and may be a symbol of coming hope and comfort. Kent therefore calls upon it in a dark world, know-ing that in the world he lives in, misery by its very nature generates the saving impossibility, and that the very lowest on Fortune's turning wheel can move only higher. The hope of miracle is echoed in Cordelia's letter, where the words have overtones of more than mortal powers at work. Though the state is enormous, though only the miracle of love could note obscure courses and the fall of a sparrow, yet it shall find time to give "losses their remedies." The universal symbol, however, must not frighten or puzzle ordinary men. Men tire, eyes grow heavy even at the promise of miracle, sleep blots out shame. And Kent falls to com-mon slumber at the end of a scene which—placed before Lear's suffering, before he has been bound (the image of bondage again) upon another wheel than Fortune's, the wheel of fire—fore-shadows Lear's redemption.

What power or powers rule this world? Shakespeare has been accused of mocking ambiguity. Are they the conventional Roman gods, Apollo, Jupiter, Juno, that are called upon in oaths? Or is it Nature, whom Edmund in his crude materialism takes as his goddess? Or is it a fatalistic world ruled by fear and superstition as Gloucester sometimes believes, a world in which omens are potent and planetary influence has cracked nature into ruinous disorders, "the images of revolt and flying off"? Or is the governor that hate which Gloucester, his eyes torn out, sees so clearly: human beings are flies mutilated and destroyed for the amusement of the callow gods. Or is Fortune tiptoe on a tickle globe, blindfolded, her wheel crazily spinning?

All of these conceptions, in the larger framework, are symbols of carelessness, ignorance, unrest, disease, or pain. Shakespeare deliberately mutes the Christian references or overtones, and pluralizes and depersonalizes the heavens and the gods. Fortune with her wheel may be the intermediary between divinity and man, as she had been in the millennium since Boethius; but above Fortune are inscrutable powers. As all the references to the gods build up,[8] they appear clearly as implacable instruments of justice and age-old order. But also they are allied with patience and mercy.

Shakespeare's dual themes of personal love and the stable social order here blend into a single embracing conception, whose symbol is the family. All of the principal characters belong by allegiance, marriage, or blood to one of two families, and the families are interwoven by the lust that couples and destroys the evil children, the loyalty of Gloucester to his outcast master—even in such small details as that Edgar is Lear's godson. The imaginative identification between the father-child symbol and the conception of universal harmony or universal discord is a bold one, but it is made so easily and confidently that when a father misjudges his daughters, "machinations, hollowness, treachery, and all ruinous disorders follow us disquietly to our graves." The speaker of these words is himself a father who misjudges his children, and the play is given its breadth of statement by the fact that every father whose children appear in the play errs in appraising them, and every child whose father appears in the play is paternally rewarded or cast out inversely according to his deserving. The fathers cannot distinguish merit or ingratitude, which accounts for the persistent symbols of eyesight and blindness. "See better, Lear!" says Kent in the first scene, and "I'll see that straight," Lear says at the conclusion. Clearer seeing is the burden of the play, whose final couplet is:

> The oldest have borne most; we that are young
> Shall never see so much, nor live so long.

In its initial course, the blind fathers banish their loving children and friends, and heap honors on their hard-hearted progeny. These paternal judgments, however, are carried out in the mixed world of practical action, and Shakespeare takes pains to set up a sharp boundary between practical consequences and spiritual realities. Thus, when Lear exiles Kent's "hated back" and "banish'd trunk," Kent in farewell says: "Freedom lives hence, and banishment is here." [9] Gloucester first sees truly immediately after he has lost his eyes. To make the moral distinction unmistakable, Shakespeare uses an ironic and surprising recognition and reversal: Regan, to increase his suffering, pitilessly reveals to the blind father that Edmund hates and has betrayed him. But Gloucester, instead of countering with hate or lamentation, responds with remorse, repentance, and prayer for his abused son Edgar:

> O my follies! Then Edgar was abus'd.
> Kind gods, forgive me that, and prosper him!

The supreme instance of the opposed worlds comes dramatically at the moment when Lear's sight is clearest. He and Cordelia have been brought in as prisoners, and his long speech to his daughter is broken once by Edmund's order to take them away to their deaths. Yet the very rhythms of

> Come, let's away to prison.
> We two alone will sing like birds i' th' cage

express an almost unbearable joy and lightness. Lear's sentence,

> Upon such sacrifices, my Cordelia,
> The gods themselves throw incense,

has little meaning in its literal context; but in the moral proportions of the whole vision, and following right upon Edmund's ominous "Take them away," it marks Lear's high point of triumph and absolution: he is identified with the gods as Oedipus was at Colonos.

What, then, are the spiritual realities of good and evil that the two protagonists in the two plots must be made to see? Evil may begin almost innocently—in the self-justifications of common sense. The talk about their father between Goneril and Regan at the end of the first scene is sound and true enough, if a trifle uncharitable; and some of Goneril's complaints about Lear's undoubtedly unruly train sound like a housewife: "By day and night, he wrongs me! I'll not endure it." Edmund's resentment against a social order that laughs in contempt at bastards might have proved the making of an independent man: "Now, gods, stand up for bastards!" But such complaints and resentment, innocuous at the start, are used to initiate and rationalize the hard cold workings of calculated selfishness.

Flattery in his daughters Lear is blind to; treachery in Edmund Gloucester cannot see. Perhaps these are weaknesses for which the old fathers cannot be blamed. Any workable world must be based upon trust of some sort or other; and flattery and treachery are worthy of their names only when they masquerade successfully as admiration and loyalty. The possible cancer at the very heart of seeming soundness Shakespeare is fully aware of, and he never tires of speculating on the relations between appearance and reality. In *Lear* he finds time for ironic puzzling—juxtaposing more than once Gloucester's clear view of Lear's mistakes with his own mistaken actions, and having the treacherous Edmund a principal mouthpiece for unctuous remarks on loyalty, justice, duty, service, and truth, or in reprehension of treason. Irony doubles upon itself as Cornwall accepts Edmund's services in what is almost a court of honor among thieves: "You shall be ours. Natures of such deep trust we shall much need." Or Cornwall to Edmund again: "I will lay trust upon thee, and thou shalt find a dearer father in my love." [10] Yet silence or blunt speech seem hardly workable defenses against the forays of flattery, and it would be a somewhat mute and ungracious world if every honest soul followed Cordelia's philosophy: "What I well intend, I'll do 't before I speak."

Evil, it would appear, is relatively harmless or not easily detectable in the external world—until it secures the collaboration of the potentially good. Lear co-operates to the full, and the seeds of evil are strong within him. He is ignorant of his own nature: "he hath ever but slenderly known himself." He acts with "hideous rashness," for "the best and soundest of his time hath been but rash." Anger and pride hold him as their slave, and when they are roused, he looses his hate upon others in order to preserve his wilful dominance. This is no picture of old age, as the Dowager Countess of Rossillion, or Polonius for that matter, could tell us. Ironically, but in keeping with the timelessness of the thought, it is the picture of a spoiled child, whose early aberrations have been protected by a position of unquestioned authority, until they have turned into "the imperfections of long-ingraffed condition." What is his "unruly waywardness" but childish unconsciousness, childish tantrums, soothed or hurt pride? Is he more than a heedless and wanton boy—magnified, of course, as Shakespeare magnified all his principal figures—in his reckless curses? [11] The impossible opening scene of the dividing of the kingdom is given some semblance of reality by interpreting it as a kind of public game Lear has thought up to flatter himself, a birthday party he has decided upon, a ceremonial playing of Post Office, with presents thrown away for every kiss, a Question-and-Answer where the rules are that each tall compliment must exceed the last, and where Lear saves his joy Cordelia for the final sweet of the banquet. He does not disown Cordelia because he thinks she does not love him. He knows that she does. But she has humiliated him in public, and his feelings are deeply hurt. After getting even with her by humiliating her before her suitors, he says in reckless dislike and annoyance—on such infantile first motivations does this great tragedy turn—

Better thou
Hadst not been born than not t' have *pleas'd* me better.

Cordelia had been able to say nothing. Nothing? Nothing.
The word burns into Lear's memory and the minds of the
auditors. It reverberates through the play in unexpected places.
Lear answers Cordelia's "Nothing" in an ominous nursery tag:
"Nothing can come of nothing." His saying is true only in the
world of barter. He is to find out, when he himself has become
"an O without a figure," that the world of spiritual values is not
that of the counting house. In the mathematics of generosity, his
"nothing" in lands and position and power is worth paying the
price of exile, or one's eyes, or one's life; and the Fool, Kent,
Gloucester, Edgar, Albany, and finally Cordelia gather round
him, not to be rewarded with "something," but because they are
themselves.

Honeyed words are nothing to Cordelia's heart. Her silent love
is nothing in the world of candied tongues and absurd pomp.
Goneril has protested her love for Lear as "dearer than eyesight, space, and liberty"; Regan echoes her sister in her "true
heart." Now that such usurping words have been regally accepted
as the glittering raiment of true love, Cordelia shows a more than
homespun bluntness. She speaks to her father and sisters with a
stubbornness and angry disapproval and a touch of that pride
which make her her father's child; or, if her adorers insist upon
her perfection, she speaks in the simplicity of truth:

I love your Majesty
According to my bond; no more nor less.

Here, expressed with more than the severity of Spartan and Stoic,
is love, allegiance, responsibility, and faith. Her love is a duty,
but it is willingly assumed; it is responsible enough to contemplate
future allegiance to a husband, and strong enough to vent its present helplessness in the prim lecture of a schoolmistress. Cordelia's
"bond" is not the shackles of a slave, but the knitting of human
brotherhood realized by her free spirit.

This wider conception of love as a social obligation is seen also in terms of the state, though it is framed in the symbols of the larger cosmos as well as the smaller unit of the family and its dependents.[12] In this sense, the theme of the play is authority and allegiance. *Lear* is not the tragedy of old age (Lear himself has the most energetically youthful spirit of anyone in the play except possibly Edmund). But old age is chosen as the symbol for natural authority. The just and powerful gods in this tragedy themselves are old. The positive ideal of mutual respect and common responsibility existing among rulers and subjects is made firm in the images. Cordelia says:

> You have begot me, bred me, lov'd me; I
> Return those duties back as are right fit,
> Obey you, love you, and most honour you.

Lear reminds Regan of:

> The offices of nature, bond of childhood,
> Effects of courtesy, dues of gratitude.

And Kent wishes only to serve where he stands condemned. The necessity for allegiance is not even argued in this play (except by the villains, who do not intend to practice it). To the well-intentioned it is as natural as breathing. On the other hand, Lear learns—but only through his suffering and madness—that authority should command allegiance only because of knowledge and fellow-feeling—"O, I have ta'en too little care of this!"—and that otherwise it is merely the monstrous mask of fear and power, "the great image of authority: a dog's obey'd in office."

A play that contains such persistent, deeply felt, and closely related moral thoughts must be organized with superb art if it is to seem a tragedy and not a collection of ethical observations. In part, the ideas loom even more powerfully in action than in words: true love in Cordelia; true service in Kent; true allegiance to the old gods in the servant who rebels against his master Cornwall; true humility in the many kneeling scenes; true insight after the plucking out of Gloucester's eyes.

One further device Shakespeare hits upon: the choric comment on the total action is relegated principally to the subplot. Since the governing ideas are made verbally clear in this less important part of the piece, the main action can present them in terms of pure character, emotion, and story. We have seen (Note 10) how Lear's madness is explained most directly by Gloucester's self-analysis: that grief has almost unsettled his own mind. Similarly, the protecting spirit of love for the outcast Gloucester is concentrated almost solely in his highly articulate son Edgar, whereas for Lear it is diversified among Kent, the Fool, Cordelia, and other followers. In an important aside, Edgar says:

> Why I do trifle thus with his despair
> Is done to cure it. (IV, vi, 33–4)

He has not tried to drive out his father's bitter emotions with weak philosophy; instead, he has led him to the cliff of suicide, and will not restrain him. The theme of the good and the wise deliberately teaching the weaker through painful experience—a theme that Shakespeare had first used in his early *The Two Gentlemen of Verona*, that had filled *Measure for Measure*, that remained in his last play *The Tempest*—is again repeated. Reason is of no avail against a strong destructive emotion, which can only be expelled by a stronger emotion. And now Gloucester is on his knees in prayer before his attempted suicide. His earlier generalizations on the nature of destiny had shown in weaker form Lear's temperamental variability. His intellect does not function consistently, for he prays to "shake patiently my great affliction off" in the impatient act of suicide. He falls and swoons. The awful setting of the will to negate existence, the discovery that life nevertheless persists—these may constitute an earthquake of the spirit, a shattering of the pattern which will allow, after the short fit of madness, a truer pattern to be constructed out of the shards. Edgar zealously proceeds as a physician of souls:

> Thy life's a miracle. . . . Therefore, thou happy father,
> Think that the clearest gods, who make them honours
> Of men's impossibilities, have preserv'd thee. . . .
> Bear free and patient thoughts.

Gloucester responds to Edgar's imaginative picture of the tempting fiend that followed him to the cliff's edge with the resolution henceforth to bear affliction.

It is a hard lesson to learn, and the miracle has not made a happy father. In the same scene he meets the mad Lear, that "ruin'd piece of nature," and broods that even so this great world will wear out to nothing. He prays for death, though he will not allow his "worser spirit" to tempt him to suicide again. And when Oswald, secure in Gloucester's blindness, draws his sword to kill the "old unhappy traitor," he greets it as drawn by a "friendly hand." His despair has not been cured. Again Edgar's hand saves him, when Edgar assumes still another disguise, as if to convince his father against his will that the common people of the earth are friends to wretchedness. And Oswald once dispatched, hand in hand father and son leave the scene.

The remorseless course of the overpowering fifth act is interrupted by a single short scene between the two. Edgar leaves his father with the promise, if he ever returns, to bring him comfort. With an ironic contrast which Shakespeare consistently uses in *Lear*, between spoken words and immediately subsequent actions, between the realm of values and the world of facts, Edgar returns at once with the news of defeat in battle. In his recurrent despair, Gloucester will not budge. "No further, sir. A man may rot even here." But endurance is not the equivalent of supine despair. Edgar answers again with the lesson of true patience in action:

> What, in ill thoughts again? Men must endure
> Their going hence, even as their coming hither; [13]
> Ripeness is all. Come on.

The little scene of eleven lines is a comment on the entire play. Gloucester accepts Edgar's truth—"And that's true *too*"—but only as a partial truth. He has thought and prayed for Edgar, he has asked for forgiveness for his own blindness, but he is a lonely man as again hand in hand with his unknown son he leaves the stage. Then, though it is not presented, we are told how grace comes smiling to his desperate remorse and loneliness. Edgar before the avenging battle, hopeful but not certain, asks his father's blessing and reveals to him how he "became his guide, Led him, begg'd for him, sav'd him from despair." And Gloucester's flawed heart

> 'Twixt two extremes of passion, joy and grief,
> Burst smilingly.

The union, the revelation of hidden and persistent loyalty, the reciprocation of love, is too much of joy, a content too absolute for the weak hearts of mortals. But it is a truth of experience. And without this formal parallel comment—since at the moment of supreme climax Shakespeare writes in hints and leaves us few stage directions—Lear's ecstasy of joy at the point of death could not be understood.

The great images of moral truth (so complete is Shakespeare's dramatic art) control the development of themes through the structure of the whole play. The framing idea of ordered justice opens and closes the tragedy with formal scenes, almost exactly balanced in length, of the division of the kingdom and its reunification. The powers of government are displayed; trumpets flourish for the withdrawal of Lear, and sound again for the approach of retribution in the last tourney.

Yet the ordering of the state must be acted out in smaller terms of fathers and children, brothers and sisters. The world picture, therefore, of a scourged nature, "in cities, mutinies; in countries, discord; in palaces, treason," magnifies in thought the actual scenes of "unnaturalness between the child and the parent." The mental picture is an "image of horror" [14] comparable to the end of the world, yet it is specifically generated by "banishment of friends." The first act, therefore, finds Lear making Cordelia a stranger to his heart in the terrible monosyllables:

> So be my grave my peace as here I give
> Her father's heart from her!

Kent is banished for his dutiful reproof of majesty falling to madness and folly; and Edgar is quickly cast out from his father's mind, with a rashness as hideous as Lear's, as an "unnatural, detested, brutish villain!"

These banishments recoil in the second act in the counterbanishment of Lear to the elements, an act which ends "Shut up your doors. . . . Come out o' th' storm." The play, which Shakespeare—carefully for once—divided into acts and scenes, follows these two acts of hateful banishment and counterbanishment with a middle act which shows the dissolution of the world in Lear's mind; a fourth act of rescue and the recovery of a truer world; and a final act of retribution, realization, and restoration of stability.

The world from which Lear is so cruelly banished is the same world from which he and Gloucester banished Cordelia, Kent, and Edgar. Since the court of Britain is full of oily cunning and unnatural ingratitude and power that is heartless because it is powerful, the world of outcasts is a better realm. Gloucester learns that

> Full oft 'tis seen
> Our means secure us, and our mere defects
> Prove our commodities. (IV, i, 19–21)

Lear varies the same thought:

> The art of our necessities is strange,
> That can make vile things precious. (III, ii, 70–1)

In these words, Lear is still using the language of the heartless court, that might well consider straw in a hovel vile. But he is finding, in the world of necessity and suffering, precious symbols of brotherhood. And he is using an image drawn from the language of alchemy: the needful brotherhood of the poor knows that strange art of love which can transmute base dross to gold.

In one sense, *Lear* is a reworking of the theme in *As You Like It*—exiles to the greenwood. "Freedom lives hence, and banishment is here," Kent says, adding of himself in farewell: "He'll shape his old course in a country new." To be sure, the stormy heath and the Dover cliffs are no Forest of Arden, but it remains true that nature is less unnatural than man, and that

> Here shall he see
> No enemy
> But winter and rough weather.

And it is *As You Like It*, not *Lear*, that contains the lines:

> Blow, blow, thou winter wind,
> Thou art not so unkind
>   As man's ingratitude. . . .
> Freeze, freeze, thou bitter sky,
> That dost not bite so nigh
>   As benefits forgot.

The reaction against the first banishments proceeds in the second act, then, through the hunting of Edgar, the stocking of Kent, and the belittling of reverence for Lear by the action of whittling down his retinue, to the final casting out into the storm. In his unnatural and bemadding sorrow, where he strives to outscorn the wind and rain in his little world of man, Lear is surrounded by beggars, wretches, tenants, peasants, servants, by an eyeless and discarded old man, by a fool who follows a great wheel down hill, and by a naked madman in "the basest and most poorest shape that ever penury, in contempt of man, brought near to beast."

Yet Lear is not fit to learn from this community of the wretched until his anger and pride have been exposed to trials. The final scene of the second act is a long series of tests of his patience, a cunning juxtaposition of flickering moods of anger and painful strivings to comprehend humility and sympathy. He is driven near to madness, as he himself realizes, by the cold pressure of his heartless daughters, but his impotent rage conspires with their selfishness to drive him into the storm. Nevertheless, the struggle for patience is there. It first glints with startling unexpectedness in the midst of an angry speech against Cornwall:

> Fiery? the fiery Duke? Tell the hot Duke that—
> No, but not yet! May be he is not well.

It has been unmistakably learned through his own experience:

> We are not ourselves
> When nature, being oppress'd, commands the mind
> To suffer with the body. I'll forbear;
> And am fallen out with my more headier will,
> To take the indispos'd and sickly fit
> For the sound man.

And it swells to a major chord in his prayer to the gods for patience. Yet the prayer for patience asks the gods to touch him with noble anger, and the terrors of his revenges are broken by his tears. With a child's petulance and need, he demands the love of one daughter while heaping hateful curses upon the other. In bitter mock humility, he imagines and acts out the kneeling to his daughter to ask forgiveness for his age, which is the only sin he sees in himself. His struggle to attain this strange new mood of patience is painful, and Shakespeare never wrote a scene in which conflicting qualities of good and evil were more fully realized. To the end of the play, Lear's passionate spirit flares into anger.

But his pride is tamed, and consciously tamed by love in the person of the Fool. The central scene here is the fourth of the first act. In at least a score of instances, the Fool compels his King to remember the consequences of his headstrong proudness. The Fool is Lear's conscience, and though his remarks sting home like lashes and cut Lear to the brains, Lear himself knows their healing necessity, calls for his Fool, tends him in the storm, and would have him whipped if he should tell lies. As a prelude to the Fool's appearance, one of Lear's knights says, "My duty cannot be silent when I think your Highness wrong'd," and Lear answers, "Thou but rememb'rest me of mine own conception." The Fool puts into practice what Edgar had phrased in words: "Why I do trifle thus with his despair is done to cure him." Therefore again and again the Fool calls Lear back to an acknowledgment of his pride, his hasty temper, his mistaken judgments, his humiliation, his shadowy nothingness, his ignorance, his folly, his nakedness, and his own responsibility for his unnatural position under the power of his ungrateful daughters. The first step in Lear's regeneration— and it occurs within the first act—is his listening to his faithful follower, who out of love foolishly reproaches his master.[15]

Most of his own follies and errors Lear's pride learns to face, even with a certain willingness that makes repentance possible.[16] But there is one error that Lear's proud mind refuses to confront directly, for it is a sin against love and out of pride—the rejection of Cordelia. The curse against love had been terrible and deliberate, when he could openly proclaim that he had no such daughter, "nor shall ever see that face of hers again." Shakespeare is at his subtlest in suggesting how this preys upon Lear's mind, even while actively he is engaged in trying to convince himself of the love of Goneril and Regan. "No more of that," he says brusquely to the Knight who has dared to mention his young lady's going into France. "Nothing can be made out of nothing," he recalls in answer to the Fool's questioning. "I did her wrong," he murmurs in the midst of his Fool's jesting. And when he refuses to return to Goneril, who has wronged him, he selects as the most impossible example of humility and of the confession of his own sins, an imagined reconciliation with Cordelia:

> Return with her?
> Why, the hot-blooded France, that dowerless took
> Our youngest born, I could as well be brought
> To knee his throne. (II, iv, 214-7)

After his proud intolerance, the possibility of tenderness in others shatters his heart before he can accept it. His pride must leave its lonely castle and stoop to the hovel of brother beggars. Kent tries to shelter him from the storm, and Lear responds, "Let me alone." Kent says: "Good my lord, enter here." And Lear: "Wilt break my heart?" Yet from the shattering itself he learns brotherhood. He returns Kent's solicitude by urging Kent and the Fool to enter the hovel, while he prays his prayer for all poor naked wretches. Madness lies ahead. When Poor Tom appears— madness and nakedness, the walking symbol of "the thing itself"—

Lear's mind cracks into new crystals as if in the presence of a catalyst.

The fragmentary insane world of the central scenes sets whirling the thoughts that had been beating in Lear's mind. His own madness is orchestrated and pyramided by the Fool's comments and the assumed madness of Edgar. Images of hypocrisy, authority, and justice, of incest and adultery, of archery and war and thieves and usurers and punishers, throng his mind. There are nearly unbearable glimpses of his loneliness in a hostile world: his attempt to escape his rescuers, or the sudden imagining:

> The little dogs and all,
> Tray, Blanch, and Sweetheart, see, they bark at me.

But reason in his madness—or is it grace beyond his control?—organizes his wild sayings. His words acknowledge the bitter evils of the world; they anatomize hard hearts; they see that authority is often the prime cause and powerful aid of vice; and with the aid of joint-stools and farmhouse cats they seek for justice. The prelude to his madness is a prayer, its last act a sermon:

> Thou must be patient. We came crying hither;
> Thou know'st, the first time that we smell the air
> We wawl and cry. I will preach to thee. Mark. . . .
> When we are born, we cry that we are come
> To this great stage of fools. (IV, vi, 182–7)

Lear has learned sympathy through suffering, through the human cry that is man's common heritage. He has stripped off all false seeming and sophistication and accommodation, and has found man to be "no more but such a poor, bare, forked animal as thou art." He has experienced what "hurts the poor creature of earth," and talks with joy to the "noble philosopher" he has discovered in Poor Tom.

The drift of the play has been from the selfish court to the broad commonalty of the poor. Some of its great speeches are Edgar's pictures of basest beggars and the forsaken castaways of society;

and from these pictures rise naturally the other great speeches of Lear and Edgar and Gloucester on just distribution and sympathy and brotherhood.

> Who alone suffers suffers most i' th' mind . . .
> But then the mind much sufferance doth o'erskip
> When grief hath mates, and bearing, fellowship.[17]

Lear and Gloucester, each himself a "poor banished man," are initiated into the wide fellowship of the poor; and from the inhabitants of hovels and heaths and prisons, "from low farms, poor pelting villages, sheepcotes, and mills," from drinking the green mantle of the standing pool and being drenched by the rain and persecuted by the thunder, swell the great prayers of sympathy with human misery. Compassion builds a classless society, for in suffering all men are equal.

Lear has poured gifts and unreciprocated love on his dog-hearted daughters; he has struggled to acquire patience, and has witnessed his pride, position, and power stripped from him. Torn between his own unavailing love and his repentance for rejecting those who loved him, his mind gives way, and he lives among mad images of justice and naked truth. He finds kind hearts among the wretches of the winter world, and he responds generously. Every inch a king, his most truly regal qualities are a sensitive heart and a magnanimous mind. The generosity of his nature dwarfs even his deep faults. He has learned that all men participate in the fellowship of suffering, and he can sympathize with poor wretches without hope of reward.

His hardest lesson is ahead. A proud king may understand proudly that virtue is its own reward. Lear has learned to forgive others. Can he bear to be himself forgiven? This is the last lesson in humility, toward which the whole of the fourth act tends, in its scenes of recovery, recognition, and restoration. The evil sisters are caught more tightly in the bonds of their own passions. Cornwall is dead. Albany recognizes the monsters of the deep; the rescuing armies draw near; and in its longest scene the blind

Gloucester is led by his loving son to a discovery of his better nature, and Lear is caught by Cordelia's attendants. He shrinks from forgiveness as if it were an accusation. Kent has noted that

> Well, sir, the poor distressed Lear's i' th' town;
> Who sometime, in his better tune, remembers
> What we are come about, and by no means
> Will yield to see his daughter. (IV, iii, 40–3)

When her retainer begins a sentence with "Your most dear daughter—"Lear reacts like a wounded lone animal expecting torture or death: "No rescue? What, a prisoner? . . . Let me have a surgeon; I am cut to th' brains. . . . No seconds? All myself? . . . I will die bravely, like a smug bridegroom. . . . Nay, an you get it, you shall get it by running." And he seeks to escape from a love he cannot bear to face.

He wakes sane and rested in Cordelia's tent in a scene where Shakespeare's pathos approaches the celestial. The images become almost directly Christian to show the abyss Lear senses between the angelic vision of his daughter and his own scalding tortures. Having lived so long in a world of selfishness at the top and misery at the bottom, a world where trust is repaid by cold hate, he shudders away from the mockery, the laughter, the abuse that might follow if he should again show faith. Yet as he wakes to the reality of his surroundings, he gradually approaches the awful daring of a moment's surrender:

> Do not laugh at me;
> For (as I am a man) I think this lady
> To be my child Cordelia.

This expression of trust as he the tormented sinner throws himself upon compassion, is the final gesture of his humility. He has learned that harder lesson for a proud man cut to the brains: that there is a fellowship in joy as well as in suffering. The old Lear is gone, and the meek have inherited the earth.

The last act confirms the exaltation. The stiff old fairy story of Leir and his daughters has been transformed into a story of spiritual grace and compassion. The two short opening scenes balance the drums and colors of the opposing powers. In one we see the increasing discord and division between the serpent sisters; in the other the ministrations of young love to age.[18] The final scene presents father and daughter "as prisoners"; it has passed beyond tragedy to beatitude, and Lear never speaks with greater lightness or a more childish trust. They are bound to each other forever, by ties that transcend age or place or duty:

> When thou dost ask me blessing, I'll kneel down
> And ask of thee forgiveness.

The old world has lost all significance, and when Cordelia says, with still a trace of her youthful rectitude, "Shall we not see these daughters and these sisters?" Lear answers gaily: "No, no, no, no!"

Well, but they *do* see them, or at least the bodies of Goneril and Regan, destroyed by their interacting heartlessness, are brought on the stage as mute witnesses to the promised end. Death is neither reward nor punishment, since it is incident to good and evil alike. The spirit of the play would be destroyed if Shakespeare had returned Lear to power. Cordelia did not come back from beyond the seas to restore her father to robes and furred gowns. (She had said to Burgundy: "Since that respects of fortune are his love, I shall not be his wife.") She returned to restore herself to his heart, and she gave her life to affirm their union. As for rewarding (or degrading) Lear with a kingdom after his blessedness—no, no, no, no! He has his reward in Cordelia, doubly precious because it was unsought, unbargained for. Cordelia—the name might be one of those anagrams of the Elizabethan love-sonneteers for the Idea of the Heart—has garnered up his entire life, and when he bends over her body, his agonized imaginings, his creative desires, cause him to say:

> This feather stirs; she lives! If it be so,
> It is a chance which does redeem all sorrows
> That ever I have felt.

And though for moments he is swept by the desolation of absolute loss, his final mood redeems all sorrows that he has ever felt, his last words realize that she lives:

> Look on her! look! her lips!
> Look there, look there!

The *hysterica passio* of grief that earlier had welled up to his throat has now become a choking ecstasy of joy, and his flawed heart bursts smilingly.

A close student of Shakespeare has found this death most desperate, in that Lear's last joy is an illusion. But the world of spirit is made up of values, not of temporal accidents and spatial quantities. In the moral world, Lear's last thought is not an illusion, but a creation. Love, God, and the artist are the three creators: they do not imitate, they *make* something which would not otherwise exist. The play itself has been removed from history. Time has been destroyed through the use of the symbol of the family, where neither "the oppression of aged tyranny" nor "The younger rises when the old doth fall" offers a solution. The human family is united in and through time, generations bound to generations in equality, so that father and child are not ultimately differentiated, for all are children in the hand of God. The artifices and distinctions of society have crumbled; the trappings of power and position have been stripped from men to reveal the naked self; only those who cast out the world and are cast out by the world can see truly; and men are united in a communion of poverty, of suffering, but of infinite possibilities for compassion and sacrifice.

The old theme that love can create love is given one last twist in a startling intimation. The opening subject of the play was heartless laughter at the bastard Edmund and the sport at his making. Edmund, lonely exile from the world, fights society with its own weapons and its own rules for the survival of the fittest. Now the wheel has come full circle. Dying—since selfish interests are no longer relevant—he observes the passing time; knowing that his own life is passing, he even forgives the unknown man who has dealt him the deathstroke. He hears Edgar's tale of his ministering to the father who has wronged him, and muses: "This speech of yours hath mov'd me, And shall perchance do good." He hears of the deaths of Goneril and Regan, and the theme of unity re-appears in this harsh key: "I was contracted to them both. All three Now marry in an instant." And again:

Yet Edmund was belov'd.

The theme of love is here distorted, the four little words carry complicated emotions, but they give Edmund at least a pitiful moment of assuagement. The slave is for a moment free. Shakespeare knew how imperfect a mirror man is for his own ideals, and might have said with Dante: "The eternal light always kindles love; and if anything your love should lead astray, it is not without some gleam, ill understood, that still shines through." However it may be, from whatever mixed motives of altruism and personal passion, Edmund suddenly attempts to repeal his writ upon the lives of Lear and Cordelia. "I pant for life," he says, a remark as significant in the symbolic as the literal world. "Some good I mean to do, Despite of mine own nature." And despite his own nature, warped by the evil of others and his own counter-evil, he repents in a moment, and by this action is an exile no longer, but a man within the brotherhood of men. It is the last miracle in the play, except for the resurrection of Cordelia in the mind of the desolated Lear. The tragedy generates miracles through misery. But the miracles are no less true than the misery; and the gods, kind and avenging, seek to give losses their remedies.

MACBETH

This picture of blood in the night is not only the shortest but also the simplest of the great tragedies. From the general view of the world in *Lear*, it again narrows its focus, like *Othello*, to the scrutiny of individual destiny. It is even narrower than *Othello*, whose three main characters are here replaced by a single figure and his feminine counterpart. As greater frames, to be sure, the cosmic order and the political order are still present, but Shakespeare's certain touch merely sketches them in as unobtrusive orienting outlines. His images were never used with greater economy: the ill-adjusted clothes that suggest a violation of the fit and proper; the many night-pieces; the hidden, peering stars; the muffled and blanketed and strangled world of dark deeds; the thickening and stickiness of blood; the visions of fear; all the ill-omened birds of prey and creatures of the night—crows, rooks, ravens, kites and hellkites, falcons, vultures, owls and bats.

The simple central idea—that the moral order exists in the microcosm, that there is no escape from conscience, that man is at once a criminal and his own executioner—is realized in pure dramatic form, so that the introspective nature of the proposition is hardly noticed by reader or spectator, and is never stated directly. The theatre of the essential struggle is in Macbeth's mind. This concentration places the tragedy in a unique position (*Richard III* is a possible parallel), in that there is no main antagonist to oppose the hero. Macbeth is his own antagonist, and fights a doomed battle not only against the world but against himself. To balance having a villain-hero, whose mental struggle and defeat are repeated in his wife's conscience, the other characters in the play are well-meaning and decent, so that the usual Shakespearean conception of tragedy—a hero basically better than the world he lives in—is turned upside down. Morally considered, the play is nevertheless more than a melodrama because the villain *is* the hero, who suffers more from his own vice than from external retribution.

The play is not rich in generalized statements, and favorite quotations from *Macbeth*, which usually spring from the particular mental state of the hero, are as easily misapplied as the famous "One touch of nature makes the whole world kin" from *Troilus and Cressida*, which merely points out our common weakness for novelty. The general order of the world, therefore, must be found in the dramatic structure itself. The development of the story shows that eventually evil is destroyed both in the practical and psychological spheres. But outside Macbeth's mind, higher forces are given a voice only in the three witches.[19] The witches have an objective existence, unless Banquo who sees and hears them is a figment in the minds of those who know him. Dramatically they are excellent. Philosophically considered, they are puzzling. Their significance and consistency may have been sacrificed to some extent to showmanship. Born of the superstitions of the English countryside, out of the Scandinavian Wyrd sisters, they have an overlay of malice and triviality that merits the ducking-stool. Yet even while they are involved in such fascinating work as brewing together the eye of a newt and the toe of a frog, they know on Macbeth's entrance that "Something wicked this way comes." And one of them, on a mission of sheer vengefulness against a sailor's wife, knows that the sailor's ship cannot be lost. Two points are clear: they foresee the future; and they do not attempt to influence Macbeth. Translated, this may mean no more than that the order of the world is determined in the sense that predictable consequences follow causes, and that man's nature is part of the predictable single order, the moral law operating without outside intervention as inexorably as the law of gravity, so that "supernatural soliciting," however it might be conceived, need and can do no more than point out what in essence is already present. Such a conception Shakespeare underlines by having Banquo note Macbeth's immediate response to the triple prophecy:

> Good sir, why do you start and seem to fear
> Things that do sound so fair? (I, iii, 51–2)

"Fate and metaphysical aid" create effective scenes on the stage, but they are present in Macbeth's half-hidden thoughts of the future before they speak to him on the blasted heath. The witches aid Macbeth much as Pandarus aids Cressida: by voicing a secret impulse already existing.

Not only the Weird Sisters, but the state of Scotland also furnishes a frame and a metaphor for the personal moral drama. One half of the idea of mutual responsibility between rulers and subjects is seen fully and clearly by Macbeth himself:

> The service and the loyalty I owe,
> In doing it pays itself. Your Highness' part
> Is to receive our duties; and our duties

> Are to your throne and state children and servants,
> Which do but what they should by doing everything
> Safe toward your love and honour. (I, iv, 22–7)

The other half of the ideal order of the state lives in the person of Duncan. The king is the soul of the political structure. When Duncan is murdered,

> Confusion now hath made his masterpiece!
> Most sacrilegious murther hath broke ope
> The Lord's anointed temple and stole thence
> The life o' the building! (II, iii, 71–4)

The awful nature of the act is imaged in Duncan's horses that eat each other up after his assassination, "Contending 'gainst obedience, as they would make War with mankind." The killing of a king is a multiple crime, for it destroys the central order on which subject parts depend for their individual existences.

Such philosophizing on the state is thoroughly consistent with Shakespeare's political ideas. Yet in this tragedy of crime and punishment in man's soul, regicide is used as a kind of parallel over-symbol in the external action for what is happening in Macbeth's own being. At the beginning of the play, Macbeth deliberately tries to kill what he recognizes as the ruling power in his nature—his soul or conscience. The following action witnesses his conscience still moving like a ghost, while the subordinate parts of his nature approach dissolution now that their crown is gone:

> As from your graves rise up and walk like sprites
> To countenance this horror! (II, iii, 84–5)

Long before Macbeth's actual death in battle, the life of the building is gone. The whole tragedy is an expansion of Brutus' anguished imagining:

> Between the acting of a dreadful thing
> And the first motion, all the interim is
> Like a phantasma or a hideous dream.
> The genius and the mortal instruments

Are then in council, and the state of man,
Like to a little kingdom, suffers then
The nature of an insurrection. (*Julius Caesar*, II, i, 63–9)

But Brutus follows his conscience, while Macbeth strangles his. Before the assassination, in a soliloquy that parallels that of Brutus, Macbeth wishes the deed done quickly; he wishes it successful and final. Even while he brushes aside the possibility of an after-life, he knows that "We still have judgment here," and that insurrection breeds chaos. He analyzes the deep damnation of regicide in general and of killing this particular king in these particular circumstances. He is aware of pity, of the universal sentiment against such an act, and belittles the only motive he can find to spur him on—ambition. To act after such consciousness is to kill the best in himself. Until he had created an irreparable breach in nature, conscience did not make Macbeth enough of a coward.

Why did Macbeth and Lady Macbeth murder Duncan? Shakespeare does not explain the origin of evil as he does in *Othello*, where it springs from a contemptuous ignorance of virtue, or as in *Lear*, where proud anger burns the heart and selfishness freezes it. In fact, he scarcely explains their deed at all. Macbeth and his lady understand what is virtuous; they are neither uncommonly proud nor selfish nor unfeeling nor passionate. If we may judge by their talk and their meditations, "ambition" is no answer. The horror is in the sudden unopposed flourishing of evil in a man and a woman of such potentialities for good. Seeking reasons for their act is motive-hunting among motiveless somnambulists, for they are left essentially unmotivated.

Perhaps this is just as well. The mystery in evil remains, or should remain, greater than that in virtue; for if evil had reason to support it, it would cease to be evil. Neither Macbeth nor Lady Macbeth explains their purpose or seeks to justify their deed—as if the mere arguing of hideous purposes would present them too clearly to allow action. They can act only when they refuse to consider, only when they concentrate on some subordinate virtue, such as unwavering resolution or courage, while throttling the reigning conscience. Such a mutilation of nature must lead to a deliberate duplicity. His wife is aware of Macbeth's double nature: he is too full of the milk of human kindness for effective aggrandizement; he wishes at once to be great but innocent, high but holy, fortunate but true, successful but God-fearing. He worships simultaneously in the temples of the Goddess Fortune and of the spirit. She will upbraid him with the valor of her tongue; she will give steel nerves to his infirm purpose. She responds to the news that Duncan is coming to their castle—"Thou 'rt mad to say it!"—with the frightening immediacy of Macbeth's reaction to the prophecy. Yet her dire instinct to help fate needs strengthening; and she is unaware of her own double nature, or of how hard it will be to kill the better twin, as she voices her terrible prayer that she may lose all tenderness and remorse:

> Come, you spirits
> That tend on mortal thoughts, unsex me here. (I, v, 39–55)

The world, and her own character, she feels, may be stamped by an act of the iron will. She believes that there's nothing either good or bad, but thinking makes it so. She lashes her husband into seeing his scruples as craven fears. In her imagination she thinks she has the power to dash out her babe's brains; she wills herself to believe that "the sleeping and the dead are but as pictures" while the grooms are smeared with blood; that "a little water clears us of this deed"; and that Macbeth's haunted imagination is "the very painting of your fear"; she tries resolutely to maintain the outward appearance of order at the ghost-ridden royal feast; in her sleep-walking she argues that power need not feel fear. Yet she cannot will herself into heartless action for more than a moment. Both her normal self and external facts oppose and overcome the unbending determination of which she had imagined herself capable: she would have killed Duncan had he not resembled her father! "Who would have thought the old man to have had so much blood in him?" Her resolution in evil breaks sooner than Macbeth's, because her imagination, limiting her to an illusion of ruthless power, is not congruent with her own nature.

Macbeth may be seen in his wife, who has no name but his. They are bound in a terrible sympathy, each being to the other not only (in Macbeth's phrase) the "dearest partner of greatness" but of fallen grace. The two of them are but man-and-woman variations on the blank desire for evil, the inexplicable negative principle, the frequent insanity that believes the will can change the very pattern of nature. But Macbeth's imagination ranges forward and backward in time; and an act, even before it is done, enlarges in frightening import and flares its glaring consequences in his mind. Nevertheless, he too seeks to impose his will upon the unrolling of time. "If chance will have me king, why, chance may crown me," he argues openly, while his actions show him to believe neither in chance nor the resigned will. He tampers with order and futurity. He insists on arranging his destiny. He secures the witches' assurance that no man of woman born shall harm him, and he reasons that therefore he need not fear Macduff. "But yet," he adds, "I'll make assurance double sure And take a bond of fate. Thou shalt not live!" And in a final assurance that he shall never be vanquished until Birnam Wood moves against Dunsinane, he is still unsatisfied. "Yet my heart throbs to know one thing," he insists, and when the Weird Sisters in unison warn him: "Seek to know no more," he continues: "I will be satisfied. . . . Let me know." The procession of the kings of Scotland in answer to his questioning leads him only to a more merciless butchery, and to a resolution "But no more sights!" Neither in his thoughts nor his deeds is he willing to accept the natural order. His spiritual ambition soars beyond Doctor Faustus, and he wills that fate itself shall give him bond. Yet in the drama of his mind, he finds himself ultimately subject to that ruling conscience which he had denied and tried to murder. Insurrection and regicide shake "the single state of man."

To Macbeth and Banquo each of the Weird Sisters addresses a prophecy. Four of these six utterances deal with position in the material world, and over these Macbeth broods. He ignores the other two sibylline pronouncements to Banquo, that express the double judgments of *virtù* and of virtue:

Lesser than Macbeth, and greater.
Not so happy, yet much happier. (I, iii, 65–6)

In his first soliloquy, his mind is troubled like a fountain stirred, and he himself sees not the bottom of it. "This supernatural soliciting," he whispers to himself, "cannot be ill; cannot be good." By his own worldly judgment, how can it be ill, since it promises him success which is already partially founded in fact? By the standards of conscience, how can it be good when his hair stands up and his heart knocks at the "horrible imaginings" of murder? He is losing his bearings in the bewilderment of "Nothing is but what is not." Fair is foul, and foul is fair.

But the "murdering ministers" continue to act through the dedicated person of his "dearest love," as she drugs him, drunk with hope, even as she had drugged the grooms with wine into "swinish sleep." Murder, which in her phrase of "this night's great business" appears ominously neutral, will give them "solely sovereign sway and masterdom." In her appeal to his courage and desire, she taunts him into unifying his nature in merciless resolve. When he objects that he dares to do all that befits a man, she asks ironically what beast it was, then, that made him confide in her. Manhood is unscrupulous daring "to be more than what you were." Memory and reason may be drugged; power may instill fear and silence in others. Guilt may be washed off with a little water, or passed on to others by gilding their hands with blood.

While their resolution congeals, short scenes are interjected in contrast: Lady Macbeth's smiling reception of the gracious king; Banquo's warning that he will take counsel with his friend Macbeth so long as he may keep his "bosom franchis'd and allegiance clear." But his friend's bosom is already choked with perilous stuff, his mind is diseased, his clear allegiance murky. As his dark decision silhouettes itself, as he moves toward the deed he will not scrutinize, the frantically wilful gesture in the dark— accusing nightmare images rise to torture him and show that the ghost of conscience still dwells in the deserted house of the soul. Visions outweigh reality in this spiritual tragedy, that begins with witches, and proceeds through "strange images of death," "horrid image," "horrible imaginings," "horrible shadow! unreal mockery!" "fatal vision," "slumb'ry agitation," "thick-coming fancies," "horror, horror, horror!" air-drawn daggers, hands and oceans stained with blood, ghosts, apparitions, omens, a third mysterious murderer as if slaughter itself could not be trusted, and inexplicable voices that cry in the night—to a final lassitude and inanition. Here are none of Lear's and Othello's purging tears, but a slow dessication. Blood thickens, light thickens, the milk of human breasts dries up, "The spring, the head, the fountain of your blood Is stopp'd, the very source of it is stopp'd," and vision turns to stoniness at sight of "a new Gorgon." The intensity of this one murderous deed infects creation, so that while "wicked dreams abuse the curtain'd sleep" in Macbeth's mind, "Nature seems dead"; and Macduff rouses all sleepers to "see the great doom's image!"

To confirm his act, Macbeth nerves himself to destroy the principle and innocence of life itself—women and children, the lineal flow of blood, "the very firstlings" of the heart. But though his hand may act the murder of infants, his imagination sees pity as a naked new-born babe, allied with the elements to publish his guilt universally. Whatever brazen show of terror he may force upon the court of Scotland, in his own mind Macbeth cannot "equivocate to heaven." He cannot say "Amen!" nor can he take his wife's counsel to forget his uneasiness. At times he dares to face the truth that his "eternal jewel" has been "given to the common enemy of man"; he dares to see that "both the worlds suffer"; he dares to know that his course is hopeless and that the snake which he has scotched will close again and be herself. He dares to know that "Blood will have blood." He learns, and admits, that the world of brute fact is for him unreal, and that spirit may fill a chair when the flesh lies safe in a ditch. In the olden time, men died when their brains were out; "now they rise again."

Macbeth and his wife struggle pitifully to enhearten each other, but their joint terrible deed has condemned them each to expiate his crime in solitude, each one keeping alone and making companions of his sorriest fancies. Macbeth's deepest tragic sincerity wells in his longings to call back the irrevocable: "Wake Duncan with thy knocking! I would thou couldst!" Since "What's done is done," then there is left only the terrible yearning for forgetfulness:

> Better be with the dead
> Whom we, to gain our peace, have sent to peace.

But Macbeth, who has murdered sleep, will sleep no more; and the play is a long diminishing agony of "these terrible dreams that shake us nightly."

He cannot share Banquo's conviction that "In the great hand of God I stand," nor Banquo's humility in hiding self-acknowledged "naked frailties," for his own unacknowledged deformities are hidden under the desecrated robes of the good king. Instead, he must lie "on the torture of the mind in restless ecstasy," until torture itself finds sordid relief in the multiplication of acts of butchery which habit renders almost meaningless. Before the world he excuses his stricken conscience as "a strange infirmity," but he and his wife know that he has fallen into a feverous fit that cannot be cured. Immediately after the first deed—"from this instant"—he had realized that

> There's nothing serious in mortality;
> All is but toys; renown and grace is dead;
> The wine of life is drawn. (II, iii, 98–100)

He learns early that his crown is fruitless and his sceptre barren. The stupid dullness of life (if he could forget the nightmare visions) steels him to mechanical acts of safety, and he resolves that

> For mine own good
> All causes shall give way. (III, iv, 135–6)

His "initiate fear," when he was "but young in deed," must be hardened by action. As his soul dries up and atrophies, he knows that he must not look to have what should accompany old age—"as honour, love, obedience, troops of friends." Lady Macbeth, whose body walked long after her spiritual suicide, and who in her fear of darkness took to sleeping with a light by her continually, is now dead; and the news of her death he receives with something far other than the controlled stoicism of Brutus on Portia's death, for he has lost the capacity to feel. The disease, as even the physician knows, is of the spirit, and the patient must minister to himself. His desperation leads to final scenes of meaningless anger, impatience, weariness, or indifference. He has supped so full of horrors that they can no longer startle him; his soul is callous before life, which has become for him the idiot's tale of no significance. If the report that Birnam Wood moves is false, then hang the messenger! If it is true, Macbeth does not care if he himself is hanged. The brief candle gutters out in sluggish bestial images: Macbeth thinks of his "fell of hair" as though he were a beast; and sees himself tied to a stake like a bear surrounded by dogs. In the last scenes he is a husk of habits, the ghost of a suicidal soldier, a dead man walking. When he learns from "the angel whom thou still hast serv'd" that his avenger Macduff was not of woman born, he curses the "juggling fiends" who paltered with him in a double sense.

But the fiends in reality were within him, self-approved. Macbeth's blindly insurgent will is the dwarf tyrant and usurper that disorders the harmony of his soul. The long battle between daring and fearing is at last over; and he is left at the end with nothing but the desperate courage of the trapped animal, unable to be thankful—for in his self-destruction, to whom can he pray?—even for death.

The first surging back of the ordered world that began with the knocking at the gate, has swelled until the stage is filled with God's soldiers. The tragedy closes on the themes of measure and "the grace of Grace." Yet external circumstance, though it may oppose or coincide with the decisions of the mind, can at best merely parallel or supplement the healings of virtue and the fevers of vice. In the portrayal of the main characters who absorb our interest, though we are looking at the dark side of the moon, moral certainty is strong and hopeful: they dared attempt the destruction of their vivid consciences; and their undying con-

sciences destroyed their warped wills. Macbeth and his lady suf-
fered in their own spirits. Had they been less sentient or less
morally sensitive, *Macbeth* would not have been a tragedy, but
the melodrama which it is sometimes termed. The two principal
figures are the greater and the nobler, even in their severed love,
because they learned through their mental suffering that the moral
world cannot be outwitted or outwilled.

The dark tower of tragedy is mysterious. It is a proud tower,
menacing, closed in upon itself, almost windowless, built in stony
isolation. The perilous approach to it may—must—be made. And
the trustful and generous and gentle man, the chivalric champion
of larger interests than his own, confronts it undaunted.

CHAPTER SIX

Roads to Freedom

FROM THE apex of the great tragedies, any possible change in Shakespeare's art and understanding might seem to be of necessity a falling off. *Macbeth* itself appears narrower and more negative when it is considered close to *Lear*. But the subtle vitality of Shakespeare's mind creates new possibilities and new patterns. The creative energy is not yet willing to rest; and in the three plays of *Timon of Athens, Antony and Cleopatra,* and *Coriolanus,* he is not content to die into mere imitation, or simplification, or forgetfulness. *Timon* will be a sketch, an essay in dramatic form that allows him to judge in retrospect his own temperament and career. The writing of *Timon* frees him from himself to such a degree that he is able, in his last two tragic visions, to pour his passion into his art and to use his knowledge to achieve a kind of impersonality.

The art itself has become a moral act. Its greatest beauty is the exact delineation of complex characters and events, the undeviating assessment of devious values. Sympathy does not lead him to the shielding of weakness; nor does his moral sense permit him to designate for all eternity the rescued and the lost. In the world of his complex speculations, there is no decisive closing of the

Book of the Dead. He establishes frames for moral action and judgment, and within these frames his characters move free and independent. Knowledge of humanity could not be more comprehensive or more faithful. He returns to his favorite themes: the miracle of love between two human beings in *Antony and Cleopatra*, the solidarity of society in *Coriolanus*. Yet neither theme is considered exclusively: the state is of importance in the tragedy of the two lovers; and in *Coriolanus*, the fate of Rome depends upon family relationships. These tragedies seem more relaxed only in comparison with Shakespeare's greatest work. Since no man can bear for long tragedy at white heat, Shakespeare has learned to observe the fading coals from a distance, and with a certain detachment. Every quality carries with it its own defect: though his open nature instinctively leads Shakespeare to care for every human being he creates, his imaginative experience is now teaching him ways not to care. In compensation for the loss of intensity Shakespeare gains clarity of judgment: the love-story of a queen is overwhelmed in history by an indifferent empire; Coriolanus' ideal of a republican Rome (in comparison, say, with a realized England in *Henry V*) appears unrealizable and cold.

TIMON OF ATHENS

Like some of the plays of the dark period, *Timon* seems written more from personal need than from dramatic inspiration. It lacks drama; it lacks characters except for Timon and Apemantus his churlish counterpart, and perhaps Timon's steward Flavius. Apparently Shakespeare tossed it to his hungry company unfinished, despairing of making a stageable piece of work out of an anecdote that had fascinated him.[1] Though he had succeeded in shaping a play out of the interior drama of Macbeth's conscience, he is less lucky in realizing the conversion of Timon to misanthropy. The simple plot seems providentially designed to illuminate a part of his own experience: the generous lover and truster of men falls on evil days, learns that men are hypocritical and

selfish, and dies hating and cursing the human race. All that Shakespeare need do is to reproduce imaginatively his own shift in mood
from the golden comedies to the dark plays. First the rose and
then the canker. But Shakespeare no longer lives in either of his
earlier convictions. They are over and done with. It is as if, though
he can understand and portray any new or imagined attitude, his
own past beliefs in their original forms are sloughed off like dead
skins. They cannot be reproduced or repeated successfully.
Timon, either as the simple lover or the simple hater of men, turns
out to be too naïve to arouse sympathy. Paradoxically, what
should be an interior tragedy of recognition and reversal comes
to depend upon outward chances. The external symbols do not
seem good enough, are not tied in inevitably with the changes in
Timon's mind. They cause the change, rather than symbolize
it—as if a noble character could be destroyed by a handful of gold-
pieces. The great themes of generosity and bounteous human
nature, or of small weaknesses twisted by desire or need or indecision into fatal ruptures, are vulgarized into banquets in rooms
of state, or the queuing up of bill collectors.

Of his hero, Shakespeare can say: "The middle of humanity
thou never knewest, but the extremity of both ends." Even by
implication the play hardly offers a corrective for such extremities, for the speaker of the above sentence is Apemantus, the "poor
rogue hereditary"; and opposed to Timon's reckless veerings (except for a handful of loyal and powerless underlings) there are no
characters but this "churlish philosopher," flatterers, tradesmen,
mistresses, maskers, thieves, usurious senators, and an angry renegade soldier. Shakespeare does not here look with sympathy upon
remembrance of things past. The complete philanthrope and the
complete misanthrope appear alike uncongenial in the extremity
of their convictions. Though the play falters as a positive statement of convictions, nevertheless it serves as a coda that allows
him to repeat outgrown themes and to dismiss them from his mind
in favor of the complicated harmonies of the last romances. The
playwright may say with Antony, "Things that are past are done
with me," and after this final *reprise* of earlier movements, turn

with freedom to his vivid dreams of Antony and Coriolanus.

Though in *Timon of Athens* he did not create a good play, Shakespeare exercised his art in finding structures for the old beliefs. Intuitions are marshalled into forms. Once again experience, not precept, must be the teacher. "He will not hear till feel." Timon's reckless liberality must be squared with the penny-pinching selfishness of the world; he must learn that his own desire for a brotherhood of free-hearted gentlemen does not remake society. Bounty creates its own warm kingdom: "Being free itself, it thinks all others so"; but the actual world is full of prudent men who are not their brother's keepers. In three successive scenes, Timon's indebted friends refuse to help him. The play is developed musically, so that after the first act of prodigality, and the second act of warning that an incredulous Timon brushes aside, the third act introduces this opposing theme of self-interest, triply repeated in short scenes. For the time being, and for the purpose of clear development, "This is the world's soul." So sharply have bounty and parsimony, trust and self-interest, been presented singly and then opposed, that one may say:

> Is 't possible the world should so much differ
> And we alive that liv'd? (III, i, 49–50)

The ideas are given human flesh and movement—in the processions of sycophants and retainers, in the great banquet and its opposed cynical travesty, in the flatterers' "serving of becks and jutting-out of bums" contrasted later with their "certain half-caps and cold-moving nods" that freeze Timon's steward into silence. In its context, there is implicit criticism even of Timon's noble outpouring to his friends, friends, friends: the "very soul of bounty" would deal kingdoms to his companions, as if he believed with Lear that love may be bought by the giving of lands. Like Satan tempting Christ in *Paradise Regained*, he extends the worlds of the senses and of art and luxury to cement allegiance. Timon "outgoes the very heart of kindness"—but the gloss on such praise is that "Plutus, the god of gold, is but his steward." Poets and painters and jewellers court Timon; the companionable guests speak of a brace of greyhounds and "four milk-white horses, trapp'd in silver"; Cupid's masque presents the five best Senses to gratulate Timon's plenteous bosom; and in the ocean of his indulgence Timon dares to believe "Faults that are rich are fair."

Parallel with the opening theme of opulence runs a counter-pointed melody, or cacophony. "Like madness is the glory of this life." Apemantus, the sneering commentator, is "opposite to humanity," say Timon's flatterers; and Timon himself chides Apemantus for his uncompromising cynicism: "Y' have got a humour there Does not become a man; 'tis much to blame." Apemantus is confident that friendship is full of dregs, that men are deaf to counsel but not to flattery, that the strain of man is bred out into baboon and monkey: "I wonder men dare trust themselves with men." He trusts no man, prays for no one but himself, and limits his needs to honest water and "a little oil and root." Though his philosophy is based upon suspicion and denial, his position in the play is ambiguous. His unhappy revelling in unhappiness places him at an extreme, but some things he sees clearly. He knows the creditors' servants to be "Poor rogues and usurers' men! bawds between gold and want!" His penury of soul makes him a gifted critic of all excess, of extravagance and gluttony. He sees "what a number of men eats Timon," and Timon in his mad misanthropy appropriates this counsel to pass on to the bandits: "You must eat men." At the heart of the play, the two contrasting melodies join in a duet, in the contest between Apemantus and Timon before the cave in the woods near the seashore. *Timon of Athens* uses over again much of the material of *Lear*, as if that tragedy, in spite of its two parallel plots, were so huge in scope that its mere leavings might furnish forth another play.[2] Just as Lear in his exiled madness is set in contrast with Edgar and the Fool, so Timon in his agonized revilings is played against the professional cynicism of Apemantus, until he too has learned to strip the false world to mere necessities, to see through men to "the things themselves," and to gnaw on one poor root.

Who is the greater misanthropist? Shakespeare was ironically aware that it is easy for the dispossessed to curse: "Who can speak broader than he that has no house to put his head in? Such may rail against great buildings." And Apemantus takes savage joy in pointing out to Timon that Timon is a misanthrope by necessity, who would rather be a courtier than a beggar. But Timon answers (and it is a belief that every play by Shakespeare exemplifies) that a state of being is most poignantly realized through contrasts. Apemantus' nature commenced in sufferance and was hardened in time. "Why shouldst thou hate men? They never flatter'd thee." But Timon, who has had "the world as my confectionary," has been exposed by a single stroke,

> bare
> For every storm that blows—I to bear this
> That never knew but better, is some burthen. (IV, iii, 265-7)

The generous and trusting man can be hurt far more than the niggard soul. "What has thou given?" Timon asks Apemantus. Shakespeare adds accuracy to Tennyson: it is bitterer to have loved and lost than never to have loved at all.

Timon in each of his moods is intransigent. The "starlike nobleness" of his trust is as far removed from reality as the annihilating fury of his curses, when he would sweepingly destroy mankind and the destroyers of mankind together. Surrounded by flatterers, he proclaims "I am wealthy in my friends." He is no more mistaken here than when, surrounded by faithful servants, he generalizes that men are like swallows, fleeing the winter and following the warmth: "Such summer birds are men." Being a man, he is unnatural and ill at ease both as the angelic rewarder of angels and the scourge of God against ungrateful beasts. Repeatedly he reminds himself that he must renounce his humanity. Pity is womanish. His grace before meat invokes the gods to prepare man for destruction. His prayer calls for a universal confusion and an all-embracing hatred that extends "to the whole race of mankind." To the "visible god" of gold, the sweet king-killer, he prays for that rebellion and chaos that will give to beasts "the

world in empire." His theme is renunciation, never reconciliation: if Athens is to be destroyed, he cares not, cares not, cares
not. And out of kindness to anyone who suffers from what
"nature's fragile vessel doth sustain In life's uncertain voyage,"
Timon tells of a tree where that man may hang himself. In his
fevered nightmare, the sun breeds nothing but rottenness; and
the earth, that common whore, brings forth abhorred births in
profusion.

Since plenty multiplies monsters, Timon's only course is the
whittling away of desire, the contraction of the heart, the wither-
ing and dessication of the spirit, the concentration on nothingness, the anatomizing of a wretched corpse bereft of a wretched
soul:

> My long sickness
> Of health and living now begins to mend,
> And nothing brings me all things. (V, i, 189–91)

Poverty and nakedness are his discoveries; "a dedicated beggar
to the air," he will embrace the wintry world as the true one;
his radical misanthropy will dig in the fecund earth for nothing
richer than one poor root; and the gold which his grave need
uncovers will be used to corrupt mankind.

The extraordinary negation of Timon's "latter spirits" is resolved only by death, and the drive of the play remains ambiguous. The piece appears an exercise in purgation, personal to
Shakespeare rather than dramatically controlled. The destructiveness of unchecked sympathy and overmastering hatred will
be channelled off by giving them both free flow, even if a dramatic vehicle must be sacrificed in the process. The ordered
world was never envisioned more fully than in Timon's
paean:

> Piety and fear,
> Religion to the gods, peace, justice, truth,
> Domestic awe, night-rest and neighbourhood,
> Instruction, manners, mysteries and trades,
> Degrees, observances, customs and laws. (IV, i, 15–9)

Yet it is constructed by Timon only in order that his curse may strike it down with infectious fevers and general filths. "The commonwealth of Athens is become a forest of beasts," and every beast is subject to some more potent bestiality, or to the final horror of falling into "the confusion of men." The irreconcilable visions strike each other off in vivid contrast, and the intensity of Timon's giddy rage, after his pure trust is shattered, may turn a disaffected soldier and a handful of gold into a cosmic image of destruction:

> Be as a planetary plague when Jove
> Will o'er some high-vic'd city hang his poison
> In the sick air. (IV, iii, 108–10)

The structure confirms some moral judgments and denies others. "Three strangers," for instance, serve for a moment as a chorus uninvolved in the action, to comment on heartless flattery as the soul of the world, to express admiration for Timon's bounty, nobility, and illustrious virtue, and to state nevertheless that now men must learn to dispense with pity, since "policy sits above conscience." Or again, Timon's complaint that the nature of man is to promise friendship and never to perform it might be considered part of his insane misanthropy, if it were not reinforced by the next scene in which the false poet and painter plan again to hoodwink Timon with expectations. They are redundant in their disenchanted glee: "promising is the very air of the time"; performance is dull; only in plain and simple people do words and deeds square; "to promise is most courtly and fashionable"; but performance argues a great sickness in judgment.

If shaping the incidents here is cynical, so is assigning to the timorous and money-loving senators speeches of excellent moral advice. Timon might well have listened to the words of one senator:

> He's truly valiant that can wisely suffer
> The worst that man can breathe, and make his wrongs
> His outsides, to wear them like his raiment, carelessly,
> And ne'er prefer his injuries to his heart,
> To bring it into danger. (III, v, 31–5)

Or again: "To revenge is no valour, but to bear." The three senators are answered by Alcibiades, as hot for honor and blood as
Troilus. "If wisdom be in suffering," he argues, why should not
soldiers "let the foes quietly cut their throats"? Why is not the
ass more captain than the lion? Almost eagerly, Alcibiades accepts man's imperfections as the basis for action:

> To be in anger is impiety;
> But who is man that is not angry?

In fighting against the cold prudence of the senators he finds a
cause worthy of his "spleen and fury," and the final scene of the
play allows him to enter Athens in triumph over its governors.
They are like Polonius in their impotent decaying wisdom, like
Angelo in their mechanical application of the law, like the
burghers in *King John* or the citizens in *Coriolanus* in their time-
serving worship of power. Yet in the wallets of the sapless senators are the scraps of wisdom.

In one respect, however, the structure of the play modifies the
inflexible bitterness of Timon's thought. Timon in his opulence,
weeping tears of joy, had seen men as brothers commanding one
another's fortunes. His radical opinion was a mistake, but his
rigid reaction was no less a mistake. In his overthrow, his loyal
servants actually find fellowship in misery. "We are fellows still,
Serving alike in sorrow." The certainty of life is dissolving, their
ship is sinking, and they all, "poor mates," must part into "this
sea of air." Yet in parting, the steward Flavius asks that "for
Timon's sake Let's yet be fellows"; they embrace one another;
and Flavius, in exquisite criticism of the needless lavishness of
earlier scenes, divides the last of his money with his comrades:

> Let each take some.
> Nay, put out all your hands. Not one word more!
> Thus part we rich in sorrow, parting poor. (IV, ii, 27-9)

Flavius has the self-forgetful integrity of Horatio, of Kent, of
Cordelia and the Fool, of Viola, of the old servant Adam (whose
part Shakespeare himself is reputed to have played) who follows
Orlando into exile in the forest. Flavius alone is able to break

through Timon's unyielding misanthropy. His genuine service
and love cause Timon to say:

> Forgive my general and exceptless rashness,
> You perpetual-sober gods! I do proclaim
> One honest man. (IV, iii, 502–4)

And though Flavius is powerless to melt Timon further, though
Timon blesses him with riches coupled with the precept to "show
charity to none," his place in the action and his victory over
Timon's all-embracing hatred entitle him to speak as close to
the voice of truth. He knows what mockery it is to live "but in a
dream of friendship." He knows "the fierce wretchedness that
glory brings us." He is fully aware of the nature of his world:

> What viler things upon the earth than friends,
> Who can bring noblest minds to basest ends!
> How rarely does it meet with this time's guise
> When man was wish'd to love his enemies!

Yet he knows equally his own integrity and honest grief, and
he prays sincerely that he may love those that would mischief
him. Out of his own charity toward his "dearest master" he presents the truest sketch of Timon:

> Poor honest lord, brought low by his own heart,
> Undone by goodness!

For Shakespeare, in this piece even more than in most of his
plays, cannot entirely free himself from his own predilections.
He can judge Timon as rash both in the moods of adorer and
vilifier of mankind, yet at the same time allow himself some
identification with his maimed hero. He can find both pleasure
in loyal love and relief in universal curses. He can summon up
to the sessions of his thought the themes of trust and of treachery
that he has played over singly, and by objectifying them in one
figure, by placing them in keen contrasts, can free himself from
their single tyrannies.

Nevertheless, in this play of pity and fury, his balanced judgment at times blurs the clarity of the oppositions: Timon's curse of the courtesans wavers into Lear's pity of the miserable:

And thatch your poor thin roofs
With burthens of the dead—some that were hang'd.
No matter! (IV, iii, 143–5)

Timon is a *tragédie manquée* because the hero's "dangerous nature" corrects one error by falling into another. The end of *Timon* is only death, whereas the end of tragedy is the transcending of death in the discovery of truth. Of man's littleness Timon is safely aware by the end of the play; but to man's capacities for good, he is irrecoverably blind, for

His discontents are unremovably
Coupled to nature. (V, i, 227–8)

Yet Shakespeare himself, from his own experience, has pity on Timon's fury. He will exalt this little world of man by coupling Timon with nature, with the sun, the moon, the earth, and the "marbled mansion" of the sky, in the image of Timon's grave, of

his everlasting mansion
Upon the beached verge of the salt flood,
Who once a day with his embossed froth
The turbulent surge shall cover.

"Rich conceit," he writes—and it is Shakespeare's own conceit, verging upon sentimentality, that creates the image—

Rich conceit
Taught thee to make vast Neptune weep for aye
On thy low grave, on faults forgiven.

What faults, and whose, are forgiven? The sea had been an image of boundless love in the generous certainty of the early plays. In the tragedies, all great Neptune's ocean will not wash away the blood of a murderer. Perhaps in *Timon* faults are forgiven in death, in a sea of forgetfulness, since evil is not operant in the "wretched corpse," which is no longer either an arch-villain or an arch-sufferer. Perhaps also Timon's faults, of too much and too little trust, are forgiven of necessity, because they had been Shakespeare's own.

Timon's gravestone is the oracle of this play. Its theme is the death of something noble, but the epitaph is not written in the spirit of tired senescence. Although in general

> Nature, as it grows again toward earth,
> Is fashion'd for the journey, dull and heavy,

Timon himself never becomes a dull and heavy old man: even in death he wishes his bitterness to be remembered. There is in this play too much fury, too determined an effort to throttle pity, to leave an impression either of indifference or resignation. Shakespeare is aware of beggary and bounty, of fierce wretchedness and the riches of our friends. He projects this awareness of irreconcilables in the person of a lord of Athens who is lord only of extremities, and who dies unreconciled. "With a wound I must be cur'd." (*Antony and Cleopatra*, IV, xiv, 78) The mere presentation of this wounded failure, this fanatically pure spirit who demands a single simple interpretation of life, may have allowed Shakespeare to lay old ghosts and to proceed, in the plays to come, toward acceptance, instead of denial, of the enigma and the mystery.

ANTONY AND CLEOPATRA

No play of Shakespeare's surpasses *Antony and Cleopatra* in grandeur of scope and scale. Only *Lear* equals it. For the last time Shakespeare exercises simultaneously all of his magnificent powers. *Antony and Cleopatra* is not always grouped with the great tragedies partly because it escapes from any easy category. The subject is suited to tragedy; yet Shakespeare flushes it with an elusive mood that makes the tragic suffering relatively unimportant; and he permits his two lovers to come "smiling from the world's great snare uncaught."

In the very style and structure of the play Shakespeare shows the certainty of his approach. Coleridge, *feliciter audax* in his criticism, sensed the "happy valiancy" of the verse. Shakespeare here surpasses himself in the complexity of his characterization, the comprehensive awareness of all moral values, and the richness of his poetry. Ironically, the play is often considered a formless chronicle precisely because its subtle shaping is so close to perfection. It is developed as is a musical composition—by opposed movements, and repetitions, and the tone coloring of reiterated and varied symbols—rather than by the discursive narrative and direct argumentation of playwrights who are less gifted as poets. And as we watch the dramatic presentation through characters who change, slip, and slide each in apparent autonomy, we do not notice the firm governing structure.[3] Yet Shakespeare himself has given *Antony and Cleopatra* a proper classification: it is a "scene individable, or poem unlimited."

The outlines are sure. The wheel comes full circle in the plot: Antony and Cleopatra are together at the beginning and are reunited at the end; the main course of the play records their temporary separation, in space and then more significantly in spirit. Power and love fight for dominance. Octavius is pure empire, Cleopatra "the finest part of pure love," and in neither character is there a tragic conflict. The struggle that shakes the world is merely the outward result of the interior conflict in Antony's mind. Power establishes its empire in the Roman world, while love sets up its triumphant kingdom in the hearts of the two lovers. As a focus in which the main presented action may be scrutinized in miniature (Shakespeare had used the trick before), Enobarbus is created so that loyalty and worldly success, "will" and reason, may war within his breast to a conclusion.

Shakespeare takes the classical tragic theme—the conflict between love and duty—and treats it romantically. The classic solution is the triumph of duty over love. The call of duty or honor—since it is nobler, or at least quantitatively is bigger, usually involving the welfare of more individuals—must outweigh personal desires, for the whole is greater than any of its parts.

But Shakespeare is no rational or mechanical moralist. He dares to reverse the classic tragic pattern, to suggest that the quality or intensity of an emotion is superior to the counting-house reckoning of the social reason. He wagers all for love. Shakespeare is at one with Aristotle in holding that in the truly moral nature instinct and intelligence are in harmony, as in Cleopatra. But in this play he is a romantic rather than an Aristotelian in believing that if they cannot be harmonized, then instinct must be chosen. Perhaps he is creating a dream of freedom rather than a way of life. It is a dangerous doctrine, for it depends upon the unverifiable quality and integrity of a particular passion, when passion in general may more frequently degrade than exalt. And it requires his greatest persuasiveness, in reshaping the old story of the royal courtesan and the great man ruined by lust.

Just as in the portrayal of Timon's unbridled misanthropy he had shown sympathy with a position whose weaknesses he knew, so in *Antony and Cleopatra* he dares to defend the illicit passion that set the halves of the world at war and destroyed its possessors. How may he hope to be felicitous in such boldness? The writing of the play constitutes in itself a moral act of judgment. Deliberately he takes four steps: he must demonstrate that "reason" is mistaken; he must belittle or blacken the cause of empire; he must make passion larger than the world; and he must spiritualize and ennoble an historical liaison until it appears as the true quality of love.

Enobarbus serves as the moral microcosm for the play. He is heart and head, personal confidant and impersonal chorus. In one rôle he is loyal follower and friend—the Horatio or Emilia or Kent or Menenius of the tragedy. In his other rôle he is the hard-headed soldier, like Philip the Bastard in *King John*, roughly breaking through the surfaces of diplomacy and convention to expose the true springs of human conduct.[4] He makes no mistake in his political forecasts, and his analyses of the relations among Antony, Octavius, Lepidus, Pompey, and Octavia are just. In his first scene, speaking of women, he knows that "between them and a great cause, they should be esteemed nothing." Yet what is the tone of his succeeding description of Cleopatra to Antony?

Her passions are made of nothing but the finest part of pure love. We cannot call her winds and waters sighs and tears. They are greater storms and tempests than almanacs can report. This cannot be cunning in her; if it be, she makes a show'r of rain as well as Jove. (I, ii, 151-7)

And in what spirit does he answer Antony's wish never to have seen Cleopatra? "O, sir, you had then left unseen a wonderful piece of work, which not to have been blest withal would have discredited your travel." There is mockery here, but like one of Cleopatra's attitudes toward Antony, it is mockery mixed with admiration. Enobarbus is Antony's ironic intimate. This is the man who is confident that Antony will not leave Cleopatra for Octavia: "Never! He will not." This is the man who in his own person can say of the lovers: "He will to his Egyptian dish again" and yet describe Cleopatra in the barge passage in willing enchantment. He is equally familiar with "affection" and "occasion."

Lepidus, and all reasonable men, know that "small to greater matters must give way." But Enobarbus in his answer, "Not if the small come first," bases his judgment on human experience rather than on reason. Lepidus may reprove him with "Your speech is passion," but reproof cannot change Enobarbus' double nature of seeing clearly and feeling deeply. He is in reality what Iago simulates—the bluff soldier whose rough cynicism hides a loyal heart. He enjoys his plainness. As the play develops, he is thrown the lines that criticize Antony's errors, and draws apart from his master as Antony loses his "absolute soldiership" and "would make his will Lord of his reason." Shakespeare develops in Enobarbus, as he does in Octavia,[5] the tragic choice between two opposing goods; and like Octavia, he can find "no midway 'Twixt these extremes at all." Repeatedly he presents them to himself, only to place heedless loyalty above the calculated saving of his own skin.

> Mine honesty and I begin to square.
> The loyalty well held to fools does make
> Our faith mere folly. Yet he that can endure
> To follow with allegiance a fall'n lord

> Does conquer him that did his master conquer
> And earns a place i' th' story. (III, xiii, 41–6)

For a while he holds to his allegiance: "I'll yet follow The wounded chance of Antony, though my reason Sits in the wind against me." But finally—and still in terms of formal contrast between passion and reason—he makes his fatal decision:

> I see still
> A diminution in our captain's brain
> Restores his heart. When valour preys on reason,
> It eats the sword it fights with. I will seek
> Some way to leave him. (III, xiii, 197–201)

In the moulding of his theme, it is one of Shakespeare's finest touches that Enobarbus first hints at his desertion of Antony when he witnesses Cleopatra temporizing with Caesar's messenger:

> Sir, sir, thou art so leaky
> That we must leave thee to thy sinking, for
> Thy dearest quit thee.

In this single instance, Enobarbus is mistaken in his judgment, failing to distinguish between one more of Cleopatra's surface "becomings" and her underlying constancy. It is a failure in trust, of the same sort as Othello's, and Shakespeare makes the most of it. Enobarbus furnishes a unique instance in Shakespeare of the loyal follower who deliberately chooses to forsake his master. His decision allows his creator to magnify Antony in his extreme defeat: "Go, Eros, send his treasure after. Enobarbus!" And the death of Enobarbus, "a master-leaver and a fugitive," who knows himself to be "alone the villain of the earth," intensifies in action Shakespeare's own moral judgment between passion and reason, between the loyalty of fools and the self-interest of knaves. He dies with "Antony" on his lips—"Nobler than my revolt is infamous." In the comedies, smiling common sense knows that men do not die for love. But in this fiction, in this dream of passion, intensity of emotion ambiguously blurs with realism, and the physical cause of Enobarbus' death is not specified.

> This blows my heart.
> If swift thought break it not, a swifter mean
> Shall outstrike thought; but thought will do 't, I feel.

One is at liberty to believe that remorse no less than swords may pierce the heart, as joy and grief flawed Gloucester's and Lear's.

What kind of world does the repentant Enobarbus renounce? Shakespeare paints it as a society of cold self-interest and prudence, occasionally shaken by the accidents of personal whims. It is Edmund's world of "The younger rises when the old doth fall." The "boy Caesar" icily calculates his policy. He sells his beloved sister to Antony in a state marriage, in order to present a united front of triumvirs against the dangerous Pompey. He concludes a peace with Pompey which lasts only until he can safely defeat him in battle. Getting there first with the most men, he finds it laughable that "the old ruffian" Antony should try to engage him in personal combat by appeals to honor and taunts of cowardice. The stability of the Roman empire is consolidated by a combination of accidents and of Octavius' cool littleness of spirit. The course of history, as Shakespeare shapes it, might have been changed on board Pompey's galley, if Pompey's captain had quietly slit the throats of the triumvirs. Pompey forbids the assassination on a point of honor: "In me 'tis villany; In thee 't had been good service" (though like Henry IV he regrets that murder had not been done unknown to him); and Pompey is lost. The wild revel of the rulers of the world on Pompey's galley is immediately succeeded by a contrasting scene in which a soldier extends the empire. But Ventidius too is cautious in his power politics. He is cynically aware that Caesar and Antony have ever won more through their lieutenants than in their own persons; but he refrains from too brilliant a conquest for fear that he may arouse Antony's jealousy.

The world which Pompey had thrown away in chivalry Octavius carefully appropriates by seizing the weak triumvir Lepidus on trumped-up charges. Against Antony and Cleopatra he proceeds with all the devices of the police state. Antony's deserters are planted in the van of battle in order to take the heart out of him. A wedge is to be driven between the allies by according Cleopatra all concessions if she will dismiss or kill Antony. She is taken into custody by force while she listens to fair speeches. Fear and favors alternate in the best fashion of totalitarian government: she is threatened with harm to her children; yet she is soothed with soft words as if she were a stupid animal to be caged and fattened for a parading triumph: "Feed and sleep."

It is a slippery world, in which not even policy may count on reward: the deserters from Antony are forced to fight against him, or are hanged, or have no honorable trust from Caesar for their pains. And Shakespeare's thoughtful deliberation, rather than carelessness, may explain the fact that though the dying Antony counsels Cleopatra to trust none about Caesar but Proculeius, it is Proculeius who bands with Caesar to betray her, and Dolabella from whom she learns, almost accidentally, Caesar's purposes.

As Shakespeare here distorts for his own ends his usual conception of the great firm Roman state, Caesar becomes an "ass unpolicied," and the world apart from Antony and Cleopatra is a "great snare," a dull spot "no better than a sty," a "vile world" in which there is no reason for lingering. There can be little remorse in a hero's mind for failing society, when society is made up of drunkards and cutthroats and little men of policy, contributing their mite of glossy speech and guarded actions to a megalochaos of accidental judgments and casual slaughters. If Antony is to fail tragically, it must be because he is false to his own conception of himself rather than false to his social obligations, for Shakespeare has intentionally portrayed a political world that "is not worth leave-taking."

And if Antony is to fail tragically, he must be built up to towering stature. His own integrity as a soldier must outweigh the world's opinion, and his love for Cleopatra must outweigh his integrity. He is larger than the world, and his love is larger than himself. The technique of magnification swells through the play, from Caesar's full-length portrait of the hardened campaigner in the first act to Cleopatra's contrasting dream of Antony in the last scene, in which his face is the heavens, his eyes the sun and moon, his voice the music of the spheres, his generosity Ceres and the sea, his raiment kingdoms, and realms and islands the small coins in his pockets. Her vision ends in an involved superlative: the mere remembrance of Antony, "past the size of dreaming," triumphs over any conceivable work of fancy or of nature or of the shadows of our night. His soldiership is twice that of Octavius and Lepidus put together; Hercules his forebear and Mars are associated with him until the trinity moves as one; while his ancestor Bacchus is casually disregarded. A daemon guards him, "noble, courageous, high, unmatchable"; he quarters the sea with his sword, and with ships makes cities on green Neptune's back; and his schoolmaster Euphronius knows that in comparison with such magnanimity he himself is no more than "the morn-dew on the myrtle leaf To his grand sea."

The images jet like fountains in Cleopatra's agony over the dying prince of the world. He is "noblest of men," and in his death the crown of the earth melts, the garland of the war withers, the soldier's standard falls. Distinctions are levelled, the odds are gone, all is but naught, and within the great sphere of the moon's orbit nothing is left that is remarkable.

Antony's great spirit glitters in all the facets that Shakespeare can conceive. The fifteen short surging scenes of the fourth act show him from many angles—pitied by the efficient Caesar; sentimentally sad enough to make his followers onion-eyed; deserted by the god Hercules, whom Antony loved, to the accompaniment of mysterious music in the air, under the earth; as a workmanlike hopeful soldier teasing his squire Cleopatra while she buckles on his armor; as the unreproving rewarder of the corrupted Enobarbus and as the cause of Enobarbus' heartbreak at the desertion of such a "mine of bounty"; in battle and in triumph; in rage and defeat; in murderous anger against Cleopatra; in resolution and reunion in the arms of death.

Caesar may well say that "The death of Antony Is not a single doom; in the name lay A moiety of the world." For Antony dominates his followers whether they are hacked to pieces in battle like Scarus, or commit suicide like Enobarbus out of guilt at deserting him, or like Eros out of love for "that noble countenance Wherein the worship of the whole world lies." His name echoes through the fifth act, after he is dead. His enemies are compelled to praise him: "A rarer spirit never Did steer humanity." And Caesar, who can afford regret when Antony is dispatched, knows him to have been "my brother, my competitor In top of all design, my mate in empire, Friend and companion in the front of war, The arm of mine own body, and the heart Where mine his thoughts did kindle"—though Shakespeare cannot resist an ironic twisting of the dagger by having Caesar break off his eulogy to attend to an Egyptian messenger.

Perhaps Antony is the most comprehensive character that Shakespeare set his hand to. The supercilious Caesar tells us at the beginning that in Antony

> You shall find there
> A man who is the abstract of all faults
> That all men follow. (I, iv, 8–10)

Yet Lepidus caps Caesar's estimate in one of his rare lucid moments of preferring truth to compromise, and says, in a cosmic simile characteristic of the play:

> I must not think there are
> Evils enow to darken all his goodness.
> His faults, in him, seem as the spots of heaven,
> More fiery by night's blackness.

His sovereignty of nature ignores consistency and scorns self-justification. He is equally natural in his dignity—"Fulvia is dead," or "I am not married, Caesar"—and in his childish and impotent rage: "He makes me angry with him. . . . He makes me angry." His is the nature of "infinite variety." Since his vitality is so enormous that it cannot be governed by lesser men, he is his own only possible master and judge. His lieutenant Canidius knows that Actium would have gone well "Had our general Been what he knew himself." Repeatedly, Shakespeare voices the idea that "none but Antony Should conquer Antony." [6] Even his enemies acknowledge that his greatness can be destroyed only by himself:

> He is dead, Caesar,
> Not by a public minister of justice
> Nor by a hired knife; but that self hand
> Which writ his honour in the acts it did
> Hath, with the courage which the heart did lend it,
> Splitted the heart. (V, i, 19–24)

Basically, Shakespeare makes confidence into a moral quality in Antony. He has no lack-luster doubts or palterings. No matter how rapidly his moods shift, no matter how recklessly he remains a "child o' th' time," at every moment he is master of himself and others. This headlong certainty of purpose is here interpreted as but another manifestation of generosity, magnanimity. Antony's character once again may be illuminated by words describing Cleopatra, who "being royal, Took her own way."

The tragic theme of the play lies in Antony's painful struggle to renounce his former greatness and accept his present enchantment. Shakespeare's dramatic equity was never stronger than in his allowing full expression to the world's opinion as to Antony's course. Antony in Egypt is a lascivious wassailer, a strumpet's fool, an instrument for a gypsy's lust. The sensual chattering Egyptian court affords him "present pleasure." [7] More important, Antony himself at times, sobered by far-off events, sees his course of life in Egypt as idleness, and determines that "I must from this enchanting queen break off." The violence of his passion draws him back to Cleopatra. Like Othello, he must sacrifice to love his occupation as a soldier. The wrench of renunciation is not presented in formal speeches but dramatically—in the anguished throes of his own dissolution. It is given a great symbol at Actium, when his doting sails turn away from a possible world-victory to follow Cleopatra. It is keyed low in his shame in the ensuing scene: "I have offended reputation—A most unnoble swerving." And it is presented without compromise as a hideous and degrading agony in three scenes: his vile upbraiding of Cleopatra when he is jealous of Caesar's messenger; his unreasoning rage in defeat, when he drives Cleopatra away as "the greatest spot of all thy sex"; and his resolution that she shall die the death for betraying him. The swift succession of scenes in the fourth act is designed to show the melting away of his soldiership and of his faith in Cleopatra, until the fragments may be formally collected in Antony's own image of his nature—shifting as the clouds, indistinct as water is in water, unable to hold a visible shape.

His picture of himself is not completely true. With equal formality, Shakespeare shows that at all moments of crisis Antony obeys a force more firm and fixed than his own self-esteem. The multiple conflicting tides of his sea are subject to the pull of the moon, of Isis, from whom Cleopatra is descended. Over his spirit she exercises full supremacy; her summons might command him away from the bidding of the gods. After the disgrace of Actium, hesitant to approach each other, and sharing a common shame, the weeping Cleopatra for once is almost at a loss for words, and Antony is too deeply hurt for recriminations. His dazed reproaches melt away into the moral intuition of the play:

> Fall not a tear, I say. One of them rates
> All that is won and lost. Give me a kiss.
> Even this repays me. (III, xi, 69–71)

The motif is repeated in a wilder, ampler vein when Antony has Caesar's messenger whipped. He flagellates Cleopatra with words, in a rage before which she stands helpless until it has spent itself. Yet when she says simply:

> Not know me yet?

he finds his heart again in her unswerving love, and again sets his hope upon victory after conflict—with its reward, "once more To kiss these lips." The third return of this motif of passion-followed-by-peace is the clearest and most melodramatic of all. In his unreasoning rage, Antony vows to Cleopatra's messenger: "She has betray'd me and shall die the death." It is too late. Cleopatra has played out her last "becoming," and through her messenger Mardian has dared to ask the final question: What would you do, what would you feel, if I were dead? "Dead, then?" are Antony's words. And, once more given the assurance of death which itself is but a shadow (for Cleopatra yet lives), Antony is certain of his course:

> Unarm me, Eros. The long day's task is done,
> And we must sleep.

He will overtake Cleopatra, and weep for her pardon, as she had wept for his.

But the play does not end in tears. Passion is not only larger than the world; it is spiritualized, ennobled, triumphant. Cleopatra throughout is "marble-constant" in her love. From her first wranglings to her last contrived fit of temper against her treasurer, her every action purposes continued union with Antony. He is her single thought. To consider the play as showing the final regeneration of a coquette is grossly to misread the text. Her nobility is evident and natural in the face of death, for she can rise to any occasion; but she, no less than Antony, has such innate and lavish regality that neither is in danger of confusing nobility with a grave primness, and even in the parting moments she may joke with a clown.

Having no inner conflict, calamity for her depends on external circumstance—separation from Antony. She bends all her efforts to hold him. She is a prestidigitator with moods. But her infinite variety is on the surface, and is directed to one sole end. In the third scene, when her becomings all fail, when she knows that Antony will leave her, when he chides her with idleness or frivolity, she drops every mask, reveals her secret, and greets like a queen the death of her one desire:

> 'Tis sweating labour
> To bear such idleness so near the heart
> As Cleopatra this. But, sir, forgive me;
> Since my becomings kill me when they do not
> Eye well to you. Your honour calls you hence.

She yawns out the great gap of time during his absence; she unpeoples Egypt with messengers as the filaments of her love; she matches his jealous rage by whipping her own bearer of unwelcome news; her femininity cheers itself uneasily with belittling of Octavia, as earlier she had derided Fulvia; she whiles away the hours (which are at last idle) with velleities—"Let him for ever go!—let him not!"—and with dreams of Gorgon or Mars, and with the detailed accounts of her messengers, and with recollections of times past. Her powerless waiting is at last rewarded. Her firmness keeps his circle just, though Athens and Rome are on the arcs, and makes him end where he began.

The love which Cleopatra never loses, to which Antony returns, and from which in spirit he is never long absent, is exalted by all the art at Shakespeare's command. At the very start, we learn that "There's beggary in the love that can be reckon'd" and that to set limits to the love of this noble pair requires the finding out of "new heaven, new earth." The kingdoms of the world are clay, the wide arch of empire falls, when such a twain embrace. "Here is my space. The nobleness of life is to do thus." When they are together, eternity is in their lips and eyes, and none of their parts so poor but that it is a race of heaven. If Enobarbus as an onlooker can know that defects in Cleopatra turn to perfection, that vilest things become themselves in her, and that she makes hungry where most she satisfies, how multiplied must such attraction be in the bounty of love! Shakespeare develops the idea in formal antiphony, and projects into dramatic figures the wonder he had himself expressed in the sonnets:

> What is your substance, whereof are you made,
> That millions of strange shadows on you tend? (LIII)

If Antony may admire his taunting queen

> Whom every thing becomes—to chide, to laugh,
> To weep; whose every passion fully strives
> To make itself, in thee, fair and admir'd! (I, i, 49-51)

Cleopatra senses the same glory:

> O heavenly mingle! Be'st thou sad or merry,
> The violence of either thee becomes,
> So does it no man else. (I, v, 59–61)

She is his Thetis, he the demi-Atlas of this earth. He makes her his "absolute queen"; to her he is "that great medicine" or "Lord of lords! O infinite virtue!" All the East shall call her mistress; they exchange kingdoms as remembrancers. The theorem that Shakespeare works out is that the greatness of their love may be demonstrated in objective terms by presenting the greatness of the empire that is thrown away recklessly for its sake.

More important than material symbols are the mental images. Significantly, their passion is almost invariably presented—in this play so often misapprehended as a portrayal of libertinism and lust!—in terms of the wedding of true minds, in contrast, for instance, with the sensuous descriptions of beauty and love in *Romeo and Juliet*, or with the emphasis upon sensual passion in *Troilus and Cressida*. Significantly also, their suffering from physical separation is trivial compared with their suffering when they are separated in spirit—when Antony in his thunderbolt moods, in his agonized change from conqueror of the world to servant of love, destroys himself and Cleopatra in his tortured ragings. Antony's heart makes wars only on Cleopatra, when in despair he feels that this false soul of Egypt, "Whose bosom was my crownet, my chief end," has beguiled him "to the very heart of loss!"

But this is transient nightmare. Though his temporary failure in trust is actually in part responsible for their physical deaths, the spirit of love in all important moments conquers and calms them. The estranged Cleopatra sends her messenger with the news of her supposed suicide and the foreboding command: "Bring me how he takes my death." She is brought in grim irony the dying Antony. He has given her himself. He has given her the losing of the world—a harder gift, from less ambiguous motives, than that of winning a world. This deliberate losing, when to hold both the world and Cleopatra is past the size of dreaming, shows the spaciousness of his spirit. Antony could have won the world from Octavius if he had so chosen; but Octavius could never have lost the world for anyone. More important, Antony's final gifts to Cleopatra are his solicitude for her honor and safety, and his laying at her feet of his best self, not base, not cowardly, but valiant: "the greatest prince o' th' world, The noblest." She must forget the miserable change of his last days, and please her thoughts by feeding them on Antony's former fortunes.

The union of their minds, the mutual planetary pull of their thoughts, is shown in the echoing motifs. It is Antony in his curses that first imagines Cleopatra displayed monster-like to the shouting plebeians in Caeser's triumph; but it is Cleopatra, preparing for her death, who again lets her mind play with Antony's hateful pictures. The poignancy of this echo does not lie in the shameful pageant the Romans plan—for Cleopatra had decided earlier to "conquer their most absurd intents"—but in her recollection of Antony's momentary spite.

Each moves toward death under the inspiration of the other. Antony, thinking Cleopatra dead, falls upon his sword when "My queen and Eros Have by their brave instruction got upon me A nobleness in record." And as its complement, Cleopatra's resolution is given its strength through Antony's suicide:

> what's brave, what's noble,
> Let's do it after the high Roman fashion
> And make death proud to take us. (IV, xv, 86–8)

Her attendants move in sympathy with her resolve, and almost in Antony's words and rhythm Iras responds:

> Finish, good lady. The bright day is done,
> And we are for the dark.

Union becomes reunion as Cleopatra knows that "I am again for Cydnus To meet Mark Antony."

"The secret house of death" is a welcome refuge and hospice.

Passion is transformed into the finest part of pure love by removing it from the world in the repeated theme of love-in-death and death-in-love.[8] Even Eros is dismissed by Antony—"From me awhile"—before his secret communion with his dead queen. Shakespeare's tragedies have depended upon moral values that may be found in the world of experience. But love in this play is so spacious that the mortal world is not enough, and images of a future life rise in dreams. Antony moves toward Cleopatra:

> I come, my queen. . . . Stay for me.
> Where souls do couch on flowers, we'll hand in hand
> And with our sprightly port make the ghosts gaze.
> Dido and her Aeneas shall want troops,
> And all the haunt be ours. (IV, xiv, 50–4)

And Cleopatra, after Iras, like Eros, has gone as a vanguard to death, moves toward Antony:

> If she first meet the curled Antony,
> He'll make demand of her, and spend that kiss
> Which is my heaven to have. (V, ii, 304–6)

Cleopatra's desire is realized for each of them in a death which is both life and love: "Die where thou hast liv'd! Quicken with kissing." The integrity and intensity of her passion give her the right to the words:

> Husband, I come!

Resigning their other elements to baser life, the lovers have become fire and air.

Antony and Cleopatra is less a tragedy than a victorious vision, a fulfilment of immortal longings. Desire is sharp and pure; and Cleopatra is "a most triumphant lady." In the sense that its protagonists finally create their own glowing worlds, the play is not the next-to-the-last of the tragedies, but the first and greatest of the dramatic romances. The tragic notion of acceptance and abnegation is given expression.[9] But in contrast, the idea that imagination and resolution may reshape or transcend life is whispered, and man is seen as the creator of his fate:

On!
Things that are past are done with me. (*Antony*, I, ii, 100–1)

Well, I know not
What counts harsh fortune casts upon my face;
But in my bosom shall she never come
To make my heart her vassal. (*Pompey*, II, vi, 54–7)

Not Caesar's valour hath o'erthrown Antony,
But Antony's hath triumph'd on itself. (*Antony*, IV, xv, 14–5)

Make not your thoughts your prisons. (*Caesar*, V, ii, 185)

This, then, is one road to freedom. A generous nature, sheer greatness of spirit, may overwhelm any accompanying fault. That Shakespeare should so admire the spaciousness and variety of his heroes' minds leads toward a moral principle that is positive: he is less interested in the eradication of faults than in the free development of men's best impulses. The mind is creative, building a towered citadel or a cloud that's dragonish, making an opulent cosmos out of a little world.

Yet for true freedom, the mind must have a center, and a center outside itself. In this play that center is the marriage of true minds, exalted above all faults and accidents. Love is a creative force, both for Antony and Cleopatra, within the mind. It allays anger, gives medicine to shame, repays all loss, and multiplies its miracles. While each has the other's heart, a million more hearts are annexed unto the lovers'. Love can take as husband the defeated and the dead. The world is not large enough to contain it; nature lacks stuff to equal such dreams; the shadows of mere mortal life must be dismissed as inadequate. In one sense, the play drifts toward a withdrawal from the world which is itself a dream: in experiencing the tragedy, the reader himself may feel:

Hark! The drums
Demurely wake the sleepers.

The asp brings Cleopatra "liberty." Death is not negation, but a liberation that finds new heaven, new earth, and an assurance of a reunion which alone gratifies immortal longings.

CORIOLANUS

Shakespeare's *Antony and Cleopatra* and *Coriolanus* have seldom been classed with his very greatest work. A more accurate
judgment might be that although they show little flagging of his
powers, each falls short of the full expression of the tragic spirit.
The reasons for the two failures are diametrically opposed. Indeed, if these two Roman plays could in some way be melted together, the tragic world would again be complete. *Coriolanus* may
even be considered as the complement and contrast to *Antony
and Cleopatra*—a last stone, perfectly wrought, to complete the
arch of Shakespeare's tragedies.

It has been argued in these chapters that the essence of tragedy
is the simultaneous awareness of man's weaknesses and infinite
possibilities. Man's "infinite virtue" is so presented in *Antony and
Cleopatra* that the play transcends—or falls short of—tragedy,
and emerges as a triumphant romance. The bias is personal, favor-
ing the lovers. In *Coriolanus* the bias is social. The state is more
important than any of its members. Man, even the hero, appears
little in contrast with "renowned Rome"

> whose course will on
> The way it takes, cracking ten thousand curbs
> Of more strong link asunder than can ever
> Appear in your impediment. (I, i, 71–4)

Coriolanus alone has an adequate and exacting social ideal; but
his defects of temperament place him among all those who would
"sack great Rome with Romans." In consequence, the play seems
cold in its passions. The balanced exercise of pity and fear is not
fully effected. Centrifugal terror outweighs centripetal compassion. If sympathy draws the reader in triumph toward Antony
and Cleopatra, cool judgment holds him at a distance from Coriolanus. In one play a dream of love is created; in the other a dream
of the state is destroyed. One play is suffused with imperial opulence; the other has the gray ground-tones of the early Roman
republic.

The play is a continuous quest for a responsible authority. To whom or to what should allegiance be accorded—in the state, in the family (that microcosm of the state), in the hierarchy of man's own faculties? The idea finds its repeated symbol, so natural to Shakespeare's mind, in the image and action of kneeling:

> for in such business
> Action is eloquence. (III, ii, 75–6)

Volumnia implores her son to kneel to the plebeians, "Thy knee bussing the stones"; Coriolanus bitterly imagines his armed knees bent to receive an alms; the citizens speak of their families and themselves praying for the tribunes on their knees; Menenius scornfully suggests that the tribunes fall down a mile before the tent of the avenging Coriolanus "and knee The way into his mercy"; Cominius the general recounts how he has knelt before Coriolanus. Not in words, but on the stage, Caius Marcius, returning in triumph to Rome with his newly won surname of Coriolanus, kneels before his mother. All necessary preparation has been made for Shakespeare's presentation of moral ideas through pantomime in the climactic scene. When "the most noble mother of the world" comes to her son's tent, Coriolanus kneels before her:

> Sink, my knee, i' th' earth;
> Of thy deep duty more impression show
> Than that of common sons. (V, iii, 50–2)

In a reversal that horrifies him, in order that she may "unproperly show duty" and may indicate how the natural order of obedience has been overturned, Volumnia kneels to her son. It rouses Coriolanus to a speech whose intense cosmic imagery is quite uncharacteristic of him:

> What is this?
> Your knees to me? to your corrected son?
> Then let the pebbles on the hungry beach
> Fillop the stars! Then let the mutinous winds
> Strike the proud cedars 'gainst the fiery sun,

> Murd'ring impossibility, to make
> What cannot be, slight work!

When the continued pressure of all her arguments and passion cannot move him, and Coriolanus turns away from his supplicants, Volumnia at the crucial instant has recourse again to pantomime, to the scornful image of allegiance disregarded: "Down, ladies! Let us shame him with our knees. . . . Down! An end! This is the last." Virgilia, Volumnia, and Valeria are on their knees. But the final trifle that tips the hovering scales, in this drama of filial piety, is the kneeling of his young son:

> This boy, that cannot tell what he would have
> But kneels and holds up hands for fellowship,
> Does reason our petition with more strength
> Than thou hast to deny 't.

His mother needs but one more idea of desolating bitterness: Is Coriolanus banished in his own spirit as well as in fact? Is his separation from his own past and from the fellowship of Rome an actual estrangement on the deepest levels of truth? Does Rome no longer flow through the rivers of his blood? Must all men and women and children withdraw from this lonely dragon? The threat of this withdrawal is in reality the last hypothesis:

> Come, let us go.
> This fellow had a Volscian to his mother;
> His wife is in Corioles, and this child
> Like him by chance.

The struggle is over. "He holds her by the hand, silent." But he has lost his battle—or won his victory.

Pantomime plays its part in the significant ordering of the dramatic action: in the kneeling, the doffing of caps in fear or humbleness, the throwing aloft of caps in victory, the donning or casting off of the "gown of humility," in the treading or standing on the prostrate, in the massing of soldiers or senators or plebeians, in the formal processions of state triumphant or suppliant, and in the deliberative councils.

As in *Antony and Cleopatra*, the purpose of this play is made certain by the structure. Such ambiguities as it possesses are consciously developed; they are not careless inconsistencies, but parts of the ironic comprehensiveness of the author's vision. The welfare of the state is the basic standard, to which every action is ultimately referred. Coriolanus, its chief defender, is flawed in character; his defects and qualities are explicitly assessed in accordance with a conventional theory of tragedy. The whole production is given coherence and clarity by the dominating metaphor of the body and its parts, by imagery selected from the work-a-day world and sauced with Roman details from Plutarch, and by a formal concentration, proportioning, and ordering of the scenes.[10] Shakespeare may well have admired the antiquarian accuracy and dramatic economy of his friend Ben Jonson in *Sejanus*, and may have determined to add such virtues to his own scene-making.

Rome—"the Roman state," "the country," "our country," "thy country"—is the hero of this play. In one sense Rome is not so much a *patria* as a *matria*, like the England of the history plays:

> This nurse, this teeming womb of royal kings, . . .
> Dear for her reputation through the world.

Volumnia is one projection of "the country, our dear nurse"—so that when she gloweringly imagines that Coriolanus may "triumphantly tread on thy country's ruin" and in succeeding lines that he may "tread on thy mother's womb that brought thee to this world," the two ideas are interchangeable. But in another metaphor, the dominant image of the play is of the great impersonal body of Menenius' opening parable. Shakespeare expands what he finds in North's Plutarch until the body politic of the fable controls the thought of the play; and the harmony of all its parts, interdependent and interacting, becomes the virtuous end of all deeds.[11]

Menenius in his fable upholds the politic view of common sense. Like so many of Shakespeare's old counsellors, he is too ripe in wisdom and compromise; he sees so much that he loses the name of action. Between the rabble-rousing tribunes and the bluntly contemptuous Coriolanus, the old senator is impotent.

Coriolanus is presented as the soul of the Roman republic. His political theory, if it could be separated from his personality, is admirably noble and altruistic. In his own mind, he is the servant of a state in which all citizens should be servants. Yet his idealism is uncompromising. He gives again the old answer to the old question: What would happen if someone told the truth? In politics—at least in Rome and in Shakespeare—absolute truth-telling will not work.

Coriolanus is modest because he is the servant of the state. In Shakespeare's iridescent thought, such a statement is not the whole truth; and often enough this modesty is presented as a trick of inverted pride, so that Coriolanus sounds as conventional as a football captain before a microphone.[12] Yet there is principle back of his brushing aside the recounting of his exploits—"Will the time serve to tell? I do not think." He sees himself and others as natural parts of a common effort: "I have done As you have done—that's what I can." And he renounces a special share of booty in order to stand upon his "common part." He had rather have his head scratched in the sun than hear his nothings monstered, and precipitately he leaves the stage when he is about to be praised. Cominius, knowing that a state should reward merit in its citizens, may be right in reproving his young lieutenant for too much modesty and for too much cruelty to his good name: "You shall not be The grave of your deserving." But the cunning tribunes are surely wrong in their analysis of Caius Marcius' acceptance of a subordinate position under Cominius; their motive-hunting reveals only their own foxships. Caius Marcius acted as a soldier, whose satisfaction and pride spring from a job well done. He "rewards His deeds with doing them."

Coriolanus is the watchdog of Rome. Or in terms of the images in the play, he is not the "lamb that baes like a bear" as the tribunes would have him, but the "bear indeed, that lives like a lamb" as Menenius sees him. He clamors and fights only against those who, as he sees it, would destroy the state. Service is all he desires—

not power.[13] But the service must be on his terms. Though he shudders away from appearing before the undeserving populace, his response to the senate upon being made consul is unaffected and simple:

> I do owe them still
> My life and services. (II, ii, 137–8)

Before the respected senators, therefore, he will passionately plead that they must not throw away the safety and health of Rome because of fear or lenity or ignorance. The whole of the third act is a tumultuous presentation of clashing theories of governance. When Coriolanus is unprovoked, his prayer for Rome glows with noble sincerity:

> Th' honour'd gods
> Keep Rome in safety, and the chairs of justice
> Supplied with worthy men! plant love among 's!
> Throng our large temples with the shows of peace
> And not our streets with war! (III, iii, 33–7)

But he is constantly provoked—by the tribunes who place the good of their class and their own personal power above the welfare of Rome. Coriolanus fails to see how they play upon his own personal weaknesses. The senators in turn fail to see the fundamental political weakness that is opening a chasm in the state. Coriolanus talks to the air. The senators are good but most unwise, grave but reckless; their softness is dangerous. As the tribunes, those Tritons of the minnows, move toward absolute power, Coriolanus poses an unanswerable dilemma: "You are plebeians If they be senators."

> When two authorities are up,
> Neither supreme, how soon confusion
> May enter 'twixt the gap of both and take
> The one by th' other. (III, i, 109–12)

Coriolanus' conception of the state is not left for speculation. It is developed fully, with all its reasons and purposes. To grant privileges to the citizens, instead of exacting services, is to nourish disobedience and feed the ruin of the state. *Panem et circenses!* Such temporizing gifts to the clamorous multitude debase the nature of government, and will only be interpreted as the concessions of fear. "We are the greater poll." The well-proportioned figure of the state will turn into a megacephalic idiot. This "double worship" of conflicting governing powers can only increase the opposition between disdainful patricians and insulting plebeians. The genuine needs of government will come to depend upon unstable slightness, when action can be concluded only "by the yea and no of general ignorance." "Nothing is done to purpose." Those "that love the fundamental part of state" must therefore take radical action to rescind the mistakes precipitated by emergency and rebellion. They must restore a responsible and unified authority, and "Let what is meet be said it must be meet."

This patrician's idealism, which escapes being despotism only because it is based on the firm conviction that the senators are the born and trained servants of the state, is too extreme for practical politics. Temperance, when it is presented in the play, goes unheeded in the conflict for absolute authority. Coriolanus "cannot temp'rately transport his honours." "Being once chaf'd, he cannot Be rein'd again to temperance." "Nay, temperately! Your promise," says Menenius just before Coriolanus' wildest outburst. And the old senator ruefully remembers that Rome, peaceful for a moment under the exultant tribunes, might have been much better if Coriolanus "could have temporiz'd." It is impossible. Coriolanus' intolerant altruism clashes against the opposite extremes of popular appetite; the city is unbuilt and laid flat; violent ideals generate opposed violent action; and as the rabble shouts "Down with him! down with him!" against Coriolanus, poor Menenius disappears in the maelstrom with the disregarded advice of "On both sides more respect."

Nevertheless, Shakespeare's conservative and aristocratic cast of mind takes its own pleasure in shaping events. He goes out of his way to develop an incident to show that Coriolanus does not hate the people and the poor as a class, but the sloth, vacillation, stupidity, and greed which he finds so frequently among them: the only gift that Coriolanus begs of his general after the victory at Corioles is freedom for "a poor man," "my poor host," a stranger among the Antiates whose very name Coriolanus in his weariness cannot recall. The voice of the people is doubled in triviality, halved in dignity, by being assigned to the indistinguishable twin tribunes Brutus and Sicinius. The plebeians themselves are dangerous—not less so because they are often well-meaning. They are again and again allowed to speak like kindergarten pupils or morons:

Ingratitude is monstrous; and for the multitude to be ingrateful were to make a monster of the multitude, of the which we being members, should bring ourselves to be monstrous members. (II, iii, 10–4)

The unsteady people and the villainous tribunes are sketched in to the verge of caricature. The final touch is given in workmanlike fashion when a civil servant, an impartial spectator, is allowed to say that Coriolanus' "noble carelessness" frankly reveals to the people "the *true knowledge* he has in their disposition."

Yet Shakespeare's even-handed justice, his sense of the almost infinite complexity of any specific moral decision—or his superb dramatic sensitivity, which is much the same thing—compels him to put in caveats and demurrers. In these later plays, Shakespeare is steadily moving toward a world where the important values lie entirely within the individual mind. The inner and outer worlds are therefore sharply separated. This is true even in this subtlest of his political studies of the state. It is true even while Coriolanus stands for consul in the Forum, and the electors dissolve into air, into thin air: thirty times in a single scene they become no more than "voices," voices, voices. It is true even while we see the great body of Rome turn into a thousand-tongued monster tettered with measles, a many-headed multitude, a Hydra. It is true at the turning-point of the play, when the absolute popular "shall" overwhelms reason and banishes Rome's defender as "enemy to the people and his country." Coriolanus turns on all Rome and says in his magnificence: "You common cry of curs, . . . I banish you!" In order to make his portrait of Coriolanus a pure demonstration of inner conflicts Shakespeare stacks the evidence: the popular cause is shown as stupid, sordid, and selfish; Coriolanus is given a nobly unassailable theory of government. He banishes Rome and withdraws into "a world elsewhere." Within his own nature he finds defeat and victory.

Once the problem is so set, Shakespeare does not spare his hero. Though Coriolanus may be granted "true knowledge" of the people's fickleness by one spectator, another immediately answers: "To seem to affect the malice and displeasure of the people is as bad as that which he dislikes—to flatter them for their love." Cominius has already reproved him at length for his impatient modesty. His impassioned plea for the safety of the state is broken across by the comment:

> You speak o' th' people
> As if you were a god to punish, not
> A man of their infirmity. (III, i, 80–2)

Does the hero act in choler or within reason? Even in the words of praise at the end, as his "noble corse" is borne off to the sound of a dead march, we are reminded of "his own impatience."

His integrity seems absolute. "He is himself alone." Coriolanus will not divide himself with the world. Though the world may be filled with beggars and cowards and curs, it is dangerous to call them by their names. Nor is it charitable. Coriolanus remains adamant; he is "what he cannot help in his nature"; he will be the people's servant in his own way or no servant at all. He cannot be ruled; he cannot dissemble with his nature as his mother can with hers; he cannot understand why his friends would have him false to his beliefs; his attempt to exchange his disposition for a "harlot's spirit" must obviously end in failure because of the very mood in which it is undertaken; he thinks continually of the "sign of what you are." His narrow rigidity is summarized clearly in Aufidius' formal character sketch, which points out his

> nature
> Not to be other than one thing, not moving
> From th' casque to th' cushion, but commanding peace
> Even with the same austerity and garb
> As he controll'd the war. (IV, vii, 41–5)

He mars his fortune because "His nature is too noble for the world." His greatest lovers—Menenius, Volumnia, Aufidius—in the very heart of their admiration are aware that pure nobility may itself be a disastrous extreme. Volumnia tells him flatly:

> You are too absolute;
> Though therein you can never be too noble
> But when extremities speak. (III, ii, 39–41)

His mother, out of ambition for her son, gives him worldly advice, though it dishonors her more to beg of him than for him to beg of the people:

> You might have been enough the man you are
> With striving less to be so. (III, ii, 19–20)

Yet they cannot help glorying in his excess. Volumnia flaunts the tribunes:

> As far as doth the Capitol exceed
> The meanest house in Rome, so far my son . . .
> Whom you have banish'd does exceed you all.

To Aufidius, embracing him as dearer than a wedded mistress, he is "most absolute sir." And Aufidius, even when he has become jealous of Coriolanus' prowess as an ally, must admit:

> I think he'll be to Rome
> As is the osprey to the fish, who takes it
> By sovereignty of nature. (IV, vii, 33–5)

Whatever may be his particular fault, Aufidius knows that "he has a merit To choke it in the utt'rance."

His merits admitted, Shakespeare seeks from beginning to end for the tragic fault. At the very start, one of the citizens sees that the people need not thank Coriolanus for his service, since "he pays himself with being proud." And as for his military accomplishment, "he did it to please his mother and to be partly proud, which he is, even to the altitude of his virtue." In formal summation, before the final trial of his nature, Aufidius scrutinizes the character of his great foe. It is characteristic of Shakespeare that the tragic flaw is not to be reduced to a single ruling passion, but is multiplied into several hypotheses:

> Whether 'twas pride,
> Which out of daily fortune ever taints
> The happy man; whether defect of judgment,
> To fail in the disposing of those chances
> Which he was lord of; or whether nature,
> Not to be other than one thing, . . . but one of these
> (As he hath spices of them all, not all,
> For I dare so far free him) made him fear'd,
> So hated, and so banish'd. (IV, vii, 37–48)

Pride? Lack of policy? Intransigence? Or some hypothetical combination among them?

It is also characteristic of Shakespeare that the last catastrophe results from a far more tragic theme than the textbook punishing of peccadilloes. Shakespeare reverts to his conception—it was clearly present in *King John*, and embryonic even in *The Two Gentlemen of Verona*—that the truly tragic choice is between two irreconcilable goods, one of which must be abandoned. He prepares for Coriolanus' decision by displaying Volumnia's parallel decision. She compels him to think with himself "How more unfortunate than all living women" is her feminine embassy in their divided allegiances. Her painful choice is presented in such certain balance and with such driving reiteration that it must be quoted in full:

> For how can *we*,
> Alas, how *can* we for our country pray,
> *Whereto we are bound*, together with thy victory,
> *Whereto we are bound?* Alack, *or* we must lose
> The country, our dear nurse, *or else* thy person,
> Our comfort in the country. We must find

An evident calamity, though we *had*
Our wish, which side should win; for *either* thou
Must as a foreign recreant be led
With manacles thorough our streets, *or else*
Triumphantly tread on thy country's ruin
And bear the palm for having bravely shed
Thy wife and children's blood. (V, iii, 106-18)

How can Shakespeare make credible a tragic split in a character of such unyielding integrity as that of Coriolanus? To answer
such a question one must turn back through the play to see the
little tricks by which a full personality is revealed. Coriolanus has
made himself into the professional soldier. He hurriedly throws
off the gown of humility in order that he may know himself again,
for his armed knees bow but in his stirrup. He does not care for
the good opinion of amateurs, but for Aufidius, the second soldier
of the world—"Spoke he of me?" The emulation between these
two is played up throughout: Coriolanus wishes for another war
that he might again drive Aufidius from the field; and Aufidius
views his rival with varying admiration and jealousy. When
Coriolanus defeats him—the forewarning comes in the first act—
Aufidius will give up his honor for wrath or craft, in order that
he may wash his "fierce hands in 's heart."

Yet Coriolanus is so absolute in his soldiership that he cannot
be defeated in arms. He is the "flower of warriors." He knows
that "brave death outweighs bad life," and that his country is
dearer than himself. Death lies in his "nervy arm"; his sword is
"death's stamp"; he is "a thing of blood" and strikes Corioles
"like a planet." The first third of the play is given over to the
exaltation of Rome's defender, until it seems undeniable that
"valour is the chiefest virtue and Most dignifies the haver." He
drives himself and others unsparingly. The soldiers before Corioles
know how impossible an example he may set for others to follow,
and he is rough on those closest to him even in jocular triumph: he
greets his wife as "My gracious silence," and turns to his anti-
quated friend Menenius with the words: "And live you yet?"

Even his language is in the lineage of the Shakespearean sol-

diers—Philip the Bastard, Hotspur, King Harry, Enobarbus—
and modifies by attraction the diction of the entire play. To the
flourish of trumpets and the sound of drums he is ceremoniously
hailed by his new-won name of Caius Marcius Coriolanus. He
answers:

> I will go wash.

When his old friend counsels him to speak courteously to the
citizens, his impulse is to "Bid them wash their faces And keep their
teeth clean." Contrasted with the glow of war, the ground-
images of the play are drawn from the hearth, the family, and
small homely events.

The thoroughbred has had training as well as breeding. The
tribunes themselves are aware not only of the long line of his
noble ancestors, but also "How youngly he began to serve his
country." Cominius recounts his exploits at the age of sixteen,
when he entered "his pupil age" as a man. His mother has devoted
her life to fostering his warlike traits. The comeliness of youth
was not enough for the only son of her womb: she was pleased
to let him seek danger. With a more than Spartan savagery, she
exults in the renown, honor, and fame of her "man-child." "To a
cruel war I sent him." From his mother he had learned that brave
death outweighs bad life—for she professes sincerely: "had I a
dozen sons, each in my love alike, and none less dear than thine
and my good Marcius, I had rather had eleven die nobly for their
country than one voluptuously surfeit out of action." Her contempt for all cowards, Romans or Volscians, that run from her
son's exploits "as children from a bear," her magnifying of her
son's sole valor, rise to a vertiginous dream of slaughter and a
grim picture of her son as death the reaper:

> His bloody brow
> With his mail'd hand then wiping, forth he goes,
> Like to a harvestman that's task'd to mow
> Or all or lose his hire. (I, iii, 37–40)

And when Coriolanus' wife shudders at the imagination of blood,
his mother scornfully turns her aside:

> Away, you fool! It more becomes a man
> Than gilt his trophy. The breasts of Hecuba
> When she did suckle Hector, look'd not lovelier
> Than Hector's forehead when it spit forth blood
> At Grecian sword, contemning.

Blood and mother's milk are mingled, and we are prepared for Valeria's miniature of the young Marcius, "the father's son," who in his rage at falling down in the pursuit of a butterfly, sets his teeth and tears the butterfly to pieces. His grandmother remarks complacently: "One on 's father's moods."

This young boy Marcius (perhaps the youngest character with a speaking part in all of Shakespeare's plays) is no accidental addition. He is the needed symbol of a developing theme. He is "a poor epitome of yours" as Volumnia reminds Coriolanus, urging the boy to speak because

> Perhaps thy childishness will move him more
> Than can our reasons. (V, iii, 157–8)

And as the whole family plead before the avenging soldier, the boy's one speech contains all of his father's fighting independent spirit:

> 'A shall not tread on me!
> I'll run away till I am bigger, but then I'll fight.

There is something boyish about Coriolanus' honor and bravery and anger and stubborn temper.[14]

If Coriolanus is to be swayed from the vengeful purpose which he has deliberately fostered in himself, it must be because of something deeper, more elemental and primal and atavistic, than rational argument. It need not be something great—for the asp in *Antony and Cleopatra*, the handkerchief in *Othello*, has shown "What poor an instrument may do a noble deed!" (or an ignoble). Coriolanus himself knows the "slippery turns" of the world, which may alter the destinies of states "by some chance, Some trick not worth an egg." In the deciding moment, his resolve turns upon his boyish relations with his mother. He had been bewildered and hurt that his mother had not approved his actions

before the plebeians; he shrank from her chiding, and for her sake
and her praises, he tried to change his nature: in a tantrum of rage
he resolved to act "mildly." Now, with supreme dramatic irony,
he is shown instinctively expecting his mother at the very moment he has determined to see no further embassies from the city.
He can resist all her arguments that glance at his honor and integrity, for he has fought them out within himself. He steadies
himself by swearing that determination shall subdue warm impulse:

> I'll never
> Be such a gosling to obey instinct, but stand
> As if a man were author of himself
> And knew no other kin. (V, iii, 34–7)

But he is not self-sufficient; he is still bound to his mother; he has
no answer but silence when she turns scold and dares to assume
the last posture, so unnatural for her, of pitying herself. The
trick not worth an egg is played in the image of a mother hen
clucking at her chicks:

> Thou hast never in thy life
> Show'd thy dear mother any courtesy,
> When she (poor hen), fond of no second brood,
> Has cluck'd thee to the wars, and safely home
> Loaden with honour.

He learns pity from the mother who has taught him to be pitiless.
His choice is made clear-eyed: Rome will live even though its
sons and daughters are trodden upon. So also that miniature of
the state, the human family, is greater than any of its members:

> O my mother, mother! O!
> You have won a happy victory to Rome;
> But for your son—believe it, O believe it!—
> Most dangerously you have with him prevail'd,
> If not most mortal to him. But let it come.

The tragic choice between two goods is formally underlined
by the witnessing Aufidius in an aside:

> I am glad thou hast set thy mercy and thy honour
> At difference in thee. Out of that I'll work
> Myself a former fortune.

The temporal victory of the smaller man over the greater is brought about by a touching again upon the quick of the hero's nature, and by weighing the little things not worth an egg against the affairs of the world. Three times Aufidius displays to the Volscians the balanced scales:

> At a few drops of women's rheum, which are
> As cheap as lies, he sold the blood and labour
> Of our great action. Therefore shall he die.

> He has betray'd your business and given up,
> For certain drops of salt, your city Rome
> (I say 'your city') to his wife and mother.

> at his nurse's tears
> He whin'd and roar'd away your victory.

Though in the tragic inner world a tear may be worth all that is won or lost, it cannot answer in Corioles. Coriolanus defends himself by calling upon the war-god, but Aufidius' answering taunt compresses into a single line the moral complexities of the whole action:

> Name not the god, thou boy of tears!

"Boy! . . . Boy! . . . Boy!" Coriolanus cries, and loses himself in the same rage of hurt pride which his son displayed in mammocking the butterfly to pieces. The childish fury is all that Aufidius needs, and to cries of "Tear him to pieces!" "He kill'd my son!" "He kill'd my father!" the conspirators dispatch Marcius, and Aufidius stands on the body. For the last time, Shakespeare has set inner integrity in tragic contrast to the slippery turns of the world. For the last time the dying hero has returned to his earliest instincts and deepest loyalties. For the last time Shakespeare has used his image of a nature too noble for the world destroyed by its very magnanimity, its death closed over by the life of the worldlings. The long procession is finished—Henry IV after Richard, Antony after Caesar, and Octavius after Antony, Fortinbras succeeding Hamlet, and Cassio Othello, and Albany Lear.

Yet the vistas of freedom may be seen even by the earthbound. The ideal of a perfect state may be held and defended in a city of apron-men and garlic-eaters. Integrity of purpose may still be translated into action and be admired. At the painful moment of choice, it may even rise above itself in a realization of blood brotherhood, in the acceptance of the human family for its miserable weaknesses and thwarted desires as well as for its capacities and aspirations. Human solidarity is such a final good that Shakespeare is even willing to extol war above peace in transient speculations, for peace "makes men hate one another. Reason: because they then less need one another." No man is author of himself, nor can any man afford to know no kin. The strongest man must learn to kneel. And if in these plays there are no gods beyond himself to kneel before, then he must kneel to himself in others. Shakespeare's tragic world stretches as far as the human eye can see in height and width, its vertical warp of passion held firmly in place by the horizontal weaving of compassion.

CHAPTER SEVEN

A World of Images

"Thou god of this great vast, rebuke these surges."

"This cannot be. My daughter's buried."

"Thou that beget'st him that did thee beget."

"In feather'd briefness sails are fill'd,
    And wishes fall out as they're will'd."

"Pure Dian, bless thee for thy vision!"

PERICLES, PRINCE OF TYRE

PERICLES is an old story. In Latin and perhaps in Greek, it whiled away the time of readers in the late Roman Empire, and sprang to life again in late Anglo-Saxon, and again in many medieval versions in many countries, and again in Renaissance England. The adventures of Pericles, or of Apollonius King of Tyre (for the name does not matter in the Greek romances or in their descendants), are as complicated, interminable, and about as convincing as those in a modern soap-opera. Whoever writes it, he may once again, "by relating tales of others' griefs, See if 'twill teach us to forget our own."

Shakespeare tells it as if it were an old story, watched over by the quaint guardian spirit of the medieval poet John Gower. The glow of his poetry, in the two or three scenes where the play catches fire, contrasts with the flat compressed narrative of most of the play almost as deliberately, it might be argued, as Hamlet's Hecuba soliloquy is set against the stilted rhetoric of the players at Elsinore.[1]

The story, for Shakespeare, is "this great miracle." It begins with the escape of the hero from an enchanter's palace of incest, where the speechless semblances of death-pale martyrs slain in Cupid's wars surround the adventurous knight. It continues in flight, in exile, and in cold shipwreck, until Pericles among the poor fishermen—miracle again!—recovers from the sea the rusty armor bequeathed him by his dead father. The hero wins a wife, only to lose her to death and tempest and the sea. Thaïsa is nevertheless miraculously restored by music and the art of Aesculapius, and is given to Diana as priestess. His daughter, too, Pericles loses to the murderous envy of Queen Dionyza—yet once more, in stormy intervention, she is saved by the pirates.

This is the incredible world in which one may die in childbirth and be cast into the raging sea in a coffin—yet, at the end, live again. The gods give man, after trial, his own.

> The rough seas, that spare not any man,
> Took it in rage—though, calm'd, have given 't again.

Proud enemies are burned in their palace, or a fire from heaven shrivels their bodies even to loathing. As for the good characters, everyone will turn out to be royal or wedded to nobility. Though Pericles himself cannot but think it the rarest dream that ever mocked sad fools, his lost daughter, his lost wife, are restored to him.

But the real miracles in this fairy-story are miracles of the spirit. They are presented as sudden illuminations; psychological realism, the slow preparation for an inevitable action, are sacrificed—almost purposefully, in order to make the magical changes more purely magical. Shakespeare no longer appears primarily interested in showing the subtle gradations by which a mind takes on new direction and decision. In *Pericles* there are none of those masterful persuasion scenes, no more dialogues of the mind with itself as it reaches toward a painful choice. The reversals in situation come like bolts of lightning. Men are struck without reference to their own wills; their faults and virtues do not lie in themselves, except for a predisposition to evil or good; free will in the piece exists beyond men, in the stars. In thunder and sudden vision, a mysterious moral order actualizes what has been hidden in man's mind; even as Pericles speculates helplessly on what might happen "Were my fortunes equal to my desires," the sea casts up his deliverance.

One may say, for instance, that when Helicanus refuses sovereignty offered him by the lords of Tyre—"For honour's cause forbear your suffrages"—his loyalty to his lost master Pericles is not even a minor miracle, for similar devotion is a thread through all Shakespeare's thought. But more typically in this play, the sudden flash of virtue in a dark world comes when it is least expected. Thus, Simonides wilfully dissembles his feelings toward his daughter Thaïsa and toward Pericles, much as Prospero harshly tests the loyalty of Miranda and Ferdinand. He threatens to tame his daughter to subjection; he brands Pericles as a wizard, liar, and traitor—only to end his tirade with the sudden smiling reversal:

> Therefore hear you, mistress: either frame
> Your will to mine—and you, sir, hear you,
> Either be rul'd by me, or I'll make you—
> Man and wife. (II, v, 81–4)

Here in a brief four lines is the doctrine of obedience to a power assumed beneficent even when its ways appear bewildering or hostile, followed immediately by a blessing.[2]

Marina has her victories as well. Surrounded by the bawd, the pander, his servant, and the powerful Governor of Mytilene, Marina is to be no Philomel, no Procne. She has only to voice her simple prayer to the gods that she be changed "to the meanest bird That flies i' th' purer air," and it is the importunate Governor who changes—he who had been jokingly asking her keepers the price of a dozen of virginities:

> Had I brought hither a corrupted mind,
> Thy speech had altered it. Hold, here's gold for thee.
> Persever in that clear way thou goest,
> And the gods strengthen thee! (IV, vi, 111–4)

He, too, never dreamed that she could speak so well. Though the sinister bawd and pander are in despair at the destruction of their trade and set on their servant to violate Marina, the brute world of Boult itself yields to her innocent eloquence. In this play as well as in the magic circle of *Comus*, heaven stoops to protect virtue.

The final miracle of the spirit occurs on Pericles' sable-bannered ship, where for three months the hero has lain motionless and silent in his sorrow. Marina wakes him to new life, delivered in his tears; and like a kind of Beatrice prepares the way for the celestial music, unheard by the others, and for the vision of Diana that will reunite him with his lost wife. Marina's natural instinct of love, which leads her to reveal for the first time the secret of her birth, is reinforced and guided by a power outside herself:

> I will desist;
> But there is something glows upon my cheek,
> And whispers in mine ear 'Go not till he speak.'

Over the rippling surfaces of the plot the dramatist glances as swiftly as a water-spider. The story is merely a plane on which he may set up focal points of rest, not to develop believable characters, but to return to central ideas—of integrity, man's helplessness, immutable order, obedience, patience, prayer, healing, and new life—and to the images which support these recurring and interrelated ideas: the sea and the sun, music and the gods. Or, to say the same thing in another mode, here is another book of the *Faerie Queen*, dramatized, in which the hero is a further aspect of Arthur or Magnificence, his wife the True Florimel, Antiochus a Busirane and his daughter an Acrasia, and Marina—how Spenserian even in name!—playing the rôle of a young Britomart or Belphoebe in the brothel scenes. Or to phrase it in still a third way, though this play contains small but distinct echoes from the earlier great tragedies,[3] it is *King Lear*, with its themes of the outcasts in the storm and of restoration to lost love, which is here transposed to another key—as, for example, the poignant compression of Lear's waking in Cordelia's tent is here drawn out lingeringly in the rousing of Pericles from his long dream.

Pericles, then, is neither a comedy nor a tragedy nor a realistic drama nor a problem play nor a morality play. It is a miracle play based upon a Renaissance romance. It is a piece of music. And it sets sharply and unwaveringly the mode for Shakespeare's final moral thought. The device upon the hero's shield is "A withered branch that's only green at top" (II, ii, 43). Many of Shakespeare's own earlier preoccupations still cling like dead leaves— the love-lust contrast, the fatal likeness between hypocrisy and truth, the old sense of sin and tragedy.[4]

But at the top the branch is green. The gods are powerful (though they choose at times to operate through human agents), and they will rescue those of upright mind.[5] A man is saved or damned by his inner intuitions, so that it is enough that Pericles may say: "My actions are as noble as my thoughts," or Marina: "Yet my good will is great, though the gift small." And on the other side, Cleon and Dionyza are condemned for their evil though unfulfilled intentions, no less surely than Christ judged those who sinned only in the spirit:

> The gods for murder seemed so content
> To punish them—although not done, but meant.

A human creature may be a symbol, a walking image, of abstract qualities, as Marina appears to Pericles:

> Falseness cannot come from thee; for thou lookest
> Modest as Justice, and thou seem'st a palace
> For the crown'd Truth to dwell in. (V, i, 121–3)

There is an immutable order in nature, of which man may make himself an active part through knowledge and obedience. Thus Pericles, when his wife is restored to him, wishes to know "who to thank Besides the gods, for this great miracle." He has Cerimon to thank, that follower of Apollo and Aesculapius, who exalts virtue and knowledge above worldly honor and riches, for he knows that

> immortality attends the former,
> Making a man a god, (III, ii, 30–1)

and has learned to "speak of the disturbances That nature works, and of her cures." The good man knows and accepts his place in the universe; [6] he does not scorn those below him nor envy those above him; he recognizes necessity, and renders to it glad obedience.

> Be quiet then, as men should be,
> Till he hath pass'd necessity,

is Gower's advice to the audience. Pericles himself acknowledges the inevitable, and says to the angry stars: "I, as fits my nature, do obey you." Cast away by the sea, made the ball for the waters and the wind to play upon in "that vast tennis court," his beggared want teaches him to think of what he is, and he knows that

> We cannot but obey
> The powers above us. Could I rage and roar
> As doth the sea she lies in, yet the end
> Must be as 'tis. (III, iii, 9–12)

Not only integrity, then, but patience, may make a man ruler over himself, and worthy of salvation.[7] Patience becomes (Shakespeare had already developed the image in *Twelfth Night*) a triumphant and breathing figure:

> Yet thou dost look
> Like Patience gazing on kings' graves and smiling
> Extremity out of act. (V, i, 138–40)

Patience must needs be strong, for all extremities are touched on in this play—death, murder, defilement, treachery, separation, exile, and envious and calumniating time. Yet Pericles in his patience has learned to accept open-eyed even the rule of Shakespeare's arch-enemy:

> I see that Time's the king of men;
> He's both their parent, and he is their grave,
> And gives them what he will, not what they crave. (II, iii, 45–7)

Before the omnipotent gods show their compassion, they test Pericles with trials equal to Job's or Griselda's. "Lady Fortune" orders or disorders the day. Life is envisioned as a sea, fickle, treacherous, always changing, and more tempestuous and ever-present than in that other sea-play *The Tempest*.[8] Man is no more than a sailor "With whom each minute threatens life or death." The raging battery and huge billows and masked calm of the ocean furnish the images of existence. Sea-tossed Pericles rides out three tempests. Clasped to the mast, he "endures a sea that almost burst the deck," while "from the ladder tackle washes off A canvas climber." In such mastering storms "The seaman's whistle Is as a whisper in the ears of death, Unheard." Oceanic terrors are realized with such prolonged intensity that we may feel with the shuddering fishermen, "Master, I marvel how the fishes live in the sea." And we may extend Pericles' observation about the fishermen to include Shakespeare himself:

> How from the finny subject of the sea
> These fishers tell the infirmities of men,
> And from their wat'ry empire recollect
> All that may men approve or men detect! (II, i, 52–5)

Man's common infirmities, yet his aspiration to win victory in spite of his shabby equipment, strengthen human sympathies—until even the crowd will cheer a forlorn hope: "Great shouts, and all cry 'The mean knight!' " Men become strangers and cast-aways,[9] tossed up on foreign shores, and suffering Marina's illusion:

> This world to me is like a lasting storm,
> Whirring me from my friends. (IV, i, 20–1)

There is no course for the hero but to accept his own exile—
"Tyre, I now look from thee then"—and to center his compassion
upon others.[10]

Who through his own power can quiet the storm? The bases
for building a new life are the recognition of human sin—"the
earth is throng'd By man's oppression, and the poor worm doth
die for 't"—the recognition of such sin in one's own nature (since
experience teaches "My frail mortality to know itself"), and
finally the taking on of an absolute humility.[11] Worldly greatness, however exalted, is "no guard To bar heaven's shaft," and
the villains themselves know that "The gods are quick of ear."
Naked and alone, "having all lost," the lowest and most dejected
thing of fortune must constantly acknowledge and submit to the
justice of all-powerful gods.[12] The readiness is all.

Having abandoned his wilful pride but not his integrity, man
may become, like Helicanus and Cerimon, an instrument
"through whom the gods have shown their power." He may become their voice, their mirror, and their consciousness. This is
no play of agonized questionings, of rational debates, and of independent decisions; it is a succession of prayers,[13] from Pericles'
second speech in the play—

> You gods that made me man, . . . be my helps
> As I am son and servant to your will

—to his last: "Heavens make a star of him!" Three of the best
scenes (II, i; III, i; V, iii) open with prayers, and it is the hero who
offers them.

In *King Lear*, when a prayer is voiced for Cordelia—"The gods
defend her!"—immediately her dead body is borne on the stage.
It is not so in *Pericles*. Weak and friendless, surrounded by enemies, Marina utters her prayer—"The gods defend me!"—and
it is answered. The admirable characters in this play kneel and
trust and hope; their belief is answered by the compassion of the
gods.[14] The hero is rewarded "in no wise Till he had done his
sacrifice," but the sacrifice is offered gladly, and the reward is

freely bestowed. Fortune, "tir'd with doing bad," smiles once more, and turns her wheel:

> I'll show you those in troubles reign,
> Losing a mite, a mountain gain. (II, Prologue, 7–8)

The "rapture of the sea," ambiguous in its meaning, leads finally to delight and honor. The mysterious questionings—"Did you not name a tempest, A birth, and death?"—flash into almost unbearable joy:

> No more, you gods! your present kindness
> Makes my past miseries sports. (V, iii, 40–1)

And the play rises in superlatives to ecstasy. Marina, who is "a princess To equal any single crown o' th' earth I' the justice of compare," is now "all happy as the fairest of all." Pericles' wife, lost so long to the kingdom of death—"This queen, worth all our mundane cost"—is restored to his arms, where the gods would do well, he prays,

> That on the touching of her lips I may
> Melt and no more be seen.

This is the apotheosis of joy, long delayed and seemingly impossible. From such heights it is necessary, if the play is to be rounded off to its conclusion, to return to the certain moral tags of Gower. The audience must be told that it has seen

> Virtue preserv'd from fell destruction's blast,
> Led on by heaven, and crown'd with joy at last.

The moral outlines of this piece of music are clear: desperate trials borne unflinchingly; the acknowledgment of sin; humility and patience never abandoned; willing obedience to an irresistible order; self-forgetfulness, as man realizes himself to be an instrument played upon by unseen virtues; trustful prayers to gods believed to be just; hope and integrity freely rewarded by unlooked-for compassion and joy.

Such a pattern of themes fails to describe the moral effect of the play adequately, for it is at once too neat and not vivid enough.

On one side, all of the elements described are present in full measure (as following out the notes to this chapter should make abundantly clear), but an unescapable causal sequence and relationship is never distinctly set. Shakespeare realizes, or has here learned to imagine, the sudden descent of unexpected joy; and the play reaches its height of passion in the two scenes of restoration to lost happiness, or more accurately, of discovery of a happiness previously unsuspected. Yet these scenes are revelations, or smiling hypotheses—not the culmination of an ordered analysis and understanding. With the same materials, Shakespeare reaches clearer conclusions—perhaps through the mere reworking of his own thoughts—in the plays yet to be considered. *Pericles* falls short in comparison, because even in this world of miracle, where spiritual mysteries are touched upon by the subtlest of minds, the inevitability of moral cause and effect may be more sharply set forth.

On the other side, the threads of the thought as traced so far are lusterless in comparison with the play itself, which is a tapestry glinting and glowing with colors and shot through with gold. *Pericles* is not an abstract preachment, but an embodied intuition. Part of its moral thought results from its incarnation or visualization of intangible values in human subjects and in the symbols of nature—so that joy is felt, not discussed, and the experience of happiness after grief is set above any arguing about it. Sorrow is no allegorical figure, but a weeping prince, or the injunction to a silent nurse, "O, no tears, Lychorida, no tears!" Or the quality of healing that is the promise of the play finds outward expression in the "sacred physic" of actual ministrants—Helicanus, Cerimon, and Marina. Or beneficent effluence loses its abstraction in the image of the sun that gives nourishment to the plants of the earth, the sun that stands on a chivalric shield above a black Ethiope who reaches toward the light as if it were his life, the sun that attracts the reverence of the lesser stars.[15]

But the great symbols of this play, that give both a supernatural sanction and a visible nature to the theme of a rough world conquered by purity of spirit, are the sea-god Neptune and Diana goddess of chastity. The two climactic scenes of recognition and recovery are set at God Neptune's annual feast at Mytilene, and within the Temple of Diana at Ephesus. Neptune rolls and thunders through such lines as "Thou god of this great vast, rebuke these surges!" [16] And "bright Diana, whom we honour all," the vestal goddess, "Celestial Dian, goddess argentine," whose votaresses yet wear her silver livery, "immortal Dian!" "Pure Dian!" is the theme of every tongue, not only of Simonides and Pericles and Thaïsa and Cerimon and Gower, but of the incestuous Antiochus who pays her hypocritical tribute, and of the laughing libertines, and of the Bawd of Mytilene—"What have we to do with Diana?" [17] In this drama of compassion, Diana is no cool removed deity such as Valeria or the young Isabella might call upon; she is the protectress of purity of spirit, but also the beacon toward new life. Her divinity manifests itself at the climactic moment, to enjoin Pericles in a dream to sacrifice before her altar: "Do it, and happy—by my silver bow!" And she calls forth some of the most intense lines in the play:

> Lucina, O
> Divinest patroness and midwife gentle
> To those that cry by night, convey thy deity
> Aboard our dancing boat; make swift the pangs
> Of my queen's travails!

The two images of Diana and Neptune are so strong that they may be mingled indistinguishably in Pericles' prayer that joins them both, or in his poignant grief over his wife's senseless body:

> A terrible childbed hast thou had, my dear;
> No light, no fire. Th' unfriendly elements
> Forgot thee utterly; nor have I time
> To give thee hallow'd to thy grave, but straight
> Must cast thee, scarcely coffin'd, in the ooze;
> Where, for a monument upon thy bones,
> And e'er-remaining lamps, the belching whale
> And humming water must o'erwhelm thy corpse
> Lying with simple shells. (III, i, 57–65)

After terror and sorrow, new life.[18] The pulse begins to beat again; the eyes' "fringes of bright gold begin to part"; out of "as chiding a nativity As fire, air, water, earth, and heaven can make" comes "this poor infant, this fresh new seafarer," to become, after the decades of a further loss and death, "another life to Pericles thy father." And though the hero may have endured for years in the belief that "This cannot be. My daughter's buried," yet the countersurge is always, and finally: "This queen will live; nature awakes." The return of life expands to embrace the audience in the last line of the play: "New joy wait on you!"

Such brightening after long darkness can scarcely be credited. The atmosphere is strange and rare, and the characters glide in a dream, where the audience may "Like motes and shadows see them move awhile." [19] Pericles, like Lear, wakes to a happiness he cannot at once venture to accept: "But are you flesh and blood? Have you a working pulse? and are no fairy?" Music sounds, the music of the spheres, "most heavenly music!" to confirm the unearthly rejuvenescent joy. Pericles himself is called "music's master." [20] And the beauties of a newly flowering earth, though they are not lingered over as in the other romances, blend their sensuous images with the sweet sounds.[21]

Marina in "her sweet harmony" is the focus for these themes, to whom Thaïsa is a fainter echo. In her own person Marina unites those other images of sea and spirit. Because she was born at sea Pericles gave her her name, yet Marina pens her tributes to her mistress Diana, and calls upon the vestal guardian in her extremity. She is "absolute Marina," and all her grace "makes her both the heart and place Of general wonder." She becomes her maker's maker, the begetter of new life in her father.[22]

The harmonious blending of images with thoughts—the loyalty of friends, the overpowering inrush of joy, the symbols of shores and seas, the new life growing out of old life and old death, the thankfulness that fears the gods—only Shakespeare's own words can convey, as Pericles dares to accept his happiness as he had accepted his grief:

> O Helicanus, strike me, honour'd sir,
> Give me a gash, put me to present pain,
> Lest this great sea of joys rushing upon me
> O'erbear the shores of my mortality
> And drown me with their sweetness. O, come hither,
> Thou that beget'st him that did thee beget;
> Thou that wast born at sea, buried at Tharsus,
> And found at sea again! O Helicanus,
> Down on thy knees, thank the holy gods as loud
> As thunder threatens us. This is Marina. (V, i, 192–201)

Surely this is a fabric that expresses in visions the archetypal patterns of the human soul, its loneliness and fear and courage and hope for continuing life. It is a romance none of whose parts is so poor but is a race of heaven. And it is a dream from thick slumber. Here, more richly realized than in Spenser's House of Holiness, though their presences are iridescent and they act through human agents, are Faith, Hope, and Charity. "More is won," we learn in a strange tongue, "through sweetness than through force." Nature's lesson of fear and joy is presented through Neptune and Diana. Man's dearest, save in his own mind, is subject to loss; and he must learn to guard his rarest treasure in a world that whirs him from his friends:

> The rough seas, that spare not any man,
> Took it in rage—though, calm'd, have given 't again.
>
> (II, i, 137–8)

In hac spe vivo reads the motto on the shield of the hero. The branch may wither, yet it remains green at top.

CYMBELINE

The four final dramatic romances play variations on common themes. Since many of these themes have been treated in some detail for *Pericles*, the least known and perhaps the least rightly valued of the quartette, they can be passed over more lightly in the next two plays considered. If *Cymbeline* returns less often than *Pericles* to the ideas of wondrous miracle and music (though

it contains three songs, two of them among Shakespeare's finest),
it equals *Pericles* in dwelling upon the theme of exile, for instance,
and surpasses it in the contemplation of natural beauty or in the
insistence upon repentance.

There is little need for penitence in *Pericles:* the villains, who
are hardly developed further than the plot-outline demands, are
wiped out; while the Prince of Tyre and his wife and daughter
are rewarded for integrity that endures all trials. Pericles needs
only a change of fortune, not a change of heart. The play, therefore, comes closest of the four to the conventional romance,[23]
and serious or ambiguous moral judgments are few. But in the
other romances the principal figures must suffer a change of heart.
Cymbeline must become aware of his own rash judgments and
admit his blindnesses; Leontes must slough off jealousy, even as
Prospero renounces his isolated life of introspection.

All of the dramatic romances tell of the ruler of a country removed in time or place, who is separated from some precious
part of his inheritance, usually through his own fault as well as
the faults of others,—until after long years his inheritance is restored to him, usually through a grace or an action not his own.
Time is the healer, or the bringer of penitence and new life, for
each of the plays except *The Tempest* is split down the middle
by a gap of time long enough to allow infant or unborn girls a
chance to grow up and become heroines. *The Tempest* would
follow the same pattern also if it were constructed in Shakespeare's usual manner, instead of as the happenings of a single
afternoon, with flashbacks narrated as a *tour de force*. All of the
romances use some principle of contrast by which to heighten
the idyllic dreams. In *Pericles,* the flat narration of the first two
acts is followed by the sudden thunder of the sea at the start of
the third. Even better, the murder and lust in palace and brothel
throughout the fourth act seem deliberately drawn out and bru-
talized to afford contrast with the unearthly restoration scenes of
the close.

A dominating contrast in *Cymbeline* is between the life of the
court and the life of nature, between sophistication and simplicity.

The rude cave in Wales is far from Cymbeline's palace—as if the Forest of Arden had been discovered in some coign of Lear's harsh Britain. Or as if a fresh area of Shakespeare's mind had burst to life in the midst of what he had known too intimately and too long. The profoundest contrast is between Shakespeare Old Style and Shakespeare New Style. In this play (as in the first half of *The Winter's Tale,* and occasionally in the other two romances) he writes of the naughty world almost with his old conviction and authority. Knowing evil, caring seriously to comprehend it, he nearly achieves again; but the achievement seems principally designed to contrast the stupidly cunning and the proud with some radiant dream which, if it is not truer, is at least more intensely realized. Often, in all of these romances, Shakespeare merely sketches in quickly, in a kind of shorthand, material which he had realized solidly in earlier plays; or he assumes ideas which he had formerly argued or demonstrated. The old elements of a fallen Adam—pride, blindness, mistrust, jealousy, revenge, hypocrisy—are taken for granted without scrutiny, much as proved propositions in geometry are used to establish a new conclusion. This means, of course, that Iachimo will be a littler Iago, Cloten a smaller Ajax, and only Cymbeline's Queen without a parallel—except for Dionyza in *Pericles.*

The evil characters, nevertheless, are treated with enough respect to individualize them; and their differing ends compose a pattern of moral beliefs that Shakespeare held to consistently. The Queen, who poisons with fair words, whose purposes remain secret to the end, cannot escape the prison of her self. The last act of this "most delicate fiend" is to confess her abhorrence of her husband, a final malignant gesture which she hopes may keep her hatred alive after her death. Her only repentance is that she "repented The evils she hatch'd were not effected." So she "despairing died." Her end is expressed with moral certainty:

> With horror, madly dying, like her life,
> Which (being cruel to the world) concluded
> Most cruel to herself. (V, v, 31–3)

Iachimo is not so cabined and confined in evil. He acts on the raw and reckless assumption that no lady lives who is "fair, virtuous, wise, chaste, constant." He matches his pride in amatory exploits against the pride in possession of the young Posthumus, who allows his own reckless anger to make a wager of his wife. Iachimo is intelligent: he realizes (in the spirit of the dark comedies) "the cloyed will—That satiate yet unsatisfied desire, That tub both fill'd and running," which after devouring the lamb still longs for garbage. But confronted by the fact of Imogen, he realizes also her "most perfect goodness," and knows immediately that he must descend to lies in order to win his wager. Evil sits so uneasily upon his nature that in the last scene he is glad to utter what it torments him to conceal, and his heavy conscience—not outside force—causes him to kneel before the man he has wronged. He asks for death for his crimes, and is forgiven.

Cloten, on the other hand, is as unyielding in stupidity as his mother is in malice. He is "too bad for bad report." Shakespeare makes of him a brutal farce. He brawls, bowls, gambles, and leads every argument to a most preposterous conclusion. Of every situation, he might well say: "I yet not understand the case myself." He is too stupid even to realize his own cowardice and incompetence. Having no center, "his humour Was nothing but mutation." He is the voice of idiocy, an essential spiritual emptiness. Imogen characterizes him as "that harsh, noble, simple nothing—Cloten!" Her ironic "noble" strikes off his subservience to externals: his boasting of birth and position, his dependence upon his mother and upon his flatterers who amuse themselves with sarcasms he is too dumb to grasp, his lamenting that "I had rather not be so noble as I am," and his notion that "it is fit I should commit offence to my inferiors." In Cloten, Caliban is dressed up in Osric's clothing. When the shallow courtier and the brute are united in one person, Shakespeare comes as close to mercilessness as his nature allows. This is the nitwit that dares to imagine he dictates to the inevitable.[24] Using his nose as a moral sense, as he so often does, Shakespeare presents Cloten on his first appearance as quite literally a stinker. And as Cloten flies to pieces for his last appearance, it is an occasion for rejoicing to see his severed head brought in by Guiderius: "This Cloten was a fool, an empty purse." For Cloten is all outsides—with no more spiritual significance than his garments possess.

There is, then, no hope for the Clotens—for evil which is too stupid to con the book. Nor is there salvation for evil which is dominated by a limited intelligence, which dies despairing within its own constricted circle. But there is salvation for the evil intelligence which can learn from experience that evil and reality are not interchangeable terms, because intelligence can correct such a partial and warped belief and therefore can repent and be forgiven.

Shakespeare develops a Clothes Philosophy which does not make the practice of virtue easy. How can the well-intentioned detect virtue and truth in others? Not through externals. Posthumus cannot ferret out Iachimo's treachery, for he accepts the ocular proof, the "corporal sign" of the bracelet stolen from Imogen's arm.[25] Again, Cymbeline to the end cannot discover the real nature of his physically beautiful Queen. Is his fault, too, the "cloyed will," the desire so powerful (as in Troilus and Gertrude and Angelo) that it overrides judgment? Shakespeare does not say so. Instead, he allows Cymbeline an extraordinary bit of pleading:

> Mine eyes
> Were not in fault, for she was beautiful;
> Mine ears, that heard her flattery; nor my heart
> That thought her like her seeming. It had been vicious
> To have mistrusted her. (V, v, 62–6)

Cymbeline permits his daughter to feel that his action was folly, but concludes his defense by abandoning personal responsibility in favor of a prayer to a higher order: "Heaven mend all!" And if it was a sin in Cymbeline to trust his wife and mistrust his friend Belarius, then why was not Othello virtuous in following an opposite course?

It is true that Iachimo, dazzled by Imogen's purity (though even here he is for a moment not sure that "all of her that is out of door most rich" can be furnished with a mind of equal rarity), thinks men mad who cannot distinguish "twixt fair and foul." The eye, the judgment, even the appetite, he feels, can make the distinction; and the unsatisfied will alone could act contrary to judgment. But Troilus said as much when he trusted Cressida. And such moral certainty appears odd in the mouth of Iachimo, who has dealt wholesale in cynicisms, and who now seems a libertine intoxicated by the sight of virtue.

Shakespeare does not hold for long to any Platonic or Spenserian intuition that a beautiful soul inhabits, because it creates, a beautiful body. His ultimate simplicity, rather, is that all mistrust is vicious. How easily, then, may slander and false appearance play upon the trustful! The ideal is reciprocal trust and virtue. Yet rarely in Shakespeare's plays, including the comedies, does a perfect trust meet with an object of perfect virtue. Nor does a perfect virtue encounter a perfect trust. Troilus and King Hamlet give the rule, and the objects of their devotion are Cressida and Gertrude; the perfections of Desdemona or of Hermione have for altar ministrants Othello or Leontes; even in the lightness of the comedies the tune of *l'uomo è mobile* is laughingly played. Failure in trust can momentarily infect even the virtuous with despair, so that Imogen offers her heart to Pisanio's knife when she learns of her husband's false suspicions. Bitterly she proclaims that the traitors of the past have destroyed trust in honest men, and caused sacred pity to falter. As for her husband Posthumus: "Goodly and gallant shall be false and perjur'd From thy great fail."

But the ideal is never abandoned because it is unrealizable, and in some impossible world the turtledove of infinite trust continues to worship the Phoenix of virtue indistinguishable from beauty.

In *Cymbeline*, Shakespeare gives one last grotesque twist to his troubled thoughts on truth and semblance. That lover of appearances, Cloten, his attention riveted by a phrase of Imogen's, resolves to ravish her in the very garments of her husband Posthumus.[26] Even Imogen cannot distinguish between apparel and "the thing itself." When she beholds the headless body of Cloten, her recognition of her own husband by his outward clothes is painfully prolonged and detailed:

> The garments of Posthumus?
> I know the shape of 's leg; this is his hand,
> His foot Mercurial, his Martial thigh,
> The brawns of Hercules; but his Jovial face—
> Murther in heaven? (IV, ii, 308–12)

She acknowledges Cloten's body as "this most bravest vessel of the world." Even the purest cannot look through the deceitful garments of the world, nor escape from their own adorations and presentiments. With insistent dramatic irony, Imogen, who knows that "Our very eyes Are sometimes like our judgments, blind," falls senseless over the body of her supposed lord.

> The dream's here still. Even when I wake it is
> Without me, as within me; not imagin'd, felt.

Tangled in their own mortality, men and women must for a time act out murder in heaven on the stage of the earth.

Yet above all this subtle realization of complex evil, Shakespeare sets contrasting and conquering images of liberty, courage, patience, hope, and truth. The natural world is beautiful, and in the main beneficent; human beings are beautiful, and in the main may learn brotherhood, humility, and the necessity for repentance and forgiveness. If instinct will out, it may be noble as well as ravening.[27] Spirit scores its triumph over matter.[28] As for the temporary losing of any good, the final answer is "'Twill not be lost." The shining dream is here elevated above common earth through superlatives, which Shakespeare never used more lavishly.[29] And though his admired creations are worthy to inlay heaven with stars, though they exceed in goodness the hugeness of any villain's unworthy thinking, and though the mere thought of banished virtue and love subdues all pangs, all fears, and is past grace, obedience, and hope, yet Shakespeare can stoutly imagine, in defending the farthest reach of his description of the virtuous, that "I do extend him, sir, within himself."

The play opens in outward sorrow and drifts steadily toward revealed happiness. In its first part, evil actions prevail, the good are banished from their native land or exiled from love, the heroine is imprisoned, and the titular hero is not aware that he himself is bound to a serpent Queen who can say:

> I never do him wrong
> But he does buy my injuries, to be friends;
> Pays dear for my offences. (I, i, 104–6)

Not until the third act is the stifling atmosphere of a flattering court, a Rome full of rakes, and a stealthily invaded bedchamber finally stirred by a steady breath of fresh air. But then—in the mountains of Wales it is "great morning." The Welsh scene opens with a "goodly day" and the prayer to the sun of Belarius and his two striplings.[30] Belarius moralizes that no life compares with theirs, nobler, richer, and prouder than the life at court; while the two impatient young huntsmen and mountaineers dream of brave exploits. The freedom of Britain is threatened, and the mountain nymph, sweet liberty, is their goddess.[31] Soon they shall descend from the Welsh highlands to rouse the demoralized Britons, and make possible through their actions the final scene of triumph. Cymbeline will be rescued by his sons. The old man and the two young ones will stand in the strait lane like Horatius and his companions at the bridge. With the "forlorn soldier" Posthumus in disguise, they will turn cowards to lions and eagles. "Nothing routs us," Belarius cries, "but the villany of our fears." The triumvirate forms an image of bravery, of spirit in action conquering despair:

> This was strange chance—
> A narrow lane, an old man, and two boys! (V, iii, 51–2)

To their cave in the mountains comes Imogen, disguised as a boy. They greet each other in mutual delight as brothers. Heart-stricken and alone, Imogen can yet find new life in her brave friends, and at moments can take on some of the sauciness of Shakespeare's earlier heroines.[32] Their instinctive and reciprocated love "doth miracle itself." Imogen sweetly preaches to her brothers the simple daily life: "Stick to your journal course. The breach of custom Is breach of all." And Belarius lessons his adopted sons in reverence and forgiveness:

> Though mean and mighty, rotting,
> Together have one dust, yet reverence
> (That angel of the world) doth make distinction
> Of place 'tween high and low. Our foe was princely;
> And though you took his life as being our foe,
> Yet bury him as a prince. (IV, ii, 246–51)

After cleansing scenes of simplicity close to nature, and of dauntless action that frees men from their own bonds, the play is ready for its final movement. Shakespeare had long ago learned to avoid the long scenes that recapitulate all that has gone before, which the audience already knows too well. Now he returns with a difference to a long finale that tells over, point by point, all that has preceded. For recognition and restoration is his ending theme. Cymbeline has lost his counsellor, his Queen, his daughter, and his sons. Posthumus has lost Imogen, Imogen Posthumus. Guiderius and Arviragus have lost Fidele. Now the theme of rejuvenescence rises to a climax; [33] Cymbeline is "mother to the birth of three"; the dead rise again and are recognized. Even more important is the recognition of their own faults by Cymbeline, Iachimo, Posthumus, even Belarius. Hope is rewarded by the waking of the dead: [34]

> If this be so, the gods do mean to strike me
> To death with mortal joy. (V, v, 234–5)

Even the defeated shall taste the joy of freedom, while the victors submit to a world order (paying their wonted tribute to the Roman empire) and to a higher order in their sacrifices to the gods:

> Posthumus anchors upon Imogen;
> And she (like harmless lightning) throws her eye
> On him, her brothers, me, her master, hitting
> Each object with a joy; the counterchange

> Is severally in all. Let's quit this ground
> And smoke the temple with our sacrifices.

Faith and truth end in a religious joy.[35]

The center of Shakespeare's interest is the image of innocent truth stricken to the ground by enemies, daring to hope again, and restored at last. The contributors to this image include most of the characters of the play—Posthumus, Belarius, Guiderius, Arviragus, Pisanio, even the old King of Britain and the general of the Romans. But it is to Imogen that Shakespeare gives his devotion.

For purposes of the plot, her husband must betray her. Shakespeare, nevertheless, does what he can to make Posthumus, despite this mechanical flaw, worthy of Imogen. "By her election," we are told, "may be truly read What kind of man he is." He is "most prais'd, most lov'd"; and his very enemy proclaims that "He was too good to be Where ill men were, and was the best of all Amongst the rar'st of good ones." In his best moods, he esteems his mistress "more than the world enjoys," knowing that "She holds her virtue still, and I my mind." Furthermore, as recompense for his nearly fatal mistrust, Posthumus is given three scenes of repentance; it adds something to his worth that they precede the revelation of Imogen's innocence. When he learns the truth, he bursts into a frenzy of recrimination that matches him with the tragic heroes. His remorse at his own villainy almost makes him worthy of his wife.

Yet it must be admitted that Shakespeare tampers with the characters both of Posthumus and Iachimo in order to give Imogen her most lustrous setting. Thus Posthumus, for example, pours forth his foul imaginings and his hatred of woman's vicious inconstancy in a scene made up of a single long soliloquy, only that it may set off a succeeding scene devoted to the unswerving faith of Imogen, who is "punish'd for her truth." Or again, in the fury of his repentance, he strikes down Fidele—"Thou scornful page, There lies thy part!"—and the thought of the play is given a melodramatic final image of innocence stricken to earth. Iachimo, too, is tailored in his villainy. He is a cultured young aristocrat, confirmed in worldly cynicism, too proud to lose a wager that may be won by cunning; but he is also subtle and intelligent. Though he plays out his self-assigned part with finesse, he mixes his Mephistophelian wisdom with admiration for a newly dis-covered virtue, he pays Imogen some of her finest tributes, and he is aware of his own evil at the moment of committing it: "Though this a heavenly angel, hell is here." His evil actions torment him; and his open repentance, long-drawn-out even for the long final scene, is a handsome tribute to the heroine.

Imogen is developed to the full. Like the early heroines, in the Welsh cave scenes she is by turns appealing and independent, boyish and pathetic, even lightly humorous. Of Fidele it may be said that "Nobly he yokes A smiling with a sigh." She is idolized: she is "divine Imogen," her fair mind is a temple and her body "so divine a temple"; she is an angel, an earthly paragon, divine-ness whose adorers would free her from distress at any cost of pain or danger. The husband who has lost her knows her to be the temple of virtue—yea, and virtue itself.

Yet Shakespeare worships this image too seriously to let it pass as a dream of perfection, or to present his Imogen wholly in the spirit of romance, like some of his wistful child-heroines. He graces her love—which is "beyond beyond"—with the most ingenious and buoyant images he can master.[36] He grants to her his favorite theme—had he not assigned it to Juliet and Helena and Mariana and Desdemona and Cleopatra, even to Ophelia?— of forgiving a loved wrong-doer even while suffering from his wrongs. Imogen learns to say: "My dear lord! Thou art one o' th' false ones." And stricken down by Posthumus, she rises to embrace him with smiling confidence:

> Why did you throw your wedded lady from you?
> Think that you are upon a rock, and now
> Throw me again. (V, v, 261-3)

Yet Shakespeare sets the final seal on his adoration for Imogen in carefully worked out scenes where adroit turns of thought and shifts of mood stamp her as a rare human being and not a goddess. Her conduct during the difficult scene of Iachimo's temptation is masterfully handled: she receives the friend of her husband with high-born courtesy, yet when she understands his hinted proposal her reaction is decisive and unafraid: she calls for Pisanio and speaks out her scorn. Moreover, when Iachimo swears that his actions were but to try her virtue, she accepts the excuse at face value, for distrust is vicious.

Confronted with the crude lout Cloten, her good manners change by gradations to the blunt truth-telling that is needed to get rid of him. She is at her best in the two scenes with Pisanio. In the first, ironically contrasted with Pisanio's horror at his murderous mission, she is all laughing hope and girlish eagerness to meet her love at Milford Haven. Yet even here, her mood turns at the end to responsible decision made in the face of uncertainty:

> I see before me, man. Nor here, nor here,
> Nor what ensues, but have a fog in them
> That I cannot look through. (III, ii, 80–2)

In the other scene (III, iv), having read the letter to Pisanio in which Posthumus reveals his foul suspicion and his decision to have her killed, she ranges from self-defense, to jealous recrimination of the jay of Italy who has betrayed him, to self-pity, to reproach of her husband, to bewilderment as to the difference between truth and falsehood, to a desperate offering of her breast to Pisanio's knife, to a scornful rejection of the heretical corrupting letters, to a pathetic and almost forgiving thought of the pangs Posthumus may suffer after she is dead, and back to the proud idea of sacrifice in order to be rid of this worthless world. The lamb entreats the butcher; the elected deer stands before Pisanio the hunter. When Pisanio swears he has not slept a wink since he received command to do this business, it is a fine and unexpected touch to have her answer like some Hotspur:

> Do 't, and to bed then!

Her anger against the unjust suspicions of her husband turns subtly against Pisanio, or veers to jealousy against some Roman courtesan. By minute adjustments it is metamorphosed into new life and hope and decision, as if virtue might be best revenged on foulness by continuing its own virtuous life. "Hath Britain all the sun that shines? Prithee think There's livers out of Britain." In disguise and exile she will show a prince's courage, and one of Shakespeare's most masterfully contrived scenes is brought to a close on the note of resolution.

With such a heroine as Imogen, surrounded by her stalwart brothers and by such faithful counsellors as Belarius and Pisanio, human aspiration and integrity must necessarily play their part in the shaping of men's fates. Nevertheless, without help, men cannot with their own eyes look through the fog into the future. They are made restless by their uncertainties and by their desires. "Doubting things go ill often hurts more Than to be sure they do." A high hope itself cannot make for calm, since "most miserable Is the desire that's glorious." Jupiter must descend in thunder and lightning, sitting upon an eagle—yet even his radiant visions and great behests cannot be understood by blind and suspicious man.

> 'Tis still a dream, or else such stuff as madmen
> Tongue, and brain not; either both, or nothing;
> Or senseless speaking, or a speaking such
> As sense cannot untie. (V, iv, 146–9)

Since the action of man's life is like the vision, whatever it signifies, the dream will be treasured out of sympathy.

But if life itself is a dream, a vision, may it not be shaped? Need it be a consigning to earth of the good and the evil side by side, strewing them with herbs that have on them the cold dew of the night? Or singing in gray requiem:

> The ground that gave them first has them again.
> Their pleasures here are past, so is their pain.

Whether it be desolate or joyful, "The dream's here still." May it not be interpreted in a final oracle by some sayer of sooth, some lover of harmony, some Philarmonus,[37] who knows that man is born of a lion, that he may without seeking find, that branches after being dead many years may revive and freshly grow, that fortune and peace and plenty shall flourish again when man is embraced by the dream itself, "by a piece of tender air"?

The eyes of love, "now canopied Under these windows white and azure, lac'd With blue of heaven's own tinct"—may again open from death and sleep. Or man himself, repentant after error and strange exile, may fall into a dream, praying "O Imogen, I'll speak to thee in silence," and trusting that no wrath or justice could be so cruel but that the dearest of creatures would answer his prayer:

> Renew me with your eyes.

THE WINTER'S TALE

In the last romances, no matter how the names of the characters change, or the setting shifts from Tyre to ancient Britain to Sicily to a desert island, Shakespeare continues to write the same play. Even when there remain but a few grains of sand in the hourglass, and when he himself needs the new life of a collaborator in order to complete a play, dominant movements in his final thought stamp his work.[38]

The first scene of *The Two Noble Kinsmen*, for example, chimes with Shakespeare's thought in developing a situation in which the hero abandons his own interests to become the instrument of the gods. The marriage of Theseus to Hippolyta—"This grand act of our life, this daring deed Of fate in wedlock"—is delayed at the supplication of the three kneeling queens in black.

> As we are men,
> Thus should we do. Being sensually subdu'd,
> We lose our human title. (I, i, 231-3)

Palamon and Arcite, too, permit Shakespeare to develop ideas of honor, of patience, of self-mastery, of distilling joy in the alembic of adversity. The dialogues of Hippolyta and Emilia and of Palamon and Arcite excellently counterpoint the old comparison of friendship and love. To Chaucer's noble antique story Shakespeare adds his touches of humor, of psychological insight, of mirth mingled with sadness, of "infinite pity," of supplications that yoke immensity to the sharp little freshnesses of this world.[39] At the end, Shakespeare once more unclasps the mystery and finds joy within the tragic dream:

> O cousin,
> That we should things desire which do cost us
> The loss of our desire! that naught could buy
> Dear love but loss of dear love! (V, iv, 109–12)

Or again:

> O you heavenly charmers,
> What things you make of us! For what we lack
> We laugh, for what we have are sorry; still
> Are children in some kind. Let us be thankful
> For that which is, and with you leave dispute
> That are above our question. (V, iv, 131–6)

The Winter's Tale reworks the pattern, and is no less worthy of prolonged scrutiny. But what has been seen in detail in the other romances is true in this romance as well, and there is no need to play over minor variations on the basic melodies.

Like The Tempest, The Winter's Tale is compressed and simplified. It gets along with only fifteen scenes. Four scenes alone— of jealousy, of judgment, of feasting, and of repentance—fill three-fifths of the play. The sprawling stories of Pericles and Cymbeline give way to a piece concentrated in two equal movements; and the tighter organization here compels Father Time to apologize for the lapse of a decade or two between the halves, a lapse which in other plays Shakespeare takes as a matter hardly worth comment.[40]

If Pericles and Cymbeline are comparable to Lear in their themes and ample structures, The Winter's Tale has parallels with Othello. Its dramatic economy in setting forth its ideas is notable. The first part introduces Leontes' jealousy without delay, and sets it against purity, loyalty, and integrity. After a little transitional scene in which new helpless life is protected even in the middle of a world of storms and man-eating bears, a second part is devoted to the healing of time and the light-hearted laughter of an innocent world. The stage is set for the discoveries and forgiveness of the fifth act. Throughout, the telling scenes are set off by shorter scenes that afford breathing spells; in the fifth act, Shakespeare's recurring theorem—repentance, followed by restoration—is broken into three scenes, in which he maintains the poignant gravity of the climactic moments by interjecting a middle scene that narrates reunions and recognitions instead of presenting them.

The jealousy of Leontes is as degrading as Othello's, and is even less justifiable. It strikes him suddenly and inexplicably like a pestilence, and "infection" is Shakespeare's key-word in describing it.[41] The blight is even more fearful in Leontes than Othello, for it is almost without external support of any kind. Hermione is spotless, and everyone in the play but Leontes knows and proclaims her innocence. Leontes poisons himself; Leontes and his counsellors reverse the rôles of Othello and Iago. Paulina brands Leontes as the sole traitor, who has betrayed "the sacred honour of himself." Antigonus tells his King: "You are abus'd, and by some putter-on That will be damn'd for 't. Would I knew the villain!"

The villain is man's vile imagination, self-generating, from whose sullen embers jealousy rises like a foul phoenix. To show evil as purely subjective, the gods themselves speak flatly against Leontes' suspicion. Divine intervention here takes the form of the message from the Delphic oracle. With only enough mystification to carry on the plot for three more acts, Apollo's oracle is read aloud in the court of justice: "Hermione is chaste; Polixenes blameless; Camillo a true subject; Leontes a jealous tyrant; his innocent babe truly begotten." In the insane fury of his *tremor cordis*, Leontes blasphemes:

> There is no truth at all i' th' oracle! (III, ii, 141)

And again in accordance with the direct progress of the play, Leontes learns at once of his punishment—the deaths of the two nearest his heart—and falls immediately into self-abasement, remorse, and the desire for reconcilement. The shock opens his eyes. To that extent, his faith and love—"that which is lost"—are found before the play is half over, though he must yet persist in his repentance and woo his dead queen for longer than Jacob sought Rachel.

Leontes' self-induced jealousy is countered by the integrity of Florizel and the simplicity of Perdita, while the compromising wisdom and good intentions of the older characters bridge the pure extremes of evil and of innocence.[42] If the first half of the play carries out in fantasy Leontes' bitter assumption, "Let what is dear in Sicily be cheap," the second half reacts to reveal how what is cheap in Bohemia may be dear. For this is a drama that rings changes on the theme of spiritual integrity,[43] and insists in multiple variations that reality is mental.[44] It is a pleasurable dance of minds when Polixenes from his experience argues that man should accept the bastard mixing of base and noble, the grafting of human sophistication upon great creating nature; and Perdita, though granting his argument, immediately answers that for her part she will have none of this streaked and pied compromise. Spring is sweetly answering to the "flow'rs of winter." (IV, iv, 79) Or again, Shakespeare presents his picture of human life—observed, not argued—when Camillo tells Perdita that prosperity is the true bond of love, whose complexion and heart are altered by affliction, and Perdita answers in her young confidence:

> I think affliction may subdue the cheek,
> But not take in the mind. (IV, iv, 583–90)

"Yea? say you so?" Camillo retorts, and falls at once to the less controversial contemplation of Perdita's beauty.

Again, as in *Cymbeline*, the interlude of harmless pastoral must precede the forgiveness which is without a shadow of reproach. The play fills with floral patterns and dances and rustic gaiety;

and after the contemplation of that which is graceful and becoming and fresh and innocent, the themes of repentance and
resignation and joy mingled with sorrow lead imperceptibly to
the end.[45] Though reality is mental, it may be embodied in human
beauty. *The Winter's Tale* confirms again that Shakespeare never
tired of reading the eloquence of the human face. Florizel may
look like truth itself; he may breathe out his life in protestations;
love itself may be a statue, and that statue miraculously warm
and answering to desire; and grace, though it is a spiritual gift
from the gods, is to be found also in becoming actions and de-
portment and freedom that looks out at the eyes.

Outside the mind of Leontes, plus a casual tempest or a carniv-
orous bear, there is no evil in the play. Court and country alike
are good. Good intentions are the rule, and like Paulina, every
character can maintain that he means well, even when he does
not well. Among all who try to act as physicians to Leontes' sick
mind, Paulina is the most skilful. Pity never breaks in upon her
until her runaway tongue has compelled Leontes to confront his
fault. She knows that "You that are thus so tender o'er his follies
Will never do him good, not one of you." Her rôle as teacher and
healer parallels that of the Fool for Lear, Edgar for Gloucester,
the Duke for Isabella and Angelo, Ulysses for Troilus. But though
Leontes tells her that her bitter frankness strikes him sorely, he
confides to her truth and goodness.

The Winter's Tale is a dream of love lost only to be restored,
and of love that is never lost, and of love born afresh. Its opening
line contains a hidden image of birth, its closing prayer is Hermione's

> You gods, look down,
> And from your sacred vials pour your graces
> Upon my daughter's head!

Throughout, it tells a story to "make old hearts fresh," it deals
with "things new-born," it welcomes spring to the earth, watches
some new grace born every wink of an eye, and redeems dear life
from the numbness of death. "The doctrine of ill-doing" is part

of the dream, but is forgotten in a more enduring vision which was first and will be final: the interchange of "innocence for innocence." The reality that rules, the dream beyond dreams, is to be found in Florizel's "I am heir to my affection," and in his "I cannot be Mine own, nor anything to any, if I be not thine," and in Perdita's "By the pattern of mine own thoughts I cut out The purity of his," and in the noble line of Hermione's:

> My life stands in the level of your dreams.

Florizel knows that Perdita's dignity "cannot fail but by The violation of my faith." [46]

As love or the loss of love prevails, the play changes color. Hermione, having lost the crown and comfort of her life, cannot be frightened by the bugbear death in the flatness of her misery. Yet always hope rises above despair. Prayers spring from the grimmest situations. Antigonus, who is to be forewarned in a dream of his own death, prays for the helpless infant Perdita:

> Come on, poor babe!
> Some powerful spirit instruct the kites and ravens
> To be thy nurses! . . . And blessing
> Against this cruelty fight on thy side,
> Poor thing, condemn'd to loss!

The messengers pray that great Apollo may turn all to the best, that the desperate issue may prove gracious, sensing that "something rare Even then will rush to knowledge."

The play proceeds in its pictures: the court of justice, the reading of the oracle, the swooning of Hermione, the dancing on the shepherd's green, the unveiling of the statue with Leontes silently weeping. All is told as an old story, out of space on the seacoast of Bohemia, out of time in a pre-Christian world where nevertheless "that rare Italian master, Julio Romano" carves statues. It is "like an old tale," "like an old tale still," "like an old tale." The young son Mamillius knows that "A sad tale's best for winter," and has one of sprites and goblins that begins: "There was a man dwelt by a churchyard . . ."

The man in this play dwells not far from a church built to

Aphrodite Urania, removed by every purposeful device from ordinary life. In that temple the highest thoughts are kept in an inner shrine, the image curtained from profane eyes:

> As she liv'd peerless,
> So her dead likeness I do well believe
> Excels whatever yet you look'd upon,
> Or hand of man hath done. Therefore I keep it
> Lonely, apart.

The image is silent only not to chide; it moves, is sentient, steps from its pedestal, looks with pity from those eyes that are "Stars, stars! And all eyes else dead coals." And Hermione never spoke to better purpose (it is her own husband Leontes who recalls the words) than when she said:

> I am yours for ever.

This was "Grace indeed."

To the clear unearthly beauty of the romances, *The Winter's Tale* adds an element not notable in *Pericles* and *Cymbeline*—the element of humor. These moral, almost religious, visions may be anchored to the earth by brutal realism, as in the brothel scenes of *Pericles;* or by action, as in the battle pieces in *Cymbeline;* or by fresh and smiling character sketches, as are those of Fidele and Mamillius, or by rounded and individualized portrayals like that of Paulina. The descriptions of a harmonious nature and of rustic life, however, are not in themselves enough to relate a fairy story to the actual world, for the pastoral and the idyl are blood cousins of the romance, a cave in Wales or a shepherd's green is only the antimasque to a royal court, and mountaineers and shepherdesses may easily turn into children of the king. But in *The Winter's Tale* the spirit of pure light-hearted comedy returns, almost for the first time since *Twelfth Night.* Comedy orients the temple of love and honor in a wider world, and comments spontaneously like an unconscious chorus on the moral conclusions of the main romantic action.

In the scene that serves as a fulcrum at the play's center, Antigonus has consigned Perdita to the rough lullaby of the elements.

The storm begins, and Antigonus has gone to his own death. With a shock of contrast, we suddenly enter the world of the old shepherd—complaining, talking endlessly, finding good luck in a lost child. His son is ridiculously inept in expressing pity for the shipwrecked sailors and the slaughtered Antigonus: "The men are not yet cold under water, nor the bear half din'd on the gentleman—he's at it now." The old shepherd takes the news with the calm philosophy of Justice Shallow meditating on death and the price of bullocks at Stamford fair:

> Heavy matters, heavy matters! But look thee here, boy. Now bless thyself! thou met'st with things dying, I with things newborn.

Here is the doctrine of compassion and of hopeful action played as a rollicking scherzo. On their lucky day, the loutish son can yet remember: "I'll go see if the bear be gone from the gentleman, and how much he hath eaten. If there be any of him left, I'll bury it."

This motif of the country bumpkins, like an ebullient dance-movement in Beethoven, needs some element that will harmonize it and temper it with the rest of the symphony. Autolycus is the solution. He is as light-hearted as the lark he sings about. Spring is in his song, with doxies and thieves and tumbling in the hay. Gaiety and carelessness flood back in over the celestial mingling of tears and joy, as if they glanced at answers that Leontes and Hermione never knew. Autolycus has his own independence, like the grave-digger or Pompey Bum. Driven into a corner, he knows "I am a poor fellow, sir." The little ones of the earth may sleep out the thought of the life to come, and may acknowledge that "when I wander here and there, I then do most go right." Let the gods reward in their own way either carelessness or cunning! Professionally (and in this, does he differ from the lawyer, the teacher, the preacher, and the physician?), he must live on man's weakness and ignorance. "Every lane's end, every shop, church, session, hanging, yields a careful man work." He might say with Beowulf that Wyrd oft saves the dauntless man. Or in his own terms: "Sure the gods do this year connive at us, and we may do anything

extempore. I see this is the time that the unjust man doth thrive."
If he cannot shear the sheepshearers, then "let me be unroll'd
and my name put in the book of virtue!"

Yet he is too careless—or too devoutly obedient to higher
powers—even to defend his own professional rascality. He accepts
the fact that "though I am not naturally honest, I am so sometimes by chance." He cannot lament that he was not the revealer
of good tidings to the princess, for "it would not have relish'd
among my other discredits." Goddess Fortune is his mistress, and
whatever happens, " 'tis all one to me." Therefore, he greets again
(for he may find them lucky) his victims, "these two moles,
these blind ones," whom "I have done good to against my will."
Who can say that the shepherd and the clown are wrong in their
judgment: "He was provided to do us good"? He acts out Florizel's counsel: "Be merry, gentle! Apprehend Nothing but jollity." In the words of his own song:

> A merry heart goes all the day,
> Your sad tires in a mile-a.

With Autolycus as sympathetic midwife to bring to full birth
their "so preposterous estate," the shepherd and his son repeat
in bumptious tempo many of the main themes of the play. The
sophistications of court life may be judged with direct seriousness, as they are by Belarius or Perdita. Or they may be attacked
even more effectively by horseplay: "Advocate," the shepherd's
son explains to his father, "is the court word for a pheasant. Say
you have none." When Autolycus is "courtier cap-a-pe" in his
insolent inquiries and threats, the two rustics marvel at his startling costume: "He seems to be the more noble in being fantas-
tical." And when they too have acquired gentility in new suits
of fine clothes, Autolycus is the first to acknowledge blithely that
each is a gentleman born. "Ay," the shepherd's son reassures himself, "and have been so any time these four hours. But I was a
gentleman born before my father."

Witnessing the brotherly reconciliation of their principals, the
shepherd's son tells Autolycus that "we wept—and there was

the first gentlemanlike tears that ever we shed." The poor have
pity, and there was gentleness in the world even when Adam
delved and Eve span. Important issues may be touched upon in
humorous vein: did Shakespeare ever reconcile pity and justice?
Did he find the highest meaning of "truth" in loyalty to those
one loves, or in knowledge of a universal order? When are good
intentions good enough? There is compassionate laughter when
the shepherd's son handles the questions. He will swear to the
prince that Autolycus is a valiant fellow in action and that he
will not be drunk. But he knows that Autolycus is no valiant
fellow in action and that he *will* be drunk. Nevertheless, he'll
swear it, and he wishes that Autolycus would be a valiant fellow.
"If it be ne'er so false," he is sure, "a true gentleman may swear
it in the behalf of his friend."

> How blessed are we that are not simple men!
> Yet Nature might have made me as these are;
> Therefore I will not disdain. (IV, iv, 772-4)

These are the words of Autolycus, and it is difficult to tell
whether he is laughing at the shepherds, or whether he is laughing at himself, or whether Shakespeare is laughing at him, or
whether both together are laughing at all of us who, but for the
grace of God, would go like simpletons. Humor, which is but
another guise for humility, has again complicated the moral issues

In these noble dreams of "a world ransomed, or one destroyed,"
humor sadly reminds us that Shakespeare may have known them
to be no more than bright speculations.[47] Man may believe those
messages that happen to please him, particularly if the ballads are
"Very true, and but a month old." He may be overjoyed to find
that the ballad ends happily: "Where some stretch-mouth'd rascal
would, as it were, mean mischief, and break a foul gap into the
matter, he makes the maid to answer 'Whoop, do me no harm,
good man!' puts him off, slights him, with 'Whoop, do me no
harm, good man!'" It is possible that nature may govern "the
ordering of the mind"—but the thought is based upon an "if."
It may be argued that "art itself is nature," since "nature is made

better by no mean But nature makes that mean." Yet the mere fact that a complicated argument is necessary—which instinct proceeds to disregard—suggests that there is another side, and that nature may be insentient to man's artful choosing of the beauty that is withdrawn, the shining hope, the ending joy.

Reality remains the undiscovered country. Even to Shakespeare, the continuance in uncertainty, the constant realization of conflicting possibilities, was painful. "Most miserable Is the desire that's glorious," and April is the cruelest month. At times it seems easier to find rest in death, and to hold with Hermione in her despair, "The bug which you would fright me with I seek," or with Leontes: "Say she were gone, a moiety of my rest Might come to me again." For "While she lives, My heart will be a burthen to me."

Yet the creative force of love cannot be killed:

> Affection! thy intention stabs the centre.
> Thou dost make possible things not so held,
> Communicat'st with dreams! How can this be?

Whether it is a gracious instinct of truth or a blind movement of the independent will, man must make the assumption of life, must act compassionately, must trust that "something rare Even then will rush to knowledge." Paulina, who has done so much for others, will not be allowed to wing herself, an old turtledove, to some withered bough; she must be restored to the society of love. And for the last miracle, capable of breathing life into cold marble,

It is requir'd

You do awake your faith.

THE TEMPEST

Everything that has been said so far in this chapter points toward *The Tempest* or illuminates it. In a form peculiarly suited to the expression of his final multiplex and fragile intuitions, Shakespeare tries his hand at three dramatic romances, and then confidently creates his final masterpiece. His surety is everywhere in evidence. The play is compressed but comprehensive. It is shorter than most; its action spans less than an afternoon; yet no aspect of his art, no last appraisal of the moral issues that had occupied him for so long, is absent. With Prospero in control, recurrent themes are played on three levels: the action shifts in successive scenes from the romance of afflicted kings and scheming courtiers, to the amorous idyl of Ferdinand and Miranda, to the farce of Caliban and the drunken servants.[48] *The Tempest* is a paradigm of all types of man—written also above and below man, in figures of the air and of the earth. With unobtrusive insistence, ideas are given a dramatic body, or a musical structure, through repetitions and variations and progressions: power and patience, mutiny and providence, storm and rest, thunder and sweet airs, bondage and liberty, youth and age, physical and spiritual grace, the mad infection of despair and the healing forgiveness that follows repentance. For this occasion Shakespeare invents his own story, omitting excrescences, and setting his thoughts with the elegance of a jeweller. But his most inimitable creation is the iridescent mood of the play: imagination is the servant of the "nobler reason" in shaping images of natural beauty that vary from the delicate to the cosmic; and wondrous strange sea-music drifts through a life that is surrounded by sleep.

The Tempest is a play of memory.[49] Whatever its conscious purpose (and surely the play is too carefully wrought, its coincidences too perfect, to allow it to be dismissed as an accidental or conventional production), it glances backward over Shakespeare's whole dramatic career, and summons up for a final curtain call characters from the earlier plays.

The heroes and heroines of the early comedies have their representatives, drawn from "the dark backward and abysm of time," in Ferdinand and Miranda. But now their fresh confidence is always observed and commented upon by the older chorus of Prospero. They are given in quintessence, imperfections and idiosyncrasies ruled out, so that Ferdinand can never show himself so intractable as Berowne or Benedick; and Miranda, though she echoes Juliet's frankness in wooing her lover, has none of

Juliet's anger. She is "admired Miranda," and her short exclamations and resilient rhythms are designed to make her "the top of admiration"—in her gratitude and pity and trust and self-forgetful sympathy and tenderness and humility and innocence and youth. It is true that the lovers are warned harshly against lustful impulse, and that Ferdinand must undergo artificially created hardships. But Prospero's "trials of thy love" are prescribed by the last of Shakespeare's physicians of souls, and Prospero at the start reveals his purpose: "This swift business I must uneasy make, lest too light winning Make the prize light." If Shakespeare's imagination is no longer piqued by a cold Adonis or Rosaline, neither is it troubled by a sweatily importunate Venus. The pageant that celebrates this "contract of true love" is presided over by Mother Earth and the Queen of Heaven; the young lovers are dowered with "Honour, riches, marriage blessing, Long continuance, and increasing"; and Venus and Cupid, who thought to work "some wanton charm upon this man and maid," are specifically forbidden to appear.

The worldly cunning of the histories, the evil of the tragedies, are likewise represented, and are likewise controlled. Antonio and Sebastian and Alonso, Stephano and Trinculo and Caliban, are allowed to work out their own natures up to the final circumventions. Treachery, selfishness, brutality, and the desire for power are acknowledged. There is no closing of the eyes in order to deny sin, in a play which contains such lines as:

> A devil, a born devil, on whose nature
> Nurture can never stick! on whom my pains,
> Humanely taken, all, all lost, quite lost. (IV, i, 188–90)

Or:

> You are three men of sin, . . . you 'mongst men
> Being most unfit to live. (III, iii, 53–8)

Or:

> For you, most wicked sir, whom to call brother
> Would even infect my mouth . . . (V, i, 130–1)

But evil no less than innocence is mastered by Prospero; his power is fate; providence and destiny are his other names.[50]

If Prospero controls good and evil, how has he gained this control, and how does he exercise it? One may, of course, deny the questions, and assume that the play has no more meaning than a soapbubble. But this negative assumption hardly explains the fascination the play has held for so many readers, nor the subtle and the fantastic theories it has called forth by its "so potent art." It would seem more respectful to Shakespeare to consider the play as his last emblem, the final device upon his shield.

One theory has held that Prospero prophesies man's domination over nature through science. The theory is based largely on Prospero's control over the elements as a result of his studies. But this is to make Shakespeare into Sir Francis Bacon, reversing the usual fantasy. Actually in his plays, Shakespeare shows as little interest or skill in scientific knowledge as, in his works, Bacon shows in poetry. A different approach to knowledge is at work. The tempests and thunder that Prospero evokes are of the same sort as the storm in *Lear*, and the air of the island is gracious in the same way that the air about Macbeth's castle is nimble and sweet. When Prospero says that graves at his command have waked their sleepers, he is speaking neither of the researches of a biologist nor of the miracles of a saint. His miracles are akin to those that Shakespeare himself practised when he evoked Henry V or Antony. Memory is the storehouse of nature, and the creative artist resurrects an image from the past. One further point: Prospero exercises his power primarily to make moral truth prevail. His "nobler reason" is no scientific rationality, but an ethical control over passion. Prospero is in harmony with the gods of nature, like some Greek tragic hero, because of his long-continued search for knowledge, patience, self-control, and resignation.

When the outcast ruler and his daughter come to the island, it is inhabited by a monster and a spirit. Neither is fully human, in the sense that man is a creature *rationis capax*. Caliban is sub-human, and is not capable of reformation, though he may be forcibly controlled, and though Prospero must acknowledge as his own "this thing of darkness"—much as instinct and passion cannot be eradicated from man's nature nor changed into an identity with reason, though reason may govern them. And as for Ariel? An idea has been turned to a shape, and airy nothing has been given a local habitation and a name. Ariel has no human feelings, though he can observe them clearly. He can imagine that he would weep at sorrow, "were I human." In the dark past he has been in bondage to the foul witch Sycorax; now, for a time, Prospero commands his services; soon the spirit will be freed to the elements. He can assume all shapes, or summon them up, or annihilate time and space. His native element is the free air. He possesses that quality of disinterestedness, that freedom from personal involvement, which is a sign of beauty, the distinguishing mark of the aesthetic experience. He can be Saint Elmo's fire, or a harpy, or a wandering voice, without losing his own nature— for his nature is the Protean power to enter into any existence. He is Imitation itself. Prospero exercises his power through Ariel, just as any artist uses as his instrument the creative imagination. Prospero's moral wisdom has been attained through the imagination, or in interaction with the imagination. It fulfills itself through the imagination, which for Shakespeare no less than for Shelley is the supreme instrument of moral good.

Imagination continues to body forth the forms of things unknown. It gives that extra-dimension of suggestion to the image, the picture, or the symbol, which is denied to abstract concepts and rational argument. In the first scene, to take a small example, "patience" assumes complex reality in the differing attitudes of Gonzalo, Sebastian, and the Boatswain. Joy and fear may be presented in the great panoramas more completely than in any direct statement.[51] "Wonder" becomes more than a dictionary meaning when Caliban applies it to Stephano, and Ferdinand to Miranda and Prospero and himself, and Miranda to the brave new world.[52] Allegiance, imaged in action, is no longer a simple quality in a play where courtiers kneel before Alonso, Caliban before Stephano, and Ferdinand before Miranda.[53] Music itself may sing to the same tune the dance upon the yellow sands and the sea-change of death.

To analyze completely the implications back of "liberty" and "grace" in *The Tempest* would require the length of this chapter.[54] "Liberty" may be the unfettered play of the imagination for Ariel, or the intoxication of rebellion for Caliban, or for the finer characters the calm freedom of the spirit that comes from self-control and the recognition of necessity. In the last lines of this play, freedom results from prayer. And "grace" may be the action of a dance, or a rain from heaven, or the loyalty of Gonzalo, or the patience in trial that Alonso so sadly lacks, or a mere term of respect—or on the lips of Trinculo, of mocking disrespect. Always the higher meanings are given their validity and fullness by varying contrasts in the veins of realism or fantasy or convention or smiling humor or farce or cynicism or stupid denial.

Even in the world of romance, created by a wish, Shakespeare will not allow his judgments to become thin or facile or extreme. Common sense orients isolated pronouncements, no matter how pure and noble they may be. Somewhere in the plays there is always a Sebastian to comment on the bereaved king and the wise words of pity from his old follower: "He receives comfort like cold porridge." The heroes themselves are aware of complexity, and may, like Prospero, voice the paradox that good itself may be the matrix of evil:

> my trust,
> Like a good parent, did beget of him
> A falsehood in its contrary as great
> As my trust was, which had indeed no limit,
> A confidence sans bound. (I, ii, 93–7)

The double answer to Miranda's question as to whether foul play or blessed grace brought them to the island is "Both, both, my girl!"

Nevertheless, certain subjects have recurred so often in his thought that in his last play he expresses them with unmistakable clarity and directness. As has been often noted, they parallel the Christian pattern to a remarkable degree: despair, resignation, repentance, forgiveness, blessing. Even in this play of pastel shades, where grim issues might mar the total effect, the dark night of the soul tinges the thought: "I have made you mad; And even with such-like valour men hang and drown Their proper selves." Alonso accepts his hopelessness with a dulled and weary spirit:

> Even here I will put off my hope. . . . He is drown'd
> Whom thus we stray to find; and the sea mocks
> Our frustrate search on land. Well, let him go.

"No matter," he says, for he feels that "the best is past." "All torment, trouble, wonder, and amazement Inhabits here." But remorse inevitably rises, and patience has not yet been tried.

> All three of them are desperate. Their great guilt,
> Like poison given to work a great time after,
> Now gins to bite the spirits. (III, iii, 104–6)

In a scene of unique imagining, Prospero talks to the spellbound courtiers, who stand like manikins. They do not hear him; he is an inner voice; and if consciousness makes cowards of us all, then perhaps some hidden moral instinct may restore us. Solemn music plays, "the best comforter To an unsettled fancy," in order to cure their brains, now useless, boiled within their skulls. The dark sterility dissolves, in two natural images of the flooding back of the seas and of the morning light; and their understanding, their "clearer reason," dispels the fumes of ignorance. When Alonso returns to his despair: "Irreparable is the loss, and patience Says it is past her cure," Prospero corrects him gravely:

> I rather think
> You have not sought her help, of whose soft grace
> For the like loss I have her sovereign aid
> And rest myself content. (V, i, 141–4)

A play cannot lack deep seriousness and moral certainty when it contains such lines as:

Ling'ring perdition (worse than any death
Can be at once) shall step by step attend
You and your ways; whose wraths to guard you from,
Which here, in this most desolate isle, else falls
Upon your heads, is nothing but heart's sorrow
And a clear life ensuing.

Or:

Though with their high wrongs I am struck to th' quick,
Yet with my nobler reason 'gainst my fury
Do I take part. The rarer action is
In virtue than in vengeance. They being penitent,
The sole drift of my purpose doth extend
Not a frown further. . . .
They shall be themselves.[55]

The action of *The Tempest* is not only dominated by an old man, but is seen through his eyes. Prospero's young daughter may lament the storm and the shipwreck, but he himself knows that there is "No harm." He shares the fresh joy of the young lovers, but his sympathy is tempered by long experience:

So glad of this as they I cannot be,
Who are surpris'd withal; but my rejoicing
At nothing can be more. (III, i, 92–4)

His answer to Ferdinand's fiery vows of chastity is a mere "Well," or a "Fairly spoke" that contains aeons of ironic reservations. His comment on Miranda's raptures at sight of "beauteous mankind" (she is looking at such men as Antonio) contains the tears of things as only age knows them. Of Miranda's "brave new world," he simply says: " 'Tis new to thee."

Yet here too, part of his wisdom, part of his power, lies in his humility, his awareness of differing forms of life. He does not deny that a new king and queen should reign in Naples and Milan; he tells his children that his old brain is troubled, and begs them not to be disturbed with his infirmity. At Milan—or is it Stratford?—every third thought shall be his grave. And at last, stepping out of the play into his actual part as entertainer, casting aside the as-

sumed rôle of beneficent justicer, he begs the audience for release from the bare island of the stage. He lacks, he says, spirits
to enforce and art to enchant, and asks his audience for pardon.

It is a graceful leave-taking. Shakespeare, like Prospero, has
called up spirits by his art to enact his present fancies. (IV, i,
118–22). He has made Ariel "Come with a thought!" Through
the creative act of his imagination he is enabled to say that "At
this hour Lie at my mercy all mine enemies." And his thought,
after he has abjured the rough magic and the airy charm, is:

> Let us not burthen our remembrance with
> A heaviness that's gone. (V, i, 199–200)

He has learned to control his own desires and to quiet the beating of his mind.[56] "Though the seas threaten, they are merciful."

Fortunately, "some subtleties o' th' isle, that will not let you
Believe things certain," can never be reduced to limited moral
propositions, for they float before the eyes as images. Instead
of flat argument concerning lostness and faith, hope and wonder,
it is far more pleasant and convincing to see walking before us
Perdita and Fidele, Marina and Miranda, and to hear their individual voices. We know them so intimately as persons that we
forget that the very name of each heroine has in its setting a
clear significance. Images flash their suggestions from play to
play, increasing at once in clarity and complexity, so that the
fixed preoccupation with purity-assailed-by-tempest that has
given us pictures in action of Lear tearing off his clothes on the
heath, of Lear waking to see his daughter above him as "a soul
in bliss," of Thaïsa cast overboard in her coffin, of Marina and
Perdita as little children lost near roaring seas, and the same
combination that has puzzled so many readers of *Macbeth* with
"Pity, like a naked new-born babe, Striding the blast, or heaven's
cherubin"—these wedded opposites now find their final image
in Prospero and his small daughter, "me and thy crying self,"
"Alack for pity!" cast adrift in a rotten unrigged bark "to cry
to th' sea, that roar'd to us; to sigh To th' winds, whose pity,

sighing back again, Did us but loving wrong," where the listening
young girl's piteous sympathy at the story draws from Prospero
the words:

> O, a cherubin
> Thou wast that didst preserve me! Thou didst smile,
> Infused with a fortitude from heaven,
> When I have deck'd the sea with drops full salt. (I, ii, 152–5)

One of the subtleties of the isle is the miraculous return of new
life. The moral ideas, as we have seen, grow from age and experience and self-discipline and resignation, almost from disillu-
sion. But Shakespeare's art did not grow old. There at least,
bountiful Fortune remained his dear lady (I, ii, 178–9). The
return of fresh creative life may be the ever-renewed luck reserved exclusively for great artists; and his mastery over poetic
expression in new modes was Shakespeare's Perdita and Marina
and Miranda. Shakespeare's verse was never more alive and carol-
ing in its resilient rhythms than in Florizel's

> What you do
> Still betters what is done. When you speak, sweet,
> I'd have you do it ever. When you sing,
> I'd have you buy and sell so; so give alms;
> Pray so; and for the ord'ring your affairs,
> To sing them too. When you do dance, I wish you
> A wave o' th' sea, that you might ever do
> Nothing but that; move still, still so,
> And own no other function. (*Winter's Tale*, IV, iv, 135–43)

And never did he play with the mere sound of words, the echoing
and contrasting vowels, the slow richness of spondaic movements,
to better effect than in a play that can contain such lines as:

> And 'twixt the green sea and the azur'd vault
> Set roaring war; to the dread rattling thunder
> Have I given fire and rifted Jove's stout oak
> With his own bolt; the strong-bas'd promontory
> Have I made shake and by the spurs pluck'd up
> The pine and cedar; graves at my command

Have wak'd their sleepers, op'd, and let 'em forth
By my so potent art. (V, i, 43–50)

The art was never more powerful, or more subtle, than in the
organization of the controlling images. It is "a living drollery"
of beautiful or fantastic beings, set to "marvellous sweet music,"
isolated on its mysterious island by a never-surfeited sea, and surrounded with a sleep.[57] The sea seeps into every action and
creates new compounds, sea-swallow'd, sea-sorrow, sea-marge,
until life itself suffers a sea-change, and the still-closing waters
have become its image. The sea of life is surrounded by the
sleep of death. But to sleep is perchance to dream, and the dreams
no longer need be those of Hamlet. Instead, we have "a most
majestic vision, and Harmonious charmingly."

That it is a vision cannot destroy its reality or its value for the
speculative mind. Just as Prospero had summoned up the thin
shapes of the pageant, the cloud-capped towers and gorgeous
palaces, so Shakespeare had summoned up Prospero and all the inhabitants of his island. It is "an excellent pass of pate," but not the
final one. If the fabric of this vision is baseless, it is baseless in
the same sense and to the same degree that the world is. The great
globe itself shall dissolve like this insubstantial pageant. In the
intricate folds of the most famous lines in *The Tempest*, the
universe itself becomes a visible symbol of intelligence, a play of
thoughts in some unknown and infinite imagination. *We* are such
stuff as dreams are made on, and the inheritors of the world are
passing thoughts in the mind of God.

CODA

The development of a creative intelligence is more significant
and important than the annals of an individual. It is a bit of luck
that the accidents that happened to shape Shakespeare's life are
so nearly non-existent, for instead of daily engagements and curious anecdotes in considering "Shakespeare," we are left with central evidence: the body of his dramatic work. The impression
which that work leaves upon us as a whole is one of naturalness

and stability. He began with a vivid delight in nature, a comprehension of human beings, an awareness of the joy and consolation which art can afford. This knowledge was with him throughout his career as a writer. He was to forget nothing that he had ever felt.

But Shakespeare's "recurrences and fervors" do not indicate that he stood still. The incredible complexity of his increasing knowledge demanded continual new orderings and adjustments. His career is a constantly changing struggle to find adequate frameworks for new discoveries without abandoning what he has already found to be true. His sensibilities make repeated fresh demands upon his organizing powers as an artist. Usually control emerges victorious over proliferating sensitivity. It is a mark of his greatness as an artist—since great art implies significant form given to significant material—that he kept fully alive both his art and his sensibility.

In many ways Shakespeare's most striking trait is his sheer vitality. He remained young longer than most people, and then compressed into two decades whole lifetimes of intense imaginative experience. The outlines of this career are clear and simple. To the age of thirty-five he reflects in his work the innocence and trust of a child. He loved human life as few artists have ever loved it; he accepted human beings as delightful and ridiculous and admirable; he set up whole worlds of hope and gay confidence, where the power of love was unquestioned. Then followed the period of *Hamlet* and the dark comedies, with its overmastering awareness of mortal failure and treachery. The instinct to organize experience in a comprehensive whole led to the great tragedies, where the highest possibilities and the lowest degradations of human nature are worked into a single canvas. Again the faltering, and the reckless plunge into the despair of *Timon*, and again the re-creation, on the other side of tragedy, of a mental world that without disregarding evil "means intensely and means good."

Shakespeare's art itself is an unconscious illustration of his vital instinct. He knows that "quick bright things come to confusion," but he knows also that out of chaos may come new life and bright order. And always, in the larger integrations of his career, the brightness prevails. The dangerous destructiveness of lust in *Richard III* and the narrative poems is the ground on which the golden comedies are built. The despair of the dark period is the necessary prelude that makes possible the magnificent ordering of the tragedies. And for the third deliberate gesture, out of the black depths of *Macbeth* and *Timon* rise the final illuminations of *Antony and Cleopatra* and the romances. Jupiter had appeared to Posthumus in a dream. "He came in thunder," and as the vision fades, "The marble pavement closes; he is enter'd His radiant roof." But he leaves with Posthumus a symbolic message: "From a stately cedar shall be lopp'd branches which, being dead many years, shall after revive, be jointed to the old stock, and freshly grow."

Vitality may exhaust the reader if it is unchecked. It may become a limiting principle, so that the strenuous optimism of a Browning or a Whitman is no less irritating and monotonous than the vital, but dull and brutal, world of the modern Nietzscheans and power-worshippers. Shakespeare's view, as usual, was more comprehensive. His instinctive acceptance of life was kept sane by his dramatic sense of human variety, and by his saving grace of humor. Both are moral qualities as he exercises them.

Drama, even in its primitive forms, requires more than one actor. Since each character speaks directly in his own person, various points of view must be expressed; and a play ceases to be "dramatic" if all characters are merely mouthpieces for a single author. Shakespeare, born of the chameleon, had the instinctive knack of entering fully into other minds by an act of imaginative sympathy. His candid sense of fair play, his awareness of uncounted possibilities and idiosyncrasies in thought, compel him to present the complete case in court, not merely the verdict. He is more easily the counsel for the defense than either prosecutor or judge—for at the start he found innate worth in all men, and in mid-career he felt that brothers' faults should not be judged harshly, since all men are brothers in an original faultiness. His freedom from simple and unchanging preconceptions allowed him to present weaknesses in the most admirable of men, and to find a soul of goodness in things evil.

Drama, moreover, has a beginning, a middle, and an end: it leads to a conclusion through a recognition or a revelation of something not realized at the start. Its themes therefore develop and grow as new knowledge is added during the course of a play. The image for the drama is less a "moment's monument" than the passing of moments—the growth of an organism changing as life itself changes, subject to the accidents and additions of time that will modify its original structure. Again, Shakespeare has the innate capacity to live in a developing world. His are not the static patterns of Dante and of Milton and (structurally, at least) of Spenser, but the dynamic images of tempest and of the tide taken at flood. His nature was too comprehensive, elastic, continually growing and adventurous to rest in any end. For finality is a kind of death. Shakespeare is a master of suspended judgment, so that his moral speculations rarely settled into complacent mottoes, but were embodied in persons, developed in actions, and constantly subjected to attack or comment by other imagined persons.

His acceptance of life gives him the energy to intensify its qualities. He fashions glowing dreams and hideous nightmares; he piles superlative on superlative until Ossa is like a wart; he stretches mortal capacities toward those of gods and goddesses and devils in single scenes of such spiritual scope that the damned may look upon the angels, or the cursed slave be washed from the sight of heaven in steep-down gulfs of liquid fire.

Yet the intense dreams are tempered by humor. At its simplest, a sense of humor demands at least a double judgment, since it is based upon an awareness of the incongruity between the unruly actual and the serious ideal, between fact and convention, between truth and shadows. A sense of humor is a sense of balance, the necessary stabilizer for any practicable morality. Whether Shakespeare's paradise is lost or regained, it is always restored to this world by some little touch: Cleopatra's crown is awry and must be straightened; the grave-digger murders the English language and sends for a can of beer; Volumnia clucks like a mother hen in her indignation; Gertrude notices that her son is panting and sweating, and gives him her handkerchief. Humor becomes a moral agent: it insists that the everyday world be given its due; it relates ideals to practical action; it is no respecter of person or place; it suggests that nothing is so vile or noble as to chain us to final judgments of complete contempt or admiration. Shakespeare's most personal and intense speculations are always subject to the wider relationships and the social comments which humor affords. Who but Shakespeare would have thought of creating a jailer in *Cymbeline* who can shape the ideas of Hamlet and Macbeth within his own professional vocabulary? And who else would have dared give to such a philosophical hangman his own secret hopes, subjecting them to the corrective of humor? "I would we were all of one mind, and one mind good." The salt of wit keeps any of his idealisms from spoiling into fanaticism. Admiration, though it better suits his generous nature, is no less dangerous than satiric negation. His motto is neither *nil admirari* nor *admirari*, but *ridere atque admirari*, which is a saner moral tag because it includes more of life.

Drama, like humor, has a social basis, since it assumes more than one point of view. Shakespeare was too much of a traditionalist, too great a respecter of the past, to disregard society. To him, reverence is "that angel of the world." He revered the social order and set up his ideal of the stable state, based upon individual moral responsibility: the acceptance by the ruler of his duty to his subjects, and by the subjects of their duty to the state. This reciprocal relationship made totalitarianism as far from his thoughts as reverence for stability was close to them. Even in the tragedies, where the personal moral issues loom so large, he is always careful at the end to pick up the scattered pieces of the state. With his intuitive comprehension of individuals, and his settled conviction of the importance—to personal morality itself—of a persisting and accepted social order, one of the vitalizing dramatic motifs throughout the plays is the adjustment of the individual to society. Once more he makes the comprehensive answer: society must, and should, take precedence over the individual, but society is merely a workable association of individuals, held together ideally by an awareness of brotherhood, by responsibilities reciprocally assumed, and by mutual love.

Few readers can resist Shakespeare's sanity. He lives on so many levels at once, with such a spacious awareness, that his hopes and his speculations do not rouse suspicions that they are partial or forced. Shakespeare has been a Bible for skeptics and for believers, for those who live in the world and those who live in the spirit. The measure of his comprehensiveness is that he himself cannot be reduced to one of these tags or to any other. Yet his hopefulness, the resurgence of vital instinct, is remarkable. It shows in his open-handed creation of scores of living characters. It shows in his highest tragic theme: the conflict not between good and evil but between two goods, or between a mistaken and a valid desire for the good. It shows in the larger patterns of his development. And it explains why a poet who writes with such rich intensity can nevertheless create the impression of gentleness.

The society of love is perhaps as good a phrase as may be found to describe Shakespeare's moral world. Love is limited in its conception to a relationship between individual human beings. But within that limit it moves in many shapes: it is Viola's feeling for Orsino, Romeo's for Juliet, Helena's for Bertram, Troilus' for Cressida, Hermione's for Leontes, Macbeth's for his wife, Don Adriano's for Jaquenetta, Valentine's for Proteus, Falstaff's for Prince Hal, Edgar's for Gloucester, Prospero's for Miranda, Lear's for the poor naked wretches as well as for Cordelia, Volumnia's and Virgilia's and Menenius' and Aufidius' for Coriolanus, Henry V's for Fluellen, Horatio's for Hamlet, Emilia's for Desdemona, Philip the Bastard's for Prince Arthur. Love varies from exalted ecstasy to a comfortable understanding, from the unendurable flash of lightning to the selfless guardianship. But it too is seen most characteristically as a principle of stability, the centripetal force that binds men in brotherhood, the base for building hope and confidence and positive action. Shakespeare could rarely resist the pleasure of putting into his latest play his oldest figure—the follower who serves his loved master for the sole reward of loving him. Orlando has his old Adam, Hamlet his Horatio, Coriolanus his Menenius, Hermione her Paulina, Prospero his Gonzalo—even Timon his steward and Goneril her Oswald.

Though Shakespeare expressed all gradations of romantic love, the largeness of his conception is best shown in his continual return to the idea that love is a quality of unshakable fidelity. He holds to this idea with such a peculiar consistency that he almost slights one of the abiding moral questions: what is right action in a conflict between loyalty and truth? He suspends his judgment—or more accurately, he judges on both sides—in the case of Falstaff versus Henry V. Troilus destroys himself by forcing himself to give up his love for Cressida in the face of fact. But for this question alone, Shakespeare seems ordinarily to have closed his mind passionately and beyond argument. Characteristically, he creates a melodramatic situation to show the fatal mistake of Enobarbus in abandoning his loyalty to follow his own interests. He selects or shapes material to persuade us that loyalty is rarely mistaken in its object and never mistaken in its nature. The procession of heroines—from Helena-and-Hermia and Juliet and Viola, to Desdemona and Cordelia and Cleopatra and Hermione—offer smiling reproach and eventual refuge to the fickleness and fever of the men. Love is a goddess, not a god; and being divine, she cannot change. Shakespeare might well say with Browning, "Our gifts once given must here abide." The turtledove is his symbol, not only because it loves absolute beauty in the phoenix, but because it represents in itself absolute devotion. The word "truth" becomes, then, almost the synonym for loyalty and love, and Shakespeare's moral discoveries may be reduced to the simple equation that love is truth.

Neither the high quality of love, nor any of the other vices and virtues, is spiritualized out of existence in Shakespeare. He accepts the physical world in all its earthiness and mixed contaminations. Love itself is always represented in human alloy, with its callousness and quirks and bawdry and cruelties and coarseness and contrarieties. But though Shakespeare never wavers in his belief in the mixed nature of reality, he also never doubts the supremacy of the spirit. His greatest moral gift may well be the *certainty* with which he held that morality is a matter of individual responsibility, and that though men choose freely, they choose within the framework of invisible moral laws as inexorable as the laws of gravity. Except in the cause of loyalty, Shakespeare does not permit himself special pleading; he neither exonerates faults nor extols shoddy virtues. He usually manages to avoid sentimental luxuriating in unadulterated pity as well as its reverse: the sentimental indictment of a cold universe moved by blind forces indifferent to man. Once again, he accepts a world of moral law, no less powerful because not written down on tablets, operating in society and reproduced in the microcosmos, the mind of man.

Intelligence, therefore, is assumed as a necessary part of his morality. When we consider also his sensitivity to the physical world, to the whole gamut of instincts and emotions, and to the intractable riddle called experience, it is easy to forget that his complex plays are dominated and steadied by a conscious sense of balance, whether the balance be termed common sense or "clearer reason." Yet Shakespeare always respects intelligence, no matter to what ends it is diverted or perverted. In the moral sphere he holds it to be the agent by whose light man may see to choose rightly. His intelligence *fully* awake and *freely* allowed to operate, man cannot make the wrong decision. To the brink of the grave, therefore, to the last line of the last scene, the intelligent man may be restored by acknowledging his faults or repenting his villainies. Only for the stupid, the bestial, or the shallow creatures who vacillate in their velleities does Shakespeare occasionally allow himself to express contempt.

Moral acts are individual mental decisions, the individual is responsible, and intelligence controls the mind. The formula is simple. In operation, it would be complicated for most of us by the infinite variety of human individuals; but with Shakespeare's extraordinary gift for compassion and sympathy, variable man

presented to him no opaque riddle, but rather the opportunity
for pleasurable excitement and discovery. His thought concerning inner responsibility changed with the years. As a youthful
preacher and an artificer of happy plays, the problem of moral
accountability looked easy to him. His superficial optimism allowed him to assume that love and truth, when discovered, would
be followed without argument, for men were essentially loving
and truthful. But as the spacious mirror came to reflect more and
more of human life, expanding to include those opposing shadows
of lust and betrayal and selfishness, the recalcitrant world became more difficult to manage. One temporary expedient was to
explode in an acknowledgment of evil, openly denying the possibility of reconcilement, or rolling up a play in confused bitterness that offered no solution. But the main line of development was
toward dual worlds of matter and spirit, in which the important
actions were taken in the world of the mind, and in which the
dramatic conflict was basically between external and internal
realities. That this conflict should so frequently take the guise
of a battle between appearance and truth, between shadow and
substance, shows that Shakespeare had already accorded the victory to inner reality. "Who can control his fate?" But however unruly the accidents of existence and the wills of others
may be, man can control his own mind. And if he can, he
should.

In the last plays, Shakespeare pushes still further the assumption that mind is the valued reality. It is as if the laws of the spirit
were relentlessly operating in the drama of Shakespeare's own
development. The creator of so many imaginary worlds falls
prey to his own creations, until it becomes difficult, or unimportant, to distinguish between what is fancy and what is fact.
Partly the change in attention may have risen out of inability to
live longer in the unbearable intensity of the tragedies, with their
sharp realization of the heights and depths of human existence.
"Your Highness," one of Shakespeare's physicians says to a
poisoner, "Shall from this practice but make hard your heart."
Shakespeare as his own physician may have found it wise no

longer to harden his heart with the poisons nor dissolve it with the powerful elixirs of his tragic worlds. Having lived through such ranges of imaginative experience, even the most inexhaustible heart may seek or welcome relaxation.

> Haply this life is best
> If quiet life be best, sweeter to you
> That have a sharper known, well corresponding
> With your stiff age.

And the free imagination may still ask: "Hath Britain all the sun that shines? Day? night? Are they not but in Britain?"

The lover and the poet combine, "of imagination all compact." The harmony of love will be given the widest and most pleasant panoramas that the imagination can devise. Music will sound throughout, as the magic art that gives greatest reality to the immaterial. And if the life of the mind is the most important reality, why may not the mental leap be made and imagination be taken as the only reality? Then the tempests and the thunder-claps, separation and death and jealousy, may dissolve in a final benediction of harmony and reconciliation. In the last assumption of all, the hero may be not only in accord with a fortunate destiny, but its actual shaper, controlling the minds and actions of others as if they too were his own creations. Desire builds the world it yearns for, concentrated in beauty and grace and ending in joy, while the imagination acts as the agent of desire. This marriage of desire and imagination, "This grand act of our life, this daring deed Of fate in wedlock," Shakespeare makes on the assumption that there's nothing either good or bad but thinking makes it so; that the fault—and the virtue—lies not in our stars but in ourselves; that man, when he has learned to control his dreams, can be bounded in a nutshell and count himself king of infinite space.

> Affection! thy intention stabs the centre.
> Thou dost make possible things not so held,
> Communicat'st with dreams! How can this be?
> With what's unreal thou coactive art,

And fellow'st nothing. Then 'tis very credent
Thou mayst cojoin with something; and thou dost.

The last act in the drama of Shakespeare's thought is obliquely introspective and plays ambiguously with the questions: What is reality? And how do we recognize it? The actors on the stage— or are they the creations of Shakespeare's mind? or the creations of Prospero his own creation?—melt into air. Yet in this they are no more insubstantial than the audience, or the great globe itself, which shall dissolve without trace into the stuff of dreams. As solidity vaporizes into such evanescence, Shakespeare chooses from all the flying shapes and images those which are most beautiful and smiling. His own career ends in comedy in the sense that Dante's vision is a comedy, that the Christian story completed is a comedy. And for the long moment of the last plays, he imagines a kinship between the artist and divinity, and assumes that there is truth in his creation of a world of images.

Yet such a statement also needs its further reservations. Shakespeare's moral strength rises largely from his receptivity and from the uninsistent breadth of his thought, so that he is able to present incompatibles simultaneously, hold enigmas in suspension, and recognize mystery. Even at the end, he will not assert without qualification that life is an imaginative dream. Prospero's great speech is occasioned by his sudden start as he remembers "foul conspiracy" yet to be subdued. It ends almost in apology for the old brain which is vexed and troubled and weak, as if Prospero were trying to protect the young lovers for a time from the disturbing thoughts which they too must in part learn in the life ahead of them. His meditations are his "infirmity," and he has yet to ask pardon for his faint strength, his overthrown charms, his failing spirits and art. Shakespeare's knowledge of human weakness and evil had been so intensely experienced as true, that even the vivid dream of human good cannot be accepted as the whole of reality merely because man wishes and imagines it to be true. Man at his noblest pitch of emotion and intellect and creative imagination is still too imperfect to make the truth. An influence above his highest nature, though harmonious with it, must be summoned. The last plays are filled with divine apparitions and emanations and visions and sacrifices. The romances cannot be brought to a close until the god descends and steps from the machine.

How are these celestial actors to be taken? The thought of the romances is eminently Christian—the wandering or sinful mortals, contrition, repentance, resignation, patience, prayer, forgiveness—but the thought is not expressed in Christian terms or even with a Christian certainty. It is possible that because of skepticism, or the conventions of the Elizabethan age, or his own delicate sense of propriety, Shakespeare deliberately masked a personal Christian conviction. But it is more probable, on the indirect evidence of the plays themselves, that Diana and Apollo and the rest are not symbols of grace, but of man's need for grace, of man's need to imagine grace. In the last movement of Shakespeare's thought, it is a cause for sorrow that, though he never lost his gentleness and hope, courage and belief begin to fail. The deep tragedy of Shakespeare's mind—and it has the inevitability of tragedy—is that he lived so long in the imaginary worlds which were necessarily his worlds as a creative artist, that distinctions were lost, that all experience became imaginings, and that not only the great globe but religion itself could be conceived only as a noble dream.

Within the limits of observed humanity, no poet could go much further than Shakespeare. He possessed, and communicated, a mimicry of human actions which the simplest and the subtlest minds easily recognize as faithful, a sense of human diversity within an unescapable moral order, an admiration for courage and integrity and loyalty and love, a vibrant compassion that understood the smallest and the largest issues, humor, wit, and proportion, a joy in that exercise of impersonal control which constitutes art, a profound humility that allowed him to enter into the foibles and the crimes of others and to build from sin as well as from virtue the awareness of human brotherhood, a glorying in action and physical beauty and nature, a knowledge of human dignity only equalled by his knowledge of human ridiculousness, a delight in the play of the spirit, an imaginative fertility that kept his comprehensive sense of balance from becoming merely dull.

Above all, Shakespeare's unquenchable vitality and love of life led him to accept and absorb all experience, never to rest satisfied in any answer as final, but to shape the most painful and desperate and sordid as well as the happiest into his noble world of images. By the continual creative act of his imagination he gave shapes to enduring and inspiring thoughts. At the top the withered branch was always green.

Notes

QUOTATIONS in the text are invariably drawn from the one-volume *Complete Works of Shakespeare* edited by George Lyman Kittredge, with the generous permission of its publishers, Ginn and Company. Kittredge's numbering of the lines accords with that commonly used. I have retained Professor Kittredge's spelling and punctuation and capitalization throughout, except in a few instances where short quotations have been worked into the text, and in one or two instances of difference of interpretation of the sense.

In order to keep the text from too great a weight, only the most important quotations have been identified, and not even those if they can be located approximately from references in the text itself.

NOTES TO CHAPTER ONE

¹ In addition to the external evidence furnished by Meres and by the First Folio, Shakespeare's authorship of *Titus Andronicus* is made more probable by such a partial list of parallels as this: Isabella's plea for mercy (I, i, 117), the dirge in *Cymbeline* (I, i, 151), the kneeling family of Coriolanus (I, i, 370), Juliet's necrophobia (II, iii, 98) and Juliet's tomb (II, iii, 226), Henry VI's and Richard II's self-pitying isolation (III, i, 33), Lear's and Othello's living in hell while thinking of heaven (III, i, 149 and IV, iii, 43), Brutus' and Macbeth's sense of walking through a nightmare (III, i, 253—"fearful slumber"), Lear's all-embracing pity and savagery in madness (III, ii, 60), Lear and Cordelia telling old tales in prison (III, ii, 81),

Iago and Othello kneeling to swear a league of vengeance (IV, i, 87), the literal and illiterate clown (IV, iii, 80 and 101), Mrs. Quickly's dismissing of God except as a last resort (IV, iii, 90), Coriolanus' marching against his own city (IV, iv, 62), the final silence of Iago (V, i, 46 and 58), Hamlet's anxiety to exact a binding oath (V, i, 70), Richard III's and Iago's merriment at their villainy (V, i, 113), Puck's rural practical jokes (V, i, 132), Romeo's last kiss and Antony's (V, iii, 167), Ophelia's desolate funeral with its maimed rites (V, iii, 196), the sonnets' mourning bell (V, iii, 197); besides the recurring themes of ingratitude (I, i, 447), of music and discord (II, i, 70), of blood pulsing in the head (II, iii, 39), of fragrant rose lips (II, iv, 24), of eternal springtime (III, i, 21), of shadow and substance (III, ii, 80), and of the sea's terrors (III, i, 223).

² As examples of Shakespeare's innocent horrors, see:
the stage burial in the tomb where Titus collects his dead sons;
the protagonist's killing of his own son Mutius in a fit of annoyance;
the throwing of another corpse into a pit, in inspecting which two further characters "Both fall in";
the cutting off of Titus' hand in full view of the audience, although it won for him only the displayed heads of two more of his sons, thus increasing the "two-and-twenty sons I never wept" to the full number of blackbirds baked in a pie;
the mad scenes that result in conspiratorially butchering a fly with a knife;
the "trimmed" Lavinia, sans hands or tongue, setting up her communications system, where Shakespeare's stage directions gloatingly read: "She takes the staff in her mouth and guides it with her stumps and writes";
Aaron's blackamoor babe, which he carries around like a trophy;
Aaron's killing of the nurse in a fine Browningesque line: "Weeke, weeke!—So cries a pig prepared to the spit" (IV, ii, 146);
the Andronici shooting messages on arrows to the gods;
the near hanging—Aaron mounts the ladder—of the black Moor and his babe;
the parading of the Empress and her sons disguised as Revenge, Rape, and Murder;
the cutting of two throats and catching the blood in a basin—on the stage;
the cannibal banquet served by Titus "like a Cook";
the stabbing of the Empress, the hero, and the Emperor within the lapsed uttering of thirty syllables.

³ The plucking of white and red roses (1, II, iv); the silent fiends that foretell Joan of Arc's downfall (1, V, iii); unmasking the religious im-

postor Simpcox (2, II, i); Humphrey of Gloucester's parting from his
shamed Duchess (2, II, iv); the quarrel between the servingmen of rival
factions, blue-coats versus tawny-coats (1, I, iii), which may have suggested to him the opening of *Romeo and Juliet;* the death of Cardinal
Beaufort (2, III, iii); the death of the Duke of York after his verbal
warfare with Queen Margaret, the "tiger's heart wrapp'd in a woman's
hide" (3, I, iv).

⁴ The shadow and substance of Talbot (1, II, iii); the antitheses of
Talbot and Joan, of Gloucester and Winchester, of York and Somerset
in Part I; Suffolk's wooing of Margaret (1, V, iii); Henry VI's Queen
Margaret contesting in words with the Duke of York (3, I, iv); the fathers
and sons unnaturally at war (3, II, v); stichomythic wooing of Lady Gray
by Edward IV (3, III, ii); the full working out, in 34 lines, of the ship-
of-state image (3, V, iv); Henry VI's famous speech extolling innocuous
pastoral simplicity (3, II, v); and his prophetic praise of the future Henry
VII (3, IV, vi, 68).

⁵ *Henry VI*, Part 1, is generally assumed to have been written later than
the second and third parts. The exact order of writing is of no importance
to this argument, which assumes that the three Henry VI plays and *Richard III* were written between 1590 and 1595—generous limits—and that
Shakespeare's thought, on the evidence of the plays, did not change or
develop notably while they were being written. It also assumes that they
are almost wholly Shakespeare's, on the grounds that they are consonant
with the rest of his work, that no convincing evidence exists to disprove
their direct contemporary attribution to him, and that their ineptness
is natural enough. Oaks were once acorns, and even genius must be
allowed to start somewhere. Certain evidences in the three parts of *Henry
VI*, each perhaps inconclusive by itself, suggest fledgling attempts that
Shakespeare later developed as his own. They include the humorous
realism of his common people, not only in the Jack Cade scenes but
elsewhere (2, II, i and 2, II, iii), as well as his consciousness of popular
fickleness (e.g., 3, III, i); his critical awareness of his own use of the high-
flown "silly-stately style" (1, IV, vii, 72); the tragic ideas of acceptance
of the inevitable (3, V, iv, 37–8) and of triumph of spirit over death
(1, IV, vii); economy in character portrayal, as when four successive single lines reveal four personalities (2, II, i, 154).

But since the main argument in this section is that Shakespeare used
these history plays as textbooks—that they put ideas and themes into his
head—its point would not be blunted entirely if it were merely admitted
that Shakespeare read over these four history plays with some care.

⁶ Scene I, ii, has 230 lines devoted to this action or "persuasion"; Scene IV, iv, has nearly 300.

⁷ It is extraordinary that no one has written a book on "Kneeling in Shakespeare." No other symbol in the whole range of his dramatic composition is more constantly or strikingly used. An obvious picturing of human relationships, in supplication, loyalty, subordination, or love, he uses it for all effects—intense emotion, bitter denial, heartbreaking tenderness, despair, and dedication. Or, as here with Richard, as an ironical reversal of the actual relationship. If the extraordinary prevalence of kneeling scenes and imagery were called to the attention of a psychiatrist, the world would soon learn that Shakespeare had a fixation.

⁸ In *The Two Gentlemen of Verona*, other interesting early trials of themes later developed are: Julia in disguise revealing her own loyal love (see Viola in *Twelfth Night*); Proteus' soliloquies on discovering his own base impulses (II, iv and II, vi; see Angelo in *Measure for Measure*); and Valentine's speech in praise of love ("Love's a mighty lord," II, iv; see Berowne in *Love's Labour's Lost*).

⁹ II, vii, 18. With her, as in all Shakespeare's early plays, love is largely the delight of the senses: "O, know'st thou not his looks are my soul's food?" Julia's restrained womanly jealousy, also, is portrayed with sympathetic and humorous deftness in IV, iv, 145–210.

NOTES TO CHAPTER TWO

¹ For example, in *The Two Gentlemen of Verona, Love's Labour's Lost, Taming of the Shrew, All's Well That Ends Well, Troilus and Cressida, Measure for Measure,* and in a sense, *Hamlet, Othello, Lear,* and *Macbeth.*

² As elsewhere, I am considering *The Merry Wives* in thematic rather than chronological order. Since external evidence cannot establish its date accurately, internal evidence, or speculations concerning habits of composition, might be given a hearing: I would suggest that it was written between *Henry IV*, Part 2 and *Henry V;* in other words, in 1598–9. Its composition almost entirely in prose and its perfunctory Falstaff support the traditions of Queen Elizabeth's request and of its being written in 14 days, and indicate that it was hasty work. Pistol is not yet Mrs. Quickly's husband, as he is in *Henry V* (and as he is in no danger of being in *Henry IV*, Part 2). And the exhaustion of the Falstaff vein, which Shakespeare could sense as easily as any critic, would afford further reason for Shake-

speare's killing off in *Henry V* a character whose appearance there had been promised in *Henry IV*, Part 2.

³ There is the striking exception of *Antony and Cleopatra*, and, if one wishes to make the Trojans into respectable small-town Christians, there is *Troilus and Cressida*.

⁴ Except in the dark comedies, jealousy in Shakespeare is usually a disease which is unassailably hideous and dangerous because it is groundless. Its object has no external existence, as Page reminds Ford: "No, nor nowhere else but in your brain." (IV, ii, 166) And earlier: "What spirit, what devil suggests this imagination?" (III, iv, 230)

⁵ The ideal of "proportion" holds even in repentance. Page warns the "heretic" Ford not to swing from the extreme of jealousy to the extreme of self-abasing remorse:
> 'Tis well, 'tis well; no more!
> Be not as extreme in submission as in offence. (IV, iv, 10–1)

⁶ Time is vilified in ingenious epithets and conceits in *The Rape of Lucrece* (925–96); it is the carrier of grisly care, the eater of youth, the false slave to false delight, sin's packhorse, virtue's snare, the universal murderer. Characteristic of Shakespeare's thought, Time is dual and may act as an avenger. It is a "tutor both to good and bad," one of whose functions is "To wrong the wronger till he render right."

⁷ V, iii, 161; II, vi, 33; III, ii, 16—all Juliet's.

⁸ "Some word there was . . . That murd'red me," says Juliet (III, ii, 108–9). Variants on "banished" or "exiled" occur 31 times in III, ii and III, iii. Note also "despair" and "death" in the play.

⁹ "For aught I see," says Nerissa, "they are as sick that surfeit with too much as they that starve with nothing. It is no mean happiness, therefore, to be seated in the mean." (I, ii, 5–8) Portia is so overjoyed at Bassanio's success in choosing the right casket that the Stagirite moralist within her starts her preaching to herself redundantly:
> O love, be moderate; allay thy ecstasy;
> In measure rain thy joy; scant this excess!
> I feel too much thy blessing. Make it less
> For fear I surfeit! (III, ii, 111–14)

Even Bassanio will advise his friend Gratiano "To allay with some cold drops of modesty" (II, ii, 195, 196, 190, 194) his skipping spirit, for he considers him "too wild, too rude and bold of voice"—"Something too liberal."

¹⁰ For the casket references, see II, vii and ix. For the distrust of cunning, see Shylock's account of Jacob's peeled wand trick, I, iii, 77–91, and its reception.

¹¹ Gilded tombs enfold worms (II, vii, 69); and "the fool multitude," choosing by show, will not learn "more than the fond eye doth teach." (II, ix, 26–7)

¹² Bassanio traces how "The world is still deceiv'd with ornament" (III, ii, 74), in law and in religion, in the bearded frowning coward and the wigged beauty. Ornament may hide "a most dangerous sea," may scarf ugliness, and may be summed up as "The seeming truth which cunning times put on To entrap the wisest." (III, ii, 73–102) Antonio exclaims "O, what a goodly outside falsehood hath!" (I, iii, 103) Gratiano chooses as his most offensive hypocrites those whose solemn silence lends them the semblance of "wisdom, gravity, profound conceit." (I, ii, 88–100) Arragon says that the stamp of merit and desert does not square with estates, degrees, and offices; and rightly viewed, "the true seed of honour" might be found in "the chaff and ruin of the times." (II, ix, 38–51)

¹³ Yet order, or the law, must not be subjected even to the best of good intentions. When Bassanio, advocating any means to a good end, urges: "Wrest once the law to your authority. To do a great right, do a little wrong," the answer is clear and immediate: "It must not be. . . . It cannot be." (IV, i, 215–22) Shakespeare will be no casuist even in a good cause.

NOTES TO CHAPTER THREE

¹ Here is as good a place as any to explain the omission of Shakespeare's sonnets, except for incidental references, in this book. The sonnets are, in my opinion, personal, local, and occasional. The topic of this book is speculative no matter how carefully it is handled; it would become more so if speculation were extended to include Shakespeare's personal life. Though Shakespeare's own experience undoubtedly shaped his outlook in the drama, I have therefore limited consideration to the plays and the three poems in which Shakespeare deliberately offered his ideas to a public audience.

² It seems a continual surprise that more of *Much Ado* is in prose than of *The Taming of the Shrew*.

³ His misliking is as sudden as his liking, and at the first zephyr of suspicion he is quick to note that "beauty is a witch Against whose charms faith melteth into blood." (II, i, 186–7) Benedick sees him as a "poor hurt fowl" that will "now . . . creep into sedges." (II, i, 209–10)

⁴ Another book on Shakespeare waiting to be written is *Shakespeare's Short Speeches.* Cf. Shylock's "I am content," and the many other examples, increasing as he learns his art, in which a short speech of not more than four words, usually monosyllables, marks a turn in the action or the highest dramatic point of a scene or of a whole play.

⁵ Shakespeare does not forget the ineffectiveness of sage advice. Compare Brabantio's bitter reply to the Duke of Venice (*Othello*, I, iii, 199–219) or Hamlet's attitude toward the sage counsel of Claudius (I, ii, 87–120). See also Polonius and Laertes, the Duke of Vienna and Claudio, and the more knowing course of action Ulysses adopts toward both Achilles and Troilus.

⁶ Shakespeare will not allow us to miss the point that criticizing evil in others is usually a comfortable and false way of magnifying our own virtues. Later, when Jaques invites Orlando to sit down while "we two will rail against our mistress the world and all our misery" (III, ii, 295–6), Orlando's reply is: "I will chide no breather in the world but myself, against whom I know most faults."

⁷ The gentleness of the old servant Adam, "Who after me hath many a weary step Limp'd in pure love," has led Orlando to reciprocal action, "Whiles, like a doe, I go to find my fawn And give it food." The Duke rounds off the episode by changing his earlier argument of mutual weakness to the argument of sympathy drawn from mutual human need and suffering:

> Thou seest we are not all alone unhappy.
> This wide and universal theatre
> Presents more woful pageants than the scene
> Wherein we play in. (II, vii, 136–9)

⁸ To take an extreme case, the epilogue spoken by Rosalind is written both in and out of part, and the boy actor who Shakespeare knew would speak it says, "If I were a *woman*."

⁹ Shakespeare the dramatist is not a practising or professing Christian. Nevertheless, the characters of Viola, and of old Adam in *As You Like It*, Isabella at times in *Measure for Measure*, Hermione in her almost silent scene, and Gonzalo, show deeper insight into the Christian secrets than

many volumes of sermons, even in this period when Christianity seemed worth serious personal passion and thought.

¹⁰ See the epilogues to *A Midsummer Night's Dream*, *As You Like It*, *Twelfth Night*, as well as *Henry IV*, Part 2, *Pericles*, *Tempest*.

¹¹ For other examples of his realistic choric "observation," compare his comment on the sudden alliance of the two enemies France and England outside Angiers:

> How like you this wild counsel, mighty states?
> Smacks it not something of the policy? (II, i, 395–6)

And on the defiance of the Citizen of Angiers:

> He speaks plain cannon-fire and smoke and bounce . . .
> Zounds! I was never so bethump'd with words
> Since I first call'd my brother's father dad. (II, i, 455–67)

And on the wooing compliments of the Dauphin (II, i, 504–9), on the overpowering inevitability of the punishment for evil acts (IV, iii, 116–34), and on the "bloody Neroes" that rip up the womb of their Mother England (V, ii, 130–58).

¹² Mention need scarcely be made of the Bastard's famous concluding speech in defense of national integrity—"Naught shall make us rue If England to itself do rest but true." (V, vii, 110–18)

¹³ II, i, 66, from 40–66. See also II, i, 73–83; 93–115; 124–38; most of the scene is devoted to Gaunt's warnings.

¹⁴ To sense the full force of Shakespeare's political conservatism, the reader should consider in order the following speeches: John of Gaunt, I, ii, 37–41; York, II, iii, 83 to the end of the scene; Richard, III, ii, 36–62; Richard, III, iii, 72–126; and the Bishop of Carlisle, IV, i, 114–49, 322–3.

¹⁵ As characteristic pictures of England, see the little one-or-two-line vignettes given by: Percy, II, iii, 53; York, II, iii, 93–5; Bolingbroke, III, i, 23; Richard, III, ii, 6, 24–5; the Welsh captain, II, iv, 8; Bolingbroke, III, iii, 46–7; Scroop, III, ii, 106–7; Richard, III, ii, 42; Bolingbroke, III, iii, 43–4, 50, 52; Aumerle, IV, i, 35; and Northumberland, II, iii, 4. When his subject is the natural beauty of England, Shakespeare disregards differentiation of characters, and all Englishmen praise alike.

¹⁶ Notice Shakespeare's conscious statement of this technique, as Henry IV reviews the retributive events of his reign:

> All these bold fears
> Thou seest with peril I have answered;

> For all my reign hath been but as a scene
> Acting that argument. (2, IV, v, 196–9)

¹⁷ Ironically, Shakespeare assigns to the rebellious Archbishop of York the thought:

> A peace is of the nature of a conquest;
> For then both parties nobly are subdu'd,
> And neither party loser. (IV, ii, 89–91)

¹⁸ Plus the deathbed scene, IV, v. See especially lines 120–38.

¹⁹ Much as he idealizes Henry V, he is as much in earnest to make him human, until for some critics, in contrast to the rampageous Prince Hal, he has become too much the ordinary man, the typical blunt Briton.

²⁰ The treatment of Malvolio is analogous to Shylock, and Malvolio possibly belongs in this list of exceptions. When he answers the third-degree questions of the pranksters with: "I think nobly of the soul and no way approve his [Pythagoras'] opinion" (IV, ii, 59–60), comedy almost flies out the window. Shakespeare respects certain traits of this character to such an extent that he does not subject him to the indignity of a scambled reformation at the end of the play.

²¹ Mistress Quickly (*Henry V*, II, i, 92–3). See also Nym's "The King hath run bad humours on the knight" (127–8), and Pistol's "His heart is fracted and corroborate" (130). The suspended sympathy for Falstaff lingers in the play with dramatic irony as late as IV, vii, when Gower may say: "Our King . . . never kill'd any of his friends," and Fluellen may emphasize again the political moral: "As Alexander kill'd his friend Cleitus, being in his ales and his cups, so also Harry Monmouth, being in his right wits and his good judgments, turn'd away the fat knight with the great belly doublet" (43–51). Sometimes too much reasonable justification may have the effect of a mild reproach.

NOTES TO CHAPTER FOUR

¹ The basic principle of contrast, which Shakespeare uses in uncounted modifications, is present in his style as well. He has two styles. We have been made almost too aware of his "taffeta phrases," his rhetoric and rhodomontade. It is high time that some statistician count up the astonishing number of lines in Shakespeare's work that consist of ten monosyllabic words.

² Compare Pompey: "Truly, sir, I am a poor fellow that would live." Or: "Does your worship mean to geld and splay all the youth of the city? . . . Truly, sir, in my poor opinion, they will to 't then." (*Measure for Measure*, II, i, 235; and II, i, 242–6) And parallel to Parolles, compare Claudio: "Sweet sister, let me live!" (*Measure for Measure*, III, i, 133; see also III, i, 118–32)

³ See I, i, 90–109; I, iii, 198–223; III, ii, 102–32; III, iv, 4–17; and her conduct and words in the whole of III, v.

⁴ Since *All's Well* is little read, a few of these single jewels might be set down here:

> Love all, trust a few,
> Do wrong to none.—*Countess*, I, i, 73–4.

> 'Let me not live,' quoth he,
> 'After my flame lacks oil, to be the snuff
> Of younger spirits, whose apprehensive senses
> All but new things disdain.'—*King*, I, ii, 58–61.

They say miracles are past, and we have our philosophical persons, to make modern and familiar, things supernatural and causeless. Hence is it that we make trifles of terrors, ensconcing ourselves into seeming knowledge when we should submit ourselves to an unknown fear.—*Lafew*, II, iii, 1–6.

> All is whole.
> Not one word more of the consumed time!
> Let's take the instant by the forward top;
> For we are old, and on our quick'st decrees
> Th' inaudible and noiseless foot of Time
> Steals, ere we can effect them.—*King*, V, iii, 37–42.

> Labouring art can never ransom nature
> From her inaidable estate.—*King*, II, i, 121–2.

⁵ See the King:
> No, no, it cannot be. And yet my heart
> Will not confess he owes the malady
> That doth my life besiege. (II, i, 8–10)

The Countess, after reproving her son in her thoughts, and exalting Helena:

> Which of them both
> Is dearest to me, I have no skill in sense
> To make distinction. (III, iv, 38–40)

And, as shedding some light on Ophelia's haunting "Lord, we know what we are, but know not what we may be" (IV, v, 42–3), this dialogue between the French lords:

Now God delay our rebellion! As we are ourselves, what things are we!
Merely our own traitors. . . .
Is it not meant damnable in us, to be trumpeters of our unlawful intents?
(IV, iii, 23–4, 31–2, and the whole scene)

⁶ In V, i, 307–9, 311, his mother says:

>   This is mere madness;
> And thus a while the fit will work on him.
> Anon, as patient as the female dove . . .
> His silence will sit drooping.

Hamlet's action before and after this comment, changing from extreme
passion to hopeless brooding, bears her out.

Even more striking is his long soliloquy of self-criticism. (II, ii, 575–
616) Five times in these lines, Hamlet whips himself into hysteria, immediately followed by an unstrung revulsion of self-awareness. This burning out of his nervous energy in inaction, its very intensity causing the
following lassitude, is here so obviously and consciously marked out by
Shakespeare in periods of about eight lines that any editor who does not
set "Ha!" (602) as a separate line, an exclamation of disgust, is doing
Shakespeare an injustice.

These dizzying alternations of mood, formalized in this speech, are
worked out consistently throughout the play. If today's jargon were not
a danger, it might even be suggested that "manic-depressive" be looked up
in any dictionary, and the two parts of this modern invention be applied
with care to Hamlet.

⁷ There is conflicting evidence as to whether or not the play was performed when written (about 1602); its first publication in 1609 tells the
reader that it has never been staled with the stage.

⁸ This conflict between speech and action is dramatized, for example,
in II, i, where Ajax's only effective retorts to Thersites' words are blows.
It is expressed directly by Thersites in II, iii, 3–6: "He beats me, and I rail
at him. O worthy satisfaction! Would it were otherwise: that I could beat
him whilst he rail'd at me." Even in the rough world of hatred, actions
speak louder than words.

⁹ In this play, Shakespeare frequently abandons his usual dramatic realism in favor of a stylized formality that makes his thought clearer in
pageantry and part-song. Note particularly the introduction of the Trojan
heroes (I, ii, 201–68), the procession before Achilles' tent (III, iii), the
triple vows of Troilus, Cressida, and Pandarus (III, ii, 180–215), and the
wooing of Diomed and Cressida, commented upon by a double chorus of
Troilus and Ulysses on one side and Thersites on the other.

¹⁰Aristotle appears to be more than a name to Shakespeare. The Duke in *Measure for Measure* is as much a mouthpiece for Aristotelian temperance as for Christian forgiveness. And the Aristotelian doctrine of the mean may underlie this judgment in *Troilus and Cressida*, IV, v, 78–82:

> In the extremity of great and little
> Valour and pride excel themselves in Hector;
> The one almost as infinite as all,
> The other blank as nothing. Weigh him well,
> And that which looks like pride is courtesy.

¹¹ Compare also the statement of the idea that virtue is social use, in the Duke's speech in *Measure for Measure*, I, i, 27–41:

> Heaven doth with us as we with torches do,
> Not light them for themselves; for if our virtues
> Did not go forth of us, 'twere all alike
> As if we had them not.

¹² See V, vi, 13–4. The words of the text are meaningless here, unless the editor inserts some such stage direction as: "They fight. Achilles is disarmed."

¹³ For the descriptions of human perfection, see I, ii, 275–8; II, iii, 158–60; IV, v, 96–112; and III, iii, 169–74.

¹⁴ See particularly III, ii, 83–90; 167–77; 178–90; IV, ii, 107–11; and IV, iv, 65–6.—For the "hand" passages, see I, i, 55–9 and *Romeo and Juliet*, II, ii, 23–5.

¹⁵ Compare also the parallel introduction of Isabella, who, informed of the rules of the sisterhood of Saint Clare, expresses disappointment that there is not "a more strict restraint" to try her zeal. (I, iv, 1–5)

¹⁶ This intuition that the acknowledgment of death—or of sin—dispels anguish is reinforced elsewhere in the play. Thus, the Duke comforts Juliet by securing her frank confession of guilt, by telling her that her partner Claudio is to die the next day, and by saying: "There rest." It is negated by her reaction:

> O injurious law,
> That respites me a life whose very comfort
> Is still a dying horror! (II, iii, 35–42)

It is repeated by the Duke, speaking of Claudio: "Yet had he framed to himself, by the instruction of his frailty, many deceiving promises of life, which I, by my good leisure, have discredited to him, and now is he re-

solv'd to die" (III, ii, 259–62). And again by the Duke to an acquiescent
Isabella—he is speaking of Claudio whom she thinks dead:

> But peace be with him!
> That life is better life, past fearing death,
> Than that which lives to fear. Make it your comfort,
> So happy is your brother. (V, i, 401–4)

¹⁷ Act II, scene ii. See also Hamlet's persuasion of his mother (III, iv);
Antony and the populace (*Julius Caesar*, III, ii); Ulysses and Achilles
(*Troilus and Cressida*, III, iii); Iago and Othello (III, iii); Volumnia and
Coriolanus (V, iii). One might add Lady Macbeth and Macbeth (I, vii)
and the Fool and Lear (I, iv). In all of these scenes except that from *Troilus
and Cressida*, the views of an important character are changed radically at
a crucial point in the action because of the persuasions of another character.

¹⁸ See particularly II, iv, 1–30 and IV, iv, 22–36.

¹⁹ For instance, one of his favorite mottoes is *La fin couronne les oeuvres*,
which he leaves in French in the Second Part of *Henry VI* (V, ii, 28). In
Troilus and Cressida, IV, v, 224, it appears as "The end crowns all." In
All's Well That Ends Well, IV, iv, 35, the very title of which is a variation
on the idea of the motto, it becomes "Still the fine's the crown," which
might easily be misunderstood if Shakespeare had not returned to rephras-
ings of the idea so frequently.

²⁰ II, iii, 36, 39. Further examples:
Isabella entering after the Duke has made Claudio absolute for death:
"What, ho! Peace here! Grace and good company!" (III, i, 44)
The Duke to Claudio, regarding Isabella's rejection of Angelo's ad-
vances: "She, having the truth of honour in her, hath made him that gra-
cious denial which he is most glad to receive." (III, i, 165–8)
The Duke to Isabella: "Grace, being the soul of your complexion, shall
keep the body of it ever fair." (III, i, 187–8)
The Duke, describing himself to Escalus:

> "Not of this country, though my chance is now
> To use it for my time. I am a brother
> Of gracious order, late come from the See
> In special business from his Holiness." (III, ii, 230–3)

The Duke's soliloquy on place and greatness (IV, i, 60–5) is applicable
beyond mortal place. Though it has its perfunctory use to allow a lapse
of time in the action, the meditation is startlingly irrelevant.
Angelo in soliloquy:
"Alack, when once our grace we have forgot,

Nothing goes right! we would, and we would not!" (IV, iv, 35–6)
And elsewhere in more perfunctory use, and throughout the fifth act.

NOTES TO CHAPTER FIVE

[1] Shakespeare's distrust of moralizing may best be realized by considering the ineffectiveness *in action* of the excellent advice given by the Friar to Romeo, by Polonius to Laertes, by Claudius to Hamlet, by Duke Vincentio to Claudio, by Ulysses to Troilus and to Achilles. See also the Duke of Venice comforting Brabantio in rhymed couplets, and Brabantio's reply (I, iii, 199–219):

> But words are words. I never yet did hear
> That the bruis'd heart was pieced through the ear.

[2] That Shakespeare does not treat Brutus primarily as the traitorous assassin of the secular order, as Dante does, does not change their common assessment of the vice of treachery.

[3] Even the same small word may take on vibrant overtones, as in Othello's "Indeed?" at Desdemona's gladness over Cassio's governorship (IV, i, 249), which echoes grimly Iago's "Indeed?"—Othello had twice repeated it—when he first starts poisoning Othello's mind with his suspicions (III, iii, 101–2).

[4] On the subject of monsters, to take one image, see III, iii, 107, 166, 377, and 427; III, iv, 161, 163; and V, ii, 189. Compare also the varied animal imagery, the cleft feet of the devil-Iago, and the cannibals, anthropophagi, and "men whose heads do grow beneath their shoulders" that are part of the background of the Moor who committed the "monstrous act" of killing Desdemona—and as her father sees it, the monstrous act of marrying her.

[5] I cannot resist quoting a final *reprise* of that suspicion-rousing phrase "Look to 't," for in its context it shows also how thickly and with what seemingly natural accent and accident Shakespeare studs his plays with variations on broad governing ideas—here the images of truth or deceit. Othello suspects that Desdemona has lost the magic handkerchief which had been steeped in hallowed medicine

Conserv'd of *maidens' hearts.*
Des: I' *faith?* Is 't *true?*
Oth: Most *veritable.* Therefore *look to 't* well.
Des: Then would to *God* that I had never seen 't! (III, iv, 74–7)

⁶ As further examples of speaking two languages at once, see Othello's determination to know Iago's thoughts and the reply: "You cannot, if my heart were in your hand; Nor shall not whilst 'tis in my custody" (III, iii, 163–4), which to Othello sounds like an honest friend laboring to quell his own wicked suspicions. Iago's "I should be wise; for honesty's a fool And loses that it works for" (III, iii, 382–3), is a brazen statement of his philosophy which nearly wins an apology from Othello for mistrusting him. See also Iago's "Her honour is an essence that's not seen; They have it very oft that have it not" (IV, i, 16–17).

The double meaning, of course, can be transferred to the unconsciously ironical remarks of others, as when Othello says of Iago—and it is true in a sense that he does not suspect—"This honest creature doubtless Sees and knows more, much more, than he unfolds" (III, iii, 242–3).

⁷ See I, iii, 262–75; III, iii, 88–92; "the business of my soul," III, iii, 181; "some place of my soul," IV, ii, 52; yet also the soul and the net may blend in one ominous thought, as in Iago's "His soul is so enfetter'd to her love," II, iii, 351.

⁸ As examples:
KENT: The gods to their dear shelter take thee, maid,
    That justly think'st. (I, i, 185–6)
ALBANY: Now, gods that we adore, whereof comes this? (I, iv, 312)
EDMUND (who says these words in irony and learns their truth in action):   the revenging gods
    'Gainst parricides did all their thunders bend. (II, i, 47–8)
LEAR: You heavens, give me that patience, patience I need!
    You see me here, you gods, a poor old man. (II, iv, 274–5)
KENT's rumination: or something deeper,
    Whereof, perchance, these are but furnishings—
    But, true it is, from France there comes a power
    Into this scattered kingdom. (III, i, 28–31)
LEAR: Let the great gods . . . find out their enemies now. (III, ii, 49, 51)
LEAR's prayer that pomp, deliberately exposing itself to feel wretchedness, may "show the heavens more just." (III, iv, 36)
GLOUCESTER: Kind gods, forgive me that, and prosper him! (III, vii, 92)
GLOUCESTER: Here, take this purse, thou whom the heavens' plagues
    Have humbled to all strokes. That I am wretched
    Makes thee the happier. Heavens, deal so still! (IV, i, 65–7)
ALBANY: This shows you are above,
    You justicers, that these our nether crimes
    So speedily can venge! (IV, ii, 78–80)
GLOUCESTER: O you mighty gods!

This world I do renounce, and, in your sights
Shake patiently my great affliction off.
      . . . your great opposeless wills . . . (IV, vi, 34–6, 38)
EDGAR: Therefore, thou happy father,
Think that the clearest gods, who make them honours
Of men's impossibilities, have preserv'd thee. (IV, vi, 72–4)
GLOUCESTER: You ever-gentle gods, take my breath from me;
Let not my worser spirit tempt me again
To die before you please! (IV, vi, 221–3)
CORDELIA: O you kind gods,
Cure this great breach in his abused nature! (IV, vii, 14–5)
EDGAR: The gods are just, and of our pleasant vices
Make instruments to scourge us. (V, iii, 170–1)
ALBANY: The gods defend her! (V, iii, 256) Cordelia is thereupon
brought on the stage dead in Lear's arms. But the gods defend spiritual
integrity and the general order—not the individual life.

A similar anthology of uses of "fortune," "nature," "monster," or any of
the key-words that have been noted in the text, would establish with almost as great a certainty the general drift of the thought.

[9] Coriolanus makes the same distinction between the judgment of power
and the judgment of spiritual value at a dramatic crisis (*Coriolanus*, III,
iii, 123).

[10] The temptation is irresistible to add here a further note on the close
inweaving of structure with the dominant ideas. Cornwall's ironic promise
to be a "dearer father" to Edmund closes a short scene which is immediately followed by the entrance and opening speech of the real father
Gloucester. Near the end of the long preceding scene, Gloucester rumi-
nates on his lost Edgar: "I lov'd him, friend— No *father* his son *dearer*.
True to tell thee, the grief hath craz'd my wits." (III, iv, 173–5) Here the
theme and motivation of madness is reinforced (Gloucester had already
mentioned it in line 171) in the subplot. And the preceding scene closes
with Edgar's ravings: "I smell the blood of a British man," immediately
before Cornwall appears and says: "I will have my revenge ere I depart
his house." The reference of the pronoun "his" is identified only by context: it would sound like the "British man," the house is Gloucester's, and
Gloucester is not yet blinded.

[11] Shakespeare makes Lear's childish nature obvious, but not too obvious,
in variations on the symbol of the family. "Old fools are babes again,"
Goneril says (I, iii, 19). And the Fool: "thou mad'st thy daughters thy

mother; for when thou gav'st them the rod, and put'st down thine own breeches,

> Then they for sudden joy did weep,
> And I for sorrow sung,
> That such a king should play bo-peep
> And go the fools among." (I, iv, 187–194)

Compare also Cordelia's reference, of multiple meaning, to "this child-changed father." (IV, vii, 17)

[12] Some of the more significant lines bearing on the theme of authority and duty, in the image of master-servant, are:

KENT to Lear: You have that in your countenance which I would fain call master: . . . authority. (I, iv, 29–30, 32)

LEAR in his madness: Thou hast seen a farmer's dog bark at a beggar? . . . And the creature run from the cur? There thou might'st behold the great image of authority: a dog's obey'd in office. (IV, vi, 159–63)

EDMUND's counterfeit letter ascribed to Edgar: This policy and reverence of age makes the world bitter. . . . I begin to find an idle and fond bondage in the oppression of aged tyranny, who sways, not as it hath power, but as it is suffer'd. (I, ii, 48–57)

KENT in soliloquy: Now, banish'd Kent,
If thou canst serve where thou dost stand condemn'd,
So may it come, thy master, whom thou lov'st,
Shall find thee full of labours. (I, iv, 4–7)

KENT to Cornwall: I serve the King; . . .
You shall do small respect, show too bold malice
Against the grace and person of my master,
Stocking his messenger. (II, ii, 135, 137–9)

LEAR and the disguised Kent: What wouldst thou? —Service. —Who wouldst thou serve? —You. (I, iv, 23–28) And Lear to Kent: Thou serv'st me, and I'll love thee. (I, iv, 97–8)

GLOUCESTER to Lear: My duty cannot suffer
To . . . let this tyrannous night take hold upon you. (III, iv, 153–4, 156)

EDGAR to his father: So, bless thee, master! (IV, i, 64)

EDGAR describing Kent: who in disguise
Followed his enemy king and did him service
Improper for a slave. (V, iii, 219–21)

LEAR in madness: Come, come, I am a king;
My masters, know you that? (IV, vi, 203–4)

KENT in the final scene: O my good master! (V, iii, 267)
I have a journey, sir, shortly to go.

My master calls me; I must not say no. (V, iii, 321-2)
ALBANY at the end: For us, we will resign,
During the life of this old Majesty,
To him our absolute power. (V, iii, 298-300)

[13] Compare Lear's preaching: "When we are born, we cry that we are come To this great stage of fools." (IV, vi, 186-7)

[14] This idea is caught up at each end of the play—in Edmund's "Brother, . . . I have told you . . . nothing like the image and horror of it" (I, ii, 188-92); and in the triple choric comment as Lear enters with the body of his daughter (V, iii, 263-4):

KENT: Is this the promis'd end?
EDGAR: Or image of that horror?
ALBANY: Fall and cease!

[15] The theme of love-the-corrector is passed on to the Fool from Kent and Cordelia in the first scene, and passed back in gentler form (Lear no longer needs such severity) to Cordelia in the fourth act after the Fool has disappeared. There are good reasons to suppose that in Shakespeare's acting company the Fool and Cordelia were played by the same actor. In the moral meaning of the play, such an identity of the two is less a physical limitation in a stage production than a happy discovery. Self-sacrificing love follows Lear always, and those wandering last words of his—"And my poor fool is hang'd"—need no specific reference or explanation, for in spirit Cordelia and the Fool are one.

[16] How hard it is, nevertheless, for pride to acknowledge error is seen in an extraordinary interchange in II, iv, 12-24. Lear asks who has set Kent in the stocks, and Kent answers, "Your son and daughter." Then follows: "No." "Yes." "No, I say." "I say yea." "No, no, they would not!" "Yes, they have." "By Jupiter, I swear no!" "By Juno, I swear ay!" "They durst not do 't; they would not, could not do 't. 'Tis worse than murther to do upon respect such violent outrage." Here the rôle of physician is thrown to Kent: he must make Lear bow to reality in a brutal interchange of yes and no.

[17] III, vi, 110, 112-3. For some of the speeches on beggary and brotherhood, see II, iii, 1-21; III, iv, 134-46; IV, i, 1-9, 25-8; and III, iv, 25-36, 105-14; III, vi, 108-21; IV, i, 65-72; IV, vi, 225-8.

[18] The "hand" imagery in this play is almost as striking as that of "eyes" or "heart" and is even more unusual. Rough equivalents for heart, eye, and hand would of course be the emotions, the intellect, and the social sense. Hands are here used as effectively as in *Paradise Lost* to symbolize union or allegiance. In this second short scene, for instance (in which we

learn that ripeness is all), Edgar rouses his father from despairing lassitude with "Give me thy hand!" The same idea has already crossed the stage in pantomime (the stage directions are Elizabethan): "Enter, with Drum and Colours, the Powers of France over the stage, Cordelia with her Father in her hand, and exeunt."

19 I omit consideration of Hecate, who seems a stupid and jarring addition by some other hand, and who, together with the incongruous naïveté and prosiness of much of the fourth act, makes it difficult to find a wholly consistent pattern in the tragedy as it has come down to us.

NOTES TO CHAPTER SIX

1 The unusually full stage directions would suggest that *Timon* was written when Shakespeare himself was not in London to help produce it; perhaps, like Timon, he was in his own "cave" at New Place in Stratford.

2 The controlling parallel between *Timon* and *Lear* is, of course, the plot of the generous nature reduced to bitterness and madness by the discovery of hypocritical selfishness. In *Timon*, however, the wheel never comes full circle in the rediscovery of generous love. There are other parallels, large and small. Flavius' rôle is like Kent's: "I'll follow and enquire him out. I'll ever serve his mind with my best will." (IV, ii, 48–9.) Timon's curses and awareness of the friendly-unfriendly elements are similar to Lear's. Apemantus' "Call the creatures whose naked natures live in all the spite of wreakful heaven, whose bare unhoused trunks, to the conflicting elements expos'd, answer mere nature" (IV, iii, 227–31) is verbally reminiscent of Lear's prayer outside the hovel. The image of the doors shut against the needy wretches is repeated (III, iii, 38–42); "cut to the brains" becomes for Timon "Cleave me to the girdle! . . . Cut my heart in sums!" (III, iv, 91–2, 94); and even phrases recur, such as "ingrateful man" (IV, iii, 188) and "monster ingratitude" (V, i, 68, and III, ii, 79–80).

3 A whole book might well be devoted to the tightly interwoven structure. This note calls attention merely to the close parallels in themes and phrasing between Act IV, which centers on Antony, and Act V, which centers on Cleopatra; the imagery of kisses; the counterpoised hand-kissing of III, xiii and IV, viii, with its preparation in II, v; the parallel anger against the messengers in II, v and III, xiii, with its suggested *reprise* in V, ii, 153–8; the charioting through Rome in IV, xii, 33–9 and V, ii, 52–7, 207–26 (barely suggested earlier in III, xiii, 134–8); Cleopatra's seeing herself in IV, xv and V, ii as a simple woman, a milkmaid, and a wife, as op-

posed to her position as "Royal Egypt" or "the president of my kingdom" (III, vii, 18) and as opposed to "the false housewife Fortune" (IV, xv, 44). The intricate jewelled watch-making is best shown, however, in the interlocking small images: the repetition of "becomes" and "becoming"; the idea of conquering one's self; the symbols of emptiness when love is absent; the premonitions of Antony's death (II, v, 26–35 and IV, xiv, 120–7); the gashed overtopping "pine" of IV, xii, 23–4 that becomes the fallen soldier's "pole" of IV, xv, 65; Antony's fallen "star" in IV, xiv, 106 and Cleopatra as "O Eastern star!" in V, ii, 311. The rich imagery of wealth and precious stones, of the gods and the cosmos and the planetary bodies, is of course well known and inescapable.

⁴ See, for instance, his comments in the political scenes, II, ii, 103–14 and 181–250; II, vi, end; II, vii; III, ii; III, v.

⁵ Octavia's key passages in the amplification of the important moral conception of tragic choice are III, iv, 12–19 and III, vi, 76–8.

⁶ See also "There is left us ourselves to end ourselves," (IV, xiv, 21–2); " 'I am conqueror of myself,' " (IV, xiv, 62); IV, xiv, 68 and 99–101; "Not Caesar's valour hath o'erthrown Antony, but Antony's hath triumph'd on itself," (IV, xv, 14–5); "a Roman by a Roman valiantly vanquish'd," (IV, xv, 57–8).

⁷ The idea in this phrase of "present pleasure" is strongly and formally developed at the opening: see I, i, 47; I, ii, 128; I, iv, 32. See also its recurrence in II, iii, 40.

⁸ A partial list of the obvious and hidden variations on the *Liebestod* motif would include:
ENOBARBUS: "I do think there is mettle in death, which commits some loving act upon her, she hath such a celerity in dying." (I, ii, 147–9)
ANTONY: "The next time I do fight,
I'll make Death love me." (III, xiii, 192–3)
ANTONY: "Mine honest friends,
I turn you not away; but, like a master
Married to your good service, stay till death." (IV, ii, 29–31)
ANTONY: "But I will be
A bridegroom in my death and run into 't
As to a lover's bed. . . .
Let him that loves me strike me dead." (IV, xiv, 99–101 and 108)
ANTONY: "I here importune death awhile, until
Of many thousand kisses the poor last
I lay upon thy lips." (IV, xv, 19–21)

CLEOPATRA: "The stroke of death is as a lover's pinch,
Which hurts, and is desir'd." (V, ii, 298–9)
CHARMIAN: "Now boast thee, death, in thy possession lies
A lass unparallel'd." (V, ii, 318–9)
CAESAR: "she looks like sleep,
As she would catch another Antony
In her strong toil of grace." (V, ii, 349–51)

⁹ CAESAR to Octavia: "Cheer your heart!
Be you not troubled with the time, which drives
O'er your content these strong necessities;
But let determin'd things to destiny
Hold unbewail'd their way." (III, vi, 81–5)
ANTONY: "Nay, good my fellows, do not please sharp fate
To grace it with your sorrows. Bid that welcome
Which comes to punish us, and we punish it,
Seeming to bear it lightly." (IV, xiv, 135–8)

¹⁰ See, for instance, the certain ordering of the initial scenes: in the first, Coriolanus is presented as "chief enemy to the people" (who are already mutinous), and as a great soldier; in the second the theme of external dangers to the state is introduced; while the third inserts the familial theme before the act is allowed to proceed in multiple scenes designed to demonstrate Coriolanus' greatness as a soldier. See also the middle act, in which the middle scene centers on Volumnia's power to persuade her son (an exquisite preparation for the crucial climactic scene of V, iii), and is cradled between the two parallel scenes of Coriolanus' flaring up against the people. Act V builds toward its climax by having the unsuccessful embassies of Cominius and of Menenius precede Volumnia's successful attempt; and the procession of Virgilia, Volumnia, Valeria, young Marcius, with attendants, is given a formal choric accompaniment in an odd sort of pageant-soliloquy delivered by Coriolanus (V, iii, 22–33).

¹¹ For the fable of the body, see I, i, 92–167. None of the body's parts—not "the kingly crowned head, the vigilant eye, the counsellor heart, the arm our soldier, our steed the leg, the tongue our trumpeter, with other muniments and petty helps in this our fabric"—is self-sufficient. They may feel that they are the instruments that "see and hear, devise, instruct, walk, feel, and mutually participate"; they may believe that taken together they "minister unto the appetite and affection common to the whole body." But the mutinous members must not revolt against the belly, the source of sustenance to be sent through the blood. The belly of the state is the senate, grave and good and deliberate, "the storehouse and the shop of the whole body," which passes on to its "incorporate friends" "that natural

competency whereby they live." The health of this great body of the Roman state must not be endangered, whether by insurrection of members against the belly, or by the belly itself, or by the "great toe" of its plebeian leader, or by its own ascetically sublimated spirit in Coriolanus.

[12] As one example, see his automatic answer to the senators' extolling of his wounds before the populace: "Scratches with briers, Scars to move laughter only." (III, iii, 51–2)

[13] The idea of service is underlined in the following passages: "To gratify his noble service" (Menenius, II, ii, 44); "They ne'er did service . . . This kind of service . . ." (Coriolanus, III, i, 122, 124); "What do *you* prate of service?" (Coriolanus to Brutus, III, iii, 83); "I'll do his country service," (Coriolanus, IV, iv, 26); "my revengeful services . . . to do thee service," (Coriolanus, IV, v, 94, 106).

[14] Even the plebeians carry on the theme with their childish arguments, and are reproved by Coriolanus himself, in dramatic irony, for giving him only "children's voices." (III, i, 30) A richer texture is added by hidden references, as when Coriolanus in disguise thinks of himself slain "in puny battle" by "wives with spits and boys with stones" (IV, iv, 5–6), and Cominius catches up the anecdote of the young Marcius with: "they follow him against us brats with no less confidence than boys pursuing summer butterflies or butchers killing flies" (IV, vi, 92–5).

NOTES TO CHAPTER SEVEN

[1] Most readers will not attribute the first two acts to Shakespeare, hesitate to ascribe to him Gower's rhymed tetrameters, and are made uneasy by the brothel scenes of the fourth act. The play seems to me much more of a piece than is usually believed, marred less by another hand than by a faulty and mismetred text. It is at any rate possible to believe that the first two acts are deliberately contrived in a level, formalized, somewhat prosaic vein; that the Gower choruses are in Shakespeare's own manner when dealing with earlier English literature or with gnomic rhymes; and that no one but Shakespeare could have created the complicated tones of the brothel scenes—which, furthermore, are needful to the drift of the play. The cunning trace of alliteration in the four-beat lines, the patina of antiquity which a few ancient words establish in Gower's choruses, and the unusual play back and forth between couplets and blank verse throughout the piece, are not accidental, nor are they the signatures of an amateur or a second-rate artist.

Nevertheless, to avoid dispute as well as inferior poetry, I have not drawn upon the first two acts in discussing this play unless the quotations can be paralleled elsewhere, easily and more than once, in Shakespeare's thought.

[2] Even minor characters are infected by this quick change of heart. In a ten-line scene (IV, v), two gentlemen come out of the brothel where Marina is being offered for sale. Their gallant badinage covers their astonishment at their own reform:

"But to have divinity preach'd there! Did you ever dream of such a thing?" "No, no. Come, I am for no more bawdy houses. Shall 's go hear the Vestals sing?"

They leave the stage with a laughing resolution: "I'll do anything now that is virtuous, but I am out of the road of rutting for ever." Such a scene only prepares for Marina's clear victories.

[3] The brothel scenes, for example, have often been compared in spirit to those in *Measure for Measure*. The scene between Cleon and Dionyza (IV, iii) offers some startling parallels in construction and thought with those between Macbeth and Lady Macbeth (I, vii; II, ii); the murderer allowing his victim to pray before killing her (IV, i, 66–71) is as heart-stopping and unexpected as in *Othello* (V, ii, 24–32); and Marina "Who starves the ear she feeds, and makes them hungry, The more she gives them speech" is, in this respect at least, kin to Cleopatra (V, i, 113–4; *Antony and Cleopatra*, II, ii, 241–3). Is it Pericles or Cleopatra who at the moment of spiritual triumph takes on regality with the words: "Give me my robes"? (V, i, 224; *Antony and Cleopatra*, V, ii, 283)

[4] Amplifying passages that illustrate general statements in the text would make the discussion of this and the other romances top-heavy and harder to follow. Selected references, however, will be given in the notes, since they establish the thematic compression and surety of a play which, when plot alone is considered, is usually branded as rambling and pointless.

As examples, for the love-lust motif:

"Her face was to mine eye beyond all wonder;
The rest (hark in thine ear) as black as incest."

(I, ii, 74–5; compare I, i, 72–86.)

For appearance versus truth:

"Opinion's but a fool, that makes us scan
The outward habit by the inward man."

(II, ii, 56–7; see also I, i, 105–6; the harpy with angel's face and eagle's talons, IV, iii, 46–8; or the dumb show of Marina's tomb, where we may "See how belief may suffer by foul show!" IV, iv, 23. Contrast also the beauty of Marina with her basket of flowers, IV, i, 14–8, and the false beauty of the daughter of Antiochus, I, i, 12.)

For the sense of sin, in typical Shakespearean imagery:
> "And both like serpents are, who though they feed
> On sweetest flowers, yet they poison breed."

(I, i, 132–3; on another plane, compare IV, ii, 23–4. See also I, i, 41–2, and the *Measure for Measure* imagery of I, i, 100–4.)

[5] For various expressions of personal integrity, see I, i, 53; II, i, 171–2; II, v, 59; III, ii, 26–31; V, i, 121–3; V, iii, 87–94.

[6] For recognition of the order of nature and man's place in that order, see I, i, 76–86; II, i, 1–4; II, iii, 24–6; II, iv, 57–8; as for those who transgress the order—even the small sparrows: "The poor Transylvanian is dead that lay with the little baggage" (IV, ii, 23–4).

[7] "Patience" as a key word or idea occurs in I, ii, 64; III, i, 19, 26; IV, iv, 50; V, i, 139, 145, 146; V, iii, 101.

As for observations on the model ruler (as a contributor to order and as himself an ordered microcosm), see I, i, 50–3; I, ii, 34–65 and 122–3; II, ii, 10–3; II, iii, 59–63 (and counterpointed in this same scene, three other ideas of kingship in lines 28, 37–44, and 45–7); V, iii, 61–3.

[8] For some of the images of the sea in storm, see I, iii, 24–5, 29; II, Prologue, 27–36; II, i, 5–11 and throughout the scene; II, iii, 84–5, 88–9; II, iv, 43–4; III, Prologue, 44–60; III, i, 1–14, 57–65; III, ii, passim; IV, i, 27–9, 52–65, 99–100; IV, iv, 29–31, 39–43; V, iii, 47.

[9] Pericles sees himself as flotsam cast on a beach, II, i, 60; and is seen by Simonides and Thaïsa as "a stranger," II, iii, 67; II, v, 78. Thaïsa's casket is tossed up on shore from the sea's stomach, III, ii, 49–59; and Marina describes herself as "but a stranger," no countrywoman of Mytilene, "no, nor of any shores," V, i, 115, 104.

[10] Pericles is not given to self-pity, and his care is always for the misfortunes of others. See particularly his fear of involving others in his own destruction, which causes his first self-imposed exile, I, ii, 83–99. If this scene was not conceived by Shakespeare, he must have had a twin.

[11] For the idea of absolute loss, of being at the very bottom of Fortune's wheel, see I, ii, 46–7; I, iv, 78; II, Prologue, 33–6; II, i, 60–81; and III, i, 38–40.

[12] For the idea of overruling and overseeing powers, see I, i, 72–5 Pericles; I, iv, 33–50 Cleon; II, i, 8–11 Pericles; II, iii, 45–7 Pericles; II, iv, 1–15 Helicanus; IV, ii, 37–9 Pander; V, i, 58–61 Lysimachus; V, iii, 59–61 Thaïsa. Even Cleon, allied with evil, knows the power of the avenging heavens: I, iv, 101–4; III, iii, 23–5.

[13] The prayers are almost too numerous to list exhaustively. But as samples, see I, i, 19–24 Pericles; I, iv, 97–8 Omnes; II, i, 1–11 Pericles; III, i, 1–14 and 36–7 Pericles; III, ii, 67 and 112 Cerimon to Apollo and Aesculapius; III, iii, 4–5 and 34 Pericles; IV, i, 66–70 Leonine; IV, ii, 95 and 161 Marina; IV, vi, 114 Lysimachus and Marina; IV, vi, 155 and 190–1 Marina; V, iii, 1–13 and 79 Pericles.

[14] For the theme of hope: II, Prologue, 5–8 and 37–8 Gower; II, i, 160–72 Pericles; V, i, 49 Lysimachus describing Marina; V, i, 196–8 Pericles; V, ii, 15–6 Gower; V, iii, 33–6 Pericles and Thaïsa; V, iii, 40–1 Pericles; and V, iii, 89–90 Gower.

For the theme of compassionate gods, usually expressed in trustful prayers: I, iv, 16–7 Cleon; IV, iii, 39 Cleon; V, i, 39 and 80 Lysimachus; V, i, 199–201 Pericles; the blessings asked by Pericles in V, i, 215 and 225; and his prayers of thanks in V, iii, 57–8 and 79–80.

[15] This paragraph is built largely from the following passages: III, iii, 38–9; V, i, 74; I, iii, 66–8; III, ii; V, i, 70–80; I, ii, 55–6; II, ii, 19–20; II, iii, 39–44.

[16] III, i, 1. As in the line quoted, Neptune usually appears by indirection, but he is specifically named in such passages as III, iii, 36 Cleon; V, Prologue, 17 Gower; and V, i, 17 Lysimachus.

[17] For quotations in this paragraph, as well as further references to Diana or Cynthia, or to her aspect as Lucina goddess of childbirth, see I, i, 8 Antiochus; II, v, 10–1 Simonides speaking of his daughter Thaïsa; III, i, 10–4 Pericles; III, ii, 105 Thaïsa; III, iii, 28 Pericles; III, iv, 10, 13 Thaïsa and Cerimon; IV, Prologue, 4 and 29 Gower referring to Thaïsa and to Marina; IV, ii, 161 and 162 Marina and the Bawd; IV, v, 7 Second Gentleman; V, i, 241–50 Diana herself; V, i, 251 Pericles; V, ii, 13 Gower; V, iii, 1–13 Pericles; V, iii, 17 Cerimon; and V, iii, 37 and 69 Pericles.

[18] For the theme of new life: III, Prologue, 9–11 Gower; III, i, 27–37 and 40–2 Pericles, speaking of Marina; III, ii, 82–6 Cerimon speaking of Thaïsa; and V, i, 197–9 and 209–10 Pericles of Marina.

[19] IV, iv, 21. For the dream motif, see III, ii, 105–6, as Thaïsa wakes from sleep; V, i, 163–4 and 235–50, as Pericles rouses from his stupor, and again as he sinks into slumber before the vision of Diana; and perhaps V, iii, 13, where Thaïsa swoons.

[20] II, v, 30. For references to music: II, iii, 98 and 107, the dances at Pentapolis after Pericles wins in the tilting lists; II, v, 25–31 Simonides and Pericles; III, ii, 88–91, as Cerimon restores Thaïsa; IV, Prologue, 7–8 and

25-7 Gower describing Marina's accomplishments; IV, v, 7-8 the singing Vestals; IV, vi, 194 Marina singing and dancing; V, i, 45-8 Lysimachus describing Marina; V, i, 80 the song that wakes Pericles; V, i, 228-34 the sudden mysterious music, unheard by others, that puts Pericles in a trance.

[21] For the beauty of the external world: I, i, 12 the daughter of Antiochus as the "false Florimel"; I, ii, 4 Pericles; II, v, 36 Pericles describing Thaïsa as the "true Florimel"; IV, i, 14-9 Marina strewing her mother's grave, the sea, with flowers; V, Prologue, 5-8 Marina's skill at needlework, so great "That even her art sisters the natural roses."

[22] For quotations used in this paragraph, see: V, i, 45; III, iii, 12-3; IV, Prologue, 28-9; IV, ii, 161; IV, Prologue, 31 and 10-1; V, i, 197. Hamlet's theme of "a dear father" lost, which Marina weeps for, is felt by Pericles in his own person: II, i, 129-40 and II, iii, 37-47.

[23] *Pericles* is the only one of the four romances, by the way, which involves its leading figure in the "romance" of courtship.

[24] II, iii, 15-7 and 69-70; and III, i, passim. This paragraph on Cloten is based principally on: I, i, 17; II, iii, 80; IV, ii, 132-3; III, iv, 135; II, i, 20-1 and 31-2; I, ii, 1-5; II, i, 17-8; and IV, ii, 113.

[25] To be more exact, Posthumus is willing to allow external evidence to confirm his own internal lack of trust. The bracelet, his "manacle of love" (I, i, 122), becomes the shackle of his own suspicions. His friend Philario will not accept such circumstantial proof, and says: "This is not strong enough to be believ'd Of one persuaded well of." But Posthumus savagely casts aside his own trust with the answer: "Never talk on 't. She hath been colted by him." (II, iv, 131-3) In the mind of Posthumus, Iachimo's description of the mole on Imogen's breast "doth confirm another stain." (II, iv, 139-40)

[26] See II, iii, 137 to end; and III, v, 125-51. For garments and apparel used as symbols for Shakespeare's Clothes Philosophy of semblance indistinguishable from truth, see also IV, i; IV, ii, 80-5; IV, ii, 308; V, i, 29-30; and V, iv, 134-5.

[27] For rejoicing proofs of "How hard it is to hide the sparks of nature!" see III, iii, 79-98; IV, ii, 24-9; IV, iv; and V, v, 381.

[28] For spirit counterpoised with fact and matter, see III, iv, 34-5 Pisanio describing Imogen as she reads Posthumus's letter; III, iv, 84-9 Imogen: that traitors harm themselves more than their victims; III, vi, 65-6 Belarius: that a rude cave does not make its inhabitants churls; III, vi, 82-7 Imogen on the stoic and ascetic "great men" who served themselves and

their own consciences; IV, i Cloten's calling Imogen an "imperceiverant thing" for loving Posthumus instead of himself, when "the lines of my body are as well drawn as his"; IV, ii, 76–9 Guiderius to Cloten; IV, ii, 308–32 Imogen over the body of "Posthumus"; IV, iv, 53–4 Belarius rejoicing over his rustic sons' instincts of "princes born"; and Imogen's knowing that even eyesight is sometimes blind (IV, ii, 301–2), or that her ears must not abuse her heart (I, vi, 130–1).

²⁹ Here is God's most plentifulest plenty, in a play that contains references to "most prais'd, most lov'd," "my dearest husband," "the loyal'st husband," "sweetest, fairest," "fairest," "basest," I, i, 47, 85, 96, 118, 123, 125; "more fair, virtuous, wise, chaste, constant, qualified and less attemptable than any the rarest of our ladies in France" "the most precious diamond that is," "more than the world enjoys," I, iv, 63–6, 81–2, 86; "most perfect goodness," "worthiest," "most worthiest," and "truest," in a single speech I, vi, 156–68; "above measure false!" II, iv, 113; "O the dearest of creatures," III, ii, 43; "O sweetest, fairest lily!" "a most rare boy," IV, ii, 201, 208; "O most delicate fiend!" V, v, 47; "the best of all Amongst the rar'st of good ones," V, v, 159–60; "Two of the sweet'st companions in the world," V, v, 349. Superlatives may be gathered in a formal tribute:

> "she hath all courtly parts more exquisite
> Than lady, ladies, woman. From every one
> The best she hath, and she, of all compounded,
> Outsells them all." III, v, 71–4.

But Shakespeare is at his most ingenious in the implied or developed superlatives. See I, i, 17–25 and 130–7; I, vi, 15–7 and 118–21; II, iii, 137–41; V, v, 351–2.

³⁰ To show how thematic images may be used to present an argument or a moral intuition, note how references to exile cluster in the first third of the play, how those to a life lived in harmony with nature cluster in the second third, and how the themes of humility, brotherhood, repentance, and forgiveness gravitate toward the last third.

Exile, banishment, and strangers: I, i, 8 and 166; I, iii, entirely devoted to the sweet and bitter sorrow of parting; I, vi, 59; II, i, 35–7 and 70; II, iii, 46; II, iv, 60–1 and 126; III, iii, 69 and 100; III, iv, 108–10; IV, iv, 26; V, v, 261–3 and 317–9. The last two references merely recall earlier banishments in order to change them.

Beautiful or beneficent nature: I, iii, 36–7 (where, in keeping with the tone, the tyrannous North nips the buds); I, vi, 32–6; II, ii, 38–9; II, iii, 22–30, the aubade; III, iii throughout; III, vi, 94; IV, ii, 61 and 218–29 Arviragus' flower-dirge; IV, ii, 258–81 Fidele's dirge; IV, ii, 390 and 398; IV, iv, 28–9.

Human beauty, in harmony with nature: I, vi, 16; II, ii, 11–23; II, iv, 102–3; III, vi, 43–5; IV, ii, 55 and 218–29, all Imogen or Imogen-Fidele; IV, ii, 309–11, 319, and 354–5 "Posthumus"; V, v, 394–6 Imogen again.

Humility: III, iii, 1–9 and 19–21; III, vi, 32–6 and 82–7; IV, ii, 35–6 and 367–8; IV, iii, 8–9 and 45–6; V, i, 16–7; V, iii, 43–5.

Brotherhood: III, vi, 9–14 and 75–6, 80–1; IV, ii, 2–5; V, iv, 211–2; V, v, 312–5, 373–8, 399, and 422–4.

Repentance: V, i, 7–17; V, iv, 7–29 and throughout; V, v, 63–8 Cym-beline, 141–6 Iachimo, 217–27 Posthumus, and 325 Belarius.

Forgiveness: III, vi, 14–5; V, v, 417–22.

[31] For the theme of liberty, see III, i, the liberty of Britain defended at court; III, iii, 42–4 and elsewhere, the chafings of the king's sons; III, v, 4–7, the Britons again; V, v, 305–6, Guiderius' spirit. See also death conceived as liberty in V, iv.

[32] For Fidele speaking as a heroine from Shakespeare's golden comedies, see III, iv, 156–68; III, vi, 1–27 and later; and IV, ii.

[33] For the birth of new life, see: I, v, 39–44; IV, ii, 58–60, 255–6, and 403; IV, iv, 34–54; V, iii, 3–4; V, iv, 102–3; V, v, 123 and 368–9.

[34] For the hopeful turn of fortune, see IV, ii, 402–3 and IV, iii, 45–6.

[35] For the mutation of truth into religious thankfulness, see: I, i, 53–4 and 65–7; I, iv, 68–9 and 156–7; I, v, 42–4 and 75–87; I, vi, 22–5, 129–32, and 145–6; II, i, 66–70; II, iii, 112–3; II, iv, 61–6 and 106–46; III, ii, 7; III, iv, 56–66 and 83–4; III, v, 108–14 and 162–8; IV, ii, 318 and 379–81; IV, iii, 41–2; V, i, 32–3; V, iv complete; V, v, 65–6, 105–7, 220–1, 268–9, 397–8, 466–7, and 475–8.

[36] See I, i, 109–11 and 165–9; III, ii, 27–9, 35–9, 52–4 and 72–5; IV, iv, 22–9; and V, v, 261–4.

[37] V, v, 435–76. It may not be too extreme to suggest that in a play which consciously considers the meaning of the names Leonatus and Fidele, and which advances the astounding etymology that woman is tender air because *mulier* may be termed *mollis aer*, Philarmonus is a Lover of Harmony. It hardly seems beyond Shakespeare to think that Imogen herself may be an Image, an image of birth or of human life, as Posthumus certainly suggests a birth after a death.

[38] As an experiment, I read over *The Two Noble Kinsmen,* marking scenes as Shakespeare's or not-Shakespeare's on the basis of the moral ideas expressed. The ascriptions coincided remarkably with the general opinions of critics reached on other evidence, principally on grounds of metrics.

The pure Shakespearean flavor can hardly be imitated. Shakespeare, for instance, must have been the original inventor of the jailer's daughter, for no other Jacobean could have written in her first scene—considering the ideas expressed as well as the flow of the prose—such speeches as: "Nay, most likely, for they are noble suff'rers. I marvel how they would have look'd had they been victors, that with such a constant nobility enforce a freedom out of bondage, making misery their mirth and affliction a toy to jest at." (II, i, 38–43) Or: "It is a holiday to look on them. Lord, the diff'rence of men!" (II, i, 66–7) On the other hand, the daughter's mad scenes (such as IV, i) are crude imitations of Ophelia, and could not possibly be Shakespeare's. As Andrew Aguecheek says of Sir Toby Belch: "He does it with a better grace, but I do it more natural."

In both the *Noble Kinsmen* and *Henry VIII*, poetic expression—the last of Shakespeare's powers to be abandoned—is beginning to fail him. Poetically, *Henry VIII* is a dull play and irrelevant to this book. If the type of evidence on which this book depends is considered, the best assumptions might be that Fletcher wrote *Henry VIII* in the main, with some help from Shakespeare in shaping a significant structure and in developing the characters of Queen Katherine and Ann Bullen; and that Shakespeare sketched in the main scenes of the *Noble Kinsmen*, allowing Fletcher to revise them toward his own thinner clarity, helping him more than a little with some of the excellent scenes of the second act, and letting the clever and eager younger dramatist develop on his own the scenes involving the jailer's daughter (which, except when first introduced, look like clumsy structural additions to an original completed edifice).

³⁹ For such imaginative integration, see the prayers to the three gods (V, i), where Mars is addressed as:

> O great corrector of enormous times, . . . that . . . curest the world
> O' th' plurisy of people! (62–6)

And Venus:

> O thou that from eleven to ninety reign'st
> In mortal bosoms, whose chase is this world,
> And we in herds thy game. (130–2)

And Diana, "sacred silver mistress":

> O sacred, shadowy, cold, and constant queen,
> Abandoner of revels, mute, contemplative,
> Sweet, solitary, white as chaste, and pure
> As wind-fann'd snow.

⁴⁰ A summary of the scenes and their proportioning suggests the moral outlook and argument:

Scene	Subject	No. of Lines	% of Play
I, i	Courteous entertainment in Sicily	50	1.5
I, ii	Jealousy of Leontes	465	15.5
II, i	Hermione accused	199	6.5
II, ii	Prison	66	2
II, iii	Perdita cast out	206	6.5
III, i	Messengers from Apollo	22	0.5
III, ii	Trial and "death" of Hermione; reading of Apollo's oracle	244	8
III, iii	Desolating bears and rescuing shepherds in Bohemia	143	4.5
IV, i	Father Time apologizes for a 15-year gap	32	1
IV, ii	Bohemia searches for his son	62	2
IV, iii	Autolycus	135	4
IV, iv	The sheepshearing feast	875	29
V, i	Repentance of Leontes	233	8
V, ii	Narrative of reunions	188	6
V, iii	Discovery and restoration	155	5

⁴¹ For the idea of jealousy as a disease or infection, see I, ii, 145, 207, 262, 297, 305, 306, 384–6, 398, 418, 423; II, i, 39–45; III, ii, 99; and V, i, 169.

⁴² See the counterchange between idealism and experience in IV, iv, 79–103 and again in IV, iv, 491–517 and 584–88. And between unjust suspicion and acknowledged weakness in I, ii, 235–64.

⁴³ For expressions of inner integrity, see I, ii, 240 regarding Camillo; II, iii, 83–4 Leontes; III, ii, 44–6 Hermione; III, ii, 166–73 Camillo; IV, iv, 31–5 and 42–6 Florizel; IV, iv, 99–103 Perdita; IV, iv, 367–71 and 393–4 Perdita; IV, iv, 474–5 and 497–509 Florizel; V, i, 230–1 Florizel; and V, ii, 175–6 Clown.

⁴⁴ For the idea that reality is mental, see I, ii, 138–46, 292–6, and 424–31 Leontes; II, i, 100–3 Leontes; II, i, 154–7 Antigonus; II, iii, 103–5 Paulina; III, ii, 82 and 110–5 Hermione; IV, iv, 381–9 Florizel; IV, iv, 393–4 Perdita; IV, iv, 397–8 and 487–8 Florizel; IV, iv, 587–8 Perdita; V, i, 67–8 Leontes; V, i, 215–8 Florizel; V, iii, 14–8 Paulina; V, iii, 70–3 Leontes.

In some of the above passages we are close to the notion that thought shapes or creates external happenings. Is it worth noting, as reinforcements of the main action of Leontes' immediate punishment for his unjust thoughts, that Antigonus is pursued and eaten up by the well-known bear within 15 lines of voicing his belief that Perdita is indeed a bastard daughter? And that Polixenes, whose rage against his son none dares to cross—"You know your father's temper" (IV, iv, 478)—loses his son as an immediate result of such rage?

⁴⁵ For grace and "becomingness": I, ii, 80, 99, 105, 282; II, i, 121–2; II, ii, 21; II, iii, 29; III, i, 22; III, ii, 48, 65–6, 199; III iii, 21–2; IV, i, 24–5; IV, ii, 31; IV, iv, 5, 8, 76, 806; V, i, 22, 134, 171; V, ii, 119–20; V, iii, 7, 27, and 122.

For innocence, see particularly: I, ii, 69; IV, iv, 151–3 and 453–7.

For resignation: III, ii, 223–4; IV, iii, 17–8 and 30–1; IV, iv, 732–3; V, i, 34–49; V, iii, 76–7.

For repentance: I, ii, 239; III, ii, 154–73 and 237–44; IV, ii, 7 and 25–6; IV, iv, 558–66; V, i throughout; V, ii, 91–3; and V, iii, 147–9.

For joy blended with sorrow, as similarly expressed in both *Pericles* and *Cymbeline,* see V, ii, 47–51 and 79–80.

⁴⁶ Since the ideas are important and recurring, the tesselation of quotations in this and the three succeeding paragraphs might here be identified in order: V, iii, 121–3; I, i, 43; III, iii, 117–8; V, i, 151–2; V, ii, 119–20; V, iii, 102–3; I, ii, 70; I, ii, 69; IV, iv, 491–2; IV, iv, 43–5; IV, iv, 393–4; III, ii, 82; and IV, iv, 487–8.

III, ii, 95, 93 and 123; II iii, 184–91; and III, i.

V, ii, 105–6; V, ii, 30–1 and 66; V, iii, 117; II, i, 25, 28 and 30.

V, iii, 14–7; V, iii, 25–6; V, i, 67–8; and I, ii, 105.

⁴⁷ The passages on which this and the succeeding two paragraphs are principally based are: V, ii, 15–6; IV, iv, 270 and 195–200; II, iii, 105; IV, iv, 97, 89–90 and 79–103; (*Cymbeline,* I, vi, 6–7); III, ii, 93; II, iii, 7–9 and 204–5; I, ii, 138–40; III, i, 20–1; V, iii, 132–46; and V, iii, 94–5.

⁴⁸ Note how all three levels play with the ideas of liberty and bondage, of insurrection even to the extent of physical violence, of treacherous or disobedient action while authority seems sleeping, of seeking a kingship, of passion overcoming the "nobler reason," whether the passion is for power, love, or drink. The attitudes of different characters toward the same problems constitute, taken together, a complex moral judgment.

⁴⁹ For the idea of memory and remembrance, see I, ii, 38, 44, 46, 101, and 247 Prospero, Miranda and Ariel; II, i, 232–3 Gonzalo; III, ii, 156 Stephano; III, iii, 68, 73 Ariel to Alonso and his followers; V, i, 138 Alonso; 199–200 Prospero; 255 Prospero to Alonso.

⁵⁰ For some of the more direct or salient thoughts on power and providence, see: I, i, 23–6; I, ii, 159, 178–9, 372–4, 438–40, 465–6; II, i, 147–68, 251–4; III, iii, 53–82, 90; IV, i, 37–8; V, i, 33–57 and 188–9.

[51] For images of nature that convey strong images of human emotion, see: I, ii, 196–206 desperate amazement; I, ii, 321–43 primitive religion; I, ii, 462–4 "natural piety"; II, ii, 1–14 hate and fear; II, ii, 164–76 rude thanksgiving; III, ii, 144–52 "the glory and the dream"; III, iii, 43–9 wonder at man's diversity; III, iii, 95–102 fear, guilt, and despair; IV, i, 60–138 bounteous joy and blessing; IV, i, 175–85 curiosity and contempt; V, i, 16–7 pity; V, i, 33–56 awe; V, i, 65–8 and 79–82 hope.

[52] II, ii, 168; I, ii, 426; IV, i, 123; I, ii, 432; and V, i, 181. For further elaboration in this play of the strange and the wonderful, see: I, ii, 306, 426, 432; II, i, 6, 58–60, 199; III, iii, 40, 87; IV, i, 7, 124, stage directions after 138, 143, 234; V, i, 104, 117, 154, 160, 170, 177, 181, 228, 232, 242, and 290. Note how these suggestions increase toward the close, and how they are associated with the images of sleep and music, which would each require a list of references at least as long.

[53] II, i, 128; II, ii, 122; III, i, 87: a stage direction should be inserted to cover the last instance.

[54] For liberty or freedom and its opposite of bondage, see: I, ii, 245, 278, (362–4), 485–93, 498; II, ii, 184–92; III, i, 88–9; III, ii, 40–2, 48, 130–2; IV, i, 266; V, i, 7–9, 96, 166, 235, 241, 252, 317–8; Epilogue 4, 9, and 15–20.
For grace, see: (I, ii, 59–61); (II, i, 1–9, 113, 159–60); (III, i, 2–4); III, i, 75; III, ii, 116; III, iii, 84; stage directions after IV, i, 138; IV, i, 229; V, i, 70, 142, (206–8), 219, 253, and 295.

[55] III, iii, 77–82 and V, i, 25–32. For other direct expressions of patience, penitence and forgiveness, see: I, ii, 153–8; II, i, 1–9; V, i, 78–9, 109–11, 118–9, 130–2, 197–200, 293; and Epilogue, 7, 19. Stephano and Trinculo, when frightened, are not beyond prayers (III, ii, 139–41); and even the urchin-pinched Caliban decides for a minute that "grace" is the best policy (V, i, 294–5).

[56] The recurring image of the pulsing brain is so sharp and particularized, here and in other plays, that it is a wonder it has not caught the attention of some physician or dealer in psychosomatic symptoms. In *The Tempest* we hear of "my beating mind" (IV, i, 163); of brains "boil'd within thy skull" (V, i, 59–60); of the pulse beating twice (V, i, 103); of the beating pulse closely associated with madness and "the affliction of my mind" (V, i, 113–6); of infesting "your mind with beating on the strangeness of this business" (V, i, 246–7). Even Miranda, quite out of character, is given the line: "For still 'tis beating in my mind." (I, ii, 176)

[57] For human beauty and passion cast in physical images, see I, ii, 222–4 Ariel describing Ferdinand; I, ii, 408–11 Miranda opening her eyes (as

fringed as Cleopatra's or Fidele's or Thaïsa's) and describing her first sight of Ferdinand; I, ii, 421–7 and 457–9 the counterchange of wonder between Ferdinand and Miranda; II, i, 113–22 Ferdinand swimming; III, i, 33–7 the counterchange again; III, iii, 29–34 and 36–9 Gonzalo and Alonso describing the island shapes; V, i, 7–19 Ariel describing the courtiers; V, i, 181–4 Miranda's famed first view of the great world. See also the stage directions throughout.

For the importance of music, see: I, ii, 375; II, i, 184 and 297; II, ii, 44 and 184; III, ii, 130; III, iii, 18 and 82; IV, i, 59 and 106; and V, i, 57 and 88.

For sleep and slumber, usually tied to suggestions of the strange and wonderful, see: I, ii, 185, 232, 305 [after this last injunction to awake, stage directions should indicate that Miranda soon falls asleep again and wakes a second time at line 408], and 486; II, i, 190–200, 209–18, 238, 267, and 300–5; III, ii, 68, 96, 122 and 147–52; V, i, 98, 230 and 239. Aside from Ariel and Prospero, every one in the play falls into some charm or sleep—even the mariners.

Postscript

THE SUBJECT of this book needs no apology today. In the big world, political, economic, and social pressures are so strong that there seems little time for the main question: how do the best individuals think human life should be led? Literature, of course, gives the most comprehensive answers to such a question. In the smaller world of art, historical scholarship has proved so powerfully successful that we tend to assume the purpose of literature is to afford us means to reconstruct the past. In reaction, literary criticism has concentrated with equal brilliance on the pure philosophical question of what quality or qualities make writing into literature. Yet great literature has always been, in the use men have made of it, more than a branch of history or aesthetics. If it is not so today, then "pushpin is as good as poetry." Merely toward a redressing of the balance, it seems fair to ask in this book: How did Shakespeare think human life should be led? The question is worth asking.

Though I do not believe the subject needs apology, the manner of treatment needs quite a bit.

Shakespeare's moral ideas have been the primary concern. The preceding chapters constitute an attempt to present these moral ideas. This postscript, therefore, is not a part of the central theses or of the description of Shakespeare's spiritual development. It is an addition designed solely for those who wish to know the bases and principles upon which these chapters have been written, before they accept or reject the conclusions of the book itself.

As an independent essay, it might be of use if it could counteract or stem, even in small degree, the fashionable, careless, and false drift that we cannot know what Shakespeare himself thought. Popular instinct is here much sounder than professional critical opinions: successive generations would scarcely have read with delight and (so it must have felt to them) understanding a poet who outtopped their knowledge. And if the beliefs in which they have found such pleasure are not reflections of Shakespeare's own beliefs and visions, then we are dealing with a moral monster, a unique deep-sea fish who denies himself at every turn and creates not from his own experience but from unassimilated, uninterpreted, accidental scraps. The widely accepted notion of an impassive Shakespeare is one of the most cynical heresies that has ever gained literary currency.

The first assumption of this book is that *all great works of art reflect the convictions of their creators*. It is based on the antecedent assumptions that men are naturally lazy, that creation is difficult and even painful, and that therefore a powerful spark is necessary in order to stir indolent men to expression. The beauty, difficulty, and depth of great art require for its creation a powerful drive, and this can come only from the artist's inner conviction that he has something important to present. Perhaps that is the chief difference between great art and commercial art. Popular demand, current styles, the economic necessity of earning a living, are not the kind of spurs that result in anything beyond competent products. When the average is transcended, the increased reach must come from something in the artist himself.

Let us admit immediately that the artist is influenced by the age in which he lives—Shakespeare perhaps more than most. Shakespeare, for instance, uses words in their Elizabethan meanings, so that some philological study, or for the average reader at least a glossary, is necessary to know just what he is saying. Yet even without a glossary Shakespeare's language is still more readily apprehensible than is that of many contemporary poets. Again, historical studies will enable the scholar to approximate what Shakespeare meant to the Elizabethans, and this esoteric knowledge may furnish him with a rare and genuine pleasure. But we are not actually Elizabethans, even by imaginative discipline; and to most of us the fuller, more normal, and more profitable excitement comes from moving Shakespeare into our own times and thoughts rather than from attempting to translate ourselves back to the year 1600. Shakespeare survives the journey across three and a half centuries more easily than we do.

Apart from studies in linguistics and historical backgrounds (which this present study has indirectly drawn upon on almost every page), there is also the study of Shakespeare's cultural indebtedness. For the ordinary reader the most barren and dangerous practice of teachers and scholars is the pointing out of analogues, influences, sources, and Elizabethan stage conventions, devices, and stock characters or situations. This tends to make the unwary reader believe that Shakespeare is a product of his environment and predecessors. It explains everything except Shakespeare. Pushed to its extremes, as it often is, this method blithely assumes that if you look hard and far enough, whatever you find in a great artist must exist in print or manuscript somewhere before him. Great art is traced to second-rate sources, and even they probably have other sources back of them. For if Atlas stands on the turtle, what does the turtle stand on? The whole theory of borrowings and popular fashions and debts eventually drops into a void.

A variant belief among the scholars engaged in explaining Shakespeare away is the statement that Shakespeare was not a profound thinker, if he was a thinker at all. He merely assimilated or felicitously re-expressed well-worn truths. Against this, a second assumption of this book is that *style and content are basically inseparable* (though of course for purposes of temporary critical convenience, they may be considered singly). If, before a great writer phrases some idea, it was never so well expressed, then also it was never so well thought, no matter how often it was thought. Any teacher of composition knows that you cannot teach a person to write well if he cannot think straight. A few mechanical rules can be planted; but a style comes from within the writer himself; the power and integrity of his thought mould his language, excluding the vague, bewildering, or unnecessary word, reinforcing or reiterating, balancing, suggesting, selecting, proportioning, unifying. Even this description is a falsification in that it suggests the thought precedes the expression and controls it. A great thinker may imaginably and occasionally override the handicap of inferior powers of expression. But much closer to usual experience is the quip: "How can I know what I think until I hear what I say?"

A great stylist, it therefore follows from this second assumption, is a great thinker. This remains a safe generalization if we avoid two pitfalls. First, the purple passage, the deliberate essay style, and in poetry the texture and rhythm and purely technical devices, must be scrutinized carefully, for often they are not good styles, but rather, incongruously weighty words or fine phrases decking trivial thoughts that cannot support such glitter and pomp. Second, the greatness cannot be determined by the subject matter, which is not at all the same thing, of course, as the content. An original and profound thought may as easily spring from some worn region such as death or love or humble toil, as from some little trodden path such as the quincunx or the Bible in Spain.

"After life's fitful fever he sleeps well."

We cannot say that this line was written by an undistinguished thinker simply because it happens to embrace the two truisms that occur at some time to everyone, that life is hard, and that death in a sense is a restful sleep. The miracle of literary creation is that anyone could have thought-and-written that line as it stands.

A third assumption of this book, closely connected with one's feeling for the line quoted above, is that *thought transcends rational statement and cannot be limited to logic*. Reason and emotion do not oppose, but rather reinforce each other, so that ordinarily the rise or fall of one will influence the other (like wage scales and the cost-of-living graphed on a chart). In the realm of mental endowments also, the Biblical injustice applies: "To him that hath shall be given." Among the littler people we can distinguish the purely intellectual or the intensely emotional; in the greater artists and personalities, such distinctions tend to be meaningless or unnecessary. And Shakespeare's thought, though it could at times be searchingly logical, is the imaginative or poetic thought that unites heart, brain, and body, bringing to a focus all man's consciousness.

So intimately allied to the argument of the last paragraph that it needs no separate assumption is the broad meaning attached to the key phrase "moral ideas." An "idea" is here understood to be a successfully clear, organized, and fairly complete communication of anything in any medium—in Shakespeare's case a verbal or a dramatically presentational communication. It need not be schematized or systematized—in fact, one of Shakespeare's "ideas" is that to make a system is to falsify experience—and sometimes its implicit organized wholeness must be pieced together from various, often widely separated, fragments. As for "moral," it is assumed that anything that tends to make the leading of a good life easier or clearer is moral. As such, "moral" is almost opposed to "didactic," for so rebellious are we by nature, so jealous of our freedom of action and thought, that to be told directly that we should do such-and-such a thing, no matter how lofty the motive or insight of the exhorter, is usually to make such action more difficult and unpleasant, or if we accede like sheep, to deprive it of that element of free choice which is at the basis of moral action. This conception of "moral ideas" widens the field in which they operate to include almost all of human consciousness. It considers man's adjustment to himself and to the world to be the central broad question of morals, and would accept Warner Fite's definition of the ethical life as the "examined life." But in discussing moral ideas it does not attempt to construct for Shakespeare a complete integrated moral system or philosophy. Shakespeare had no such system; he had something less abstract—

a number of sharp and deeply felt insights that controlled and vitalized his art.

And how are we to arrive at those insights? There are three initial difficulties: Shakespeare's usual dramatic form, the complexity of his thought, and the changing nature of that thought over a career of twenty years. Let us consider these in order.

Those who would make Shakespeare either an automaton or a sphinx repeat triumphantly that in pure dramatic form an artist cannot express his own, lyrical, personal ideas without violating the form. Shakespeare as the supreme dramatic artist, they hold, kept his plays uncontaminated by his private beliefs and allowed each character to speak for himself. (In passing it might be noted that this assumed Shakespearean technique would in itself indicate a moral idea: that Shakespeare saw, more clearly than most dramatists or citizens, that each individual is entitled to his own opinions.) Yet instinctively we realize that the dramatist *does* express himself, and it seems as absurd to think of Aeschylus as the possible author of *The Way of the World* as to think of Congreve having written *Prometheus Bound*. If historical differences make this illustration extreme, then let us say that Ben Jonson could never be mistaken for the author of *Twelfth Night*, for there is no Ben Jonson in it; nor could Shakespeare have written *Cataline*.

How can, or how does, the artist express his own convictions in the form of drama, where everybody except the author is allowed to speak directly? First of all he chooses a subject. I am writing this book, for example, about Shakespeare's moral ideas instead of Shelley's—which are much more obvious—because I have the greatest admiration for Shakespeare's and cannot abide most of Shelley's. It would be legitimate to make deductions concerning my own moral convictions from this choice of subject. Shakespeare chose his subjects because they interested him. Sometimes this interest was so personal, as in *Timon of Athens*, that he could not work it out successfully in the form of a play. Sometimes the interest was so close to him and so unresolved or lately resolved in his own mind that he could not construct a convincing dramatic picture, as in *All's Well*, the ending of *Measure for Measure*, and perhaps also *Julius Caesar*. And sometimes, though he was the most nonchalant of all adapters, he could find nothing to his purpose and had to invent his own plot as a vehicle for his thoughts, as in *Love's Labour's Lost* and *The Tempest*. Yet he did the choosing. Artistic greatness, at least, cannot be thrust upon a man. When someone else did the choosing for him, as in the earliest histories or *The Merry Wives of Windsor*, the result is journeyman's work, perfunctory in the main drive, and lighted up only in incidental details.

The choice of a fit subject—fit for his capabilities and interests—shows the artist's mind, as the choice of clothes shows a woman's taste and temperament. Consider the care and time Milton lavished on choosing a subject for his epic! More important, however, is the shaping of the subject after it has been chosen. The protagonist in the fable of the Fox and the Grapes is a rather reprehensible and ridiculous little rationalizer cynically muttering "Sour grapes!" But with a different fabulist, the same story might leave us with a fox wholly admirable and wise, nobly renouncing the unattainable, making the best of his hard vulpine lot, and murmuring in sad abnegation, shall we say, "Ripeness is all." Here is where Shakespeare's sources are of exciting importance. That Shakespeare used other men's stories is no more than a trivial literary truism, though it must be remarked that he knew the best that had been thought and said up to his time. But that he *changed* those stories is of overwhelming interest to anyone seeking to know what he thought and felt. Here is a key to the artist's convictions. Two striking examples are *Troilus and Cressida* and *Antony and Cleopatra*. The publication of Chapman's Homer—the greatest ancient poet translated by a respected modern—was no slight Elizabethan literary event. Yet Shakespeare's Troy is not Homer's city, nor Chapman's, nor the average Elizabethan's. It is Shakespeare's, and—to the discomfiture of theorists on conventions and currents-of-influence—it is recognizably his. Again, much of the criticism of Shakespeare's *Antony and Cleopatra* is vitiated because the critics depend on traditional moral lessons in statecraft (Antony is a bad statesman) and in lust (Antony was a twice married man, Cleopatra had had other affairs, both were along in years: their attachment was an illegal, evil, lustful, destructive infatuation). But Shakespeare sees it differently, sees it consistently, powerfully, and poetically. His reinterpretation of old materials affords us insight into some of his most profound valuations of worldly power, love, reason, and loyalty. Even minor changes in plots are revealing, not only of Shakespeare's art, but of his character and beliefs. A further assumption of this study, therefore, is that *Shakespeare's modification of his sources is of importance in understanding what he is thinking.*

Now let us consider for a moment the form of the drama itself. Its material, says Aristotle, is men in action. This is also the material of morals. The first three of its six component elements, still according to Aristotle, and philosophically the most important, are plot, character (or *ethos*), and what may be called "reasoning," or the intellectual statement of a position or a belief. Most Shakespearean agnostics content themselves with considering this third element—as if a play were composed of independent opinions expressed by opposed characters, with the dramatist showing his peculiar professional powers by remaining aloof. But Aristotle seems to give precedence over *dianoia* or reasoning to the second of his elements, *ethos* or character. Surely it is an inhumane, almost fantastic, conception of the drama to suppose that the dramatist does not take sides in the portrayal of character. Is a play to be no more than a Madame Tussaud's waxworks of unrelated figures speaking their little pieces? Does the dramatist lead his reader-spectator through a menagerie saying in simple description, "This is a giraffe, a lion, a zebra"? Let us hope rather that he composes a great picture made up of individual character studies, comparable, say, to Raphael's *School of Athens* or Rembrandt's *Night Watch*. Moral ideas will shine in the characters themselves as revealed in their talk, action, and impact upon others. And not even the apotheosized Shakespeare can be so inhuman or superhuman as to leave his likings out of these portraits. It is not so simple as to say that he approves of virtue and is against sin. There is more individuality in this elusive playmaker. Why are the cards stacked so cruelly against well-meaning Polonius and the inoffensively compliant Osric? Why are the citizens in his crowds such dolts and weathercocks? Why the sympathetic weighting of the character of the Duke in *Measure for Measure*, who to the average reader seems weak, vacillating, and a refugee from responsibility? Do the unusual presentations of usual virtues and vices in almost all of his plays tell us nothing of Shakespeare's own beliefs?

In this search for moral judgment in the drama, we must accept Aristotle's discriminating discovery that the most important element is the plot. The "Et puis alors" chronicler of unrelated incidents is no plot-maker. E. M. Forster has said very neatly and simply that "The king died and then the queen died" does not constitute a plot, but that "The queen died *because* the king died" is a plot. And since the second reading is human action interpreted, it inevitably contains moral ideas—of the power of passion, of the inevitability of tragedy, of the weakness of womankind, of love as stronger than the separation of death, of whatever refinements in judgment might result from extended treatment. And the plot is the most important element because it takes the other elements—the moral natures of the characters, their reasonings, convictions, self-portrayals, and relationships, the music, the motion, and the poetry of the play—and organizes them into unity. The plot locates its self-moving and self-justifying characters within a social organism, and leads them to a foreseen end. In this sense a play is less like a cross-section sliced through a debating society than like a courtroom in which the dramatist presides as judge. If the characters get away with murder, then the judging dramatist approves of murder. He controls the destinies of his figures, and metes out to them their deserts as—this is a further assumption—he considers fit. Critics have found relatively few of Shakespeare's plays that seem to shirk this moral responsibility and disregard or skimp these final judgments. It remains necessary to say, here as always, that rarely will Shakespeare's manner be that of the judge (as it is, say, at the end of

Romeo and Juliet). The moral judgments, although they are present at the end and indeed throughout the plays, will not be issued in the form of fiats and decrees. In the happiness, torment, doubt, increased knowledge, and self-realization of the characters, in the appraisals of what they do and what they are by other characters whose worth or lack of worth is made obvious, and in the final results of their actions and thoughts, Shakespeare's moral ideas shine out for all to see.

Shakespeare is evident in the smaller parts as well as in the whole. If the form of drama requires that the *dramatis personae* speak in character, what are we to deduce when they do not? Either that the dramatist is nodding (though we still have not explained why he should nod), or that what he has to say seems more important than coherence in the characters who say it. His convictions, in other words, overrule his art. That explains why some works written in the outward form of verse-drama are actually lyric expressions of personality. There are no "characters" in *Prometheus Unbound*—only Shelley's dreams and nightmares. And everyone in *Death's Jest Book* speaks and thinks pure Beddoes. Shakespeare is not beyond such undramatic utterance. It is an assumption of this book that when characters do not speak like their consistent selves, what they say should be scrutinized to determine whether these undramatic passages represent a lapse of the poetic imagination, or, as is usually the case in the mature Shakespeare, a focussing of that imagination upon an idea that for the moment interests the writer even more intensely than the play *qua* play. The notes to this book, and particularly for the last chapter, should show how Shakespeare frequently uses many differing characters to develop a single thought; some of his plays, in fact, seem constructed to handle themes and ideas more successfully than to dispose of characters and actions. For such a practised dramatic artist as Shakespeare, only some deep conviction or recurring personal speculation could fascinate him into abandoning his instinctive and acquired art. One example is Hamlet's enumeration of the whips and scorns of time: it has become a platitude to say that Hamlet could have known little about them, but that Shakespeare had experienced them all in his own person. Or again, Caliban in character knows best how to curse; when he breaks out into some of the most glowing poetry in *The Tempest*, immortalizing the island's "sounds and sweet airs that give delight and hurt not," we must either enlarge our conception of Caliban (a possibility), or accept the passage as Shakespeare's own vision.

Closely connected with the speeches out of character are the long set-pieces that contribute little to the action or theme of the play. There are not so many of these as one might suppose—Mercutio's Queen Mab speech is one, perhaps Jaques' seven ages of man is another—but when they occur, the assumption again is that some particular side-interest has made Shakespeare forget his play. And those side-interests have proved of value to our search. Usually, however, even the long formal disquisitions, such as Berowne's on woman's love, or Ulysses' on degree and on honor, are closely related to their plays and must be considered in connection with the principal drift and organization of those plays.

Shakespeare may also be known through his repetitions. If a man repeatedly calls red green, we may be safe in assuming that he is color blind. And when characters of the most diverse sort—Romeo, Claudio in *Measure for Measure*, Lear, Antony, Cleopatra—associate death with marriage, we are forced to the conclusion that they are expressing a particular belief of their creator. J. Wilson Knight and his followers have shown how repeated dominant ideas may organize Shakespeare's plays. The single expression of an idea may be accidental or it may be dramatically appropriate; but the reiteration of the same idea in many plays and in many mouths, it is here assumed, has passed beyond coincidence to conviction.

More difficult to treat logically, but perhaps even more revealing, is Shakespeare's use of images. As Caroline Spurgeon has demonstrated, images reveal Shakespeare's ideas and predilections when they are least deliberate and direct. The argument here is that an image is used to make some statement clearer. Naturally the artist will select images only from matter which seems clear to him. As Marlowe turned to books and Jonson to textures and the feel of things, Shakespeare drew his images from the life of the body, from the daily routine of the hearth and the family, from the great country world of trees and seasons. If this is to know nothing of Shakespeare's values, then we might as well lapse into agnosticism and hold that knowledge of our neighbor is impossible.

Finally, not all types of drama are so purely "dramatic" that they allow room only for characters speaking in their own right, each figure appearing as *une force qui va* whom the dramatist watches in helpless amazement. The Greek tragic drama, for instance, was so religious and social in spirit that it may be considered as roughly presenting, morally speaking, the communal creeds and convictions of the Athenians. The formal device for such didactic (rather than dramatic) utterance was the chorus. Shakespeare uses the chorus sparingly. The similar formal device of the prologue or the epilogue he uses for moral enlightenment only on rare occasion, as in the prologue to *Romeo and Juliet*. He does not even use it often for the statement of artistic principles, as Marlowe and Jonson employed it. His characteristic prologue or epilogue serves as a kind of accompanying note to the audience, a smiling little apology or wish that the play may prove acceptable. Yet he does employ the principle of the chorus in almost every one of his plays—by creating a touchstone figure, some character of average sensibility and obvious common sense, usually somewhat aloof from the main action and sympathetically attached to the protagonist. And this choric figure—Juliet's Friar, York in *Richard II*, Touchstone, Lear's Fool, Horatio, Emilia, Enobarbus, Menenius—who appears so regularly that he would seem to be a conscious device in Shakespeare's play-making, Shakespeare exploits in a way that satisfies at once his sense of dramatic propriety and his need for personal moral comment on the scenes he imagines. The function of these choric figures goes far beyond that of the confidant in Greek or French tragedy, though it includes that aspect as well. While remaining their own dramatic selves, these figures pass moral judgments, for Shakespeare and the audience, on events and characters. They are sufficiently normal and disinterested and uninvolved in the action so that their opinions may be trusted; yet in spite of the fact that they are not notably warped by selfishness or personal passion, their sympathy toward the heroes and heroines, their awareness of the antagonists, make them into catalysts precipitating the judgments of the plays. These figures constitute one of Shakespeare's most brilliant and successful devices for moral catharsis. The reader of this book may already have noticed how, paralleling the development of Shakespeare's dramatic art to its maturity, the discussion of "moral ideas" is presented increasingly in terms of characters, images, musical organization, and details of structure.

To summarize, then, these are the roads by which Shakespeare's moral ideas may be methodically and reasonably approached: *his choice of subject, his shaping of sources, the judgments implicit or stated in the outcome of his plots, his ventriloquism when characters speak out of key, his undramatic set speeches, his repetitive ideas, his recurrent images, and his choric or touchstone figures.*

The validity of these approaches may be supported by logic. "Yes, but there *is* more." Although this book in its exploration of ideas has principally employed the methods so far described, consideration must be qualitative as well as quantitative. To use Smart's excellent phrase, in Shakespeare there are not only "recurrences" but also "fervors." When in the plays an idea is expressed fervently, at such white heat as to startle and exalt the reader-spectator, it is at any rate conceivable that Shakespeare may be doing more than magnificently implementing a dramatic puppet. He may be expressing his deepest conviction. The young, somewhat priggish, experimentalizing Edgar is no one to know in his own person that "Ripeness is all." And frequently, inevitably, some insight, some torrent of emotion stands out so sharply and clearly that the reader instinctively feels the artist himself is underlining the thought with an implicit

> If this be error, and upon me proved,
> I never writ.

Shakespeare in such passages transcends the rules of the drama. Admittedly, this is controversial and dangerous ground. Carelessly handled, it may lead to the old game of proving anything by quoting Scripture. But on the other side, let it be remembered that Shakespeare does not give these fervors to his evil characters, nor to the evil natures in his mixed characters except when he is convinced of the possible evil in all of us. We judge our acquaintances and friends, not by their inconsistencies and half-hearted utterances, but by their fervors. This is subjective judgment, granted. But it is also a subjective judgment to believe that all subjective judgments should be disregarded. It is safer here to be discriminating rather than doctrinaire.

The second great barrier in the quest for Shakespeare's thought is its extraordinary complexity. We so easily assume that thought is not thought unless it may be expressed simply and powerfully. "Whatever is, is right." Now *there* is a moral idea which we can examine, because it is succinct and direct, with no beating about the bush! But Shakespeare is always beating about the bush, to discover the choir of birds that it may contain, which are worth far more in their freedom and naturalness than any confined bird in the hand. He has the supreme imaginative power not to mar the profound moral meanings of *Othello* or *Macbeth* by reducing them to didactic tags. "Beauty is truth, truth beauty" is what everyone quotes, because it is a handy pocket-piece, and because few of us have the power to hold in a single instantaneous apprehension the imaginative thought of the whole "Ode on a Grecian Urn" which the concluding lines almost betray by translating it into another mode of thinking.

Yet poetic thought remains thought, even though it cannot be completely or adequately expressed in concepts and propositions. Poetic thought contains such concepts and implies others (one of the implied ideas being that intuitive or imaginative or poetic expression gives a truer, more complete, or more satisfactory transcript of reality than logical expression). Poetic thought is by nature connotative or suggestive. It has been my purpose to explore Shakespeare's moral ideas, to particularize some of the connotations, to develop the suggestions more formally, more directly, and more logically than a dramatist would or should. Even here, however, they cannot be outlined simply and without qualifications, for not only is Shakespeare's expression complex, but often the substance of the thought itself. The previous chapters have tried to show that, to take two extremes among his characters, Shakespeare says neither that "Iago is a bad man, is motiveless malignity," nor "Cordelia is a good woman," because he does not believe such radical simplicities. He refuses to create devils and angels in his plays, because he is working with mixed human beings. All his moral judgments are qualified, relative, complex; Shakespeare in his moral thinking is neither a pure idealist nor a pure worldling. Though he can create characters who are guided by abstract theories, he himself shuns abstract thought. His only measures are men and the world.

Between Shakespeare and Bacon as epistemologists, there could have been no controversy, for each in his own field was discovering new possibilities in empiricism. And as Bacon rejected the old natural philosophy as inadequate to describe or explain the marvellous complexities of the visible universe, so Shakespeare wrote his *Everyman* with a difference, labelling none of his characters "Good Angel" or "Bad Angel," because in the fulness of their development unexpected complexities, incongruities, and inconsistencies might discover themselves. He did not hold a set of preconceptions up to nature: he held a mirror. And since nature is infinitely complex, Shakespeare's reflections (though words necessarily simplify nature) tend toward complexity.

It is amazing that so many men could have mistaken this breadth of understanding, this receptivity of mind, for lack of moral conviction. I. A. Richards has well pointed out that irony depends upon the simultaneous realization of at least two opposed attitudes, and that tragedy possesses this irony. It is not that Shakespeare had no moral beliefs, but that he embraced so many. His ironical ambiguous attitude, which gives the illusion of suspended judgment, may have misled critics into supposing that Shakespeare's own beliefs cannot be found in his work. On the contrary, the ironical tendency of his thought shows that he is more deeply involved, and that he has been able to comprehend and absorb conflicting possibilities. And in the end, his judgments are not suspended but complex. His plays reach conclusions, and so do his judgments.

No lack of moral ideas leads an artist to write that "Naught so vile that on the earth doth live But to the earth some special good doth give," though the proposition may annoy the moralists who want their black to stay a super-ebony. Two of the greatest discoverers in Shakespeare, Coleridge and Keats, found this out long ago. Coleridge writes on the normal health of Shakespeare as a moral thinker, although even Coleridge slips into odd judgments (nominating Isabella as Shakespeare's finest heroine, excluding the drunken porter scene from *Macbeth*) because Shakespeare's moral vision is more comprehensive than Coleridge's own. And Keats, perhaps the most naturally attuned to Shakespeare of all his readers, has given us the light that most illuminates Shakespeare's manner of thought when he speaks of Shakespeare's "Negative Capability," that is, the power to live easily in the midst of uncertainties and doubts. Shakespeare founded his stability upon the accidents of the world, the inconsistencies in human nature, the nobility and treachery of man, and the terrifying flux of time.

That Shakespeare's ideas changed and developed is the last, and relatively minor, reason why some people have denied that he had any. One might on the same grounds deny moral ideas to Plato or Augustine or Rembrandt or Beethoven. Yet the strength and consistency of Shakespeare's thought at any one period is so notable that if we did not have external evidence and the technical metrical tests for dating the plays, they could be grouped, and the groups set in chronological order without serious deviation from the established and accepted series, on the basis of the substance and expression of the thought. Take the one instance of *All's Well That Ends Well*, which is uneven in style, may have been written at different periods, and wanders somewhat disconcertingly up and down the chronological canons of the scholars. A close student of Shakespeare's thinking is compelled to assign its great poetic passages to the period which included the writing of *Hamlet, Measure for Measure,* and *Troilus and Cressida.* Shakespeare's most notable trait as a thinker was his seemingly infinite capacity to assimilate human experience. Yet even Shakespeare could not assimilate everything at once. And his progress, his spiritual biography as an artist, is marked into stages: the tentative trials, the certain apprehension of man's nobility, the bitter doubts arising from new discoveries of man's flaws, the masterful portrayal of the best and worst in man simultaneously existing, a short and even more radical despair, and a final vision of man's possible redemption through grace and his own unlimited imaginings. This artist's road leads through three great periods of synthesis—the comedies and histories, the tragedies, and *Antony and Cleopatra* and the dramatic romances, separated from each other by periods of uncertainty and adjustment. Since each synthesis accepts what has been discovered before and adds new elements, the order is as irreversible as time itself. And therefore, although there is much in Shakespeare's thought that is unchanging and characteristic throughout his career, and although in each period of his life we find consistency and coherence, it is also necessary to remember that his ideas at differing stages of that career may be radically at war with each other.

We must still consider briefly the view that denies morality not only to Shakespeare but to art in general. This current fashion rises in part from the philosophical independence of aesthetics since the days of Kant and even more notably since Benedetto Croce. Delicate instruments have been perfected for considering art as art, for analyzing its structure and its characteristic qualities, and for rigorously excluding everything that is not purely art, such as history, biography, psychology, morality, society, and utility. But this is to omit the function, the drive, the creative impulse that produces art. It is analogous to surveying a locomotive, determining its metallic structure and the articulation of its parts, describing its peculiar locomotiveness in such fashion that it stands out sharply from the aeroplane, the automobile, and other locomotives—and never asking why it was made or what it is good for. Such method may excellently present pure philosophical distinctions, but it is hard on art. Some critics hold not merely that ethics are irrelevant in aesthetic discussion, but that the work of art itself actually contains little of ethical interest either to the artist or the reader. The artist's control over his materials, the certainty of his vision and the unimpassioned clarity of his expression, it is argued, show that he has disassociated himself from any moral judgments his materials may contain, and has gone beyond them to the calm plane of art.

To such a radical dissociation of art from the good life, the best answer is purely personal: "That is not the impression art makes upon me. In reading a poem, I feel emotions, I sense values, though the *expression* of those values is not in the manner of a philosopher, a preacher, a justice on the bench, or a political reformer." The purely aesthetic critics, it seems to me, unconsciously betray that they too sense moral values in art, for they tend to concentrate on the littler poets, where pure technique may be easily studied, and have neglected the major writers, whose technique is at least as good, because other elements inevitably get in their way, moral elements in which the major writers irritatingly seem to be interested.

An impersonal answer, of course, may be given to the theorists defending art for art's sake. The history of the artists themselves contradicts them. If we turn to most poets of the past and to many poets of the present, we shall find that there are moral ideas in poetry.

Another reason for denying morality to poetry comes from the modern realization of the complex individuality of *each* work of art. But this leads critics into hopeless solipsism. Nothing could be more incontrovertible than to say "A poem is a poem." And nothing could be more useless. The lover of art knows the need for analysis and partial considerations as steps toward fuller appreciation of works of art *as wholes;* and the implicit moral idea of a work surely deserves his study.

If we grant that art contains moral ideas and that Shakespeare's moral ideas may be discovered or approximated, what is the value of setting them down formally, when it is assumed that the plays themselves state them more clearly, in all the precision of their original poetic complexity? The value is that of any translation. A translation makes some aspects of a work of art available to those who can't read the original or haven't the time or patience to read it. A translation also may afford a trot for comparison with the original, making it easier to absorb the pure source. And a translation may give a quick over-all view of a difficult whole which might be missed in direct, slow, interrupted study.

Are Shakespeare's moral ideas of much significance? For all those who cannot go beyond the moral interpretation of life to the religious interpretation, it might easily be held that Shakespeare is the most precious of thinkers. Probably only the recording angel knows what influence Shakespeare has had upon the development of Occidental thought and even upon the workings of democracy, though the record might prove startling. He teaches us the possibility of living without rigid systems, for a system (any system) shuts out many other modes of life—shuts out many other systems, for that matter. Yet this elasticity of Shakespeare's, this "Negative Capability," does not leave him bewildered, floundering in chaos. His multitudinous and varied insights are organized, like the dots of a *pointilliste,* into a single vast painting so comprehensive that, as we have seen, many deny that the picture is there. This book is no final revelation of that great vision. The most such discourse can achieve is to point out some of the dominating themes—integrity, loyalty, patience, love, forgiveness, humility—that give Shakespeare's thought an ordered scope.

We need his thought today, for it is neither skeptical (except of the worth of partial judgments), nor narrow, nor rigid, nor despairing. It is doubly precious and dependable because its hopefulness and balance do not rest upon a partial consideration of human life and human possibilities. No other writer or moralist (I am excepting the religious figures throughout this study) based his conclusions on such comprehensive human experience. Some writers may have climbed higher or descended lower, but none has so great a range. No man has evidenced such sympathy, such love and acceptance of human life—and this with the open-eyed knowledge of man's imperfections and positive evil. This smiling understanding, this tolerance which is not based on laziness or lack of belief, compels us again and again to find this moralist, as his contemporaries intuitively felt, "sweet Shakespeare," "gentle Shakespeare." He insists little. But he plants the seeds of courage and faith and compassion. Though we are surrounded by currents of thought, billows of controversy, wavelets of the present and waves of the future, Shakespeare remains the "butt and very sea-mark" of our utmost sail. To an unstable world wavering between the two despairs of skepticism and fanaticism, he steadily exemplifies as his central moral belief, to use Shelley's thought, that the prime agent in moral action is the imagination. Shakespeare does us one further service: the supreme instrument of his imagination he focuses unwaveringly upon man as he is in this world.

A word, just for my own pleasure, concerning the epigraphs. They are chosen on purpose from Shakespeare's less familiar or his suspect work because I am convinced that his greatest works cannot be fully appreciated without a knowledge of his lesser works, and also because his "lesser" works so frequently contain short passages that would be household words if they appeared in *Hamlet* or *Twelfth Night*. I deliberately chose epigraphs obscure and oracular: this book has of necessity reduced Shakespeare to simplicities and to those platitudes which seem unavoidable in any talk about sane and practical morals. Actually, Shakespeare's best thought is subtle, rapid, elliptic, and muscular: anyone who absorbs *The Phoenix and Turtle*, for instance, has encountered a powerful mind that works in the mode of poetry—creating patterns of pleasurable significance out of images, hypotheses, emblems, and music. To my mind the three epigraphs govern much of the argument in this book, and the choice of mottoes of such difficulty (if they are not read simply for the surface) is my partial apology to Shakespeare for the effrontery of daring to write the book at all.

When a man writes a book about Shakespeare these days and comes to the acknowledgments, there is nothing to say except that his debts are so numerous that they cannot be recorded. A Shakespearean scholar could point out on almost any page how heavily this book has drawn upon past criticism. At the very least, however, I wish to express my thanks to the Rockefeller Foundation for a Post-war Fellowship which has helped me, as it has helped so many others, toward the early completion of plans which might otherwise have languished. I should like to dedicate this book in gratitude to about half a dozen friends, and particularly to my sister Ruth Stauffer, whose firm sense of proportion managed to exclude, in spite of my arguments from authority, many mixed metaphors. In varying degrees, I am grateful to all writers on Shakespeare I have read, for it is perhaps impossible to write a completely useless book about him; each book is a hand pointing back to Shakespeare, and that is always a public service.

Analytical Index

CHAPTER TWO THE SCHOOL OF LOVE

CHAPTER THREE   THE GARDEN OF EDEN

CHAPTER SEVEN   A WORLD OF IMAGES

A selected list of MIDLAND BOOKS

(continued on next page)